Recognising Human Rights in Different Cultural Contexts

"When the Convention on the Rights of Persons with Disabilities was accepted by the United Nations General Assembly in 2006, the work of human rights was only just beginning. This varied and fascinating book reveals some of the ways in which national contexts and cultures adopted and implemented the Convention into local use. We need urgently to understand the complexity of implementing disability equality, and this collection is of inestimable help in that task."

—Professor Tom Shakespeare, *London School of Hygiene and Tropical Medicine*

"An important addition to the field of disability rights, highlighting the role of culture(s)—legal, social, and identity—on international law-making processes, interpretation and implementation. With 'snapshots' of the journey of the CRPD post-ratification across and within nations, *Recognising Human Rights in Different Cultural Contexts* provides a first of its kind look into dynamics and embedded values that affect the struggle for human rights of persons with disabilities."

—Assistant Professor Maya Sabatello, *Columbia University*

"Culture can be a powerful influence on the way in which international law is adopted or resisted, and this book acts as a timely reminder of its importance. Drawing on evidence from the United Nations Convention on the Rights of Persons with Disabilities, the authors provide a sensitive, unique and insightful portrayal of the intersection between legislative directive and its translation into practice in different cultural contexts, within and between societies. It is a thought-provoking and interesting book that addresses complexity and diversity but in itself is well-structured and inclusive in its approach."

—Professor Pauline Heslop, *University of Bristol*

Emily Julia Kakoullis • Kelley Johnson
Editors

Recognising Human Rights in Different Cultural Contexts

The United Nations Convention on the Rights of Persons with Disabilities (CRPD)

palgrave
macmillan

Editors
Emily Julia Kakoullis
School of Law and Politics
Cardiff University
Cardiff, UK

Kelley Johnson
Social Policy Research Centre
UNSW
Sydney, Australia

ISBN 978-981-15-0785-4 ISBN 978-981-15-0786-1 (eBook)
https://doi.org/10.1007/978-981-15-0786-1

This Palgrave Macmillan imprint is published by the registered company Springer Nature Singapore Pte Ltd.
The registered company address is: 152 Beach Road, #21-01/04 Gateway East, Singapore 189721, Singapore

We dedicate this book to persons who identify as persons with disabilities and their allies who are engaged in working to achieve their human rights at global, State and local levels.

Acknowledgements

We thank the contributors for their work, commitment, and patience during the development of this book. We thank Joshua Pitt for his patience and support in the journey towards the realisation of this book and Marie Selwood for her assistance with copyediting. We also thank our friends and families for their patience, love and support in this journey.

Contents

1 **Introduction** 1
Emily Julia Kakoullis and Kelley Johnson

Part I Culture, Disability and the CRPD 17

2 **Legal Culture and the CRPD** 19
Gerard Quinn

3 **Anthropology, Disability and the CRPD** 45
James G. Rice

4 **Recognising Cultural Diversity: Implications for Persons with Disabilities** 63
Kelley Johnson

5 **A Personal Reflection on Indigeneity, Colonisation and the CRPD** 79
Huhana Hickey

Part II The Ratification Process: To Be or Not to Be? 95

6 The Failure of the United States to Ratify the CRPD 97
Arlene S. Kanter

7 The Long Road to Ratification: Ireland and the CRPD 133
Eilionóir Flynn

8 A Consultative Culture? The Ratification Process for the CRPD in Cyprus 157
Emily Julia Kakoullis

9 A Janus-Faced Affair: Sri Lanka's Ratification of the CRPD 179
Dinesha Samararatne

Part III Making Disability Human Rights Happen? Cultural Challenges to Implementing the CRPD 201

10 The 'Transposition' of Article 12 of the CRPD in China and Its Potential Impact on Chinese Legal Capacity Law and Culture 203
Huang Yi

11 Implementation of Article 19 of the CRPD in Hungary and Its Impact on the Deinstitutionalisation Process So Far 227
Magdi Birtha

12 Implementing Article 19 of the CRPD in Nordic Welfare States: The Culture of Welfare and the CRPD 257
Ciara Brennan and Rannveig Traustadóttir

13 **Article 30 of the CRPD as a Vehicle for Social Transformation: Harnessing the CRPD's Potential for Persons with Intellectual Disabilities** 269
Matthew S. Smith and Michael Ashley Stein

Part IV Monitoring the CRPD: Resolving Conflicting Interests? 295

14 **Was Ratification of the CRPD the High Watermark for United Kingdom Disability Rights? Ten Years of Monitoring Implementation of the CRPD** 297
Neil Crowther and Liz Sayce OBE

15 **The Role of Disabled People's Organisations in Promoting the CRPD in Indonesia** 333
Dina Afrianty

16 **The Process of State Party Reporting to the CRPD Committee: The Indian Experience** 353
Amita Dhanda

17 **Conclusion** 377
Kelley Johnson and Emily Julia Kakoullis

Index 387

Notes on Contributors

Dina Afrianty is a Research Fellow at La Trobe Law School, La Trobe University, Melbourne; is affiliated with the State Islamic University (UIN); and is the founder of Australia-Indonesia Disability Research and Advocacy Network (AIDRAN). AIDRAN receives funding from the Knowledge Sector Initiative partnership with Indonesia's National Development Planning Agency. Afrianty's research focuses on the intersection of law, politics, gender, and religion in Muslim societies and the human rights of persons with disabilities in Indonesia. Her publications include the book *Women and Sharia Law in Indonesia* and articles on gender, women's movements for policy reform, and disability rights movements in Indonesia.

Magdi Birtha is a Researcher at the European Centre for Social Welfare Policy and Research, a Vienna-based intergovernmental organisation affiliated to the United Nations. She is also a Research Affiliate at the Centre for Disability Law and Policy (CDLP) at the National University of Ireland (NUI). Prior to that Birtha was a Marie Skłodowska-Curie PhD Research Fellow, part of the DREAM (Disability Rights Expanding Accessible Markets) Project at the CDLP. She holds expertise in the areas of CRPD monitoring, legal capacity, independent living, accessibility, social inclusion, and political participation of persons with disabilities.

Ciara Brennan holds a PhD in Disability Studies from the University of Iceland. Her doctoral thesis *The Nordic experience of independent living and personal assistance a human rights approach* explored the complexities of implementing Article 19 of the CRPD at EU and EU Member State level. She has ten years of experience as a disability rights researcher. In 2009 she joined the National Institute for Intellectual Disability at Trinity College Dublin. Her most recent work focuses on advancing reproductive rights for women in the Republic of Ireland.

Neil Crowther is an Independent Expert on the rights of persons with disabilities and consultant supporting social change. He has led and contributed to research in the field of disability rights including into the progress of European countries in implementing the right of persons with disabilities to independent living, for the EU Agency for Fundamental Rights (FRA) and the European Commission. He has acted as specialist adviser to the United Kingdom (UK) Joint Parliamentary Committee on Human Rights and supported UK civil society to prepare its submissions to the CRPD Committee.

Amita Dhanda is Professor of Law at NALSAR (National Academy of Legal Studies and Research) University of Law, where she also heads the Centre for Disability Studies and the Centre for Legal Philosophy and Justice Education. She is an international expert in the field of disability human rights who has not just argued for the human rights claims of persons with disabilities but also demonstrated how disability human rights would strengthen the human rights of all. Her book *Legal Order and Mental Disorder* is an evidence-based exposition on how the denial of legal capacity caused discrimination to be effectuated by the law.

Eilionóir Flynn is Established Professor of Law and Director of the Centre for Disability Law and Policy (CDLP) at the National University of Ireland (NUI). Her work on disability rights is widely published, and her research interests include legal capacity, access to justice, and the intersectionality of disability, gender, and ageing. She regularly collaborates with civil society organisations and disabled people's organisations (DPOs) at national and international levels. In Ireland, she co-ordinated the Civil Society Legal Capacity Coalition to influence the drafting of the Assisted Decision-Making (Capacity) Act, and internationally she has supported the Secretariat of the CRPD Committee.

Huhana Hickey holds an LLB/BSoc Sci, LLM, and a PhD in Law and Tikanga Maori from the University of Waikato. She was a solicitor at Auckland Disability Law and a Māori Research Fellow at the Taupua Waiora Māori Health Research Unit at the Auckland University of Technology. Hickey was the indigenous peoples' representative for the International Disability Association Steering Group Caucus during the development of the CRPD. She was awarded the New Zealand Order of Merit in 2015 for her services to the Māori and disability community. She holds several governance roles, has sat on several ethics committee, and is a life member of Rostrevor House in the Waikato.

Kelley Johnson holds Honorary Professorial appointments at Deakin University and University of New South Wales (UNSW) in Australia. She is an internationally known scholar who has been a researcher and advocate with persons with disabilities for more than 20 years in Australia and internationally. Her recent previously held positions include Director, Social Policy Research Centre at UNSW, and Director of the Norah Fry Research Centre in Bristol, UK. Johnson has an ongoing commitment to inclusive research which involves persons with disabilities undertaking research on issues that are important in their lives. Her research interests include deinstitutionalisation, community participation of persons with disabilities, sexuality and relationships, and rights with a particular focus on the CRPD.

Emily Julia Kakoullis is a Lecturer at the School of Law and Politics at Cardiff University in the UK. She has worked as a research fellow at the University of Exeter and held an honorary research fellow position at the University of Bristol. Prior to a career in academia, Kakoullis worked as a researcher at the Ministry of Justice in the UK, and for a disability NGO in Cyprus where she engaged in advocacy work with persons with disabilities.

Arlene S. Kanter is the Laura J. and L. Douglas Meredith Professor for Teaching Excellence and Professor of Law at Syracuse University College of Law. She is the founder and Director of the College of Law's Disability Law and Policy Program (DLPP). The DLPP houses the United States's first joint degree programme in Law and Disability Studies. Kanter is an internationally acclaimed expert in international and comparative disability law. She publishes and lectures extensively on domestic and international human rights and disability law and policy. Her most recent book, *The Development of Disability Rights Under International Law: From Charity to Human Rights*, traces the development of the CRPD.

Gerard Quinn was the founding director of the Centre for Disability Law and Policy (CDLP) at the National University of Ireland (NUI); he now holds the Wallenberg Chair at the Raoul Wallenberg Institute, University of Lund, and also holds a part-time Chair at the University of Leeds. He holds Honorary Chairs at NALSAR, India, and Wuhan University, China. He led the delegation of Rehabilitation International and later the global network of national human rights institutions (NHRIs) during the drafting of the CRPD. He was a member of the research advisory board of the EU Agency for Fundamental Rights (FRA). His research interests include the protection of persons with disabilities during armed conflicts.

James G. Rice is Assistant Professor of Anthropology at the School of Social Sciences, University of Iceland. He received his doctorate in Anthropology from Memorial University of Newfoundland, Canada, in 2007 and has been a member of the Centre for Disability Studies, University of Iceland, since 2008. He is an academic adviser for the *Disability before Disability* project (funded by The Icelandic Centre for Research) and a member of the European Commission Marie Curie Training Network DARE (Disability Advocacy and Research for Europe). He has recently published in the journals *ALTER, Human Organization, Social Inclusion, Laws*, and *Journal of Applied Research in Intellectual Disabilities.*

Dinesha Samararatne is a Senior Lecturer at the Department of Public and International Law, Faculty of Law, University of Colombo, Sri Lanka. She is a Public and International Law scholar with expertise in human rights law. Samararatne has carried out research on the rights of rural women with disabilities in Sri Lanka and is a member of the Disability and the Global South Editorial Board.

Liz Sayce OBE is a Joseph Rowntree Foundation (JRF) Practitioner Fellow at the International Inequalities Institute, London School of Economics (LSE). She was Chief Executive of Disability Rights UK (and its legacy charity Radar) from 2007 to 2017, and she is Chair of the Commission for Equality in Mental Health, UK. Sayce is a non-executive director of the Care Quality Commission (CQC) and a member of the Disability Advisory Committee of the Equality and Human Rights Commission (EHRC), and the Committee of Healthwatch England and the Social Security Advisory Committee in the UK. She has published widely on mental health, disability, social participation, and employment. A Harkness Fellowship in the United States resulted in a book *From Psychiatric Patient to Citizen.* Sayce was awarded an Order of the British Empire (OBE) in 2009 and an honorary doctorate from the University of Kent in 2014.

Matthew S. Smith is a Research Associate with the Harvard Law School Project on Disability, where he is responsible for research, advocacy, and training initiatives in Latin America, Bangladesh, and the United States; some of his responsibilities include providing technical support to State-wide self-advocacy organisations in designing and implementing strategies for guardianship reform and providing research and expert testimony on Mexico's mental health system. He also is a senior project coordinator for Supported Decision-Making New York (SDMNY) at Hunter College, City University of New York, which provides training on and piloting of novel legal alternatives to guardianship to adults and transition-aged youth with intellectual disabilities.

Michael Ashley Stein is the Co-founder and Executive Director of the Harvard Law School Project on Disability, and a Visiting Professor at Harvard Law School. Stein participated in the drafting of the CRPD, works with DPOs and NGOs around the world, actively consults with Governments on their disability laws and policies, and advises a number of UN bodies and NHRIs. His authoritative and path-breaking scholarship has been published worldwide by leading journals and academic presses and has been supported by fellowships and awards. Stein holds an Extraordinary Professorship at the University of Pretoria's Centre for Human Rights, is a Visiting Professor at the Free University of Amsterdam, and teaches at the Harvard Kennedy School of Government.

Rannveig Traustadóttir is a Professor and Director of the Centre for Disability Studies, School of Social Sciences, University of Iceland. Her research focuses on violence against disabled women, independent living and personal assistance, and how the CRPD can be used to promote full human rights and equality. She has published 13 books and numerous articles. Traustadóttir was a founding member of the Nordic Network on Disability Research (NNDR) and served as its president for many years. In addition to her academic work, she has been an active advocate for human rights, and one of her concerns is how activism and academia can work together in bringing about social change.

Huang Yi is a Post-doctoral Researcher at the Centre of Disability Study and Public Interest in Shenzhen University, China. Before this, she received her PhD and LLM from the University of Leeds, and Bachelor of Law from East China University of Political Science and Law. Her main research interests lie in human rights law, anti-discrimination, disability rights, and Chinese law and legal culture. She also works closely with practitioners, grassroots NGOs, and advocates in disability-related areas in China.

List of Tables

Table 8.1 The processes that took place during each phase of the journey towards ratification of the CRPD in Cyprus 165

Table 11.1 The six participating institutions in the deinstitutionalisation process and the number of people leaving institutions 244

1

Introduction

Emily Julia Kakoullis and Kelley Johnson

> *While the Convention [CRPD] is important and an outstanding achievement, the distance between … an international agreement about human rights and its application for people with disabilities needs to be explicitly recognised.*
> *(Rioux et al. 2011, p. 480)*

> *One must resist the 'temptation of elegance' or the easy assumption that words alone will bring about the kind of change needed. After all, it is quite easy for persons and states to agree to language without necessarily thinking through its implications. There is no guarantee that the new values (really old values but novel in their application to disability) will be internalised and then operationalised.*
> *(Quinn 2009, p. 216)*

E. J. Kakoullis (✉)
School of Law and Politics, Cardiff University, Cardiff, UK
e-mail: KakoullisE@cardiff.ac.uk

K. Johnson
Social Policy Research Centre, UNSW, Sydney, Australia
e-mail: kelley.johnson@unsw.edu.au

E. J. Kakoullis, K. Johnson (eds.), *Recognising Human Rights in Different Cultural Contexts*, https://doi.org/10.1007/978-981-15-0786-1_1

1 Introduction

We have chosen these two statements above as an introduction to this chapter because they articulate the key issue which is the focus of this book: how the United Nations (UN) Convention on the Rights of Persons with Disabilities' (Convention/CRPD 2006) interacts with cultural contexts during its ratification, implementation and monitoring processes. The CRPD (2006) was adopted by the UN General Assembly in 2006. By January 2020, 14 years after its adoption, 181 States had ratified it, with 96 States Parties also having ratified its Optional Protocol (OP-CRPD 2006). This is an impressive record, but it also raises the issue of how an international human rights treaty interacts with, influences and is influenced by the specific cultural contexts in which it must be implemented. The CRPD (2006) has been seen as a 'paradigm shift' in relation to how persons with disabilities are constituted in their societies and as potentially transformative in changing their lives for the better (Quinn 2009; Kayess and French 2008; Scully 2012). However, its success also depends on how States Parties to the CRPD actually interpret it within their particular historical, social, economic and political contexts, and how its provisions are reflected in their domestic laws, policies and practices, in relation to persons with disabilities. The transition from the CRPD at the international level to specific action within States Parties' domestic contexts is not a simple legal process but a complex cultural one (Kakoullis 2015). It is affected by the unique nature of the CRPD that has sought to not only promote the human rights of persons with disabilities in their societies through its content, but also include them as active agents in its ratification, implementation and monitoring processes. While States Parties are responsible for the interpretation and translation of International Human Rights Law into domestic law and policy, how individuals and groups are constituted by those around them may impact on the ways in which the CRPD is interpreted and may lead to challenges and change in cultural contexts.

This book's development has been informed by a number of questions which arose from our engagement with the human rights of persons with disabilities within our own States Parties and internationally. These questions are as follows: what is meant by the concept of 'culture' in relation to the human rights of persons with disabilities set out in the CRPD? How important are cultural contexts in shaping how the CRPD's provisions are interpreted and implemented by particular States Parties? What cultural factors facilitate or challenge the process of interpreting and translating the provisions of the CRPD into action for change during the processes of ratification, implementation and monitoring? How far is the CRPD recognised as an instrument for social change in particular cultures? In this book we have sought to deepen our understanding of these questions through engaging with contributors who provide a range of perspectives to the interaction between cultural contexts and the CRPD.

In this chapter, we begin by providing a statement of our positions as editors. We then provide a rationale for the specific focus and development of this book. Finally, we describe the structure of the book.

2 The Editors' Positions

Our decision to develop an edited book that focuses on the ways in which the CRPD and cultural contexts interact originally arose from our individual experiences in working with persons with disabilities in different States and cultures. Our separate interests in the issue of cultural contexts and International Human Rights Law became a shared one as we worked together at the University of Bristol, UK. We met in 2009 when Kelley was a Professor of Disability and Policy at the Norah Fry Centre for Disability Studies, School for Policy Studies, and Emily was a doctoral researcher between the Law School and the Norah Fry Centre for Disability Studies.

Kelley is Australian, and Emily is half-English and half-Cypriot. We initially worked together in an English university context. Sometimes we found it challenging to reconcile or to make clear to each other the issues arising from our particular cultural contexts. This was of particular importance to Emily whose doctoral research at the time focused on the ratification process for the CRPD in Cyprus. During Emily's doctoral journey, we worked together to develop a shared understanding of the particular socio-historical-cultural context of Cyprus in relation to persons with disabilities and of how particular

English language concepts, such as the 'social model of disability' and 'impairment', were understood and/or did not have an equivalent meaning in the Cypriot context, including in the Greek language. Kelley came from Australia, where the social model of disability was known and used by disabled peoples' organisations (DPOs) and where the CRPD approach to human rights was familiar. In contrast, in Cyprus, the history and culture were less focused on human rights in relation to persons with disabilities, and the social model of disability underpinning the CRPD was little known or used by DPOs. From our work came an understanding of the importance of particular norms, history, language and tradition, in shaping and influencing the ways in which our cultural contexts engaged with the CRPD. Furthermore, another cultural context arose from our disciplinary backgrounds. Kelley is a social science researcher, whereas Emily is a socio-legal researcher. We had to navigate the very different disciplinary discourses, including language and terminology and the theoretical and epistemological perspectives in which we operated. From these interactions of perspectives came new learning for both of us.

That journey has largely informed this edited book as we became increasingly aware of the complexity of interpreting and translating the CRPD's provisions into States Parties' cultural contexts and saw the need for interdisciplinary approaches to exploring this.

3 A Note on Language

The CRPD recognises that the concept of 'disability' is not static but is an evolving concept (CRPD 2006, Preamble), and it employs a description of disability that although grounded in the social model of disability is also influenced by a 'minority rights approach'[1] to disability, 'person first language' (PFL) and a 'human rights approach' to disability (CRPD 2006, Art. 1; Lawson 2007; Kanter 2007; Kayess and French 2008;

[1] This is also found in the literature as the 'minority group model' or the 'minority group approach' (Hahn 1996).

Kakoullis and Ikehara 2018). The language used in this book predominantly adopts the language used in the CRPD, that of 'persons with disabilities', although the phrase 'disabled persons' is also sometimes used. Language used in relation to disability also varies depending on the cultural context.

4 Culture and the CRPD

Since the adoption of the CRPD in 2006, its importance has been recognised in the development of a large and growing body of literature largely based within a legal discourse. This has provided theoretical analyses of the CRPD itself as a whole or has focused on particular provisions and/or their domestic implementation in particular States Parties (Arnardóttir and Quinn 2009; de Beco 2013, Blanck and Flynn 2017; Fina et al. 2017; O'Mahony and Quinn 2017; Bantekas et al. 2018) including how they have been affected and interpreted by their courts (Waddington and Lawson 2018). Some of the literature combines the two approaches with an account of the CRPD and its significance, together with a focus on particular provisions (Kanter 2015). Some authors have focused on a particular aspect of the journey of the CRPD at the international level, for example, Sabatello and Schulze (2014) in their edited book are concerned with the drafting of the CRPD from the perspectives of persons with disabilities, while Flynn (2011) focuses on international responses to the implementation of the CRPD, and Rioux et al. (2015) concentrate on the issue of monitoring of the CRPD and its implications for social change. This literature is significant in providing an account of the progress of the CRPD since its adoption. Within legal and anthropological discourses more generally there has also been voluminous literature that documents the debate on the universality of human rights and cultural relativism, which suggests a tension between the universal respect for human rights on the one hand and cultural diversity on the other hand (Addo 2010), a debate once considered irreconcilable but now considered more theoretical (de Varennes 2006). Amongst these bodies of literature we have found little that explores different perspectives to the complexity of cultures as central in a discussion of the CRPD (Scully 2012) or which analyses the interaction between the CRPD and the domestic cultures in which it is ratified and implemented (Kakoullis 2015). These issues seem to have important implications in the practice of human rights for the lives of persons with disabilities.

As social, and socio-legal, researchers, respectively, we believe that focusing on the 'socio-cultural' as well as the 'legal' is an important addition to our knowledge of the CRPD. We have therefore sought to take an interdisciplinary approach to this edited collection. In developing it we did not provide our contributors with a guiding definition of 'culture', but we indicated that we were interested in the interaction between the CRPD and particular cultural contexts. We return to this in the Conclusion to this book, where we will discuss how the concept of 'culture' was explored and analysed from different perspectives.

Further, while the previous literature has focused on specific provisions of the CRPD (2006) and on different aspects of States Parties' progress, there has not been any literature to our knowledge that provides 'snapshots' of the journey of the CRPD through ratification, implementation and monitoring. This book aims to examine some of these 'snapshots' from the stage of a State making a commitment to the CRPD by its ratification, through implementation of the CRPD's provisions, to monitoring the implementation of the CRPD, to better understand how cultural factors may interact with the CRPD's journey into States Parties' domestic contexts.

5 Book Structure

This book is divided into four parts. It begins with reflections on culture, disability and International Disability Human Rights Law from different disciplinary perspectives (Part I). It is then organised as 'snapshots' of the journey of the CRPD from the international level to the domestic, that is, the process of ratification (Part II), the process of implementation of certain of the CRPD's provisions (Part III) and then the process of monitoring the CRPD's implementation in States Parties' cultural contexts (Part IV). The book's structure brings together cultural reflections of the journey of the CRPD from the international level to the domestic. It provides a series of in-depth accounts of how different States' domestic cultural contexts facilitated or led to particular challenges in the CRPD's interpretation and translation from an international treaty into practice. In this book we have given freedom to the contributors to consider the cultural issues that they thought were most important in the journey of the CRPD rather than imposing a particular theoretical perspective. We bring the themes that arise from these chapters together in the Conclusion to the book.

5.1 Part I: Culture, Disability and the CRPD

This part provides an interdisciplinary approach to analysing the nature of the concept of 'culture' and its implications for persons with disabilities and their human rights. In developing this part, we sought to explore the meanings given to 'culture' from various perspectives. This led to consideration of the complexity of the concept, particularly how its meanings have changed over time including within particular disciplines. It also led to a consideration of different 'cultures' including those which may be dominated or practised by particular disciplines, for example, 'legal culture', 'disability culture/s' and the importance of belonging to more than one 'culture'. In this part the authors have considered the implications of their analyses of culture for the human rights of persons with disabilities in relation to the CRPD.

In Chap. 2, Gerard Quinn advances the proposition that there is a 'legal culture', which consists of unstated values and institutional expectations that underpin legal orders and constitute a 'morality' which enables law to be possible. He focuses on the CRPD, in particular on Article 12—Equal recognition before the law, to discuss the limited power (to date) that it has had in dislodging fundamental assumptions in legal cultures concerning legal capacity. Quinn uses the example of legal capacity in Article 12 to show how changes to ideas of legal personhood and mental capacity are difficult to achieve because of 'legal fictions' that lie at the heart of legal systems' legal cultures. Quinn puts forward some suggestions to dislodge the historical 'legal fictions' embedded in legal culture.

In Chap. 3, James Rice uses an anthropological perspective to explore some of the cultural implications of the CRPD. He uses content analysis, of the Reservations, Declarations and Objections made to the CRPD by some States, to identify a number of tensions between the human rights of persons with disabilities as set out in the CRPD and the broader cultural values and priorities of particular States. Rice argues that any human rights convention has to negotiate with local cultural norms, including that of the CRPD.

In Chap. 4, Kelley Johnson considers the complexity of the concept of 'culture' and some of the ways in which its different meanings have impacted on the human rights of persons with disabilities. In particular she considers the diversity of cultures which may be included within any nation State and how the interaction between these various cultures may affect the human rights of persons with disabilities. The chapter considers the development of disability culture(s), including Deaf Culture, the cultural model of disability and the development of human rights based cultures by persons with disabilities.

In Chap. 5, Huhana Hickey provides an account of the different ways in which indigeneity has been defined historically and in contemporary contexts. She uses her own experiences to provide a particular case study of Maori perspectives to disability and the impact of colonialism on the lives of persons with disabilities who are also members of indigenous cultures. Hickey argues that the effects of colonialism on persons with disabilities who are members of an indigenous culture continue to the present through Government and community failure to both take account of, and respect, the cultural values and beliefs of Maori people and the continuing discrimination they face. As someone involved in the drafting of the CRPD she explores the attempts made to give the rights of indigenous people with disabilities stronger representation in its provisions and provides a reflection on the consequences of the failure to do so.

5.2 Part II: The Ratification Process: To Be or Not to Be?

This part provides an interdisciplinary approach to exploring the ratification process States undergo to become States Parties, that is, to be bound under International Law, to the CRPD. The act of signature at the international level is the first stage in the journey of introducing human rights norms from the international to the domestic level and it indicates a State's intention and promise to ratify the convention in the future (VCLT 1969, Art. 18(a); Achiron 2007; Kallehauge 2009). Ratification at the international level is the act through which a State establishes 'its consent to be bound' by a convention at the International Law level (VCLT 1969, Art. 11). Following ratification, the State becomes a party to, and is required to observe the convention's provisions 'in good faith' and implement them (VCLT 1969, Art. 26). However, before a State can ratify a convention at the international level, it must first meet requirements and undergo processes at the domestic level. This ratification process provides States with time to acquire the necessary approvals, where necessary to enact domestic legislation (UN 2012; Aust 2011) and to think about implementation. The chapters in this part reveal the complexity of issues which may delay the ratification process for the CRPD or lead to no ratification.

In Chap. 6, Arlene Kanter explores the paradoxical historical position of the United States (US) which has failed to ratify most international human rights treaties while at the same time being one of the architects of the UN. The chapter explores the contemporary history of the failed attempts to achieve ratification of the CRPD. Kanter provides an overview of why States ratify human rights treaties, followed by a short summary of US treaty ratification history. It then describes the failed CRPD ratification process in the US Senate, including an analysis of the arguments that were presented for and against ratification. The chapter discusses the reasons for the failure of the ratification in the US and what this failure means to persons with disabilities in the US and to US foreign relations.

In Chap. 7, Eilionóir Flynn focuses on the ratification process for the CRPD in Ireland. In the chapter she considers the domestic cultural context—in terms of the legal and political landscape, which shaped the process of the CRPD's ratification leading to a long time elapsing between signature and ratification. The chapter shows some positive effects from the length of time taken to consult and to examine domestic laws, in terms of their consistency with the CRPD, but also the increasing frustration at the delay to ratify. Flynn's chapter reveals the factors leading to Ireland finally ratifying the CRPD without completing the promised legislative reforms.

In Chap. 8, Emily Julia Kakoullis discusses the journey towards ratification of the CRPD in Cyprus and considers how the Cypriot context struggled to embrace the consultative and participatory culture that is found in the Convention. The chapter shows that where States create formal structures for consultation these may be inadequate to truly embed the spirit of the Disability Movement's mantra 'Nothing About Us Without Us!', if the Governmental will is not there. Kakoullis's chapter also reveals that despite the challenges during Cyprus's ratification process there was some change regarding the practice of consultation with DPOs.

In Chap. 9, Dinesha Samararatne focuses on the impact of the CRPD on Sri Lanka and reveals the importance of action taken by civil society and persons with disabilities regarding the achievement of ratification of the CRPD. The chapter explores both the ways in which the CRPD has been received by the Government of Sri Lanka, and the incentive the CRPD has offered DPOs and activists to take action to work for the human rights of persons with disabilities. Samararatne's chapter reveals that even when ratification does not have immediate effects in terms of legislative or policy measures regarding persons with disabilities, it can lead to the mobilisation of advocacy on the ground.

5.3 Part III: Making Disability Human Rights Happen? Cultural Challenges to Implementing the CRPD

This part provides an interdisciplinary approach to exploring the implementation of the CRPD. In this part all four authors chose to focus on one CRPD provision: the first chapter discusses the implementation of Article 12—Equal recognition before the law, the second and third chapters discuss the implementation of Article 19—Living independently and being included in the community, and the last chapter in this section discusses Article 30—Participation in cultural life, recreation, leisure and sport (CRPD 2006). The chapters in this section reveal the influence of particular cultural contexts in implementing the CRPD's provisions and that some CRPD provisions tend to be particularly challenging for some States Parties.

In Chap. 10, Huang Yi provides an account of empirical research about the practice of guardianship and legal capacity to better understand the challenges of implementing Article 12—Equal recognition before the law, in China. She identifies and examines key cultural issues that affected the implementation of Article 12 in China. Yi's chapter provides an account of both the systemic issues that affect the way in which persons with disabilities are constituted within the 'culture of the law' in China, and the moral and relationship issues to which they are subject. She argues that in order to achieve the implementation of Article 12 in China not only a comprehensive understanding of Article 12 is needed but also that Chinese social and cultural contexts need to be taken into consideration.

In Chap. 11, Magdi Birtha discusses the implementation of Article 19—Living independently and being included in the community in the context of the continuing segregation of many persons with disabilities in large institutions, and the beginnings of deinstitutionalisation processes in Hungary. The chapter reports on research which studied the first six deinstitutionalisation projects designed to close large institutions in Hungary, an initiative largely driven by the ratification of the CRPD. Birtha takes a socio-historical-cultural approach to explore why institutions are still present in Hungary, and reflects on the challenges faced in closing six institutions. The chapter also discusses the role of the European Union (EU) and the importance of the European Structural and Investment Fund (ESIF) in providing incentives for implementing Article 19 in Hungary. Birtha's chapter reveals that the six deinstitutionalisation projects were not underpinned by an understanding of Article 19.

In Chap. 12, Ciara Brennan and Rannveig Traustadóttir provide an account of research carried out in three Nordic welfare states, Iceland, Norway and Sweden, which explored the challenges of implementing Article 19—Living independently and being included in the community. These States have historically been regarded as 'leaders' in the area of deinstitutionalisation and community living. The chapter explores how the human rights approach of the CRPD 'fits' with the culture of the

Nordic welfare states. Brennan and Traustadóttir's chapter identifies a Nordic 'welfare culture' as the main obstacle to the implementation of Article 19 in Iceland, Norway and Sweden.

In Chap. 13, Matthew Smith and Michael Ashley Stein explore through a discussion of Article 30—Participation in cultural life, recreation, leisure and sport, how theatre can be used particularly by persons with intellectual disabilities to provide unique opportunities for (re) negotiating their rights-holder status with society at large and to politically engender and support the social transformative change promised by the CRPD. The chapter discusses how three theatre groups in Bangladesh, the United States and Switzerland create spaces for dialogue that empower theatre performers with intellectual disabilities to convey political messages to their audiences. Smith and Stein argue that Article 30 if fully harnessed provides powerful opportunities for persons with intellectual disabilities and that human rights practitioners would do well to follow such theatre groups' lead and direct more attention to the role of theatre in the CRPD's implementation.

5.4 Part IV: Monitoring the CRPD: Resolving Conflicting Interests?

This part provides an interdisciplinary approach to analysing the monitoring process of the CRPD's implementation in which States Parties to the CRPD, their national human rights institutions (NHRIs), civil society and DPOs are engaged (CRPD 2006, Art. 33; 35). Each State Party to the CRPD has an obligation under Article 33—National implementation and monitoring—to establish independent mechanism/s to monitor the implementation of the CRPD (2006, Art. 33(2)) and civil society and DPOs must fully participate in the monitoring process (Art. 33(3)). Furthermore, States Parties have an obligation under Article 35—Reports by States Parties, to submit State Reports to the CRPD Committee on the measures they have taken to implement the CRPD. The chapters in this part reveal the power plays at work in the monitoring process and the important role DPOs play in the process.

In Chap. 14, Neil Crowther and Liz Sayce provide a detailed account of the activities that have taken place in the United Kingdom (UK) since the CRPD was ratified in 2009 with a particular focus on monitoring. They describe how the ratification of the CRPD came at the end of a period characterised by progress on disability rights and thus can be seen as a high point. They then document the negative effects of the subsequent austerity measures on the lives of persons with disabilities. In focusing on monitoring, Crowther and Sayce's chapter discusses the UK Government's examination by the CRPD Committee following the submission of its State Report, the UK's response and DPO's reactions, and shows that the CRPD Committee's examination revealed interesting dynamics between the different stakeholders.

In Chap. 15, Dina Afrianty focuses on the roles played by persons with disabilities and their DPOs in ongoing monitoring at national and provincial governmental levels in Indonesia. The chapter considers the history of perspectives to disability within the cultural contexts of Indonesia and how these impact on the CRPD. It describes how DPOs have been collaborating with other human rights organisations in Indonesia to support the implementation and monitoring of the CRPD. Afrianty's chapter illustrates how ratification of the CRPD has provided DPOs with support to development campaigns designed to change attitudes and new legislative frameworks in Indonesia in relation to persons with disabilities.

In Chap. 16, Amita Dhanda provides an account of the preparation of the Indian Government's State Report to the CRPD Committee as part of its monitoring obligations. The chapter discusses how the Centre for Disability Studies, at the NALSAR (National Academy of Legal Studies and Research) University of Law, was contracted to prepare India's State Report and discusses the political and ethical challenges involved in working with the Government, civil society and DPOs in order to provide a comprehensive and balanced State Report. Dhanda's chapter considers the systemic factors that make the preparation of a useful and independent State Report challenging to fulfil, and concludes with some suggestions as to what can be done to make State Reporting a deliberative process, rather than an inquisitorial exercise.

6 Conclusion

We anticipate that this book will serve as a starting point for discussions at the domestic and international levels about the importance of recognising the different cultural contexts in which the CRPD, and other international human rights conventions, are implemented. We consider that such discussions are of crucial importance in the journey towards the successful implementation and practice of the human rights of persons with disabilities. We also hope that this book will assist persons in developing ways in which the CRPD may be used more effectively within their particular cultures. Our contributors provide diverse accounts of the discussions that have been held (or not held) in different States and cultural contexts about how provisions of the CRPD have been interpreted (or misinterpreted) and the implications flowing from this for the ratification of the CRPD, its implementation and its monitoring. Lastly we hope that this book will contribute to these discussions, and that they may be extended and further developed and contribute to the success of the implementation of the CRPD wherever it interacts with particular cultural contexts.

References

Achiron, M. (2007). *From exclusion to equality realizing the rights of persons with disabilities handbook for parliamentarians on the convention on the rights of persons with disabilities and its optional protocol.* Geneva: Secretariat for the Convention on the Rights of Persons with Disabilities, United Nations Department of Economic and Social Affairs, Office of the United Nations High Commissioner for Human Rights, and Inter-Parliamentary Union.

Arnardóttir, O., & Quinn, G. (2009). *The UN convention on the rights of persons with disabilities. European and Scandinavian perspectives.* Leiden: Martinus Nijhoff Publishers.

Aust, A. (2011). *Modern treaty law and practice.* Cambridge: Cambridge University Press.

Bantekas, I., Stein, M. A., & Anastasiou, D. (2018). *The UN convention on the rights of persons with disabilities: A commentary.* Oxford: Oxford University Press.

Blanck, P., & Flynn, E. (2017). *Routledge handbook of disability law and rights.* London: Routledge.

CRPD (United Nations Convention on the Rights of Persons with Disabilities). (2006). *Adopted in 2006 by the United Nations general assembly.*

de Beco, G. (Ed.). (2013). *Article 33 of the UN convention on the rights of persons with disabilities: National Structures for the implementation and monitoring of the convention.* Leiden: Martinus Nijhoff Publishers.

Fina, D., Cera, V., & Palmisano, G. (2017). *The United Nations convention on the rights of persons with disabilities a commentary.* Cham: Springer.

Flynn, E. (2011). *From rhetoric to action. Implementing the UN convention on the rights of persons with disabilities.* Cambridge: Cambridge University Press.

Hahn, H. (1996). Antidiscrimination laws and social research on disability: The minority group perspective. *Behavioral Sciences & the Law, 14*(1), 41–59.

Kakoullis, E. J. (2015). *A shift from welfare to rights: A case study of the ratification process for the convention on the rights of persons with disabilities in Cyprus.* Ph.D. Thesis, University of Bristol, Unpublished

Kakoullis, E., & Ikehara, Y. (2018). Article 1 Purpose. In I. Bantekas, M. Stein, & D. Anastasiou (Eds.), *The convention on the rights of persons with disabilities a commentary.* Oxford: Oxford University Press.

Kallehauge, H. (2009). General themes relevant to the implementation of the UN disability convention into domestic law: Who is responsible for the implementation and how should it be performed? In G. Quinn & O. M. Arnadottir (Eds.), *The UN convention on the rights of persons with disabilities: European and Scandinavian perspectives.* Leiden: Martinus Nijhoff Publishers.

Kanter, A. (2007). The promise and challenge of the United Nations convention on the rights of persons with disabilities. *Syracuse Journal of International Law and Commerce, 34*, 287–321.

Kanter, A. (2015). *The development of disability rights under international law. From charity to human rights.* Abingdon: Routledge.

Kayess, R., & French, P. (2008). Out of darkness into light? Introducing the convention on the rights of persons with disabilities. *Human Rights Law Review, 8*(1), 1–34.

O'Mahony, C., & Quinn, G. (2017). *Disability law and policy. An analysis of the UN Convention.* Dublin: Clarus Press.

OP-CRPD (United Nations Optional Protocol to the Convention on the Rights of Persons with Disabilities). (2006). *Adopted in 2006 by the United Nations general assembly.*

Quinn, G. (2009). Resisting the 'temptation of elegance': Can the convention on the rights of persons with disabilities socialise states to right behaviour? In

O. Arnardottir & G. Quinn (Eds.), *The UN convention on the rights of persons with disabilities. European and Scandinavian perspectives* (pp. 215–256). Leiden: Martinus Nijhoff Publishers.

Rioux, M. H., Pinto, P. C., & Parekh, G. (Eds.). (2015). *Disability, rights monitoring, and social change building power out of evidence*. Toronto: Canadian Scholars' Press.

Rioux, M. H., Basser, L. A., & Jones, M. (2011). *Critical perspectives on human rights and disability law* (pp. 479–491). Leiden: Martinus Nijhoff.

Sabatello, M., & Schulze, M. (2014). *human rights and disability advocacy*. Philadelphia, PA: University of Pennsylvania Press.

Scully, J. L. (2012). The convention on the rights of persons with disabilities and cultural understandings of disability. In J. Anderson & J. Philips (Eds.), *Disability and universal human rights: Legal, ethical, and conceptual implications of the convention on the rights of persons with disabilities*. Utrecht: Utrecht University Netherlands Institute of Human Rights.

UN (United Nations). (2012). *Treaty handbook* (pp. 1–72). United Nations, Treaty Section of the Office of Legal Affairs. Retrieved from https://treaties.un.org/pages/Publications.aspx?pathpub=Publication/TH/Page1_en.xml.

VCLT (Vienna Convention on the Law of Treaties). (1969). United Nations.

Waddington, L., & Lawson, A. (2018). *The UN convention on the rights of persons with disabilities in practice a comparative analysis of the role of courts*. Oxford: Oxford University Press.

Part I

Culture, Disability and the CRPD

2

Legal Culture and the CRPD

Gerard Quinn

Fictions are to be found not only in the opinions of judges, but in critical treatises written by men free from any of the influences which supposedly restrain the judge and warp his expression. Even the austere science of jurisprudence has not found it possible to dispense with fiction. The influence of the fiction extends to every department of the jurist's activities. Yet it cannot be said that this circumstance has ever caused the legal profession much embarrassment.
(Fuller 1930, p. 363)

G. Quinn (✉)
University of Leeds, Leeds, UK

Raoul Wallenberg Institute, University of Lund, Lund, Sweden
e-mail: gerard.quinn@nuigalway.ie

E. J. Kakoullis, K. Johnson (eds.), *Recognising Human Rights in Different Cultural Contexts*, https://doi.org/10.1007/978-981-15-0786-1_2

1 Introduction

In this chapter, I advance the proposition that there is such a thing as 'legal culture'.[1] Like all cultures, legal culture can act as a filter to expand, enrich, distort or narrow the reception of new ideas—especially new ideas that challenge important and foundational concepts that lie at the heart of that culture. Legal culture is real and usually involves a set of unstated values that underpin the legal order as well as a set of assumptions that guide how legal institutions like courts ought to behave. These often unstated values and institutional expectations can be peculiar to one country or they can be more or less shared across regions and sometimes even across the world. In the famous language of Lon Fuller (1964), these foundational values (whatever their provenance) constitute the 'morality' that makes law possible. How they come about, how they change, whether at least some parts of them remain constant and whether they can be intentionally changed are matters of systemic importance. Certainly, the power of new law, whether international or domestic, on its own to simply dictate change in the fundamentals of legal culture is itself questionable. The deep structure of domestic legal culture seems oddly immune to new legislation and even new international human rights treaties when the fundamentals are at stake. That is not to say that it cannot change or be changed. But something else besides fresh legislation or a new treaty is probably needed to change the underlying basis of the legal culture and make way for radical innovation.

To be more specific, this chapter concerns the (so far) limited power of the United Nations (UN) Convention on the Rights of Persons with Disabilities (CRPD) to dislodge a fundamental assumption implicit in nearly every legal culture. The UN CRPD is widely seen, though not unanimously so, as advancing the novel idea that every person with a disability (no matter how severe) has the legal capacity to make decisions for themselves and to direct their own lives (CRPD 2006, Art. 12). This stands in stark contrast to the positive laws of most countries in the world, which operate to transfer decision-making power to a substitute

[1] Perhaps the most seminal law review article on the concept of legal culture is Friedman, L., '*Legal Culture and Social Development*,' 4 Law & Soc'y Review 29 (1969).

decision-maker (like a guardian) on a showing of a severe cognitive impairment. These laws are not in themselves the obstacle. Laws can be changed. What is crabbing these innovations is a set of 'legal fictions' that lie at the heart of State's legal culture.[2] In effect, these 'legal fictions' confine personhood (and the full rights of personhood) to those with higher levels of cognitive ability. Put another way, they privilege those with higher levels of cognitive ability. It is hard to replace one set of 'legal fictions' with a completely new set.

The traditional assumption that cognitive ability and rationality mark out persons from others (or other things) is deeply embedded in nearly every legal culture. It helps explain why the vast majority of States Parties that have engaged in law reform in this field since the adoption of the CRPD ten years ago have not yet opted to completely abandon guardianship regimes.[3] Rather, many States have narrowed down the scope of application of traditional guardianship whilst opening up some new space for supported decision-making regimes. This does not necessarily evince an unwillingness to engage in law reform. Instead, it represents a hedging of bets—reforming on the basis of completely new 'legal fictions' (supported decision-making) whilst also preserving the essence of an old set of practices (limited guardianship) based on an earlier set of 'legal fictions'. Here we can see the prevailing legal culture cabining change—tilting in its direction but then tying it back to the values and precepts of an older legal culture. Since 'legal fictions' are fictions, the clash of fictions will not necessarily be resolved inevitably in favour of the new 'legal fiction'. They could go on co-existing indefinitely. But they can and do change. Indeed, their transition is the very stuff of legal history.

This chapter is inspired by the work of Karl Klare on legal culture (1977–1978). His essay *'Judicial De-Radicalization of the Wagner Act and the Origins of Modern Legal Consciousness'* (1977–1978) set the standard

---

[2] Legal fictions were long ago recognised by Sir William Blackstone in his 'Commentaries on the Laws of England'. Lon Fuller revived an interest in the role of 'legal fictions' as a foundational part of legal culture in (Fuller 1930–1931).

[3] The apparent exception is the reform of the Peruvian Civil Code in 2018: see https://www.ohchr.org/EN/NewsEvents/Pages/DisplayNews.aspx?NewsID=23501&LangID=E. More typical is the 2015 legislative reform in Ireland which innovates with assisted decision-making but which also preserves a reduced form of guardianship: Assisted Decision-Making (Capacity) Act 2015—available at—http://www.irishstatutebook.ie/eli/2015/act/64/enacted/en/html.

for scholarship on legal culture. His central thesis was that progressive and even radical legislation stands very little chance of effectuating profound change unless the underlying postulates of legal culture change and the courts acknowledge it. If they do not, and the courts continue to look on new legislation through the prism of orthodox values then, slowly but surely, through case-law the courts will narrow down the new legislation to the point of impotency. In Klare's (1977–1978) analysis, he highlights the importance of legal consciousness as a drag on innovation. Implicit in his analysis is that it does not matter that the innovation has been democratically sanctioned. It is pretty plain that some innovations of the CRPD do not fit with orthodox legal culture. It is no surprise therefore to see States hedging their bets when it comes to law reform.

Part 1 of this chapter unpacks the notion of 'legal culture'. Does it exist relative to other cultures? What does it entail? What core *legal fictions* drive it? How and why do they emerge and how do they change? A larger and transcendent question implied by the subject matter of this chapter is whether, and to what extent, legal culture can be intentionally changed to make way for completely novel ideas or practices. If the values at stake are so well settled, so deeply interwoven into law and practice, then it is hard to see wholesale change coming about simply from new law and even an international treaty like the CRPD. Yet, unless and until the underlying legal culture changes, very little space will exist for wholesale innovation. The hedging of (legislative) bets will continue.

Part 2 of this chapter will set out some of the background assumptions embedded in traditional legal culture—in most parts of the world—on the notion of who counts as a person. These assumptions have taken decades, if not centuries, to crystallise. It is remarkable the degree to which nearly all legal cultures embed and internalise a sense of the centrality of cognitive ability as the essence of what it means to be a human agent—a person in law. There is a curious symmetry of purpose between the Irish common law and the Chinese Civil Code when it comes to the core issues at stake. While it is hard to be definitive, I will suggest some possible reasons for this symmetry. But the symmetry itself cannot be denied.

Part 3 sets up the contrast between the narrow 'legal fictions' about personhood in traditional legal culture and the radically new 'legal fictions' propounded by the CRPD. Here we see the old 'legal fictions' narrowing the reception of new ideas. Most States to date interpret the CRPD to preserve intact the old 'legal fictions' despite the gradual but unmistakable emergence of a more expansive interpretation by the CRPD Committee. Hence it is no surprise that current law reform strategies in most countries proceed as if the old 'legal fictions' remain intact. Here we see legal culture filtering out some of the more radical turns in the CRPD.

Part 4 reflects on this evident filtering. It is not wholly unexpected. But it does beg a bigger question. How can one set of 'legal fictions' (universal legal capacity) replace another (capacity withdrawn from those with lower cognitive ability)? It is clear that 'legal fictions' can and do change. But legislating for change, for example, through international treaty law, has its limits. The assumptions that characterise the old 'legal fictions' are not so easily dislodged. It is suggested that a range of argumentative strategies are required, beyond the ritual incantation of treaty law, to change the underlying 'legal fictions' and halt the narrowing effect of the filter against change.

1.1 Legal Culture as a Constraint on Legal Change

The term 'legal culture' implies a set of values that exist largely outside the legal realm but which help to give it structure and orientation. Often these unstated values transcend even constitutional texts and, at the end of the day, help decide key legal issues. For example, most rights under the European Convention on Human Rights (ECHR 1950) can be limited if, inter alia, this is consistent with the exigencies of a '*democratic society*' (Zand 2017). This is nowhere defined in the ECHR itself but really comes from a shared understanding that one of the key purposes of the ECHR is to preserve an open and responsive democratic order, in contrast to the People's democracies then emerging in the 1950s across Eastern Europe. These values imply a certain image of democracy as a process, for example, how it should work, who can participate. They also imply a set of values that underpin democracy and also limit it. None of these are spelled out in the text of the ECHR. However, by allowing for limits on rights provided they are consistent with the exigencies of a democratic society, the text of the ECHR actively invites the judges to draw on the deep well of these values at key inflection points. That is, even if that invitation were not textually plain, it is clear that the judges would nevertheless have do so since the whole purpose of the ECHR is to prevent a slide back into the authoritarianism that doomed Europe to conflict in the 1930s.

These underlying values have a filtering effect. They can pre-dispose the legal order against alien values that do not fit. They can trigger defensive responses in the system against alien ideas. This operates at a subconscious level. Even when enacted into law, new ideas can be marginalised and not allowed to uproot the foundations of the underlying legal culture. This can be done through applying interpretive techniques that have a narrowing effect on the reach of the new ideas. Hence the system can right itself by deflecting incompatible norms. Of course, this can also work in reverse. If the new ideas help develop core norms, then they are not only allowed but actively welcomed.

The same filtering device helps to police the internalisation of new international legal norms like those of the CRPD. In point of fact, most of the CRPD norms are perfectly compatible with most legal systems. That is because every legal system at least purports to be based on a theory of human equality, and the CRPD is said to be essentially a thematic equality treaty on the ground of disability. However, some of the personhood norms—especially in Articles 12—Equal recognition before the law, and Article 19—Living independently and being included in the community, are much more challenging to most legal cultures since they directly challenge some long-standing assumptions or prejudices about the capacity of persons with disabilities to exercise these rights.

Parenthetically, an expansive view of Article 12 of the CRPD not only finds little fit with existing legal culture, as exemplified in domestic law and practice in most States. It also fails the filter test with other UN human rights treaties (A/CN.4/L.682 2006; Sandland 2017). To put this another way, those other UN human rights treaties themselves reflect and embed traditional legal culture with its emphasis on cognitive ability as the essence of personhood and moral agency.[4] What is more, some other human rights treaty monitoring bodies in the UN human rights treaty system do not take the view of the CRPD Committee as dispositive. To those who seek to advance the CRPD view, they must face the fact that their normative turn cuts against the grain of both domestic law as well as much existing international human rights law. That is not to say they are wrong. Far from it. But it demonstrates the power of traditional legal culture even among the other UN human rights treaties. The challenge is to nudge not just domestic law to the contrary but to change the overall thrust of existing international human rights law. This is not an easy task, but it is a necessary one. Intriguing though this inter-treaty competition is, it does not form part of the core focus of this chapter. Rather the fact that the older view is reflected in a range of UN human rights treaties, which again is not unexpected, demonstrates the difficulty of the task in changing the underlying 'legal fictions' of both the domestic and international legal orders.

Filtering is not a one-way street: from international to domestic. It also works the other way around especially in the drafting of treaties. The very process of crafting the CRPD was itself a product of filtering: from domestic to international. The CRPD is itself an artefact of a legal culture—or a combination of world legal cultures. It did not come from a vacuum. Most negotiators were aware that they were creating something new—something transcendent—something that could be used to shine a light on current domestic practices and subvert them at least in part. But they were also alert to the need to reduce this disruptive element to the minimum with respect to existing State practice. That is to say, they negotiated from the perspective of creating something new whose critical bite could be securely narrowed when it came to their existing practices. So, there is always a natural undertow to make the new cultural artefact, a treaty in this case, subservient to State practice rather than be overly critical of it. The CRPD is both the product of a 'legal culture', or combination of 'legal cultures', and a set of elevated benchmarks that have the

[4] Article 15 of the Convention for the Elimination of all forms of Discrimination against Women (CEDAW 1979)—is the closest analogue in the other UN thematic human rights treaties to Article 12 CRPD (2006).

potential to directly challenge or subvert existing 'legal cultures'. Indeed, that is exactly why the text of Article 12 contains much constructive ambiguity, either in the hope or in the expectation that it would be interpreted narrowly, and thus poses no threat to orthodox legal culture. And if it were interpreted expansively then States could apply a web of tools to narrow down its application to them, including through Declarations, Reservations and Understandings. This is exactly what many States have done.[5]

'Legal culture' is relatively autonomous and distinct from 'culture' more generally. This is important since it goes to the limits and possibilities of new peremptory norms, like Article 12 (CRPD 2006), to change the underlying legal culture. Famously, during a transformative period in the common law in the early 1600s, Chief Justice Coke admonished the King for purporting to second guess legal outcomes in the courts. Coke C.J. said (*Dr. Bonham's* case):

> His Majesty was not learned in the laws of his realm of England, and causes which concern the life, or inheritance, or goods, or fortunes of his subjects, are not to be decided by natural reason but by the artificial reason and judgment of law, which law is an art which requires long study and experience, before that a man can attain to the cognisance of it. (Brudner and Nadler 2013, p. 46)

Unpacked, what this means is that there is a world of difference between the 'natural reasoning' of those uninitiated in the law and the 'artificial reasoning' of the law, and lawyers. Those who are uninitiated in this 'artificial reasoning' of the law, unlike legally trained lawyers, are not therefore best placed to provide a telling critique. Only those acculturated in the priesthood of the law could be allowed do so. Here the substantive and methodological autonomy of the law is insisted upon.

Substantive autonomy means that the underlying postulates of the law stand apart from other postulates, in politics or ethics or in otherwise grounded disciplines. This is so, even when they have been historically

[5] Full text of the various Reservations, Declarations and Understandings lodged by States Parties (RUDs) is available here: https://treaties.un.org/pages/ViewDetails.aspx?src=IND&mtdsg_no=IV-15&chapter=4&clang=_en.

derived from outside the law. Procedural autonomy means that the characteristic methodology of the law, that is, formal legal reasoning, stands apart from other kinds of reasoning, for example, in politics or ethics, and court outcomes that are fairly derived from it should be respected even when those outcomes offend against 'natural reasoning'. Coke C.J. not only stands as a clear statement for the autonomy of the legal realm, or legal culture, but also as a clear statement about the autonomy (and distinctiveness) of the legal profession.

All of this is really a belief system—a series of 'legal fictions'—and can be contested. The underlying legal postulates of today often resemble the underlying political or ethical postulates of yesterday. When courts pronounce they may even be unselfconsciously taking sides among warring creeds. When courts rationalise certain outcomes their formal rationality may conceal as much as it reveals about the true cause of judgment. Legal reasoning is not so different from other forms of reasoning and can be cross-contaminated. The pretensions of the law to be wholly autonomous in form, as well as procedure, can be seen as just that—a pretension. Yet there can be no doubt that Coke's move gave life to the idea of the 'rule of law' and has often served as a useful brake on the improvident use of power. This relative autonomy of the law and legal culture makes it doubly hard to displace its foundational values. These embedded values are therefore hard to dislodge and have a history of their own. They may well have emanated from a variety of sources, such as from religion, ethics, political culture and popular culture. But once they enter into legal culture they assume a life of their own and seem remarkably impervious to critique and change.

To coin the language of Professor Lon Fuller, they become 'legal fictions' at the base of the legal order. One cannot do better than to quote Fuller:

> Probably no lawyer would deny that judges and writers on legal topics frequently make statements which they know to be false. These statements are called "fictions." There is scarcely a field of the law in which one does not encounter one after another of these conceits of the legal imagination. (Fuller 1930, p. 363)

The power of these fictions is not to be tested relative to their truth. Probably, they come from a deeper well of ideas or values characteristic of the underlying culture. And probably they come from some utilitarian calculus—for example, the 'fiction' of a corporation as a person helps increase the wealth generating capacity of an economy. Or maybe it is a mix of the two. Fuller (1930) was at pains to demonstrate that although they are in some important sense untrue does not necessarily rob them of their power to inform and structure the legal realm. They certainly are not directly dislodged by a new law, even at the higher level of an international treaty, which seeks to uproot them. Something else is needed to shift them apart from the ipse dixit of international law.

This notion of a legal culture underpinning, structuring and bounding a legal order and populated by 'legal fictions' or useful legal myths is strongly supported by Dean Roscoe Pound—the father of Sociological Jurisprudence. His legal writings were aimed at breaking through ideas about legal formalism as a block on progressive change. He saw the courts as deploying formalistic methods of interpretation in order to retard the introduction of new legal ideals and to preserve older ones—and thus illegitimately take sides in broader socio-economic disputes. He stated that the ultimate aim of the new sociological approach to law was to enable the felt needs of the time to be the true basis of law reform. He said:

> The sociological movement in jurisprudence is a movement for pragmatism as a philosophy of law; for the adjustment of principles and doctrines to the human conditions they are to govern rather than to assume first principles; for putting the human factor in the central place and relegating logic to its true position as an instrument. (Pound 1908, pp. 609–610)

Conscious that he might be seen as endorsing a form of legal Darwinism, a legal order without any fixed anchorage points, he was careful to assert that there were some constants in the process of change—and that these constants came from outside the law and helped to give the field structure and direction (Pound 1908). He never himself identified these core postulates but posited their existence as the very foundation of the legal order. Indeed, in a similar vein, Lon Fuller (1930) postulated the existence of a kind of morality that 'makes law possible', which of course emanates from outside the law itself. An observation that 'legal fictions' exist and help explain legal change (or the lack of it) is not the same as subscribing to cultural relativism in law. Neither Pound nor Fuller would have endorsed this.

So, there is no doubt that a distinctive legal culture exists. It is usually the pale shadow of ideas that have emanated elsewhere and then become ossified over time in the law. There is then a natural drag between major cultural shifts in society and changes in underlying legal culture. The latter does not necessarily follow the former and may take a lot longer. This might even be rationalised as a good thing in democratic societies since it acts as a brake on radical change, which may turn out to be wrongheaded.

2 The Primary Legal Fiction in Our Legal Culture: Cognitive Ability and Rationality as the Essence of Personhood

What 'legal fictions' lie at the heart of our legal culture on the issue of 'personhood'? The underlying 'legal fictions' seem remarkably uniform throughout the world. It is intriguing to observe just how central the foundational 'legal fiction' of 'cognition' and 'rationality', as the essence of what it means to be a 'person' is to nearly every legal culture in the world. What emerged from, or at least was crystallised in, the Enlightenment, and what was eventually operationalised in law, was a highly atomised conception of the person. That is, the proverbial masterless man or woman, with no organic ties to others and wandering abroad seeking (self-seeking) his/her own fortune.

Within classic ethics the 'morally considerable person', that is, the person that the system of justice acknowledges, respects, protects and supports is the person capable of self-reflection, self-direction and self-control (Feder-Kittay and Carlson 2010). To him or her (and only to him or her) is due a wide margin of latitude to make their own way in the world—whatever we may think of the wisdom of their life plans. To entities that fall short they are designated as of no moral considerability—objects or things, like a stone, and not subjects (Bernstein 1998). The person is a subject, not an object. Those who are constituted as in between, for example, persons with intellectual disabilities, are deemed persons of 'lesser moral worth'. Unlike objects, they are due respect and protection because they are recognisably human. However, within classic ethics they are not entitled to the wide margin of latitude on personal decision-making that is only allowed for full persons.

Strangely enough, this foundational '*legal fiction*' permeates nearly every legal culture in the world despite other wide ideological differences. It is beyond the scope of this chapter to explain why this is so. Perhaps it has something to do with the emergence of commercial societies some 300 years ago. The re-making of the world into public and private spheres in the 1700s privileged the private sphere and de-legitimated public power. The intent was to create a private sphere of unencumbered individuals acting autonomously and at arms-length from each other. If legitimate obligations were to be assumed by individuals, they would be assumed voluntarily with each other. There grew up the notion of the 'will theory of contract', to explain and justify private obligations enforceable through contract provided there was a genuine 'meeting of the minds'—a sort of mutual surrendering of rights and assumption of obligations. Naturally, only those who had capacity for this 'meeting of minds' could enter into contractual relations. In addition, third parties had a 'reliance interest' in such transactions being deemed valid. No such 'reliance interest' could arise unless one could assume that the parties were capable of entering into contractual relations (Fried 2015).[6] Put another way, one might rely on the outward appearance of contractual relations but only provided the parties were capable of acting autonomously. Otherwise no reliance interest could arise. Of course, the reliance interest can bear another interpretation. If outward behaviour gives rise to a legitimate expectation of contractual obligations, then they might be deemed to arise regardless of capacity.

One also suspects that the gradual rise of the welfare State may have strangely copper-fastened the 'legal fiction' of the rational person as the only morally considerable person. The original purpose of the welfare

[6] For a history of the reliance interest notion see Hudec, R., '*Restating the Reliance Interest*,' 67 Cornell L. Rev., 704 (1981–1982).

State was to provide for, that is, to compensate for, a deficiency. Implicit in this was that any loss was not to be allowed to lie where it falls—it was in a sense to be socialised. That being so, why allow space for the person with the presumed deficiency, in this case a decision-making deficit, to make mistakes for which the public (taxpayer) would have to pick up the tab. As a counsel of prudence, the predictable 'damage' could be foreclosed by limiting the decision-making options of the individual who bore the deficit. The prophylactic was to foreclose decision-making that could lead to such costly mistakes.

Whatever the ultimate historical reason/s for the narrowing down of personhood into essentialist criteria like rational or cognitive ability, its implications were stark. If some humans are excluded from personhood, then individuals will have to be tested to see on what side of the line they fall. The mere presence of a serious cognitive deficit became a proxy for lacking the essentialist indicia for personhood. This was the essence of the 'status-based' approach. Or, working backwards, if a pattern of improvident decisions were observable, then that might be interpreted as evincing some underlying cognitive frailty. This too could be used to place someone on the wrong side of the line. The point is, legal culture posits a line and, that being the case, it is natural to test to see where particular individuals fall on either side.

The key ingredients of the 'legal fictions' underpinning traditional legal culture came about long before international human rights law came into its own in the mid-twentieth century. Interestingly, a consciousness that regimes of legal incapacity might give rise to human rights concerns did not come until the 1990s—long after the adoption by the UN of the two major UN human rights covenants (ICCPR 1966; ICESCR 1966). It is fair to infer that it had simply been assumed that the values that supported legal incapacity regimes were woven deep into the intellectual structure of these treaties and were left undisturbed by them. Such was the power of the 'legal fictions' underpinning much domestic law at the time.

This began to change in the late 1980s and early 1990s. Quite why it only began to happen then is open to question. Certainly, the re-examination of civil commitment laws as a result of Soviet abuses of mental health law was an early spur from the late 1970s (Fitzpatrick 1988). Certainly, the rise of the anti-psychiatry movement with its objection to paternalism and protectionism had something to do with it. And certainly, the rise of disability civil society, stirred into life by the UN 1981 World Programme of Action on Disabled Persons, had something to do with it.

The first (pre-CRPD) wave of human rights responses to regimes of legal incapacity took place in the 1990s and indeed continues. The main point about this framing is that it is perfectly compatible with the 'legal fictions' of the traditional legal order, which is why so many States prefer it to the CRPD. It emanated from the various organs of the Council of Europe (CoE) and especially in an important set of policy guidelines in 1999 issued by its Committee of Ministers (CoE 1999). It accepts that the withdrawal of voice and capacity raise profound human rights issues. Re-framing the issues as ones within a human rights frame, rather than a protectionist or welfare frame, is already an advance. However, saying that legal incapacity regimes beg justification is not the same as saying they lack justification. What the first wave of human rights-based reform did was (1) to narrow down to the bone those instances where guardianship can be imposed, and (2) to tighten up on the applicable due process requirements. Emblematic of this approach is the famous Recommendation (99)4 of the Committee of Ministers of the Council of Europe of 1999 (CoE 1999). Among many things, this policy recommendation which was intended to guide law reform laid down the principles of necessity and proportionality in response to incapacity, as well as the maximisation of respect for human rights. Flipped, however, the logic reveals an openness to legal incapacity in certain reduced instances. One innovation was to suggest that persons might be incapacitated for some functions and not for others. Therefore, any measure of intervention should be narrowly tailored to exactly where the functional limitation arose, hence the term 'functionalism'.

It might be said that this first wave of a human rights response, and framing, helped to modernise and refine the underlying 'legal fictions'. However, it did not—and does not—fundamentally challenge them, whereas the CRPD does.

3 The Janus Face of Article 12: Reflecting and Reinforcing Traditional Legal Culture or Transformative of It?

Most States probably entered into negotiations on Article 12 (CRPD 2006) on the assumption that there would, and should, be a movement away from traditional guardianship towards something like a 'functionalist' approach, as outlined in the Council of Europe Recommendation above (CoE 1999). Part of the motivation to do so is the natural tendency for States to negotiate for norms that would have the least amount of disruptive effect on existing laws and practices.

Embedding a 'functionalist' approach would not displace the traditional 'legal fictions'. Indeed, it left them largely intact because if there was an objective showing of a decision-making deficit, then an appropriate displacement of legal capacity was authorised. So, although the 'functionalist' approach narrows the traditional precepts, it does not fundamentally challenge them. However, the text of Article 12 (CRPD 2006) is ambiguous—pointing at one and at the same time backward towards traditional 'legal fictions', and also pointing forward towards a completely different 'legal fiction'. Ambiguity is of course natural and even normal in treaty language. Usually, however, the ambiguity exists at the edge of a rule—hinting at the outer limits of its reach or application. Seldom does it point at the heart of a rule—hinting at two completely different sets of underlying values or 'legal fictions'.

States responded to this ambiguity by entering Declarations and Understandings to the effect that the first or less disruptive interpretation was to be preferred. Certainly, that comported best with existing State practice. Typical of this is the Declaration and Reservation entered by Ireland:

> Ireland recognises that persons with disabilities enjoy legal capacity on an equal basis with others in all aspects of life. Ireland declares its understanding that the Convention permits supported and substitute decision-making arrangements which provide for decisions to be made on behalf of a person, where such arrangements are necessary, in accordance with the law, and subject to appropriate and effective safeguards.

> To the extent article 12 may be interpreted as requiring the elimination of all substitute decision making arrangements, Ireland reserves the right to permit such arrangements in appropriate circumstances and subject to appropriate and effective safeguards. (https://treaties.un.org/pages/ViewDetails.aspx?src=IND&mtdsg_no=IV-15&chapter=4&clang=_en#EndDec)

So, it declares that both supported and substituted decision-making are allowed under Article 12 (CRPD 2006), one 'legal fiction' sitting uncomfortably alongside another. And, to the extent to which the UN Committee on the Rights of Persons with Disabilities decides otherwise, Ireland hedges its bet by entering a Reservation to the effect that substitute decision-making is still allowed at least for it. In as much as law reform is happening, States Parties tend to hedge their bets by narrowing down guardianship, as per the functionalist approach, and opening up some new space for supported decision-making. In other words, they have hedged their bets in law reform too.

In a sense, the CRPD represents a second wave of human rights response to legal incapacity. The essence of the second wave is to view the entire enterprise of guardianship as illegitimate. There is no replacement of guardianship as such. Rather an entirely different regime is required to use new techniques of discovery to unveil the will and preference of the person—and to respect it. This, most assuredly, is not consistent with the 'legal fictions' of traditional legal culture. How does Article 12 (CRPD 2006) point in two directions with two seemingly incompatible value systems and 'legal fictions'?

The first paragraph (CRPD 2006, Art. 12(1)) states the obvious and is notable simply because it was felt necessary to state the obvious in the first place—namely that persons with disabilities have a right to recognition as 'persons' before the law. It does not qualify itself by saying that some or even most persons with disabilities count as persons. This hints strongly in the direction of a new 'legal fiction' to replace the old—that everyone has legal capacity. But it also leaves some space for the older view that while all persons with disabilities are persons, some persons are 'less morally considerable' than others (to use the strangely clinical and somewhat offensive language of ethics). This is so because it does not stipulate in so many words that personhood is a unitary concept meaning the same thing in all times everywhere in the world. Instead (as per the next paragraph) persons with disabilities are assured their rights 'on an equal basis with others' which allows for distinctions to be made.

The second sub-paragraph (CRPD 2006, Art 12(2)) assures persons with disabilities a right to enjoy legal capacity 'on an equal basis with others' and in all spheres of life (CRPD 2006, Art 12(2)). The reference to 'on an equal basis with others' interjects equality analysis into the frame. Of course, it is open to States Parties to assert (and many of them strenuously do) that there are significant material differences between persons with severe intellectual disabilities and others. These differences, in turn, are said to fully justify the withdrawal or limitation of legal capacity. That is because many States still see, as under the traditional 'legal fictions', cognitive ability as the essence of personhood. Therefore, equality analysis, on its own, will not necessarily change this. Indeed, by inviting an exploration of material differences, equality analysis seems to create space for it to count.

However, the third sub-paragraph (CRPD 2006, Art. 12(3)), which is perhaps one of the most discussed provisions in any modern international human rights treaty, points to a new departure point in the context of personhood and decision-making frailty. It speaks of a right of 'access' to 'supports' to enable a person to 'exercise' their legal capacity. The overall thrust of Article 12(3) is unmistakable. At the first sign of frailty, States should not resort to guardianship. Instead, the States Parties should endeavour to promote 'access' to a web of supports to enable a person to exercise their inherent legal capacity (CRPD 2006, Art. 12(3)). This notion of 'support' to 'exercise legal capacity' embraces (CRPD 2006, Art. 12(3)), but also goes beyond, simple supported decision-making. It may even involve sparking the will and preference of the person, or developing new tools of discovery in order to be able to access the persons' will and preference. In point of fact, most States do not object to the introduction of supported decision-making regimes. Rather, what they typically insist on is the latitude to introduce such regimes whilst at one and the same time retaining the option of guardianship as a last resort and in compliance with the functionalist model as above. On the other hand, sub-paragraph 3 does not, at least on its face, proscribe guardianship.

Many 'reforming' States have latched onto this. That is to say that they have enacted legislation that narrows down but does not eliminate guardianship. A prime example of this is the Irish Assisted Decision Making (Capacity) Act of 2015. Much of the Act innovates in respect of assisted decision-making. However, Section 38 still allows for the possibility of guardianship.

Sub-paragraph 4 (CRPD 2006, Art. 12(4)) also points in both directions at once, that is, the continuance of guardianship but with safeguards, and the introduction of supported decision-making also with safeguards. The various safeguards envisaged in sub-paragraph 4 do seem to contemplate the continuance of some form of substitute decision-making, thus present an interesting interpretive conundrum for the treaty monitoring body. Sub-paragraph 4 famously interjects the language of 'will and preferences' of the person. This is a curious formula that also seems to point in two different directions. The mention of 'preferences' seems to assume a traditional 'functionalist' approach whereby it is assumed, until proved to the contrary, that the person can rationally process his/her options and rationally pronounce a preference. However, the mention of 'will' seems to point in exactly the opposite direction—towards naked preferences formed more by instinct and impulse than by rationality. This tension aside, most people use the term 'will and preferences' as a term of art, which refers essentially to the choice of the person (howsoever formed) as distinct from choices imposed upon the person by a third party.

Sub-paragraph 5 (CRPD 2006, Art. 12(5)) deals with the right to legal capacity in the context of decision-making over property and financial affairs. Strictly speaking, this was not necessary since the reference to 'all aspects of life' in sub-paragraph 2 (CRPD 2006, Art. 12(2)) should have been sufficient to cover it. What probably moved the drafters to include a specific provision on it was the widespread prevalence of financial abuses.

Janus is the old Roman God of gates, transitions and beginnings. The UN Committee on the Rights of Persons with Disabilities (Committee) has discarded one face of Janus—pointing away from the old 'legal fictions' and towards a theory of universal legal capacity. As if to underscore Article 12 as the fulcrum of the whole convention, the UN Committee chose to issue its very first General Comment on it in 2014.[7] Though not, in a strict legal sense, legally binding, General Comments put forward a treaty monitoring body's understanding of a provision and the correlative obligations incumbent on States Parties. The General Comment opens by asserting that there has been a:

> general failure to understand that the human-rights based model of disability implies a shift from the substitute decision-making paradigm to one that is based on supported decision-making. (CRPD/C/GC/1 2014, Para. 3)

Actually, the accepted wisdom up to that point was that the human rights model of disability required a move to the functionalist model. The General Comment continues by asserting that the right to equal recognition before the law:

> implies that legal capacity is a universal attribute inherent in all persons by virtue of their humanity and must be upheld for persons with disabilities on an equal basis with others. (CRPD/C/GC/1 2014, Para. 8)

In point of fact, equality analysis can point in both directions. Most States understood the notion of 'on an equal basis with others' to allow them to identify 'material difference' and to legislate accordingly. The philosophy of 'universal' legal capacity is simply posited. The reasoning is a little conclusory since being a human does not necessarily mean that one was a full legal person in law in the past. And indeed, some entities are persons in law despite not being human at all, for example, corporations.

The General Comment dissolves the age-old difference between 'holding' a right and 'exercising' a right (CRPD/C/GC/1 2014, Para. 12). This runs directly contrary to the view taken in many civil law jurisdictions. That does not make the position wrong—but it is clear that the Committee's understanding is far ahead of much State practice and legal culture. Further, the General Comment separates out tests of 'mental capacity' from the question of 'legal capacity', which it assumes is universal

[7] UN CRPD Committee General Comment 1, Equal Protection before the Law, (2014): available at https://www.ohchr.org/EN/HRBodies/CRPD/Pages/GC.aspx.

(CRPD/C/GC/1 2014, Para. 13). Rather than fused or connected categories, it sees both as hermetically sealed from each other. It adds to this an implacable opposition to 'functionalism' (CRPD/C/GC/1 2014, Para. 15). The General Comment asserts that 'will and preferences' should replace the old theory of 'best interests' (CRPD/C/GC/1 2014, Para. 21). In other words, the process of exploring or excavating the 'self' and identifying his/her own choices is primary. The endeavour of controlling the actions of substitute decision-makers through the application of controlling notions like 'best interests' is not only not secondary—it does not exist.

Let me repeat, all of the above jurisprudence of the UN Committee seems starkly ahead of State practice and is a direct challenge to dominant legal culture. If you bring the assumptions of the traditional 'legal fiction' of personhood to it, then it probably does not work for you. If you have already began to move away from the traditional 'legal fictions' about personhood, then it begins to make sense.

Will the jump by the UN Committee trigger deep and wide change? If State practice is anything to go by, probably not. The underlying legal culture has not changed—most States still see cognitive ability as the essence of personhood. The view of the UN Committee really represents what the *outcome* of a change of legal culture would look like; however, it does not in itself change legal culture. Nevertheless, legal culture must be changed to make space for new ideas.

4 Nudging Legal Culture to Support a Theory of Universal Legal Capacity

It is plain that law on its own is not enough to change legal culture, especially where the 'legal fictions' of that culture are anchored deep in its substrata. And yet, unless and until that legal culture changes there will be little space for a more expansive view of personhood and legal capacity to trigger a non-guardianship future. All of which begs the question—how can we change legal culture and especially its underlying 'legal fictions'?

The ritual incantation of international norms will not do—at least not on its own. The circularity of equality analysis means it can be flipped both ways. Nor will the deployment of slogans like 'universal legal capacity' work, since they do not budge States from the view that cognition is the essence of personhood and that any law must reflect and respond to real differences.

Yet legal culture does change. How can we accelerate that change to make for more receptive ground for the CRPD? It is suggested a broader repertoire of arguments are needed to explain why the predicates of the underlying 'legal fictions' no longer make sense (if they ever did), and why their utility value has also declined. Even then, we still need to convince States that the alternative is well grounded and would generate no additional problems of unknowable magnitude. The first is probably easier than the second; however, both must be prosecuted to make space for the culture shift of the CRPD.

As to the first, there is now overwhelming scientific support for the proposition that decision-making does not rest on exaggerated expectations of cognitive ability or rationality. Modern science is displaying in brilliant technicolour the true extent to which the 'self' is a social construct. At one extreme is the field of socio-biology or evolutionary psychology. It can lead to the view that the 'self', like the 'mind', is an illusion. Certainly, if taken to such extremes it places not just an asterisk but also a huge question mark over **all** decision-making whether by 'normal' people or persons with intellectual disabilities alike. My intent in mentioning socio-biology is not to deny the existence of a 'person' or the 'will' or the 'mind'—although some do. Rather my intent is to place notions like autonomy and mind in context, and to show how the standard account of it is far from monolithic (Midgley 2014).

Additionally, much neuroscience is yielding new theories of the mind which have been conspicuously absent from orthodox debates about the 'self', including decision-making. Antonio Demasio, for example, is famous for his thesis that the brain is 'wired to connect' (Demasio 2012). He does not say that the brain of those with higher cognitive functioning is 'wired to connect', rather that all brains are wired to connect (Demasio 2012). In essence the 'self' emerges from these connections. Our 'selves' are inter-subjective from the outset and our autonomy is fundamentally 'relational'. Similarly, Bruce Hood (2013) develops the idea of the 'social brain'. The point is that modern neuroscience debunks the 'standard account' of a hermetically sealed and disconnected mind. What it points to instead is the quality of the social connectors in our lives and especially in the life of the mind (Hood 2013).

One pithy way of putting this is that our personhood is primarily shared—although it is necessarily experienced individually. It is probably the normal interplay of support and threat that 'others' pose in relationships that helps form (and subtly change) our sense of 'self' and maintain a baseline identity through time. This is another way of making sense of the support paradigm in Article 12 (CRPD 2006). McSherry's perceptive article (2015) shows how the new 'discovery' techniques being opened up by neuroscience have positive potential into the future to reveal formerly unknown and unknowable persons accordingly, as the science evolves.

Even before the emergence of new scientific insights questioning the centrality of cognition, the humanities have long challenged excessively atomistic conceptions of human autonomy. For example, Davy (2015) captures brilliantly the notion of inter-subjectivity or shared personhood in feminist legal and political thinking and applies it to the sphere of intellectual disability. Although not directly concerned with the notion of support as understood under Article 12 of the CRPD (2006), her survey of the idea of our inter-subjective 'selves' reinforces the move towards a support paradigm—especially when one realises the supports occur naturally in the community.

Added to recent literature in clinical psychology is the burgeoning field of behavioural economics. The standard account of mind, consciousness and rational decision-making underpins much classical economics and animates many econometric models. Yet the explanatory power of these models has been found deficient. Contemporary economists have been reassessing the role of rationality in economic decision-making. Indeed, the latest 2015 World Bank Development Report focuses on exactly this 'Mind, Society and Behaviour' (World Bank 2015). The Report characterises decision-making (for all people) along three axes: (1) automatic decision-making, (2) social decision-making and (3) mental decision-making. It insists that the vast majority of decisions are made automatically with little or no in-depth deliberation (World Bank 2015). By social thinking is meant the reflex in all of us to fit with and be valorised by our group affiliation, if we are lucky enough to have one (World Bank 2015). Lastly the Report insists that we come to decision-making with mental baggage—narrow windows through which we make sense of the world, bypassing our cognitive functioning (World Bank 2015). The 'rational economic man' has not disappeared—but he just got radically contextualised!

Peeling away the many layers of analysis—what are these disciplines really telling us? They are telling us loud and clear that cognition is just one part of a menu of capacities that most humans possess. They are telling us that personhood is primarily shared and that it is wholly natural to focus on the dialectic between supports and threats that are integral in all our decision-making. They are telling us that new discovery techniques are available and are evolving to enable us to divine the will and preference of the person, even in circumstances where we thought they were unknowable to us. That should be enough to force a thoroughgoing reconsideration of traditional 'legal fictions'. Why persist with laws and policies that rest on assumptions that are plainly at odds with new insights from the hard sciences? If there ever was 'evidence-based policy-making', then clearly our old policies stand in clear need of reform.

It seems that the insights and advances mentioned above are highly corrosive of the old legal culture—and go especially against the myth of cognition as the essence of personhood. One missing element in our armoury for change has been the effective use of such insights to undermine the foundations of legal culture. This is a much more direct way of challenging legal culture than positing its non-existence through law (World Bank 2015).

One blind-spot induced by legal culture has to do with our restricted imagination for alternatives. Even if policy-makers are convinced that their predominant 'legal fictions' lack any foundation whatever, which is what the science is tending to say, then they may still demur by doubting the practicality or wisdom of the alternatives. This is of course perverse. It predisposes one not to see the alternatives in their own right but sets them against the known and more knowable set of current practices. Typically States worry that the new discovery techniques that allow us to peer into a person's soul and divine their will and preference are not yet so well settled as would give confidence. In other words, unless and until the new techniques are better grounded, they pose as many dangers as solutions. Further, these new techniques are only useful in as much as we can usefully screen out ambient noises from third parties who, through their 'support', may in fact be unselfconsciously interpolating their own will and preference. In situations where the person's will and preference are not presently discoverable and where the very stuff of the self needs to be built up and augmented, for example, post long-term institutionalisation, there is a standing danger of 'manufacturing' the self through 'supports'. This evokes images of the intentionally contrived 'socialist man' in Honecker's East Germany—something to be avoided at all costs. And lastly, there is the fear that the inevitable mistakes will somehow have to be absorbed, accommodated or paid for by public institutions—causing more disruption than at present.

5 Conclusion: Towards a Broader Agenda to Change Legal Culture to Give Breathing Space to the UN CRPD

It seems obvious that a dual-track strategy for change is needed to dislodge the old 'legal fictions'. First of all, their 'legal fictions' have to be challenged from the perspective of the new insights emerging from the social and natural sciences. If public policy is to be truly evidence based, then the evidence points convincingly away from the atomistic and rational decision-maker—not just for persons with disabilities but for everyone. And second, law reform models that eliminate guardianship have to steadily prove themselves. New problematics will emerge. For example, how do we protect the process of discovering the person from cross-contamination? It is obvious that protection as a value has not gone away. In the newer legal culture, protection should no longer be about compounding the problems of a weak voice by taking it away altogether through guardianship. The urgent task of protection becomes one of protecting the process of discovery of the self. This has everything to do with giving efficacy to rights, rather than policing the processes by which they are taken away.

The prize of a new legal culture based on a different set of 'legal fictions' is big, and not just for persons with disabilities but also for older persons. In this 'kulturkampf' all disciplines have to be harnessed and not just the law. If Homes (1896–1897) was right in saying that the law is the external deposit of communities' morality, then that morality must change to make way for greater receptivity to Article 12 (CRPD 2006). A more realistic appraisal of the limits of law is needed since the law itself will not necessarily change the underlying legal culture.

References

A/CN.4/L.682. (2006). *Report of the study group of the international law commission: fragmentation of international law—Difficulties arising from the diversification and expansion of international law*. International Law Commission (2006). Retrieved from http://legal.un.org/ilc/documentation/english/a_cn4_l682.pdf.

Assisted Decision Making (Capacity) Act of 2015. (2015). Retrieved from http://www.irishstatutebook.ie/eli/2015/act/64/enacted/en/html.

Bernstein, M. H. (1998). *On moral considerability: An essay on who morally matters*. New York: Oxford.

Brudner, A., & Nadler, J. (2013). *The unity of the common law*. Oxford: Oxford University Press.

CoE (Council of Europe). (1999). *Recommendation no. (99)4 of the committee of ministers to member states on principles concerning the legal protection of incapable adults*. Retrieved from https://search.coe.int/cm/Pages/result_details.aspx?ObjectId=09000016805e303c.

CRPD/C/GC/1. (2014). *(Committee on the rights of persons with disabilities) general comment no. 1 (2014) Article 12: Equal recognition before the law*. Retrieved from https://www.ohchr.org/EN/HRBodies/CRPD/Pages/GC.aspx.

Davy, L. K. (2015). Philosophical inclusive design: Intellectual disability and the limits of individual autonomy in political and moral theory. *Hypatia, 30*(1), 132–148.

Demasio, A. (2012). *Self comes to mind. Constructing the conscious brain*. New York: Vintage.

Feder-Kittay, E., & Carlson, L. (Eds.). (2010). *Cognitive disability and its challenge to moral philosophy*. Oxford: Wiley Blackwell.

Fitzpatrick, C. A. (1988). *Soviet abuses of psychiatry for political purposes*. Report Prepared for U.S. Helsinki Watch Committee. Retrieved from http://digitalcollections.library.cmu.edu/awweb/awarchive?type=file&item=543132.
Fried, C. (2015). *Contract as promise: A theory of contractual obligation* (2nd ed.). Oxford: Oxford UniversityPress.
Fuller, L. (1930). Legal fictions 25. *Illinois Law Review, 25*(4), 363–399.
Fuller, L. (1964). *The morality of law*. New Haven and London: Yale University Press.
Homes, O. W. (1896–1897). Path of the law. *Harvard Law Review, 10*, 457.
Hood, B. (2013). *The self illusion: How the social brain creates*. Oxford: Oxford University Press.
ICCPR. (1966). *International covenant on civil and political right*. New York: United Nations.
ICESCR. (1966). *International covenant on economic, social and cultural rights*. New York: United Nations.
Klare, K. (1977–1978). Judicial de-radicalization of the Wagner act and the origins of modern legal consciousness. *Minnesota Law Review, 62*(3), 265–340.
McSherry, B. (2015). Decision making, legal capacity and neuroscience: Implications for mental health laws. *Laws, 4*(2), 125–138.
Midgley, M. (2014). *Are you an illusion?* Abingdon: Routledge.
Plucknett, F. T. (1926). Bonham's case and judicial review. *Harvard Law Review, 40*(1), 30–70.
Pound, R. (1908). Mechanical jurisprudence. *Columbia Law Review, 8*, 605–610.
Sandland, R. (2017). A clash of conventions? Participation, power, and the rights of disabled children. *Social Inclusion, 5*(3), 93–103.
World Bank. (2015). *World Bank development report mind, society and behaviour*. Retrieved from http://www.worldbank.org/en/publication/wdr2015.
Zand, J. (2017). The concept of democracy and the European convention on human rights. *The University of Baltimore Journal of International Law, 5*(2), 15–42.

3

Anthropology, Disability and the CRPD

James G. Rice

1 Introduction

The United Nations (UN) Convention on the Rights of Persons with Disabilities (CRPD) (2006), which is the first UN international human rights treaty of the twenty-first century, is progressive and innovative in its scale and scope, not only in regard to furthering the rights of persons with disabilities but for human rights in general. Theresia Degener (2016) argued that when the CRPD was conceived, it did not intend to create any new human rights, or rights particular to persons with disabilities, but to ensure that persons with disabilities are protected by the human rights conventions that have been ratified by their State. However, Degener continues that the CRPD goes beyond this and that it does introduce "new equality and non-discrimination concepts into international human rights law" (Degener 2016, p. 15). One reason is

J. G. Rice (✉)
School of Social Sciences, University of Iceland, Reykjavík, Iceland
e-mail: james@hi.is

E. J. Kakoullis, K. Johnson (eds.), *Recognising Human Rights in Different Cultural Contexts*, https://doi.org/10.1007/978-981-15-0786-1_3

that it has to, if implementation of the vision of the CRPD is to be possible.

The articles that comprise the CRPD reveal that behind the laudable ambition to ensure that persons with disabilities enjoy the same level of human rights protection as anyone else, the realisation of this is predicated upon an international and cross-cultural consensus about a wide range of matters, ranging from cultural worldviews, to that of fundamental aspects of social organisation, like marriage and the family. The CRPD engages with a broad range of issues involving rights and equality, which extend beyond those more specific to disability. Change in these areas is also required if the CRPD's vision of equality and inclusion of persons with disabilities is to be implemented and sustained. Critical Disability Studies scholars generally agree that disability is in many ways a social construct, though they differ on whether this refers to a set of power relationships, a cultural concept, an identity category, a label or signifier, or some combination thereof (Goodley 2011). As a social construct, the concept of disability is thus also a product of local cultural worldviews, histories and socio-economic and environmental conditions. It has been argued (Ingstad and Whyte 2007) that as the result of international forms of knowledge and governance, the CRPD being one example, the World Health Organisation (WHO) and its International Classification of Functioning, Disability and Health (ICF) being another, there is the potential for an international convergence in the definition of what disability means, but this has not been realised (Iriarte 2016). Disability as such remains a culturally emergent and mutable concept, dependent upon manifold systems of meaning as well as material, environmental and socio-structural factors, at the local as well as the global levels.

The key purpose of this chapter is to explore some of the cultural implications of the CRPD from an anthropological perspective. This will reveal that some of the articles of the CRPD may be in tension with or in contradiction to wider cultural values and beliefs. For example, Article 23—Respect for home and the family (CRPD 2006)—makes reference to concepts such as 'marriage' and 'consent' in such a way which implies that their meanings are straightforward and universally shared. These tensions may also be apparent in the Declarations, Reservations and Objections made by Signatories and States Parties (UN 2019a). The

CRPD is thus an example of the long-standing dilemma in Anthropology concerning the discussion of human rights, "the dilemma of universalism versus cultural relativism" (Dahre 2017, p. 611). No attempt at a solution is offered in this chapter other than the suggestion, in support of Dahre (2017), that the strong dichotomy between universalism and cultural relativism can be called into question, as all human rights treaties predicated upon notions of universalism will always confront local norms and values in the process of their negotiation and implementation.

The tension between universalism and cultural relativism in the context of the CRPD may be observed at a fundamental level, that of the understanding of the concept of 'disability' itself. The cultural variability of the 'disability' concept is something that has been observed by anthropologists for some time, notably in the edited volume by Ingstad and Whyte (1995), and this discussion has since continued (Hershenson 2000; Ingstad and Whyte 2007; Kasnitz et al. 2001; Rapp and Ginsburg 2001; Reid-Cunningham 2009; Staples and Mehrotra 2016). It has also been argued that the attempts to create a universally applicable definition of disability, whether within academic circles or governmental, are often situated in, at least up to recent years, that of a white, urban and middle-class perspective located in the Global North (Devlieger et al. 2007). The cross-cultural implications of disability pose some challenges for the CRPD. Although this issue was identified early in the process of drafting and negotiation and, as some have suggested, it may not be such an insurmountable problem—unless one adheres to an extreme view of cultural relativity that is more akin to cultural incommensurability (Bickenbach 2009). However, the issues raised here are broader than that of the cross-cultural understanding of the 'disability' concept itself; rather these issues are as broad as the concept of 'culture'. For example, when teaching undergraduate students about the 'culture' concept in Anthropology, one early goal is to instil critical thinking about the constructivist nature of 'culture'. Another is to draw attention to the problem of ethnocentrism, in which cultural values or practices of the 'other' are viewed from the perspective of one's own cultural location. Ethnocentrism may lead to value judgements and even notions of cultural superiority, various degrees of which have been noted in classic anthropological studies (Hsu 1979). The discipline continues to grapple with this legacy. It is also important to reinforce the idea that for anthropologists the considerations of 'culture' are indeed quite broad, encompassing, among others, the material, the symbolic and the socio-structural. E.B. Tylor's (1871, p. 1) classic definition of 'culture' as "that complex whole which includes knowledge, belief, art, morals, law, custom, and any other capabilities and habits acquired by man as a member of society" is usually provided as a starting point, as well as a stepping stone for the inevitable criticism to follow. A Tylor-esque understanding of the broader view of 'culture' is indeed suggestive of how the problematics of the CRPD extend beyond that of understandings of the 'disability' concept and matters narrowly specific to disability. This is perhaps what Shaun Grech (2016) was thinking in the introduction to a volume about disability from the perspectives of the Global South when he asked: "Can we really define and contain disability across cultures, contexts, ideologies, (geo)politics and socio-economic terrains?" (Grech 2016, p. xiv). The focus within the CRPD on achieving a universal vision of human rights for all, including persons with disabilities, could be interpreted as demanding adherence to a particular, and situated, perspective upon many other aspects of human socio-cultural life. These include but are not limited to gender relations, kinship, economic production, jurisprudence, marriage, sexual practices and mores, language, nationalism; and local, national and international politics and governance, such as border security, not to mention the notion of human rights themselves. The tensions within Anthropology between relativism and universalism are also apparent within the CRPD to an extent, but certainly in some of the reactions by Signatories and States Parties to it.

2 The CRPD

One of the strengths of the CRPD, and which allows it to offer far more than bland platitudes about respect for this or tolerance for that, is that it demands change in a wide range of areas of socio-cultural life, which are required to realise its vision in practice. It has been argued that this is indeed an important point of the CRPD, that is, to carry forward certain 'legacy values', such as "dignity, autonomy, equality and social solidarity … squarely to the heart of the disabilities field" (Quinn 2009, p. 246).

That strength, however, is also a potential weakness, as the very notion of a 'legacy value' contains within it the assumption that this value system is universally shared, or should be shared, and it overlooks how these values are also products of particularly situated worldviews. For example, some of the CRPD's fundamental building blocks that play a central role in a number of its articles, such as 'community', are not clearly defined (e.g. in Articles 19 and 24), while others reflect an understanding of 'gender', or 'marriage', or 'the family' or 'independence' (e.g. in Articles 19, 23 and 29), which are rooted, arguably, in a set of values and a worldview situated in the urban, Global North. This situatedness of UN conventions has been noted by anthropologists since the early discussions leading up to the UDHR and subsequent conventions. Montgomery (2001) contends that, for example, fundamental concepts such as 'childhood' underlying conventions such as the UN Convention on the Rights of the Child (CRC 1989) can be subjected to such a critique: "the ideal of childhood that it represents is based on a Western model which may not be appropriate for all societies" (Montgomery 2001, p. 83). There is a need for caution, though, as it has also been argued that the 'Western' perspective underlying UN conventions has been overstated. Arat (2006) contends that there are dangers in continuing to promote the idea that the various human rights treaties put forth by the UN are a reflection of the values of the Global North. Partly because this is false, in that from the UN Universal Declaration of Human Rights (UDHR 1948) onwards, these treaties have been negotiated by actors comprised from diverse national and cultural backgrounds. Furthermore, Arat (2006) also argues that presenting human rights as a 'Western' discourse can serve the agendas of repressive regimes to justify discriminatory and oppressive practices in the name of resisting Euro-American hegemony. Arat (2006) further concedes that one cannot ignore the history of European colonialism and its 'civilising' missions, and that the scepticism about the motives of international bodies in the formerly (or currently) colonised world is understandable. However, she remains adamant that all notions of human rights sit within cultural and historical contexts, and that the recognition, protection and enforcement of human rights treaties demand "the transformation of not only cultural norms but also their material foundations"

(Arat 2006, p. 424). While Arat is writing primarily about the history of the UDHR (1948), this applies to the CRPD as well.

3 The Anthropology of Disability

The Anthropology of disability, which is a small but growing body of work, has staked out cultural relativity as one of its key contributions to the study of disability; however, that is not the entirety of its contribution or implications for the matters at hand. In the context of teaching Anthropology, as well as Disability Studies, I have often drawn upon Ingstad and Whyte's (1995) edited volume to make a point to Anthropology students about the cross-cultural variability of often taken for granted concepts, and to Disability Studies students about the relativity, and situatedness, of the concept of 'disability'. An interesting example to demonstrate this point comes from a study of the Kel Tamasheq people of North Africa in which the researchers attempted, using WHO guidelines, to understand how 'disability' was understood locally (Ingstad and Whyte 1995). One issue that arose was that of language translation, as there was great difficulty in finding comparable terms for 'disability' or 'impairment'. This question was finally settled, on a notion of 'faults' of the body (Ingstad and Whyte 1995). Here culture also became significant, as the Tamasheq informants listed age, that is, infants and elderly people, 'excessive freckles', 'illegitimate birth', a 'protruding navel' and 'flabby or small buttocks' as faults, roughly approximating impairments (Ingstad and Whyte 1995, p. 6). There is no disability pension system that I am aware of where points would be awarded for freckles or a protruding navel. However, within the Tamasheq worldview this was entirely logical because, lacking a comparable terminology and conceptualisation of 'disability', the research participants listed factors that rendered individuals in their society as 'socially anomalous', because these people are either seen as 'dependent', such as elderly people and children, or as 'difficult to marry', as certain physical attributes were not seen as attractive in a society in which not being married was not a tenable position. None of these factors would be seen as embodied impairments or as disabling factors within the bio-medical understandings of disability typical of the

Global North. While the cultural relativity of the concept of 'disability' has gradually been incorporated into the discipline of Disability Studies, the situatedness of Disability Studies itself in the Global North has also been criticised (Connell 2011; Meekosha 2011; Grech and Soldatic 2016). Much as with international forms of knowledge and governance, the social scientific premises of northern Disability Studies, despite their differences, still draw upon a shared intellectual and cultural heritage which influences their interpretation and understandings of disability.

Despite the relevance of the 'culture' concept and cultural relativity, Anthropology has been generally meagre in its contribution to Disability Studies. There are a number of reasons raised as to why this may be; however, part of the problem perhaps lies within the discipline itself. Despite differences in interpretation and that of social effects, all human societies encounter impairment in some form or another, ranging from birth or acquired, as the result of accidents, injuries, illness, warfare or during the process of aging. In this sense impairment is a human universal. Nevertheless, in my education in Anthropology, the concepts of 'impairment' and 'disability' were entirely ignored. Staples and Mehrotra (2016) suggest that one reason that the discipline of Anthropology may have overlooked disability is that not many anthropologists are disabled and are simply not interested or motivated to do research in this area. Another issue could be disciplinary boundaries (Staples and Mehrotra 2016). For example, the interests of medical anthropology and the body intersect in similar ways as that of disability; however, they generally remain focused on illness and health rather than disability. Despite the relevance of cultural relativity to understanding disability, Anthropology's claim to fame as a study of the 'other' may not sit well within Disability Studies where 'otherness' is seen by some authors as one of the roots of social exclusion. Oliver and Barnes (2012), writing from the perspective of Disability Studies, situate Anthropology as the study of the 'other', specifically the 'pre-modern' 'other', that is, as 'rural, Global South', and relegate Sociology to the study of contemporary society, that is, as 'urban, Global North'. This is partly because of how Anthropology positioned itself in the early twentieth century; however, this is hardly how anthropologists work or think of their discipline now. In plumbing the corpus of early and mid-twentieth century ethnographies for examples of impairment, Oliver and Barnes (2012) neglect to reference the late twentieth century work in Anthropology that explicitly focuses on disability (e.g. Ablon 1984; Groce 1985; Murphy 1990), as well as more recent work that existed during their time of writing and which often engages with Disability Studies, such as Shuttleworth (2000) on disability, masculinity and sexuality, and Kohrman (2005) on the bureaucratic governance of disability in the People's Republic of China, as well as the edited volume by Ingstad and Whyte (2007). Oliver and Barnes (2012) highlight the contribution from Anthropology that disability and impairment vary contextually in terms of culture, place and history, and contend that this is generally ignored in the disciplines of Medicine and the Social Sciences.

Oliver and Barnes's (2012) other criticisms though, bear closer consideration for the matters at hand. They reserve a great deal of attention in their text to criticisms of the WHO's ICF but pay little attention to the CRPD—aside from commenting that it is difficult to enforce and, in their view, has had little impact upon the lives of persons with disabilities (Oliver and Barnes 2012). However, they raise an important point about the focus on culture and disability in Anthropology, or more specifically on that of religion and disability. Oliver and Barnes (2012) concede that cultural or religious ideology is often cited for variations in local explanations for disability, for example, witchcraft, taboo violation, notions of karma, but they suggest that accepting local explanations for disability is problematic, as it is deterministic and simplistic, and "In so doing it sidesteps other factors such as the workings of the economy, power relations and structural inequality" (Oliver and Barnes 2012, p. 34). However, it is important not to assume that the cultural and the material are easily divorced, and that anthropologists consider these to be distinct phenomena; as these are complementary, not antagonistic, analytical approaches. There is a tendency within Disability Studies to focus on the cultural or the material as distinct avenues of inquiry (Waldschmidt 2018). For example, a material (or social model of disability) approach to independent living would seek to explain what barriers are in place that inhibit or restrict self-determination; "In contrast, an approach indebted to the cultural model strives to understand what personal autonomy and independent living mean in a given culture and society" (Waldschmidt 2018, p. 77). Both are critically important, and complementary, points of view but far too often the 'cultural' is synonymous with meaning, symbolism or the analysis of discourse, "where analyses of fine art, theater, films and literature tend to be privileged at the expense of studying everyday life" (Waldschmidt 2018, p. 78). Staples and Mehrotra (2016) raise another relevant tension between Anthropology and Disability Studies: the universal; "This, we would argue, is because the tendency of [Disability Studies] to seek out universal analytical categories through which disability might be better understood jars with contemporary anthropology's focus on the local and the particular" (Staples and Mehrotra 2016, p. 45).

A global, transnational orientation has become quite mainstream in Anthropology for the last two or three decades (Appadurai 1996). Nevertheless, Staples and Mehrotra (2016) raise a profound point with regard to universalism. The very notion of 'a universal' is admittedly rather anathematic to Anthropology, but universalism is a significant feature in the arena of international human rights law. For example, while certain practices such as marriage appear universal within the literature, the specific forms that marriage takes are not. Some of the articles contained within the CRPD display evidence of universal thinking and arguably certain values associated with the Global North, which explain why some of the cultural implications of the Convention are susceptible to such an anthropological critique.

Dahre (2017) has recently summarised Anthropology's relationship with international human rights law and reports that while the divide between universalism and cultural relativism may be somewhat exaggerated, it nevertheless lingers within the discipline (Dahre 2017). Dahre continues that some scholars in the discipline prefer to focus on issues such as the translation of human rights in differing cultural contexts, while others opt for an ethnographic, descriptive approach that draws a distinction between the universal intention of human rights treaties with practices on the ground. The CRPD and its commitment to universal 'legacy values', as denoted by Quinn (2009), creates a tension with traditional anthropological thinking concerning ethnocentrism and its sensitivity towards the legacy of European colonialism and cultural imperialism. As important as these concerns are, all forms of knowledge are situated and it is naïve to assume that so-called universal values are not cultural constructs themselves, and it would also be naïve to assume that the processes of signing, ratifying and implementing an international human rights treaty is going to be a top-down, linear process. Cultural values and worldviews will be in dialogue with every step of the process. Anthropological perspectives can reveal that there are indeed some troubling aspects of the CRPD in this light and they need to be articulated. In consideration of the Reservations, Declarations and Objections to the CRPD that have been made, these suggest that some Signatories and States Parties are also aware of these tensions. However, it is also important to avoid the older problematic views that some peoples are bound by culture and religion, whereas other worldviews are predicated upon objectivity, science and reason. The content of the Reservations, Declarations and Objections to the CRPD reveals that some States Parties to the Convention take issue with some of its articles as the result, arguably, of cultural or religious worldviews, and this includes States Parties of the Global North and South. Further, some Reservations that appear to be based upon religious grounds could also be concerned with a variety of other matters. It is important to consider the 'universal' values of the Convention as situated forms of knowledge, which will be interpreted as such by States Parties to the CRPD.

4 Reservations, Declarations and Objections to the CRPD

There are certain issues in implementing the provisions of the CRPD where they may be in tension with or in contradiction to wider cultural values and beliefs. For example, Article 23—Respect for home and the family, is necessary and it is important for the CRPD (2006) considering the extent to which persons with disabilities have been denied the right to marry and have families. However, the language of the article needs to be examined carefully for its implications. For example, Article 23(1)(a) holds that the "right of all persons with disabilities who are of marriageable age to marry and to found a family on the basis of free and full consent of the intending spouses" (CRPD 2006, Art. 23(1)(a)), is striking in the cross-cultural context considering the range of how the concept of 'marriage' is viewed and practised outside of the Global North, and sometimes in it. Marriage is not always seen as a union between individuals, but sometimes seen as a union of kinship groups in which, disabled or otherwise, the 'free and full consent' of the intended spouses may not be much of a consideration, if at all. Marriage may be far more concerned with building alliances or with property rights and inheritance (see Bossen 1988; Grossbard 1978). An example from an introductory text in Anthropology is evidence of this thinking about the variety of the form and function of marriage that has long been a staple of the discipline. Hendry notes that "marriage means different things in different societies" and that "we must look at marriage as part of the wider society where it is found, at how it fits into wider systems of exchange and political allegiance" (Hendry 1999, p. 197). It is simply not tenable to assume that persons with disabilities will have the right to choose their marriage partners, a marriage based on 'free and full consent' of all parties, if the general population of certain societies do not enjoy this right. This would be a scenario in which persons with disabilities would have rights not just specific to them, but beyond those of the larger society. This is unlikely to occur, and this problematic scenario has been noted. For example, Monaco articulated full support for human rights and fundamental freedom for persons with disabilities, "but that the Convention does not imply that persons with disabilities should be afforded rights superior to those afforded to persons without disabilities" (UN 2019a). In consideration of the Declarations, Reservations and Objections that have been recorded pertaining to the CRPD, it is evident that a number of Signatories and/or States Parties have indeed taken exception to the implications of some of the articles within the CRPD.

What follows is a content analysis of the Reservations, Declarations and Objections made concerning the CRPD, which considered the predominant Convention Articles that were the focus of the Declarations and Reservations. The analysis in turn is then further sub-divided into the major themes pertaining to the specific issues that were raised. The content was retrieved from the website of the United Nations Treaty Collection, "Chapter IV, 15. Convention on the Rights of Persons with Disabilities" (UN 2019a). As a number of these appear to have been made fairly recently, the content analysed only includes entries made up to, and including, the time of writing. For the sake of clarity, as well as simplification, 'Declarations' can refer to a Signatory or State Party clarifying its understanding of some element of a treaty, whereas a 'Reservation' is stronger, as a State Party seeks to legally exclude the application of some specific aspects of a treaty that it has otherwise generally agreed to (UN 2019b). An 'Objection' refers to a signatory or State Party's objection to the reservation made by another State Party. Furthermore, "The objecting state may further declare that its objection has the effect of precluding the entry into force of the treaty as between objecting and reserving states" (UN 2019b).

4.1 Reservations and Declarations

Article 23—Respect for home and the family, particularly paragraph 1(a) and Article 25—Health, particularly paragraph a (CRPD 2006), were a significant focus of the Reservations and Declarations made by Signatories and States Parties, which could be interpreted as pertaining to cultural values. Most Signatories and States Parties broadly supported fundamental disability human rights, though expressed cautions concerning the financial implications of full implementation, or else articulated specific concerns such as they declared their understanding that Article 12—Equal recognition before the law (CRPD 2006), allows for the retention of substituted decision making, for example, Canada and Ireland (UN 2019a). As stated above, it would be obvious to many anthropologists that Article 23(1)(a) would run counter to the range of marriage practices that exist around the globe, especially pertaining to how the choice of marriage partnership is determined. For example, Israel made a Reservation that pertained to Article 23(1)(a) concerning marriage (UN 2019a). It is not entirely made clear as to the specific nature of Israel's Reservation beyond the statement that Israel expresses its Reservation: "to the extent that the laws on personal status, which are binding on the various religious communities in Israel, do not conform with these provisions" (UN 2019a). While lacking in detail, one possible interpretation is that there is a concern that Article 23(1)(a) could be interpreted in such a way as to impact upon the right of religious communities in Israel to govern the practices of marriage according to their traditional norms.

Article 25—Health, specifically paragraph a, repeatedly made an appearance in the list of Reservations and Declarations (UN 2019a). Article 25(a) specifies that States Parties shall "Provide persons with disabilities with the same range, quality and standard of free or affordable health care and programmes as provided to other persons, including in the area of sexual and reproductive health and population-based public health programmes" (CRPD 2006). The intention is that persons with disabilities around the world should enjoy the same level of healthcare as persons without disabilities, as inequities in healthcare provision to persons with disabilities remain a concern of international bodies like the UN and the WHO (WHO 2011). However, the text "including in the area of sexual and reproductive health" caught the attention of a number of Signatories and States Parties as it moved the discussion beyond disability to that of broader norms and mores. The CRPD's position is understandable in light of the repression of the sexualities and reproductive capabilities of persons with disabilities, particularly those who resided within institutional environments. However, the area of sexual and reproductive health is not culturally neutral or value free. Even if most nations broadly supported the universal spirit of the Convention pertaining to disability rights, nevertheless specific aspects of the Convention were interpreted, as expected, though a national or local perspective. Malta, for example, recorded a Reservation that Article 25(a) "does not constitute recognition of any new international law obligation, does not create any abortion rights, and cannot be interpreted to constitute support, endorsement, or promotion of abortion" (UN 2019a). Further, "Malta's national legislation, considers the termination of pregnancy through induced abortion as illegal" (UN 2019a). This is an example where we find evidence of a cultural, and possibly a religious, value system which intersects with national law and that takes priority over the CRPD's universalistic vision in a specific area. Other States Parties expressed similar sentiments, such as Monaco: "the Prince of Monaco considers that Articles 23 and 25 of the Convention must not be interpreted as recognizing an individual right to abortion except where expressly provided for under national law" (UN 2019a).

4.2 Objections

Particularly revealing are some of the Objections submitted by Signatories or States Parties, towards the Reservations and Declarations made in a blanket manner by Brunei Darussalam and the Islamic Republic of Iran. Brunei succinctly stated a blanket Reservation about the entirety of the CRPD as follows: "The Government of Brunei Darussalam expresses its reservation regarding those provisions of the said Convention that may be contrary to the Constitution of Brunei Darussalam and to the beliefs and principles of Islam, the official religion of Brunei Darussalam" (UN 2019a). Iran also issued a blanket Declaration: "the Islamic Republic of Iran declares that it does not consider itself bound by any provisions of the Convention, which may be incompatible with its applicable rules" (UN 2019a). Rather than singling out specific articles, or sub-sections within articles, these two nations opted to argue that they did not intend to be bound to any provisions that would be contrary to norms and values of each specific national context. It is interesting to note that the majority of Objections to Brunei and Iran's Reservations were made by nations in the Global North, which were primarily concerned about the blanket manner in which these Reservations were made. Belgium was one of a number of nations that lodged such an Objection: "This reservation effectively subordinates the application of all the provisions of the Convention to their compatibility with the Constitution of Brunei Darussalam, and to the beliefs and principles of Islam" (UN 2019a). Further, "such a reservation seeks to limit the responsibilities of the Sultanate of Brunei Darussalam under the Convention through a general reference to national law and Islam without specifying its contents" (UN 2019a). The Reservations are so broad that the other States Parties have inadequate information with which to evaluate the Reservations, with the effect that subordinating the CRPD to Islam renders the Convention meaningless in this context. Although it is only possible to speculate with the limited information available, it could be argued that the Reservations reflect opposition to universal principles, which may be perceived as the product of the Global North or perhaps as a form of resistance to European hegemony. Based on the Objections raised, it would appear that a number of European nations viewed this tactic as an example of 'bad faith'. However, in a nation whose official religion is Islam, which intersects with the national legal structures, it is difficult to see how it could be otherwise. In other words, all elements of the CRPD among all State Parties will engage with the CRPD in terms of their national legal structures as well as localised norms. Laws are cultural, as Sally Moore argues, laws are 'enforceable norms' (Moore 2005, p. 1), and this applies to all national contexts within which the CRPD must enter into dialogue, including national and municipal level legal structures. Mohammed M. Ghaly (2008) has argued that jurists in the Islamic world have long debated matters of disability in terms of how impairments should be treated but also what disability means, and that there is no homogeneous 'Muslim' view of disability, considering the different schools of thought on the issues. Although much of the CRPD may not contravene Islamic principles, Brunei's Reservation could be interpreted as a reasonable response in light of this complexity.

5 Concluding Remarks

Anthropology brings a number of strengths to understanding the concept of 'disability', such as cultural relativism. Anthropology also articulates a number of cautions that should be well heeded, such as concerns about geopolitical hegemony and cultural imperialism. The CRPD represents an exceptional achievement in the arena of disability rights. However, for anthropologists such as myself who strongly support disability rights, the universalism contained within the Convention is at odds at times with concerns about ethnocentrism, cultural imperialism and the problematic divide between universalism and cultural relativism. Dahre (2017), however, has suggested that this anthropological tension has been somewhat misconstrued. He writes, "Instead of seeing universalism and relativism as two opposing forces, we should see them as parts of an ongoing social process in which universal and local values are negotiated and evaluated in relation to each other" (Dahre 2017, p. 626). Cowan et al. (2001) articulate similar thoughts: "Rather than seeing universalism and cultural relativism as alternatives which one must choose, once and for all, one should see the tension between the positions as part of the continuous process of negotiating ever-changing and interrelated global and local norms" (Cowan et al. 2001, p. 6). As shown in this chapter the tension between universalism and cultural relativity can be revealing of some of the problematic aspects of the articles of the Convention. However, the analysis of the Reservations, Declarations and Objections suggests that concerns about ethnocentrism and cultural imperialism imposed from the Global North may be overstated. Any human rights law convention will have to negotiate with local cultural norms, and this clearly applies to realising the vision of the Convention in a universal manner for all persons with disabilities.

References

Ablon, J. (1984). *Little people in America: The social dimensions of dwarfism*. New York: Praeger Publishers.

Appadurai, A. (1996). Global ethnoscapes: Notes and queries for a transnational anthropology. In *Modernity at large: Cultural dimensions of globalization* (pp. 48–65). Minneapolis, MN: University of Minnesota Press.

Arat, Z. F. K. (2006). Forging a global culture of human rights: Origins and prospects of the international bill of rights. *Human Rights Quarterly, 28*(2), 416–437.

Bickenbach, J. E. (2009). Disability, culture and the UN convention. *Disability and Rehabilitation, 31*(14), 1111–1124.

Bossen, L. (1988). Toward a theory of marriage: The economic anthropology of marriage transactions. *Ethnology, 27*(2), 127–144.

Connell, R. (2011). Southern bodies and disability: Re-thinking concepts. *Third World Quarterly, 32*(8), 1369–1381.

Cowan, J. K., Dembour, M. B., & Wilson, R. A. (2001). Introduction: Rights and culture as emergent global discourses. In J. K. Cowan, M. B. Dembour, & R. A. Wilson (Eds.), *Culture and rights: Anthropological perspectives* (pp. 1–26). Cambridge: Cambridge University Press.

CRC (United Nations Convention on the Rights of the Child). (1989). Adopted in 1989 by the United Nations general assembly.
CRPD (United Nations Convention on the Rights of Persons with Disabilities). (2006). Adopted in 2006 by the United Nations general assembly.
Dahre, U. J. (2017). Searching for a middle ground: Anthropologists and the debate on the universalism and the cultural relativism of human rights. *The International Journal of Human Rights, 21*(5), 611–628.
Degener, T. (2016). Disability in a human rights context. *Laws, 5*(35), 1–24.
Devlieger, P. J., Albrecht, G. L., & Hertz, M. (2007). The production of disability culture among young African–American men. *Social Science & Medicine, 64*, 1948–1959.
Goodley, D. (2011). *Disability studies: An interdisciplinary introduction.* London: Sage.
Grech, S. (2016). Disability and development: Critical connections, gaps and contradictions. In S. Grech & K. Soldatic (Eds.), *Disability in the global south* (pp. 3–19). Cham: Springer.
Grech, S., & Soldatic, K. (Eds.). (2016). *Disability in the global south.* Cham: Springer.
Groce, N. E. (1985). *Everyone here spoke sign language: Hereditary deafness on Martha's vineyard.* Cambridge: Harvard University Press.
Grossbard, A. (1978). Towards a marriage between economics and anthropology and a general theory of marriage. *The American Economic Review, 68*(2), 33–37.
Hendry, J. (1999). *An introduction to social anthropology: Other people's worlds.* London: Macmillan Press.
Hershenson, D. B. (2000). Toward a cultural anthropology of disability and rehabilitation. *Rehabilitation Counseling Bulletin, 43*(3), 150–157.
Hsu, F. L. (1979). The cultural problem of the cultural anthropologist. *American Anthropologist, 81*(3), 517–532.
Ingstad, B., & Whyte, S. R. (Eds.). (1995). *Disability and culture.* Berkeley, CA: University of California Press.
Ingstad, B., & Whyte, S. R. (Eds.). (2007). *Disability in local and global worlds.* Berkeley, CA: University of California Press.
Iriarte, E. G. (2016). Models of disability. In E. G. Iriarte, R. McConkey, & R. Gilligan (Eds.), *Disability and human rights: Global perspectives* (pp. 10–32). London: Palgrave.
Kasnitz, D., Switzer, M., & Shuttleworth, R. P. (2001). Introduction: Anthropology in disability studies. *Disability Studies Quarterly, 21*(3), 2–17.

Kohrman, M. (2005). *Bodies of difference: Experiences of disability and institutional advocacy in the making of modern China*. Berkeley, CA: University of California Press.

Meekosha, H. (2011). Decolonising disability: Thinking and acting globally. *Disability & Society, 26*(6), 667–682.

Montgomery, H. (2001). Imposing rights? A case study of child prostitution in Thailand. In J. K. Cowan, M. B. Dembour, & R. A. Wilson (Eds.), *Culture and rights: Anthropological perspectives* (pp. 80–101). Cambridge: Cambridge University Press.

Moore, S. F. (2005). *Law and anthropology: A reader*. Malden, MA: Blackwell Publishing.

Murphy, R. (1990). *The body silent: An anthropologist embarks on the most challenging journey of his life: Into the life of the disabled*. New York: W.W. Norton.

Oliver, M., & Barnes, C. (2012). *The new politics of disablement*. New York: Palgrave Macmillan.

Quinn, G. (2009). Bringing the UN convention on rights for persons with disabilities to life in Ireland. *British Journal of Learning Difficulties, 37*, 245–249.

Reid-Cunningham, A. R. (2009). Anthropological theories of disability. *Journal of Human Behavior in the Social Environment, 19*, 99–111.

Shuttleworth, R. P. (2000). The search for sexual intimacy for men with cerebral palsy. *Sexuality and Disability, 18*(4), 263–282.

Staples, J., & Mehrotra, N. (2016). Disability studies: Developments in anthropology. In S. Grech & K. Soldatic (Eds.), *Disability in the global south* (pp. 35–49). Cham: Springer.

Tylor, E. B. (1871). *Primitive culture: Researches into the development of mythology, philosophy, religion, language, art, and custom* (Vol. 1). London: John Murray.

United Nations. (2019a). *United Nations treaty collection. Chapter IV—Human rights: 15*. Convention on the rights of persons with disabilities. Declarations and reservations [online]. Retrieved January, 22, 2019, from https://treaties.un.org/Pages/ViewDetails.aspx?src=TREATY&mtdsg_no=IV-15&chapter=4&lang=_en&clang=_en.

United Nations. (2019b). *Glossary of terms relating to treaty actions* [online]. Retrieved January, 22, 2019, from https://treaties.un.org/pages/overview.aspx?path=overview/glossary/page1_en.xml#objection.

Waldschmidt, A. (2018). Disability–culture–society: Strengths and weaknesses of a cultural model of dis/ability. *Alter, 12*(2), 65–78.

World Health Organization. (2011). *World report on disability* [online]. Retrieved January 22, 2019, from https://www.who.int/disabilities/world_report/2011/report.pdf.

4

Recognising Cultural Diversity: Implications for Persons with Disabilities

Kelley Johnson

[P]ersons with disabilities have the right to access and participate in society from their own cultural perspective, as long as it is compatible with universally recognized human rights. Continuously questioning the norms and processes and giving more thought to how every person can be fully included while respecting their inherent dignity is necessary to ensure the effectivity of universal human rights in ever-changing contexts and realities.
(Bennoune 2018, Art. 61, p. 18)

1 Introduction

Bennoune (2018), the United Nations (UN) Special Rapporteur in the field of cultural rights, emphasises that while it is important to change attitudes and social processes that deny persons with disabilities their human rights to participate in society, full achievement of these rights will not be experienced until individuals are accorded dignity and respect and

K. Johnson (✉)
Social Policy Research Centre, UNSW, Sydney, Australia
e-mail: kelley.johnson@unsw.edu.au

E. J. Kakoullis, K. Johnson (eds.), *Recognising Human Rights in Different Cultural Contexts*, https://doi.org/10.1007/978-981-15-0786-1_4

are able to participate from their own particular cultural perspectives. This statement raises important questions which are explored in this chapter: what does the concept of 'culture' generally mean in relation to persons with disabilities? What do the cultural perspectives of persons with disabilities mean to them and to others? What is their significance in relation to the Convention on the Rights of Persons with Disabilities (CRPD 2006)? Each of these questions is complex and contested, and consequently, this chapter is a voyage of exploration rather than a journey's end.

This chapter provides a reflection on each of these questions drawing on the literature from interdisciplinary perspectives in relation to the nature of culture generally, the consideration by disabled writers and advocates of the nature of disability culture(s) and the importance of considering intersectionality in relation to cultural perspectives of persons with disabilities.

2 The Concept of 'Culture' and Its Impact on the Lives of Persons with Disabilities

This section of the chapter is concerned with a consideration of what is meant by the concept of 'culture' and how different conceptions of it impact on the lives of persons with disabilities. 'Culture' is a complex and problematic concept and has been defined in many different ways depending on the context in which it is being considered and the disciplinary perspective of the writer (Kasnitz and Shuttleworth 1999, Kasnitz, Switzer and Shuttleworth 2001; Klotz 2003; Devlieger 2005; Eagleton 2018). In the past and sometimes contemporarily, it has been seen as constituting a common shared view held by groups of people, sometimes at a national level. This view defines 'culture' as providing "a world view for a particular group or collective, comprised of a system of beliefs, values and behaviours which delineates their reality" (Yoshida et al. 1999, p. 322). Such a world view is perceived to be "coherent, homogenous, consensual, and static" (Donnelly 2007, p. 296). More recently some anthropological definitions of 'culture' (Donnelly 2007; Aldo 2010; Afshari 2015) conceptualise it as symbolic and constructed and consisting of "a repertoire of deeply contested symbols, practices and meanings over and with which members of a society constantly struggle" (Afshari 2015, p. 877). Such a view of 'culture' also implies agency by those participating in it so that it becomes a site of constant change and at times subversion.

The UN Committee on Economic, Social and Cultural rights (2010, p. 1182) provides a more detailed account of the constituents of 'culture' that "encompasses, inter alia, ways of life, language, oral and written literature, music and song, non-verbal communication, religion or belief systems, rites and ceremonies, sport and games, methods of production or technology, natural and man-made environments, food, clothing, shelter, and the arts; in short, all customs and traditions through which individuals and communities express their humanity and build their worldview". This is a very comprehensive list. In contrast, some writers emphasise that 'culture' has been more narrowly defined to focus on the arts, sports and leisure. For example, Stevenson comments that the concept of 'culture' "is usually associated with a mix of public and private institutions including museums, libraries, schools, cinemas and the media while more specifically being connected with the dialogic production of meaning and aesthetics through a variety of practices" (Stevenson 2003, p. 4). He goes on to distinguish between 'culture' on the one hand and 'citizenship' (membership, belonging, rights and obligations) on the other but argues that these concepts are no longer separate in contemporary, more fluid and information-based societies (Stevenson 2003).

Another complex issue in considering 'culture' is its relationship to the nation or State (Eagleton 2018). While older definitions of 'culture' could be loosely equated with nations as a mono-culture, this view is less viable as many nation States have become multicultural in nature. However, States are still described as reflecting and promoting cultural values which are national in nature through law and policies (Haslam 2017) and through the exercise of governmental power. This issue is particularly important since it is only through the translation of international into domestic law that human rights conventions can be implemented (Kanter 2015). Consequently, the nature of the relationship between culture and State gains particular importance in the debates about universal human rights law and the idea of cultural relativity and diversity. The tension between the ideas of universal human rights applicable to all persons and the view that the nature of particular cultures has precedence or will determine the way universal law is interpreted have led to issues in the translation of international human rights conventions into domestic law and culture.

Some cultural relativists have argued that universal human rights as evidenced in International Law and conventions can be seen as reflecting a western based set of values and involve a post-colonial imposition of them which devalue or ignore the cultural values and traditions of particular States or nations (see Arat 2006; Bickenbach 2009; Benhabib 2011a; for a more detailed discussion). Some writers have sought to resolve the tension between the universality of human rights and the particular cultures of States or nations (Aldo 2010; Afshari 2015; Arat 2006; Benhabib 2011b; Donnelly 2007; Harris-Short 2003). While these writers suggest some possible solutions for this tension, the debate continues.

2.1 Cultures and Persons with Disabilities

One of the important issues in considering the nature of cultures is that they all have boundaries which define those who are seen as 'other' and who are marginalised or excluded (Stolcke 1995; Riddell and Watson 2003; Reid-Cunningham 2009; Benhabib 2011b). These boundaries differ in different cultures and change over time. This is particularly important in considering issues in relation to persons with disabilities. Studies which focus on the nation State to define culture reveal that from this perspective persons with disabilities are often excluded from belonging and are constituted as 'other', sometimes on the basis of very different beliefs or values (Ingstad and Reynolds Whyte 1995; Snyder and Mitchell 2006; Haang'andu 2018). There are variations in ascribed meanings of disability across national cultural boundaries but the result for persons with disabilities is often the experience of oppression and exclusion. The consequences of these forms of exclusion or marginalisation are documented in the World Health Organisation (WHO 2011) *Report on Disabilities* which concludes that persons with disabilities in the global context are affected negatively by significant social barriers. The consequences of these barriers are poor health outcomes, lower educational achievements, less economic activity, higher rates of poverty and barriers to living independently or participating in their communities (WHO 2011, p. 263).

A further consequence of the exclusion of persons with disabilities through law and national policies has been labelled 'civil death' (the loss of personhood and the accompanying rights to make personal decisions or to exercise legal capacity; Quinn 2011, 2015). To return people to 'civil life' requires not only changes to their material lives but changes in the way in which they are valued and constituted within their society.

This section has provided a brief view of the complexities of culture(s) with some reference to the ways in which more traditional views of it can be seen as affecting the lives of persons with disabilities, particularly in relation to various forms of cultural oppression. The next section of this chapter considers the cultural perspectives which have developed specifically in relation to persons with disabilities both in terms of models of disability and ideas of disability culture(s).

3 Cultural Perspectives of Persons with Disabilities

There are a number of different approaches to reflecting on what 'disability cultures' might mean to persons with disabilities and to others. In this section I consider: the cultural model of disability and the development of disability cultures, and the implications of persons with disabilities belonging to more than one culture.

3.1 Culture or Cultures?

> (a) all people and all peoples have culture, not merely certain categories or geographies of people; (b) cultures are human constructs constantly subject to reinterpretation; and (c) while it is customary to do so, referring to culture in the singular has problematic methodological and epistemological consequences. It must be understood that culture is always plural. "Culture" means cultures. (Bennoune 2018, para. 8, p. 17)

Bennoune's (2018) statement reflects the symbolic and socially constructed view of 'culture' discussed in the previous section of this chapter. In stating that all people have culture, or as she would argue, cultures, a legitimacy is given to the possibilities of recognising multiple cultures which may develop from particular group experiences, for example, disability, which would not be possible from a 'static, monocultural or national perspective'.

Strong arguments have been made for the development and growth of 'disability culture(s)' with Cunningham (2009) noting that 74% of Americans with disabilities identify as having a particular cultural identity as 'disabled', and 45% see themselves as a 'minority group'. This raises the question of how disability culture(s) should be defined. Some writers have seen disability cultures as arising from the politicisation of persons with disabilities (Barnes and Mercer 2001; Devlieger et al. 2007) in particular the shared experience of oppression in other cultural contexts:

> With the recent politicization of disabled people, a stimulus has been given to the formation of a disability culture. The aim has been to counter the individualization and medicalization of disability, the essentialist and determinist definitions of disability, the moral laden character of "normalcy" and negative stereotyping of disabled people as well as disability as a metaphor for social exclusion and the lack of subjectivity and agency among disabled people. (Barnes and Mercer 2001, p. 531)

This view of disability culture motivation is strongly political with its challenge to oppressive practices and ideologies emanating from other cultures towards persons with disabilities. The development of this culture is seen to be based on a "sense of common identity and interests" (Barnes and Mercer 2001, p. 522) among persons with disabilities which separate them from persons who are not labelled as 'disabled'. A characteristic of this cultural development is a positive sense of identity and pride in the capabilities and resilience of persons with disabilities and a shared cultural history and common experiences (Barnes and Mercer 2001; Brown 2002; Jakubowicz and Meekosha 2003).

> Disability has its own cultural history, not just the cultural perceptions of disability by the wider society. It has its internal narratives, its own meanings and its own yet-to-be unearthed histories. (Jakubowicz and Meekoscha 2003, p. 193)

As this quote suggests, self-identification, as a defining characteristic of this culture, is extremely important for persons with disabilities who have often been assigned an externally defined 'culture' which excludes them from others (Snyder and Mitchell 2006).

The development of disability cultures is seen not only as related to history and shared history. Theatre, art, music, literature and dance have all been part of the contribution and the shared culture of people with disabilities:

> We generate art, music, literature, and other expressions of our lives and our culture, infused from our experience of disability. (Brown 2002, p. 48)

The shared expression of the arts also serves to challenge the prevailing norms of other cultures by affirming "different embodiments through literature, drama, sport and music" (Jakubowicz and Meekosha 2003, p. 193) and through the recognition the arts receive through festivals, exhibitions, concerts, performances and awards and the achievements of individuals (Teuben and Davey 2000; Jakubowicz and Meekosha 2003; Johnson 2009; Ledger et al. 2020, in press).

In the light of the earlier discussion of the characteristics of culture in this chapter, this brief account of disability arts, shared history and experience, political action and self-identification suggests that there is a strong argument to recognise and respect the 'cultural perspectives' (Bennoune 2018) of persons with disabilities.

3.2 Disability Cultures or Culture

It is possible to consider disability culture as a broad category which includes those who self-identify with its characteristics. However, as with other human rights cultures (e.g. women and the rights of LGBTQI) there are diverse groups which self-identify as having their own cultural perspective. One example of a particularly strong cultural perspective is 'Deaf culture' (Poitras Tucker 1997; Ladd 2003; Scully 2012) which not only has the characteristics of 'culture' listed above but also includes a distinct language in sign language, a characteristic that is unique to Deaf culture.

> Over the past several years, a growing concept of Deaf culture has taken root. Under that concept deafness is not a disability that requires fixing. Society should not focus on research to cure deafness, claim the Deaf culturists, but should accept Deaf people as composing a cultural minority and respect their right to live as Deaf persons. (Poitras Tucker 1997, p. 25)

I am somewhat uncomfortable at discussing Deaf culture in the context of disability since the perspective of many Deaf people is that they do not have an impairment but rather that they represent a culture that is different from hearing people (and this group includes disabled people who are hearing). However, as discussed later in this chapter, Deaf people have been strong advocates for their recognition in the CRPD and may claim needed supports through anti-discrimination laws (Scully 2012) or disability programmes.

In a discussion of 'deaf identities', Scully (2012, p. 111) defines culture in relation to Deaf people as capturing "the distinctive beliefs and practices of Deaf people that have been shaped by the dominance of visual over auditory interaction with the world". Deaf culture provides an example of why it is important to consider self-identification as an essential characteristic of disability cultures and for it to be considered with respect by others in society.

3.3 Tensions in Disability Cultures

> Beginning in the 1980s, there has been a debate about whether or not the concept of culture could be meaningfully applied to groups such as disabled people, since disability results from a wide range of mental and physical conditions and spans age, race, gender, ethnicity, social class and national boundaries. (Scheer 1994, cited in Devlieger et al. 2007, p. 1994)

While as described above there are strong arguments for recognising disability culture(s), there are also tensions and challenges in doing so. This section of the chapter considers some of the issues raised in the literature which are problematic in considering disability cultures. These include the problem of 'culture' and 'disabilities', different priorities held by persons with different impairments and the challenges of working across or belonging to more than one culture.

3.3.1 The Tensions in Conceptualising 'Disability' and 'Cultures'

As discussed above, there is evidence for the development of 'disability cultures' which share the characteristics attributed to this concept more generally. However, there are a number of tensions (as there are in other cultural movements) in conceptualising disability cultures. One of these tensions relates to a somewhat paradoxical problem in conceptualising disability cultures. While as noted in the previous section these may lead to, and be informed by, political activism and the gaining of a heard voice by persons with disabilities, they can also lead to a perpetuation of exclusion and continued oppression. So, claims of belonging to specific disability culture(s) run the risk of confirming persons with disabilities as 'other' or outsiders, thus perpetuating their segregation from other cultures (Brown 2002). The positive effects of defining oneself culturally as 'disabled' may be countered by a view by others that members of disability cultures are there as the result of a 'defect' (Scully 2012).

Differences and tensions may also arise as a necessary part of the development of cultures and their relationship to identity. For example, Davis (2014) explores the development of disability cultures and identities and argues that the first phase of their development involves the establishment of a common positive identity against former attributed negative identities.

> The first phase also implies a pulling together of forces, an agreement to agree for political ends and group solidarity, along with the tacit approval

> of an agenda for the establishment of basic rights and prohibitions against various kinds of discrimination and ostracism. (Davis 2014, p. 264)

The second phase, which occurs once a positive sense of identity has been established involves a more nuanced recognition of differences between different groups and may lead to conflict and tension between members of the group or culture. Further tension may arise in relation to the strong assertion of Deaf people that they do not identify as disabled but rather as ethnically and linguistically different (Scully 2012) and as belonging to and creating Deaf culture. However, not all deaf people adopt this position, and some do identify as disabled. Nor is the position of those who are members of Deaf culture unambiguous as they have also been strong advocates against discrimination laws and for the human rights of Deaf people (Poitras Tucker; Scully 2012) within a disability context. This adds to the complexity of considering disability cultures where within one group, in this instance deaf people, there may be divisions on how they perceive themselves and how they want to be perceived or constituted by others.

Furthermore, Riddell and Watson (2003) comment that the economic priorities of groups of persons with disabilities may differ according to their impairment in spite of a shared experience of oppression:

> Within the cultural realm, we are made aware of some of the difficulties which have ensued in developing a shared disability culture. Even though the disability movement has sought to highlight the commonalities of economic oppression which transcend specific impairments, there is a constant reminder from deaf people, people with learning difficulties and mental health service users that the problems encountered and solutions sought by different groups are not the same. (Riddell and Watson 2003, p. 15)

For example, persons with physical disabilities have campaigned strongly for the provision of accessible buildings and public transport, for some people using mental health services and the issues of involuntary confinement to hospitals are of paramount importance and for some Deaf people the educational and social recognition of sign language is seen as fundamental.

4 Cultures and the CRPD

The debates about the nature of culture(s) and their relevance to the advancement of human rights has particular resonance in relation to the ratification, implementation and monitoring of the CRPD (2006). The CRPD has been said to provide the possibility of a 'paradigm shift' in relation to how persons with disabilities are constituted for States ratifying, implementing and monitoring it (Quinn 2009; Mittler 2015). This shift involves constituting persons with disabilities as persons with human rights and stresses the right for them to be involved in decision-making about their lives and in shaping their nation's future through participation in political, social, cultural and economic issues. It places responsibility on States to work to remove the barriers which prevent the full participation of persons with disabilities in their communities. In doing this, to some extent the view of culture in the CRPD suggests that it is embodied in the States.

In developing this perspective, the CRPD promoted an approach which for some States was new and problematic. Partially for this reason the focus in much of the recent literature on the CRPD has engaged with the issues confronting States in their relationship with the CRPD (de Beco 2013; Rioux et al. 2015). While this has sometimes explicitly explored cultural diversity as an issue, this is often done implicitly rather than explicitly, focussing on the ways particular national cultures are progressing with the CRPD. In the literature there is much less emphasis on the extent to which disability itself may be seen as reflecting one specific culture or a diversity of cultures and the possible implications of this for the implementation of the CRPD. However, the emphasis in the CRPD on participation by persons with disabilities in decision-making in relation to their lives and the responsibility of States to encourage and support such participation (2006: Art. 4(3)) may also be seen as supporting the development of disability cultures which provide a basis for positive self-identity by persons with disabilities.

Further, the CRPD (2006) explicitly addresses the concept of culture in Article 30—Participation in cultural life, recreation, leisure and sport, where it recognises the human right persons with disabilities have to participate in cultural life. In this provision there is an emphasis on cultural life as including: the arts and media, sport, recreation tourism and leisure activities. However, in paragraph 4 this article also emphasises the importance of recognising the right of persons with disabilities to the entitlement "on an equal basis with others, to recognition and support of their specific cultural and linguistic identity, including sign languages and deaf culture" (CRPD 2006, Art. 30(4)). This was included following the campaigning of representatives of Deaf culture during the drafting of the CRPD (Kauppinen and Jokinen 2014).

The question can be asked: how far do any of us really belong only in one culture? The close relationship between culture and individual identity is evident in the increasing focus on intersectionality which is apparent in the statement by Bennoune (2018). We belong to some extent in different cultures even within one national society. The CRPD recognises differences between groups of persons with disabilities in terms of their membership of different groups such as women or children, and as noted above, in terms of what may be termed disability culture with a particular focus on Deaf culture. In the Preamble to the CRPD (2006), the human rights of minority groups are stated as follows:

> Concerned about the difficult conditions faced by persons with disabilities who are subject to multiple or aggravated forms of discrimination on the basis of race, colour, sex, language, religion, political or other opinion, national, ethnic, indigenous or social origin, property, birth, age or other status. (CRPD 2006, Preamble, para. p)

However, there are no specific articles in the Convention which take this further, in terms of the human rights of indigenous people or the LGBTQI communities.

5 Conclusion

Historically many persons with disabilities have experienced exclusion from their communities and other cultures. In some States their categorisation as 'disabled' has led to them being 'culturally located' in specific places or symbolic sites within a society (Snyder and Mitchell 2006). While these negative experiences inform the development of what might be termed 'disability cultures', the latter are also the result of positive self-identification of persons with disabilities. In considering these issues and disability cultures, it is important to keep in mind that all cultures are constantly evolving and changing. And that the ways disability cultures are considered and conceived will differ at different times and within the broader cultural contexts in which they exist. However, there is evidence (Soldatic and Johnson 2019) that the development of what might be termed 'disability cultures' has led to positive action for change by disabled people's organisations and persons with disabilities and made a strong contribution particularly in relation to the struggle for the human rights set out in the CRPD.

References

Afshari, R. (2015). Relativity in universality: Jack Donnelly's grand theory in need of specific illustrations. *Human Rights Quarterly, 37*(4), 854–912.

Aldo, M. (2010). Practice of United Nations human rights treaty bodies in the reconciliation of cultural diversity with universal respect for human rights. *Human Rights Quarterly, 32*(3), 601–664.

Arat, Z. (2006). Forging a global culture of human rights: Origin and prospects of the international bill of rights. *Human Rights Quarterly, 28*(2), 416–437.

Barnes, C., & Mercer, G. (2001). Chapter 21 disability culture: Assimilation or inclusion? In G. Albrecht, K. Seelman, & M. Bury (Eds.), *Handbook of disability studies* (pp. 515–5234). Thousand Oaks, CA: Sage Publications.

Benhabib, S. (2011a). From the dialectic of the enlightenment to the origins of totalitarianism. Theodor Adorno and max Horkheimer in the company of Hannah Arendt. Chap. 2 in *Dignity in adversity. Human rights in troubled times* (pp. 20–40). Cambridge: Polity Press.

Benhabib, S. (2011b). Another universalism. On the unity and diversity of human rights. Chap. 4 in *Dignity in adversity. Human rights in troubled times* (pp. 57–76). Cambridge Polity Press.

Bennoune, K. (2018). *Universality, cultural diversity and cultural rights*. Report of the Special Rapporteur in the field of cultural rights. Presented at the 73rd Session General Assembly UN.

Bickenbach, J. (2009). Disability, culture and the UN convention. *Disability and Rehabilitation, 31*(14), 111–124.
Brown, S. (2002). What is disability culture? *Disability Studies Quarterly, 22*(2), 34–50.
CRPD (United Nations Convention on the Rights of Persons with Disabilities). (2006). Adopted in 2006 by the United Nations general assembly.
De Beco, G. (Ed.). (2013). *Article 33 of the UN convention on the rights of persons with disabilities: National structures for the implementation and monitoring of the convention*. Leiden: Martinus Nijhoff Publishers.
Devlieger, P. (2005, October 14–16). *Generating a cultural model of disability*. Paper presented at the 19th Congress of the European Federation of Association of Teachers of the Deaf (FEAPDA).
Devlieger, P., Albrecht, G., & Hertz, M. (2007). The production of disability culture among young African-American men. *Social Science & Medicine, 64*, 1948–1959.
Donnelly, J. (2007). The relative universality of human rights. *Human Rights Quarterly, 29*(2), 281–306.
Eagleton, T. (2018). *Culture*. New Haven, CT: Yale University Press.
Haang'andu, P. (2018). Transnationalizing disability studies in embedded cultural-cognitive worldviews: The case of sub-Saharan Africa. *Disability and the Global South, 5*(1), 1292–1314.
Harris-Short, S. (2003). International human rights law: Imperialist, inept and ineffective. Cultural relativism and the UN convention on the rights of the child. *Human Rights Quarterly, 251*, 130–181.
Haslam, N. (2017). Australian values are hardly unique when compared to other cultures. *The Conversation*, pp. 1–4. Retrieved from https://theconversation.com/au.
Ingstad, B., & Reynolds Whyte, S. (1995). *Disability and culture*. Berkeley, CA: University of California Press.
Jakubowicz, A., & Meekosha, H. (2003). Can multiculturalism encompass disability? In S. Riddell & N. Watson (Eds.), *Disability, culture and identity* (pp. 180–189). Harlow: Pearson Prentice Hall Ltd.
Johnson, K. (2009). Reflecting on inclusion. Towards an inclusive community. In Kilkenny Collective for Arts Talent (Ed.), *Art and inclusion. The story of KCat*. Kilkenny: Kilkenny Collective for Arts Talent.
Kasnitz, D., & Shuttleworth, R. (1999). *Engaging anthropology in disability studies*. Position papers in disability studies. V. 1 Issue 1, pp. 1–37. Oakland: Rehabilitation Research and Training Center on Independent Living and Disability Policy. World Institute on Disability.

Kasnitz, D., Switzer, M., & Shuttleworth, R. (2001). Introduction: Anthropology in disability studies. *Disability studies quarterly, 21*(3), 2–17.

Kauppinem, L., & Jokinen, M. (2014). Including deaf culture and linguistic rights. In M. Sabatello & M. Schultze (Eds.), *Human rights & disability advocacy* (pp. 131–145). Philadelphia, PA: University of Pennsylvania Press.

Klotz, J. (2003, September 12). *The culture concept: Anthropology, disability studies and intellectual disability.* Paper presented to disability studies and research institute symposium. Disability at the cutting edge. A colloquium to examine the impact on theory, research and professional practice, pp. 1–31. Sydney: University of Technology.

Ladd, P. (2003). *Understanding deaf culture: In search of deafhood.* Clevedon: Multilingual Matters.

Ledger, S., Walmsley, J. with members of Access all Areas Theatre Company. (2020, in press). 'The madhouse': Working with performance artists with intellectual disabilities to share the history of institutions and increase public awareness and involvement in activism. In S. Soldatic & K. Johnson (Eds.), *Global perspectives on disability activism and advocacy.* Abingdon: Routledge.

Mittler, P. (2015). The UN convention on the rights of persons with disabilities: Implementing a paradigm shift. *Journal of Policy and Practice in Intellectual Disabilities, 12*(2), 79–89.

Poitras Tucker, B. (1997). The ADA and deaf culture: Contrasting precepts, conflicting results. *The Annals of the American Academy of Political and Social Science, 549*, 24–36.

Quinn, G. (2009). Resisting the 'temptation of elegance': Can the convention on rights of persons with disabilities socialise states to right behaviour? In O. Arnardottir & G. Quinn (Eds.), *The UN convention on rights of persons with disabilities. European and Scandinavian perspectives* (pp. 215–256). Leiden and Boston, MA: Martinus Nijhoff.

Quinn, G. (2011, April 29). *Rethinking personhood: New directions in legal capacity law and policy.* Paper, new foundations for personhood and legal capacity in the 21st century conference, p. 17. University of British Columbia. Retrieved from www.nuigalway.ie.

Quinn, G. (2015, December 20). *From civil death to civil life. Perspectives on supported decision-making for persons with disabilities.* Lecture Tbilisi State University Georgia. Retrieved from www.nuigalway.ie/cdlpgerard.quinn@nuigalway.ie.

Reid-Cunningham, A. (2009). Anthropological theories of disability. *Journal of Human Behavior in the Social Environment, 19*, 99–111.

Riddell, S., & Watson, N. (2003). Disability, culture and identity: Introduction. In S. Riddell & N. Watson (Eds.), *Disability, culture and identity* (pp. 1–16). Harlow: Pearson Education Ltd.

Rioux, M., Pinto, P., & Parekh, G. (2015). *Rights monitoring and social change. Building power out of evidence*. Toronto: Canadian Scholars' Press Inc.

Scully, J. L. (2012). Deaf identities in disability studies. With us or without us. In N. Watson, A. Roulstone, & C. Thomas (Eds.), *Routledge handbook of disability studies* (pp. 109–119). London: Routledge.

Snyder, S., & Mitchell, D. (2006). *Cultural locations of disability*. Chicago, IL: Chicago University Press.

Stevenson, N. (2003). Chapter 1 cultural citizenship. In *Cultural citizenship. Cosmopolitan questions* (pp. 4–34). Maidenhead: Open University Press.

Stolcke, V. (1995). Talking culture. New boundaries, new rhetorics of exclusion in Europe. *Current Anthropology, 36*(1), 1–24.

Teuben, S., & Davey, M. (2000). Gina's story. In R. Traustadottir & K. Johnson (Eds.), *Women with intellectual disabilities: Finding a place in the world* (pp. 162–171). London: Jessica Kingsley.

United Nations Committee on Economic Social and Cultural Rights. (2010). *Report on the 42nd and 43rd sessions 4–22 May 2009 and 2–20 November 2009*. UN: Economic and Social Council.

WHO. (2011). *World report on disability*. Geneva: World Health Organisation.

Yoshida, K., Li, A., & Odette, M. (1999). Cross-cultural views of disability and sexuality: Experiences of a group of ethno-racial women with physical disabilities. *Sexuality and Disability, 17*(4), 321–337.

5

A Personal Reflection on Indigeneity, Colonisation and the CRPD

Huhana Hickey

He waka eke noa
(A canoe which we are all in with no exception)

1 Introduction

Indigenous people are disproportionately presented in the disparity models that exist within Western law and policies. Research studies paint an appalling picture (Hickey and Wilson 2017; King et al. 2014; Wylie et al. 2013), and this is not surprising when poverty is a predominant feature of indigenous people's identity. Further, these studies show that if in addition to being indigenous, one is disabled and has experienced colonialism, the inequity has increased impact. Instead of the current practice of trying to fit indigenous persons with disabilities into Global North bio-Western disability models, it is important to examine why indigenous persons with disabilities who have experienced colonialism do not benefit

H. Hickey (✉)
Housing NZ Corporation, Wellington, New Zealand

E. J. Kakoullis, K. Johnson (eds.), *Recognising Human Rights in Different Cultural Contexts*, https://doi.org/10.1007/978-981-15-0786-1_5

well from Global North policies. This chapter explores some of these issues in the context of an increasing emphasis globally on the rights of persons with disabilities.

The United Nations' (UN) Universal Declaration of Human Rights (Declaration/UDHR 1948) did not address inequality for certain minority groups, including indigenous peoples and persons with disabilities. In recognising some of the inequities experienced by specific minority groups following the introduction of the Declaration (1948), the UN has focused on human rights treaties for minority groups requiring specific protection. This led to the development and adoption of the UN Convention on the Rights of Persons with Disabilities (Convention/CRPD) in 2006. This chapter is a personal reflection on my own experiences and understanding as an indigenous disabled woman in my role as an indigenous disabled people's representatives appointed by the UN General Assembly Ad Hoc Committee on a Comprehensive and Integral International Convention on the Protection and Promotion of the Rights and Dignity of Persons with Disabilities. In this chapter I reflect on the complex nature of indigenous culture and disability using a case study of Polynesian and Māori people in New Zealand (NZ) and relate this to my experience of the CRPD. In particular, this chapter explores the experiences of indigenous persons in NZ who have resided in the Global South and experienced colonialism and disablement. It provides an account of how they engage within and with their own and other indigenous communities in relation to understanding disability and accessing health and disability services. Here I focus on Māori due to being based in NZ.

1.1 Māori Diverse Realities

In order to understand indigenous populations and their place within the CRPD, it is relevant to first understand indigenous identity. In NZ the situation is complicated by the distinction made between Māori who are regarded as the *tangata whenua* (original inhabitants) of the land and the broader group of Polynesians (which also include indigenous people from the Hawaiian Islands and Easter Island). These latter groups when living in NZ are referred to as Pacific Islanders. In this chapter I focus particularly on Māori realities and identity.

Statistics New Zealand (2001; 2014; 2015) defines 'ethnicity' as an ethnic group or groups that people identify with or feel they belong to. Ethnicity is a measure of cultural affiliation, as opposed to race, ancestry, nationality or citizenship. Ethnicity is self-perceived, and people can belong to more than one ethnic group. From this description it can be deduced that an ethnic group is made up of people who have some or all of the following characteristics:

- A common proper name
- One or more elements of common culture which need not be specified, but may include religion, customs or language
- Unique community of interests, feelings and actions
- A shared sense of common origins or ancestry
- A common geographic origin (Statistics New Zealand 2001)

Within this context, Māori ethnic identity is a continually evolving concept (Pearson 1990; Broughton 1993; Durie 1994). Historically, the term Māori simply meant normal or usual and was not a term used by Māori to describe an ethnic identity (Barlow 1991). The use of the term Māori to describe the indigenous inhabitants of New Zealand evolved around the time Europeans began arriving in New Zealand which was around 1810 (Belich 1996). While Māori maintained their connections to their land, sea and *whānau* (family), *hapu* (sub tribe of the extended family group) through methods such as *whakataukī* (proverbs), there were multiple connections and identities that changed according to the political, social, economic and geographical environments (Ballara 1998).

The rural and urban tensions where the urban migration patterns of the 1960s led to the spread of kinship ties, going beyond the local environmental and economic patterns of the past resulted in the intermeshing of boundary, where interdependence and consciousness is constantly present (Pearson 1994; Durie 1994). The issues for Māori who do not have a direct experience of impairment are also applicable to those who do have a direct experience, due to their interconnectedness and collective approach to many issues. For example, in relation to a child with autism, both the immediate family and the extended family are impacted through local marae visits or other cultural events, as Māori gather regularly for events and cultural situations. Family is seen as an integral part of a Māori way of living, we do not act in isolation very often. This is also due to our common experience of colonisation, violence and trauma. Taking into account the factors of impairment, and now the term disability, when applying an ethnic appropriate response to meet the requirements for Māori with disabilities, the State, despite years of addressing Māori ethnic identity in policy, is failing this group (Dow 1999). For example, according to the NZ health chart book, Māori people have the highest rate of disability experiences, especially youth under the age of 25 where 46% have an impairment (Ministry of Health 2015). Yet Māori are not engaging in the NZ disability community. This is not an uncommon experience among many indigenous communities which have experienced colonisation.

As NZ became aware of Māori issues in policy, the Ministry of Māori Affairs adopted the Tu Tangata philosophy in 1977. The implementation of this philosophy led to the inclusion of Māori concepts and the devolution of State involvement in all areas of service delivery for Māori such as *Kohanga reo* (Māori language kindergartens; Fleres 1989) and *Mātua Whāngai* (Māori foster parent programmes). These community initiative programmes were expected to run on minimal State funding which has made it difficult for them to remain operational. At the same time as this was happening, the transfer of persons with disabilities from institutional to community assisted care was developing, which resulted in putting financial responsibility onto the community programmes but with less onus on State support.

For Māori with disabilities, the impact of both institutional and community care was dependent on their involvement with their *whānau* (family) and with their community (Hickey 2008).

Within Māori disability identity there are also other groups who identify as distinctive groups, and who see their impairment identity and their ethnic identity as positive aspects of themselves, whilst they see disability as a negative identity label (Padden 1996). This is particularly the case for those of Deaf cultural identity. While older Deaf persons would once identify as becoming deaf through a particular experience of impairment, younger Deaf persons simply see their identity from a cultural perspective through having a unique language and community identity. Deaf persons consider themselves to be a distinct, cultural identity and not a subculture within a culture, but equal to other cultural identities; hence the reason for the tensions that exist when trying to define culture within a Deaf contextual framework (Hickey 2015). To define 'culture' for Deaf persons is to re-examine 'culture' as a concept of ethnic identity. Whereas to define 'culture' for Deaf Māori (or Māori Deaf) is to conceptualise 'Deaf culture' also from an ethnic framework—where neither fit under the current definitions of 'culture'. Deaf persons wanting to define 'culture' for themselves are calling for a new conceptualisation of 'culture' that will allow for their own specificity as Deaf persons—without placing this identity within that of 'disability' or as a subgroup (Clifford 1988; Padden 1996).

This example of the discussion around Deaf culture outlines the difficulty of framing disability in a monocultural manner. For example, the NZ Disability Strategy (NZDS) (Office for Disability Issues 2001), although it does identify certain ethnic groups, such as Māori and Pacific Islander persons with disabilities, does not apply an ethnic specific model to its objectives for these groups, nor does it identify the specific issues for Māori Deaf people. Therefore, it exemplifies the assumption of one concept of disability throughout its recommendations regardless of both differences in the way disability may be conceived by both particular ethnic groups and some people with disabilities.

Further, the NZDS does not seek to apply its policy recommendations from the perspective of, for example, Māori with disabilities, which would involve several components, including an interdependent approach to their well-being and social integration within their cultural communities. The NZDS applies a monocultural approach to each of the groups it identifies and not a diversity approach. Also, it does not recognise the collective nature of Māori indigenous culture which is, in part, an element recognised in their cultural identity.

Māori cultural thinking around impairment, which is generally not seen as a deficit or in a negative way, may partially explain why few Māori with disabilities are involved within the disability sector. They are more focused on surviving, and not on disability or their bodies being disabled.

In other words, Māori do not see disability as a social or political identity but rather as a natural consequence of living. This appears to have similarities to other indigenous people with disabilities who do not define themselves through their impairment but through their indigenous identity. My experience in working with indigenous people with disabilities both in NZ and internationally has led me to think that indigenous people with disabilities who identify more strongly as persons with disabilities than as indigenous peoples do so because of their disconnection from their families and cultural communities. Those with disabilities who were removed and institutionalised in infancy or at birth, appear to have a greater disconnection with their *whānau* links than those who were raised with their *whānau* and within their cultural communities. To date, this is as yet anecdotal through oral stories, as little research has been done in this area.

Religion is another strong component of Polynesian identity post-colonially which affects indigenous people with disabilities. The Old Testament, in particular, plays a large part in influencing how Polynesian peoples view their family with disabilities (Hickey 2008; Kingi and Bray 2000; Collins and Hickey 2006). When missionaries came to NZ, they brought with them a biblical teaching that opposed the practice of the Māori experts in healing and the belief in Māori Gods, this influenced Māori practices and customs:

> Unlike the traders, who were motivated only by commercial gain, the missionaries were the cutting edge of colonisation. Their mission was to convert the Māori from heathenism to Christianity and from barbarism to civilisation. Underlying this mission were ethnocentric attitudes of racial and cultural superiority. (Walker 2004, p. 85)

While it is true that Polynesians were affected by these new colonial influences, it could be that Polynesians also selectively and consciously took control and selected what appealed to them (Walker 2004). Whatever the case may have been, there is no mistaking that the missionaries became effective in changing pre-colonial beliefs by providing Euro/Western medical care to the Polynesians while teaching them the Bible. They challenged traditionally held beliefs of sickness and changed many ways of thinking in Polynesian culture, which today still has a mix of traditional and Christian beliefs (Kingi and Bray 2000). This has played a large part in the thinking around indigenous people with disabilities today, in that religion, in particular the Old Testament, plays a part in the role of excluding indigenous people with disabilities from their cultural community (Elsmore 1999; Hickey 2008; Kingi and Bray 2000). This influence still permeates Polynesian cultural identity, and it is this influence that continues to divide the thinking of Polynesians around impairment today (Kingi and Bray 2000).

2 The Impact of Colonisation on Indigenous Peoples with Disabilities

Colonisation impacted heavily on indigenous populations, including indigenous peoples with disabilities when medical institutions routinely institutionalised people due to their disabilities and often subjugated them to medical treatment that was not available prior to the colonialists coming to their country (Soldatic and Grech 2016). Further, indigenous people do not receive appropriate supports from the State (Mooney Cotter 2006). Until indigenous peoples receive appropriate support, they cannot expect to see improvements in their own status. Research carried out by Durst and Bluechardt in researching the issues for Indigenous/Aboriginal Canadians with disabilities found that they experienced:

> ... the necessity of dealing with the serious problems of poverty, unemployment, social and geographical isolation, as well as inadequate living conditions. These [living] conditions continued to contribute to the high incidence of disability among First Nations people. The Follow Up Report stated that the situation of First Nations people with disabilities is not likely to improve significantly until the situation of all First Nations people improves. [It] also recognized that jurisdictional debates among government departments and among levels of government about who is responsible for providing services to First Nations people were creating incredible difficulties for people with disabilities, making it almost impossible, in some instances, to access services. (Durst and Bluechardt 2001, p. 37)

This quotation describes a situation where there is underlying systemic racism and a failure of responsibility within institutions such as health services that were introduced along with colonialism where persons with disabilities, along with indigenous peoples, were institutionalised and affected, often violently through these institutions (Soldatic and Grech 2016). The concept of 'other' has worked to subjugate and often inflict violence on those whose identity was deemed to deviate from what was considered the 'norm'. This has been carried into the institutions we know today where services such as health and disability are providing supports around those with disabilities. Unfortunately, these services still carry the historical racist practices, as the infrastructure has remained systemically discriminatory (Came and Griffith 2018; Soldatic and Grech 2016). Ghai, in describing colonisation and disability states that:

> The colonised loses its entity as a subject in its own right and remains only what the coloniser is not. It is thus an erasure both out of history and all significant aspects of development. (Ghai 2003, p. 80)

This failure to respect or acknowledge the rights of indigenous people leads to a failure to recognise the complexity of the ways disability may be seen by them. The perception of disability by indigenous people with disabilities may differ to that held by non-indigenous people (Kingi and Bray 2000). Many indigenous people with disabilities do not generally see themselves as having a disability; rather, they view their indigenous identity as more relevant to them than focusing on impairment as an identity (Gething 1995). Gething (1995) found that while obvious impairments such as amputations or severe physical impairments were easily defined by aboriginal peoples as a disability, hidden impairments such as intellectual, learning or psycho-social were not generally seen as a disability. Many of the disabilities that affect us later in life may be considered to be a 'normal' aspect of the life cycle and are therefore not singled out or isolated as belonging to a disability identity for those people; rather:

> Disability is rarely seen as a separate issue, but is seen as part of problems which are widespread and a part of the life cycle. (Gething 1995, p. 81)

It is also relevant to note the cultural diversity of diverse indigenous nations and groups which affects the definition, interpretation and attribution of factors constituting a disability (Soldatic and Grech 2016). The term 'disability' does not exist for some cultural groups, and therefore they do not consider attributing this identity to a group of people.

The diversity of understanding impairment exists within different cultural communities, for example, some indigenous peoples hold to the belief that some impairments have a social or spiritual component which affects well-being (Coleridge 1993). However, other indigenous communities sadly do not encourage the participation of their tribal members with disabilities resulting in their exclusion and isolation (Kiyaga and Moores 2003).

3 Indigenous Peoples

Defining indigenous as an identity is difficult, as there is no standard or fixed definition of it and indigenous experiences vary vastly between colonised communities and non-colonised communities. Although the UN has not adopted an official definition of 'indigenous peoples', the Special Rapporteur of the Sub-Commission on Prevention of Discrimination and Protection of Minorities, José Martinez Cobo, in his Study of the Problem of Discrimination against Indigenous Populations wrote that:

> Indigenous communities, peoples and nations are those which, having a historical continuity with pre-invasion and pre-colonial societies that developed on their territories, consider themselves distinct from other sectors of the societies now prevailing in those territories, or parts of them. They form at present non-dominant sectors of society and are determined to preserve, develop and transmit to future generations their ancestral territories, and their ethnic identity, as the basis of their continued existence as peoples, in accordance with their own cultural patterns, social institutions and legal system. (Cobo (1982), Add.6)

I would argue that the above group of characteristics is a description rather than a definition. The concept of indigenous identity cannot be a shortened or abbreviated definition, as it would otherwise remove and dilute the complexity and diversity of what it means to be indigenous. However, in a post-colonial society where indigenous people are a minority group, there are consequences in how they are described. For example, for many indigenous peoples, due to the poverty they experience, participation in society is denied. Indigenous people with disabilities face further marginalisation because as a person with a disability, it is highly unlikely they will be employed or access their health and equipment needs, so to be able to participate in employment. Therefore, they face the double jeopardy of both identities.

4 The Dominant Global North Discourse

The Global North in colonising has had a huge impact on the Global South's indigenous populations. We still face many issues over 200 years after the impact of imperial colonialism, including the issue of those not of indigenous descent who have since been born in the Global South but have ancestral ties to the Global North. Often, tensions arise between the indigenous peoples and the non-indigenous peoples who were born or have since come to these lands. In relation to disability, the worst impact is the loss of knowledge of how indigenous peoples addressed impairment historically and how they addressed the long-term care and support of their families who experienced disabilities. These areas are all now medicalised, often supported by institutions, which all have historical foundations in colonialism and violence (Hickey 2008; Soldatic and Grech 2016).

In relation to disability, NZ Government institutions with colonial influences continue to hinder the well-being of indigenous peoples with disabilities by not recognising indigenous concepts of disability. There is barely a platform in NZ that provides an indigenous disability voice at local, national and international level, nor are Māori with disabilities sufficiently represented in decision-making around disability supports and services. Ironically, Pacific Island peoples with disabilities have a Disabled Peoples' Organisation (DPO) and are resourced to ensure they have a voice at the table with the other DPOs. Other than blind and deaf/Deaf Māori, other Māori disability identities are not at that table. This is despite the Treaty of Waitangi in 1840 guaranteeing Māori partnerships, participation and protection of their rights as Māori in determining their own health and well-being pathways. Until Māori with disabilities also sit at the table as other demographic groups with disabilities do, and until they have the right to represent an indigenous perspective, then it is my belief they will struggle to achieve a reduction of the disparities and marginalisation that they currently experience.

5 The CRPD: How Do Indigenous Disabled People Fit In?

I consider that the CRPD continues the history in which indigenous cultural issues are not taken into account. During the negotiations for the CRPD, the decision was taken to accredit representatives from DPOs and human rights NGOs with observer status, and to allow them to attend future Ad Hoc Committee sessions (Lawson 2007); however, UN Member States continued to retain control over their delegation appointment processes. It is difficult to estimate the number of indigenous people's representatives who were involved in the drafting of the CRPD. Apart from the Australian aboriginal delegation, there was no official presence of indigenous rights disability groups at the UN Ad Hoc Committee sessions. However, a decision was made to develop an indigenous people's representative role for the International Disability Caucus IDC (Caucus) where myself, and aboriginal Gail Rankine, were appointed.

My experience on the Caucus led me to the view that Western values dominated the process, and that those of us who embraced other worldviews were not as easily included. For example, as members of the Caucus we were aware that indigenous communities wanted autonomy of their identities, their own access to services and to run their own services in a self-determining way. During the development of the CRPD, a group of us did try and get an article for indigenous peoples and other minorities included into the body of the Convention (Hickey 2014). This article however was rejected by the UN Member States' delegates at the time. Instead indigenous peoples and other minorities were recognised as a group that face greater marginalisation in the CRPD's Preamble:

> (p) Concerned about the difficult conditions faced by persons with disabilities who are subject to multiple or aggravated forms of discrimination on the basis of race, colour, sex, language, religion, political or other opinion, national, ethnic, indigenous or social origin, property, birth, age or other status. (CRPD 2006, Preamble, para. p)

This has not led to a development of the autonomy and rights of indigenous peoples with disabilities. For example, in NZ the statistics are revealing an increasing marginalisation of indigenous peoples with disabilities (Statistics New Zealand 2013; Ministry of Health 2015).

Therefore, the final text of the CRPD did not recognise the right of self-determination for indigenous disabled peoples. Which is in contrast to the UN Declaration on the Rights of Indigenous Peoples (UNDRIP) that was adopted a year later in 2007 and ensures that the identity of disabled indigenous peoples is protected (UNDRIP 2007, Art. 21; 222).[1] Because of this failure to recognise the right of self-determination of indigenous people with disabilities I consider that the CRPD represents a westernised construct within a colonising framework, as it does not incorporate an intersectional approach to identity except in relation to women and children (CRPD 2006, Art. 6, 7).

[1] Article 21: '(1) Indigenous peoples have the right, without discrimination, to the improvement of their economic and social conditions, including, inter alia, in the areas of education, employment, vocational training and retraining, housing, sanitation, health and social security. (2). States shall take effective measures and, where appropriate, special measures to ensure continuing improvement of their economic and social conditions. Particular attention shall be paid to the rights and special needs of indigenous elders, women, youth, children and persons with disabilities' (UNDRIP 2007, Art. 21). Article 22: '(1) Particular attention shall be paid to the rights and special needs of indigenous elders, women, youth, children and persons with disabilities in the implementation of this Declaration. (2) States shall take measures, in conjunction with indigenous peoples, to ensure that indigenous women and children enjoy the full protection and guarantees against all forms of violence and discrimination' (UNDRIP 2007, Art. 22).

6 Conclusion

The process of colonisation played a big part in causing impairment related disablement (Kingi and Bray 2000). It is clear that indigenous disabled people are dealing with a UN human rights framework that largely ignores their communities and the impact of disablement in their lives. What is not clear is why there has been so little effort to amend the UN human rights framework to better reflect the rights of indigenous disabled populations. For example, when the CRPD was first ratified by NZ there were high hopes of change by many in the community. While changes are happening for mainstream disabled people, the indigenous disabled population is experiencing increased disparities and inequities. Until there is a redesigning of the UN human rights framework, including the CRPD, there will be few changes to the issues that are causing the exclusion and disparities experienced by indigenous disabled people.

References

Ballara, A. (1998). *Iwi: The dynamics of Maori tribal organisation from c.1769 to 1945*. Wellington: Victoria University Press.

Barlow, C. (1991). *Tikanga Whakaaro—Key concepts in Maori culture*. Auckland: Oxford University Press.

Belich, J. (1996). *Making peoples: A history of the New Zealanders from Polynesian settlement to the end of the nineteenth century*. Auckland: Penguin.

Broughton, J. (1993). Being Maori. *New Zealand Medical Journal, 106*, 506–508.

Came, H., & Griffith, D. (2018). Tackling racism as a "wicked" public health problem: Enabling allies in anti-racism praxis. *Social Science & Medicine, 199*, 181–188. https://doi.org/10.1016/j.socscimed.2017.03.028.

Clifford, J. (1988). *The predicament of culture*. Cambridge, MA: Harvard University Press.

Cobo, J. M. (1982). Study of the problem of discrimination against indigenous populations: Report submitted by the special rapporteur, Mr. José Martínez Cobo, UN Doc. E/CN.4/Sub.2/1982/2/Add.6.

Coleridge, P. (1993). *Disability, liberation, and development*. Oxford: Oxfam.

Collins, A., & Hickey, H. (2006). *The role of whanau in the lives of Maori with physical disabilities*. Research Report. Wellington: Families Commission.

CRPD (United Nations Convention on the Rights of Persons with Disabilities). (2006). Adopted in 2006 by the United Nations general assembly.

Dow, D. (1999). *Maori health and government policy 1940–1940*. Wellington: Victoria University Press.

Durie, M. H. (1994). *Whanau/families and healthy development*. Paper Presented to the Fifth Annual Conference of the New Zealand College of Clinical Psychologists, Department of Maori Studies, Massey University, Hamilton.

Durst, D., & Bluechardt, M. (2001). *Urban aboriginal persons with disabilities: Double jeopardy*. Regina: University of Regina.

Elsmore, B. (1999). *Mana from heaven: A century of Maori prophets in New Zealand*. Auckland: Reed.

Fleres, A. (1989). Te Kohanga Reo: A Maori language renewal program. *Canadian Journal of Native Education, 16*(2), 78–88.

Gething, L. (1995). A case study of Australian aboriginal people with disabilities. *Australian Disability Review, 2*, 77–88.

Ghai, A. (2003). *(Dis)embodied form: Issues of disabled women*. New Delhi: Har-Anand.

Hickey, S. J. (2008). *The legal social and cultural rights of Māori with disabilities*. Unpublished doctoral thesis, University of Waikato, Hamilton, New Zealand.

Hickey, H. (2014). Indigenous peoples with disabilities. In *Voices from within: Civil society's involvement in the drafting of the convention on the rights of persons with disabilities* (pp. 157–169). Philadelphia: University of Pennsylvania Press.

Hickey, H. (2015). Tätau tätau: Engaging with whänau hauä from within a cultural framework. In J. Bevan-Brown (Ed.), *Working with Mäori chil- dren with special education needs: He mihi whakahirahira* (pp. 70–84). Wellington: NZCER.

Hickey, H., & Wilson, D. L. (2017). Whānau hauā: Reframing disability from an indigenous perspective. *MAI Journal, 6*(1), 82–94. https://doi.org/10.20507/MAIJournal.2017.6.1.7.

King, J. A., Brough, M., & Knox, M. (2014). Negotiating disability and colonisation: The lived experience of indigenous Australians with a disability. *Disability & Society, 29*(5), 738–750. https://doi.org/10.1080/09687599.2013.864257.

Kingi, J., & Bray, A. (2000). *Māori concepts of disability*. Dunedin: Donald Beasley Institute Incorporated.

Kiyaga, N., & Moores, D. (2003). Deafness in sub-Saharan Africa. *American Annals of the Deaf, 148*(1), 18–24.

Lawson, A. (2007). The United Nations convention on the rights of persons with disabilities: New era or false Dawn? *Syracuse Journal of International Law and Commerce, 34*, 563–619.

Ministry of Health. (2015). *Tatau Kahukura: Māori Health Chart Book 2015* (3rd ed.). Wellington: Ministry of Health.

Mooney Cotter, A.-M. (2006). *Race matters. An international legal analysis of race discrimination*. Farnham: Ashgate.

Office for Disability Issues. (2001). *New Zealand disability strategy (NZDS)*. Retrieved from https://www.odi.govt.nz/nz-disability-strategy/about-the-strategy/new-zealand-disability-strategy-2001/2001-strategy-readonline/.

Padden, C. (1996). From the cultural to the bicultural. In I. Parasnis (Ed.), *Cultural and language diversity and the deaf experience* (pp. 79–98). New York: Cambridge University Press.

Pearson, D. (1990). *A dream deferred: The origins of ethnic conflict in New Zealand*. Wellington: Allen and Unwin.

Pearson, D. (1994). Community. In P. Spoonley, D. Pearson, & I. Shirley (Eds.), *New Zealand society* (2nd ed.). Auckland: The Dunmore Press Ltd.

Soldatic, K., & Grech, S. (2016). *Disability and colonialism. (Dis)encounters and anxious intersectionalities*. Abingdon: Routledge.

Statistics New Zealand. (2001). *Review of the management of ethnicity background paper*. Wellington: New Zealand Government.

Statistics New Zealand. (2013). *Disability survey: 2013*. Retrieved from http://www.stats.govt.nz/browseforstats/health/disabilities/DisabilitySurvey_HOTP2013.aspx.

Statistics New Zealand. (2015). *He hauä Mäori: Findings from the 2013 disability survey*. Retrieved from http://www.stats.govt.nz/browse_for_stats/health/disabilities/He-haua- maori-findings-from-2013-disabilitysurvey.aspx

UDHR (United Nations Universal Declaration of Human Rights) (1948). United Nations general assembly resolution 217 A.

UNDRIP (United Nations Declaration on the Rights of Indigenous Peoples. (2007). United Nations general assembly resolution A/RES/61/295.

Walker, R. (2004). *Ka whawhai tonu matou: Struggle without end*. Auckland: Penguin.

Wylie, K., McAllister, L., Davidson, B., & Marshall, J. (2013). Changing practice: Implications of the world report on disability for responding to communication disability in under-served populations. *International Journal of Speech-Language Pathology, 151*, 1–13. https://doi.org/10.3109/17549507.2012.745164.

Part II

The Ratification Process: To Be or Not to Be?

6

The Failure of the United States to Ratify the CRPD

Arlene S. Kanter

1 Introduction

No country in the world is required to ratify, or even sign a treaty; yet most countries do (Kanter 2015a, 2019a). Of the 193 member states of the United Nations (UN), most have signed some, if not all, of the human rights treaties that have been adopted to date by the UN.[1] The mostly widely ratified human rights treaty is the UN Convention on the Rights of the Child (CRC 1989), which has been ratified by literally every member state, except for the United States (US).[2] Even Somalia,

[1] Of the UN's 193 member states that are eligible to ratify treaties, 192 countries have ratified the CRC 1989, 180 countries have ratified the CEDAW 1979, 175 countries have ratified the ICERD 1965, 167 countries have ratified the ICCPR 1966, 161 countries have ratified the ICESCR 1966, and 153 countries have ratified the CAT 1984 (Kanter 2015a; UN Undated-b).

[2] The US has ratified two optional protocols of the CRC but only signed the CRC. According to Philip Alston, a leading international human rights legal expert, the US reluctantly signed the CRC. The fact that "this treaty contained a number of provisions giving effect to [the Convention

A. S. Kanter (✉)
Syracuse University College of Law, Syracuse University, New York, USA
e-mail: kantera@law.syr.edu

E. J. Kakoullis, K. Johnson (eds.), *Recognising Human Rights in Different Cultural Contexts*, https://doi.org/10.1007/978-981-15-0786-1_6

the only other country that had failed to ratify the CRC for over 20 years, ratified it in 2015.

The US is one of only seven countries, and the only industrialised country, that has failed to ratify the Convention on the Elimination of Discrimination Against Women, since its adoption by the UN in 1979 (CEDAW 1979).[3] Moreover, the US is only one of fewer than two dozen countries that have not yet ratified the Convention on the Rights of Persons with Disabilities (CRPD 2006). The CRPD was adopted in 2006 and came into force in May 2008. Since then, the CRPD has been signed by 163 countries and ratified by 181 countries, but not the US.

The US has one of the worst treaty ratification records in the world. Of the nine core human rights treaties adopted by the UN, the US has ratified only three.[4] This number is strikingly low, especially in relation to other countries with whom the US compares itself, such as Australia, the United Kingdom, France, Germany and Canada, all of which have either ratified or acceded to all or most human rights treaties and their optional protocols (Kanter 2019a; Venetis 2011). By contrast, the US is now considered the country with the "poorest record of ratification of human rights treaties among all industrialized nations" (Lord and Stein 2009).[5] Some com-

on Economic, Social and Cultural Rights] was often cited as a reason for not proceeding with ratification. This was rather ironic since most of the relevant formulations had in fact been significantly watered down at the insistence of the Reagan Administration during the process of drafting the CRC in the 1980s" (Alston 2009, p. 5).

[3] The other countries are Iran, Nauru, Palau Somalia, Sudan and Tonga (UN OHCHR Undated-b).

[4] Of the nine core human rights treaties adopted by the United Nations prior to the CRPD in 2006, the ICCPR in 1966, the ICESCR 1966, the Genocide Convention 1948, the Convention Relating to the Status of Refugees 1951, the ICERD 1965, the CEDAW 1979, the CAT 1984, the CRC 1989, and the International Convention on the Protection of the Rights of All Migrant Workers and Members of their Families 1990, the US has ratified only the ICCPR (in 1992), the ICERD (in 1994) and the CAT (in 1994).

[5] The Senate has a very bad track record when it comes to human rights treaties, having only ratified three treaties and two optional protocols since the 1960s (Lord and Stein 2009). The three treaties are the ICERD, the ICCPR, and the CAT. The United States has ratified two Optional Protocols for the CRC, one concerning children in armed conflict and the other concerning the sale of children, child prostitution and child pornography (Human Rights Watch 2009). The following are some of the treaties the US has not ratified: The CEDAW, the CRC, the International Convention for the Protection of all Persons from Enforced Disappearance (ICPPED 2006), the Landmine Ban Treaty 1999, the Convention on Cluster Munitions 2010, and the Optional Protocol to the CAT 2006 (Human Rights Watch 2009). With respect to the CEDAW, there are only seven countries, including the US, that have not ratified it (Human Rights Watch 2009).

mentators have gone so far as to suggest that the failure of the US to ratify human rights treaties not only reflects poorly on the US, internationally, but also adversely affects the ability of the US to conduct foreign policy (Kaye 2013).

This chapter addresses the question of why the US has failed to ratify the CRPD, especially in light of the progress the US has made in the development of domestic disability laws. The chapter begins with an overview of why countries ratify treaties in the first place, followed by the second section that provides a brief overview of US treaty ratification history. The third section of the chapter discusses the CRPD treaty ratification process in the US Senate, including the arguments that were presented for and against ratification of the CRPD. The chapter concludes with a discussion of what the failure of the US to ratify the CRPD means to people with disabilities in the US and in relation to the standing of the US throughout the world.

2 Why Countries Ratify Treaties

At first glance, it appears counterintuitive for a country, any country, to ratify an international human rights treaty. Once a country ratifies a treaty, it agrees to comply with the laws of an international body, the United Nations. Such ratification, therefore, may be considered against the country's self-interest in preserving its own state sovereignty (Kanter 2019a). Nonetheless, a substantial number of countries have ratified most, if not all, human rights treaties.[6] Many leading scholars have sought to explain why so many countries have ratified so many treaties (see, e.g., Chayes and Chayes 1995; Hathaway 2002; Koh 2002; Hafner-Burton and Tsutsui 2005; Hafner-Burton et al. 2008; Vreeland 2008; Wotipka and Tsutsui 2008; Simmons 2009; Sikkink 2017). What they have found is that countries ratify treaties for many different reasons, but that most

[6] For example, 180 countries have ratified the CEDAW, 175 countries have ratified the ICERD, 167 countries have ratified the ICCPR, 161 countries have ratified the ICESCR, and 153 countries have ratified the CAT. For a discussion of the current debate about the efficacy of human rights treaty ratification, see Kanter (2019a, 178–184).

of these reasons have nothing to do with the country's support for the particular treaty (Kanter 2019a). Some countries may decide to ratify a particular treaty in order to gain approval by the international community, or, alternatively, to avoid being ostracised for failing to ratify a particular treaty. Other countries may choose to follow the lead of their regional neighbours; while others may ratify a particular treaty as a quid pro quo for receiving international aid (Hafner-Burton and Tsutsui 2005; Hafner-Burton et al. 2008; Vreeland 2008; Wotipka and Tsutsui 2008; Simmons 2009). The reasons for ratification also may depend on the country's own history of treaty ratification, its legal or political system, cultural and religious traditions, or how rich or poor the country is (Koh 2002). Nevertheless, scholars generally agree that most countries choose to ratify human rights treaties because it is in their interest to do so and not because they intend to comply with the terms of the treaty (see, e.g., Hathaway 2002; Kanter 2019a; Koh 2002; and Simmons 2009). Moreover, whatever the reasons may be for treaty ratification by a given country, more countries than ever before are ratifying human rights treaties, except for the US, which remains an outlier in this regard.

3 History of Treaty Ratification in the United States

The US Constitution provides a framework for treaty adoption that requires action by both the President and the Senate. According to this framework, the President signs the treaty, and then decides to transmit the treaty to the Senate, or not.[7] The full Senate must approve the treaty by a required two-thirds vote. However, the Foreign Relations Committee of the Senate ultimately decides whether to send the treaty to the floor of the full Senate for a vote (Bradley 2015).

When a treaty is sent to the full Senate, the Senate may approve it, demand changes to it, or request the addition of Reservations, Understandings or Declarations (RUDs).[8] Once a treaty is approved by

[7] For a detailed discussion of the US treaty process, see Bradley (2015).

[8] RUDs have been attached to all four human rights treaties ratified by the US (Venetis 2011).

the required two-thirds of the Senate, the Senate then sends to the President a resolution of "advice and consent" to the treaty (Venetis 2011, p. 116). At that point, the President has the option of ratifying the treaty or not. However, the Senate cannot constitutionally obligate the President to ratify a treaty (Venetis 2011).

Given the US Constitution's elaborate system of treaty ratification, one could assume that treaty ratification is part of the Senate's typical workload. However, as the record on US ratification illustrates, the Senate does not often ratify treaties. In fact, the US has not ratified most human rights treaties, including the CRPD.

Opposition to the role of treaties in domestic law began long before the ratification vote for the CRPD. Even before World War II, politicians mounted a campaign to limit the effect of international law, culminating in legislators of both parties opposing American involvement in the conflicts in Asia and Europe. For example, in 1934 and 1936, Senator Gerald Nye, a Republican Senator from North Dakota, held hearings attempting to show that America was forced into World War I by an alliance of arms merchants, bankers, and foreign influences (Cole 1962). With the attack on Pearl Harbour in 1941, these "non-interventionists," as they later became known (Cole 1983), were temporarily silenced. Further, following the conclusion of World War II when the world came together to create the United Nations, the US played a prominent role in this process. Indeed, the president's own wife, Eleanor Roosevelt, was one of the chief architects of the UN Declaration on Human Rights in 1948 (UN Undated-a).

By the early 1950s, however, some legislators in the US sought to renew efforts to block the effect of international law by refusing to ratify international human rights treaties (Venetis 2011). As one scholar has written, the US came "kicking and screaming into the modern world of international human rights treaties" (Schabas quoted in Venetis 2011, p. 100). In fact, it took the US nearly 40 years to ratify its first human rights treaty, the Convention on the Prevention and Punishment of the Crime of Genocide (Genocide Convention 1948), which is regarded as one of the least controversial treaties of all (Venetis 2011).

In the 1950s the non-interventionists introduced several proposals to amend the Constitution to limit the treaty power. These proposals, known collectively as the Bricker Amendment, were named for its sponsor, Senator John William Bricker.[9] In its original form, the Bricker Amendment would have eliminated the automatic incorporation of international law into domestic law of the US, leaving it to Congress or state legislatures to decide upon the internal enforceability of international obligations of the US (Ciment 2015).[10] Although this version of the Bricker Amendment was defeated, it was revised and presented again to the Senate in 1954. The final version of the Bricker Amendment declared that no treaty or international agreement could conflict with the US Constitution. It also provided that treaties could not be self-executing and that in order to effectuate the terms of a treaty, Congress would be required to enact separate enabling legislation. The proposed amendment also limited the president's power to effectuate executive agreements with foreign powers, except with an act of Congress.[11] This version of the Bricker Amendment, like the prior version, failed to receive the necessary two-thirds votes of the Senate; but it lost by only one vote.[12] Senator Bricker and his colleagues' effort to insulate US laws and policies from "foreign influence" failed (Ciment 2015, pp. 172–173). However, their effort exacted a price on US foreign policy. In exchange for the Senate votes against the Bricker Amendment, President Eisenhower apparently agreed not to accede to any international human rights treaty or to use the treaty power to address matters of domestic concern (Bradley 2000,

---

[9] Senator Bicker was a governor of Ohio, Republican Senator from Ohio, and an unsuccessful nominee for Vice President in 1944 (see, generally, Kaufman 1990, pp. 94–147). Some scholars argue that the Senate continues to pay homage to the "ghost of Senator Bricker" by insisting on assurances that new human rights treaty obligations will not alter existing domestic law, even if the treaty's policy objectives are considered desirable (see Henkin 1995).

[10] According to this scholar, such a change would have caused American foreign policy to return to the time of the Articles of Confederation of the eighteenth century when the US refused to adhere to its obligations under international law (Ciment 2015).

[11] Introduced into the Senate in February 1952, as Senate Joint Resolution 130, the "Bricker Amendment" to the Constitution read as follows: Section 1. A provision of a treaty which conflicts with this Constitution shall not be of any force or effect; Section 2. A treaty shall become effective as internal law in the United States only through legislation which would be valid in the absence of treaty; Section 3. Congress shall have power to regulate all executive and other agreements with any foreign power or international organisation. All such agreements shall be subject to the limitations imposed on treaties by this article; Section 4. The congress shall have power to enforce this article by appropriate legislation.

[12] Although the Bricker Amendment started out with 56 co-sponsors, it eventually went down to defeat in the US Senate, 42–50, with 4 not voting.

2015). Moreover, even with the defeat of the Bricker Amendment, hostility towards international law found expression in US law in the post-World War II years. For example, in 1957, the US Supreme Court held in *Reid v. Covert* (354 US 1 (1957)) that the Bill of Rights could not be abrogated by agreements with foreign powers. As the Court stated, "this Court has regularly and uniformly recognised the supremacy of the Constitution over a treaty" (*Reid v Covert* 1957).[13] The particular issue of that case was whether American civilians outside of the territorial jurisdiction of the US could be tried by US military courts while retaining their right to a trial by jury, as guaranteed by the US Constitution. The Court held that American citizens outside of the territorial jurisdiction of the US retain the protections guaranteed by the Constitution, asserting that no treaty could confer upon Congress the sweeping power to try civilians by military tribunal (Bradley 2015).

Thus, although the US was one of the chief supporters of the development of the international human rights regime, as well as an architect of the United Nations, itself, the US has remained divided on whether and to what extent the US should participate in international treaties. With references to the post-World War II decade, Curtis Bradley has observed that:

> Among other things, critics were concerned that the treaties would undermine US federalism by allowing the national government to regulate matters that Congress did not have the constitutional authority to regulate. There was also opposition from representatives of southern states who were concerned that the government would use treaties as a vehicle for engaging in civil rights reform that was beyond the legislative authority of Congress. (Bradley 2015, p. 36)[14]

By the 1970s, however, the US evidenced a renewed commitment to the international human rights law system. President Jimmy Carter made

---

[13] *Reid v Covert*, 354 US 1 (1957). The particular issue of that case was whether American civilians outside of the territorial jurisdiction of the United States could be tried by US military courts while retaining their right to a trial by jury, as guaranteed by the United States Constitution. The Court held that American citizens outside of the territorial jurisdiction of the United States retain the protections guaranteed by the Constitution, asserting that no treaty could confer upon Congress the sweeping power to try civilians by military tribunal (Bradley 2015).

[14] For additional discussion of the reasons for US resistance to the human rights treaties, see Bradley (2010).

human rights a central component of his foreign policy.[15] Among other actions, he submitted to the Senate for ratification four international human rights treaties: the International Convention on the Elimination of all Forms of Racial Discrimination (ICERD 1965), the International Covenant on Civil and Political Rights (ICCPR 1966), the International Covenant on Economic, Social and Cultural Rights (ICESCR 1966) and the American Convention on Human Rights 1969. The Senate ratified the ICERD and the ICCPR, but not until 1992 and 1994, respectively.[16]

The next US President, Ronald Regan, also acknowledged the importance of human rights in his Democracy Initiative that focused on support for democratic institutions.[17] In fact, during the Regan Administration, the US ratified the Genocide Convention (in 1988), the first treaty the US had ratified in decades.[18] Later, during the Clinton Administration, the US ratified additional human rights treaties, including two treaties President Carter had signed but not ratified, the ICCPR, the ICERD, as well as the Convention against Torture and Other Cruel, Inhuman and Degrading Treatment or Punishment (CAT 1984). However, with the attack on the World Trade Center on September 11, 2001, the Administration of President George W. Bush chose a different path, focusing on domestic security and not international human rights (see, e.g., Human Rights First Undated).

The US reasserted its commitment to human rights under the Obama Administration when it adopted two protocols to the UN CRC (1989), one on the involvement of children in armed conflicts and one on the sale of children, child prostitution and child pornography. In 2005, the US also ratified the UN Protocol to Prevent, Suppress and Punish Trafficking in

[15] The Carter Administration (1977–1981) made human rights the focus of his presidency (see Committee on Foreign Affairs (1974) and US Department of State (1977–1981)). Since then, former President Carter has remained a zealous advocate for human rights.

[16] See UN OHCHR (Undated-b).

[17] Two years later, in a major foreign policy address delivered at Westminster Palace before the British Parliament, President Reagan proposed an initiative "to foster the infrastructure of democracy—the system of a free press, unions, political parties, universities—which allows a people to choose their own way, to develop their own culture, to reconcile their own differences through peaceful means." See Lowe (Undated). See also Jacoby (1986).

[18] The Genocide Convention 1948 was originally submitted to the US Senate by President Truman in 1949, and resubmitted by President Nixon and President Carter.

Persons, Especially Women and Children 2000,[19] which supplements the Convention against Transnational Organized Crime 2000. President Obama also presented CEDAW and the CRPD to the Senate for ratification. Since then, however, the Senate has failed to ratify CEDAW, the CRPD or the CRC.

Despite the progress during the Obama Administration with respect to the ratification of human rights treaties, the US record on ratification remains disappointing. Not only has the US not ratified most human rights treaties, but it also has attached Reservations, Understandings and Declarations (RUDs) to the treaties that it has ratified (Bradley 1992). RUDs are attached to treaties to indicate how the country will interpret the treaty according to domestic law, once the treaty is ratified. RUDs are permitted under international law unless they are either prohibited by the treaty itself or are inconsistent with the "object and purpose" of the treaty (VCLT 1969, Art. 2(1)).[20] However, attaching RUDs to a treaty does not excuse the country from adhering to its obligations under a treaty.

The US, like any country, is free to adopt RUDS to any treaty it ratifies.[21] Indeed, many countries, in addition to the US, have included

[19] The US also has signed the following treaties, which have not been ratified: ICESCR (ratified by 167 countries) American Convention on Human Rights 1969, CRC (ratified by 193 countries) CEDAW (ratified by 187 countries) and CRPD (ratified by 175 countries).

[20] The prohibition against Reservations, Understandings and Declaration, or "RUDS" which contradict the object and purpose of a treaty was established in 1969, with the adoption of the UN Vienna Convention on the Law of Treaties. Article 2(1) (d) of the Vienna Convention defines a reservation as a "unilateral statement" made by a State when ratifying a treaty "whereby it purports to exclude or modify the legal effect of certain provisions of the treaty in their application to that State." Ibid at art. 2(1)(d). Article 19 of the Vienna Convention further prohibits any reservation that is "incompatible with the object and purpose of the treaty." Thus the Vienna Convention makes clear that RUDS may not be used to undermine the force and effect of any particular article in a human rights treaty. *Id.* As explained in the International Law Commission's *Guide to Practice on Reservations to Treaties* (2011): "[a] reservation is incompatible with the object and purpose of the treaty if it affects an essential element of the treaty that is necessary to its general tenor, in such a way that the reservation impairs the *raison d'être* of the treaty" (para. 3.1.5); see also International Court of Justice (1951):"It is the compatibility of a reservation with the object and purpose of the Convention that must furnish the criterion for the attitude of a State in making the reservation on accession as well as for the appraisal by a State in objecting to the reservation." See also Cook (1990). For a discussion of the effect of reservations on treaties, see, generally, Alston and Goodman (2012, pp. 1080–1087).

[21] The International Court of Justice addressed the question of the effect of reservations to a multilateral human rights treaty in its 1951 Advisory Opinion on Reservations to the Genocide

RUDS with their ratification of human rights treaties, including the CRPD (Bradley 2015).[22] Nonetheless, the extensive use of RUDs by the US has been criticised on the ground that it displays a lack of good faith in joining the relevant treaties.[23] As Professor Louis Henkin has written, "[b]y adhering to human rights conventions subject to these reservations, the US, it is charged, is pretending to assume international obligations but in fact is undertaking nothing" (Henkin 1995, p. 341).

In sum, the US commitment to international human rights enforcement is paradoxical. On the one hand, the US was one of the primary architects of the entire international human rights law system, including the creation of the United Nations. On the other hand, since World War II the US has adhered to a policy of exceptionalism, resulting in its failure to endorse nearly all international human rights treaties. With respect to the CRPD, in particular, the US has failed to ratify it, even while the US enjoys notoriety as a world leader in the area of disability rights. It is this relationship between the ratification history of the US and the US position regarding ratification of the CRPD that is the subject of the next section of this chapter.

Convention. In this opinion, it rejected the argument that any State is entitled to become a party to a treaty while also making any reservation it chooses by virtue of its sovereignty. As the Opinion continued, "It is the compatibility of a reservation with the object and purpose of the Convention that must furnish the criterion for the attitude of the State in making the reservation on accession as well as its appraisal by a State in objecting to a reservation." Alston and Goodman (2012, pp. 1080–1082).

[22] For example, for information about which countries attached RUDS to their ratification of the CRPD, see United Nations Treaty Collection (2006, p. 15a) Optional Protocol to the Convention on the Rights of Persons with Disabilities.

[23] According to Professor Bradley, these RUDs typically do a number of things: "First, they decline to agree to treaty provisions to the extent that they would violate individual rights provisions of the Constitution (such as the right of free speech). Second, they decline to agree to certain other provisions on policy grounds (such as provisions restricting the death penalty). Third, they purport to interpret some provisions that are undefined in the treaties (such as the phrase "cruel, inhuman, or degrading treatment or punishment" in the Convention against Torture). Fourth, they announce that the United States will implement the treaties in a manner consistent with its federal system of government. Finally, they declare that the terms of the treaties are non–self-executing" (Bradley 2015, pp. 36–37); Henkin (1995, p. 344).

4 The United States and the CRPD

4.1 The Role of the United States in Drafting the CRPD

Given the failure of the US to ratify most human rights treaties, its refusal to ratify the CRPD may come as no surprise. One could have expected the US to refuse to ratify the CRPD since, after all, it had not ratified most other treaties, and not even the CRC, which has been ratified now by every other country in the world. However, the failure of the US to ratify the CRPD was not inevitable. Unlike other treaties, the CRPD was actually based on a US law, the Americans with Disabilities Act (ADA).[24] In order to understand why the US failed to ratify the CRPD, we must first understand the role of the US in the CRPD drafting process (NCD.gov. 2012).

The United Nations convened the Ad Hoc Committee on the Comprehensive and Integral International Convention on the Protection and Promotion of the Rights and Dignity of Persons with Disabilities in December 2001. This Committee was charged with drafting the first comprehensive treaty on the rights of persons with disabilities, "based on the holistic approach in the work done in the fields of social development, human rights and non-discrimination" (Kanter 2015a, p. 292). The CRPD Ad Hoc Committee included representatives of over 40 countries, and over 400 different non-governmental organisations (NGOs) and disabled people's organisations (DPOs; Kanter 2015a). It held its first session in the summer of 2002 and met twice each year for three weeks at a time, for the next four years. The Committee thoroughly discussed, debated, negotiated, and drafted the final version of the CRPD and its Optional Protocol, which was adopted by the General Assembly of the United Nations on December 13, 2006. One of the most remarkable and now precedent-setting aspects of the drafting of the CRPD was the active involvement of people with disabilities from throughout the world. "Nothing About Us Without Us" became the rallying cry for the

[24] The ADA 1990 was one of several domestic disability laws that provided a model for the CRPD (Kanter 2015b). Although the CRPD is modeled after the ADA, there are some differences between the two documents, none of which, however, warranted the US's refusal to ratify the CRPD (Kanter 2019b).

CRPD and continues today as a slogan of the disability rights movement worldwide (Kanter 2015a).

The drafting of the CRPD occurred during the Administration of George W. Bush. Early on in the CRPD drafting process, the Bush Administration went on record stating that it would not sign the CRPD. In the Administration's view, there was no need for an international treaty because of the existence of national laws prohibiting discrimination on the basis of disability. The Administration's representative also referenced the long history of the US commitment to equal rights for persons with disabilities, and suggested that such a convention may be viewed as an unwelcome intrusion into national sovereignty.[25] Indeed, it was President Bush's father, President George H. Bush, who signed the original version of the ADA in 1990, and George W. Bush, himself, who signed the amended version of the ADA, the Americans with Disabilities Amendment Act (ADAA) in 2008 (ADA.gov Undated). Nonetheless, the Administration of George W. Bush prohibited US Justice Department attorneys from officially intervening in the CRPD. In fact, not only were the career Justice Department attorneys not permitted to formally participate in the drafting process, but they were actually replaced by a less experienced, junior-level political appointee (Stein and Lord 2009). According to those involved in the CRPD drafting process, this official had "neither substantive disability law expertise nor human rights treaty experience" (Stein and Lord 2009). Moreover, the staff change occurred just when the right to sexual and reproductive health was to be discussed (Stein and Lord 2009). Accordingly, the timing of the staff change may not have been coincidental. One of the only times during the entire CRPD drafting process when a member of the official US delegation spoke up was to join the Holy See in a statement that the CRPD should not be read to condone abortion (Kanter 2015a).

Based on this history, it appears that the Bush Administration, like Senator Bricker and his colleagues decades earlier, embraced the view that the most effective way to protect the rights of US citizens was to

[25] The US testified during the Ad Hoc Committee Meeting in June 2003. See Statement of Ralph F Boyd Jr (2003).

implement national legislation rather than enforce international treaties. According to this view, it was simply not necessary for the US to support the CRPD because the US already had the ADA 1990, which was considered "among the most comprehensive civil rights laws protecting the rights of people with disabilities in the world" (Holmes 2004).[26]

Further, if there was any doubt about the official position of the Bush Administration with respect to the CRPD, that doubt was resolved on December 6, 2006, when the Ad Hoc Committee completed its work and the US made the following statement, through its Justice Department official:

> … The United States believes that the most effective way for States to improve the real-world situation of persons with disabilities from a legal perspective is to strengthen their domestic legal frameworks related to non-discrimination and equality. That approach is rooted in our own national experience with legislation such as the Americans with Disabilities Act. We hope that the Convention will assist States in that process at the national level … My delegation reiterates its congratulations to all involved in this very significant process. (UN General Assembly 2006)

Although the Bush Administration made it clear that it would not sign or ratify the CRPD, that was not the position of most other countries in the world. The CRPD garnered more signatories on its opening day than any other treaty in the history of the UN (Kanter 2015a). Further, within three months after its adoption by the UN General Assembly, 81 countries and the European Union signed the CRPD and 44 countries signed its Optional Protocol (Kanter 2015a). By May 3, 2008, when the CRPD entered into force and became the first human rights treaty of the twenty-first century, more than 100 countries had ratified it (Kanter 2015a). As of today, 181 countries have ratified the CRPD. Thus, not only did the Bush Administration's position regarding the CRPD appear to contradict the role of the US as a world leader in disability rights at the time the

[26] Letter from Kim R Holmes, Assistant Secretary of State for International Organization Affairs, United States Department of State, to Lex Frieden, Chairperson, National Council on Disability on June 3, 2004 (Holmes 2004).

CRPD was adopted,[27] it also presented a challenge to those in the US who supported ratification of the CRPD by the US Senate.

4.2 The CRPD Comes Home

The US position towards the CRPD changed with the election of President Barak Obama in 2008. During the 2008 Presidential election, candidate Obama affirmed his commitment to the CRPD. Within a year after his election, on July 30, 2009, UN Ambassador Susan Rice signed the CRPD on behalf of President Obama.[28] At the signing, Ambassador Rice stated that by signing the CRPD, the US "once again confirm[s] that disability rights are not just civil rights to be enforced here at home; they are universal human rights to be promoted around the world. So we proudly join the international community in protecting the human rights of all" (Dale.gov. 2009).[29]

Although signing the CRPD did not bind the US to its subsequent ratification, it did evidence the Obama Administration's commitment to the goals and principles of the treaty. Thus, three years later, in May 2012, it came as no surprise when President Obama transmitted the CRPD to the Senate for advice and consent to ratification.[30] In a statement on December 3, 2012, the International Day of Persons with Disabilities, President Obama indicated his support for ratification of the CRPD, by issuing the following Presidential Proclamation:

> .... While Americans with disabilities already enjoy these rights at home, they frequently face barriers when they travel, conduct business, study, or

[27] As Lord and Stein (2009) also observed: "The Bush administration's aversion to cooperation was also particularly striking because of the references in the CRPD to American disability law (notably, the concept of reasonable accommodation) and its inherent values (such as its emphasis on independence and autonomy)."

[28] The US signed the CRPD on July 30, 2009. See Congress.Gov (2012a).

[29] President Obama issued a statement praising the CRPD by referring to the "extraordinary treaty... [that] urges equal protection and equal benefits before the law for all citizens [and] reaffirms the inherent dignity and worth and independence of all persons with disabilities worldwide." *Ability Magazine* (Undated).

[30] See, for example, Chaffin (2015) (citing Holmes 2004; indicating that the United States has chosen disability experts to participate in the Ad Hoc deliberations before the United Nations).

reside overseas. Ratifying the Convention in the Senate would reaffirm America's position as the global leader on disability rights and better position us to encourage progress toward inclusion, equal opportunity, full participation, independent living, and economic self-sufficiency for persons with disabilities worldwide. We have come far in the long march to achieve equal opportunity for all. But even as we partner with countries across the globe in affirming universal human rights, we know our work will not be finished until the inherent dignity and worth of all persons with disabilities is guaranteed. Today, let us renew our commitment to meeting that challenge here in the United States, and let us redouble our efforts to build new paths to participation, empowerment, and progress around the world. (Presidential Proclamation 2012)[31]

[31] President Obama spoke about the importance of ratifying the CRPD:
December 3, 2012: Proclamation by the President of the United States of America

Americans have always understood that each of us is entitled to a set of fundamental freedoms and protections under the law, and that when everyone gets a fair shot at opportunity, all of us do better. For more than two decades, our country has upheld those basic promises for persons with disabilities through the Americans with Disabilities Act—a sweeping civil rights bill that moved our Nation forward in the journey to equality for all. And from making health care more affordable to ensuring new technologies are accessible, we have continued to build on that progress, guided by the belief that equal access and equal opportunity are common principles that unite us as one Nation. On the 20th International Day of Persons with Disabilities, we reaffirm that the struggle to ensure the rights of every person does not end at our borders, but extends to every country and every community. It continues for the woman who is at greater risk of abuse because of a disability and for the child who is denied the chance to get an education because of the way he was born. It goes on for the 1 billion people with disabilities worldwide who all too often cannot attend school, find work, access medical care, or receive fair treatment. These injustices are an affront to our shared humanity—which is why the United States has joined 153 other countries around the world in signing the Convention on the Rights of Persons with Disabilities, which calls on all nations to establish protections and liberties like those afforded under the Americans with Disabilities Act. While Americans with disabilities already enjoy these rights at home, they frequently face barriers when they travel, conduct business, study, or reside overseas. Ratifying the Convention in the Senate would reaffirm America's position as the global leader on disability rights and better position us to encourage progress toward inclusion, equal opportunity, full participation, independent living, and economic self-sufficiency for persons with disabilities worldwide. We have come far in the long march to achieve equal opportunity for all. But even as we partner with countries across the globe in affirming universal human rights, we know our work will not be finished until the inherent dignity and worth of all persons with disabilities is guaranteed. Today, let us renew our commitment to meeting that challenge here in the United States, and let us redouble our efforts to build new paths to participation, empowerment, and progress around the world.

4.3 The CRPD in the US Senate

Two months after President Obama transmitted the CRPD to the Senate, in July 2012, the Senate Committee on Foreign Relations (SFRC) held its first hearing on ratification. Later that month, the SFRC reported the CRPD favourably to the full Senate by a vote of 13 in favour and 6 opposed, subject to certain conditions (Blanchfield and Brown 2015, p. 7; see also US International Council on Disabilities 2015). The SFRC noted that like other treaties, the CRPD is not self-executing and therefore does not give rise to individually enforceable rights in the US (Congress.gov. 2012a, b, 2014).[32] However, the Committee went on to state that given the "comprehensive network of existing federal and state disability laws and enforcement mechanisms … [i]n the large majority of cases, existing federal and state law meets or exceeds the requirements of the Convention" (Congress.gov. 2014).

On December 4, 2012, the CRPD came before the full Senate for a vote. The Senate voted down the CRPD, 61 Senators in favour of ratification and 38 opposed. With this vote, the CRPD failed to achieve the Senate's required advice and consent to ratification by only five votes short of the two-thirds majority of votes needed for Senate ratification (House of Representatives 2012).

According to protocol, the CRPD was returned to the SFRC. In July 2014, the Committee again reported the treaty favourably by a vote of 12 in favour and 6 opposed, subject to certain conditions. This time,

---

NOW, THEREFORE, I, BARACK OBAMA, President of the United States of America, by virtue of the authority vested in me by the Constitution and the laws of the United States, do hereby proclaim December 3, 2015, as International Day of Persons with Disabilities. I call on all Americans to observe this day with appropriate ceremonies, activities, and programs.

IN WITNESS WHEREOF, I have hereunto set my hand this third day of December, in the year of our Lord two thousand twelve, and of the Independence of the United States of America the two hundred and thirty-seventh. (Presidential Proclamation 2012)

[32] Harold Koh has criticised the US posture of attaching non-self-executing declarations to treaties: "[a]s Professor Louis Henkin likes to say, that in the cathedral of human rights, the United States is more like a flying buttress than a pillar- choosing to stand outside the international structure supporting the international human rights system, but without being willing to subject its own conduct to scrutiny of that system" (Koh 2002, p. 308).

however, the Senate chose not to provide its advice and consent to ratification. As a result, the CRPD was returned automatically to the SFRC at the end of the 113th Congress (see Blanchfield and Brown 2015, p. 9; US International Council on Disabilities Undated). Since then, the Senate has not taken any further action on the CRPD.

Leading the support for CRPD ratification was Senator Thomas Harkin, a long-time defender of disability rights, and the primary architect and sponsor of the original version of the ADA of 1990, as well as the ADAA of 2008.[33] The opposition to the CRPD was led by Tea Party Republican and former presidential candidate, Rick Santorum. He claimed that ratification of the CRPD would threaten American sovereignty and intrude on the rights of American parents (Diament 2012).

Senator Santorum was supported by other Republicans in the Senate, and by the Homeschooling Legal Defense Association, a US-based non-profit organisation established "to preserve and advance the fundamental, God-given, constitutional right of parents and others legally responsible for their children to direct their education" (HSLDA 2017). The HSLDA mounted a vigorous campaign against ratification of the CRPD. Its director, Michael Farris, urged "all freedom-loving Americans to contact their US senators and urge them to oppose this dangerous UN treaty" (Farris 2012).

The Republican opposition to the CRPD was not entirely anticipated for two reasons. First, two of the Senate's most prominent Republicans, Senators Bob Dole and John McCain, both former presidential nominees and both disabled as a result of military service, strongly and actively supported CRPD ratification (Lobe 2012). Second, given the similarity between the CRPD and the ADA, one could have assumed that most Senators would support a treaty that essentially codifies US law.[34] Indeed, the goals and principles of human dignity, equality and non-discrimination,

[33] A complete list of Senators and how they voted is found at US Senate (2012).

[34] According to Lord and Stein: "Where gaps arise between the two sets of legal mandates, they do so because U.S. domestic civil rights laws and international human rights laws operate from distinct, but not necessarily mutually exclusive, perspectives. Thus, U.S. law is either consistent with the mandates of the Convention or capable of reaching those levels through more rigorous implementation and/or additional actions by Congress" (Lord and Stein 2009).

and the right to reasonable accommodations and full participation contained in the CRPD are not only consistent with the US disability law but are, in fact, the cornerstones of the ADA 1990 (NCD.gov. 2008; Kanter 2015b).

As the National Council of Disability (NCD) observed, there was no legal impediment to US signature and ratification of the CRPD since "in large measure, the legal standards articulated in the CRPD align with U.S. disability law" (NCD.gov. 2008). Moreover, prior to the CRPD, the existence of a domestic law, such as the ADA, was typically a condition for US ratification, not a reason to reject it (Melish 2007). Supporters of the CRPD also argued that ratification of the CRPD would bolster existing US domestic disability laws by supporting the millions of individuals with disabilities in the US who seek employment and other opportunities outside of the US (Palmer 2013; Blanchfield and Brown 2015, pp. 17–18).

As one commentator noted, ratification of the CRPD would increase the ability of the US to improve physical, technological and communication access in other countries and to play a role in the development of international standards that are being developed on accessibility and technology access (Marcus 2013).[35] In this way, ratification of the CRPD would help to ensure that Americans with disabilities have equal opportunities to live, work, and travel abroad. Since such protections are clearly in the interest of the US and its elected officials, one would have expected Senate support for ratification.

Moreover, opposition to the CRPD cannot be explained away by Senate Republicans' hostility towards disability rights. Republicans had shown widespread support of the passage of the ADA in 1990 as well as its amendments in 2008. Thus, reasons unrelated to the substance of the treaty have to account for the opposition to ratification among Senate Republicans. As the following overview of the debate on ratification reveals, the opposition to CRPD ratification had less to do with disability

[35] For example, the Marrakesh Treaty provides an exception to domestic copyright law in order to make printed material available to visually impaired and print disabled people. It also allows for the import and export of accessible versions of books and other copyrighted works, without requiring copyright holder permission.

rights, and more to do with opposition to ratification of human rights treaties, generally, as well as the refusal of some Senate Republicans to endorse any Democratic-led proposal (Marcus 2013).

Following the transmission of the CRPD to the Senate, the hearings and debates leading up to the vote focused primarily on the role of international law on US domestic laws (Marcus 2013).[36] Opponents to ratification in the Senate argued that the CRPD, as well as other treaties, necessarily threaten US sovereignty by superseding US law (Blanchfield and Brown 2015, p. 15). They expressed their concern about intrusion into US state sovereignty and its impact on existing US laws and policies, particularly the potential authority over US law of the CRPD's monitoring body, the UN Committee on the Rights of Persons with Disabilities (CRPD Committee; SFRC Hearing Undated).

The CRPD Committee was created pursuant to Article 34 of the CRPD (2006). Today, it consists of 18 independent experts, mostly people with disabilities, who are elected by State Parties and serve in their individual capacities.[37] The CRPD Committee is charged with preparing reviews of country reports and providing "list of issues" and "concluding observations" in response to country reports. The CRPD Committee's findings and responses to country reports are, however, non-binding recommendations. Thus, even in those countries that ratify the CRPD, the Committee's findings and concluding observations have no binding authority under domestic law. The Senate Republicans' claim that the CRPD Committee would have authority under US law was simply wrong.

Eventually, most Senators from both parties agreed that CRPD posed no threat to US sovereignty, nor would ratification of the CRPD by the US undermine existing US disability laws (Blanchfield and Brown 2015, p. 16). In fact, the RUDs attached to the CRPD, specifically addressed

[36] The Senate voted in favour of going into executive session to consider ratification of the Convention.

[37] For the list of current CRPD Committee members, see UN OHCHR (Undated-a).

implementation of the CRPD in relation to US law (Marcus 2013).[38] One reservation, for example, referred to as the "federalism reservation," states explicitly that as a non-self–executing treaty, the CRPD cannot affect state laws nor be enforced in any court without prior legislative implementation (Marcus 2013; Blanchfield and Brown 2015). Thus, as one scholar has observed, "Given that the U.S. contends that appropriate implementing legislation is already in place, federalism-based comity concerns [were] simply not relevant to the ratification debate" (Melish 2007, p. 37).[39]

---

[38] The topic of RUDs is of particular interest in the debate over ratification of the CRPD because the Senate resisted ratification even with the RUDs. In addition to the reservation on federalism, the Obama Administration proposed two reservations, five understanding, and one declaration, including the following:

A private conduct reservation, which states that the U.S. does not accept CRPD provisions that address private conduct, except as mandated by U.S. law; A torture, inhuman, or degrading treatment reservation, which states that persons with disabilities are protected against torture and other degrading treatment consistent with U.S. obligations under the UN Convention Against Torture and Other Cruel, Inhuman, or Degrading Treatment or Punishment, and the International Covenant on Civil and Political Rights;

A first amendment understanding, which says that the U.S. understands that the CRPD does not authorize or require actions restricting speech, expression, or association that are protected by the Constitution;

An economic, social, and cultural rights understanding, which says the U.S. understands that the CRPD prevents disability discrimination with respect economic, social, and cultural rights, insofar as such rights are recognized and implemented under U.S. law.

An equal employment opportunity understanding, which states that the U.S. understands that U.S. law protects disabled persons against unequal pay, and that the CRPD does not require the adoption of a comparable framework for persons with disabilities A uniformed military employee understanding, which states that the U.S. does not recognize rights in the Convention that exceed those under U.S. law in regards to military hiring, promotion, and other employment issues.

A definition of disability understanding, which states that the CRPD does not define "disability" or "persons with disabilities", and that the U.S. understands the definitions of these terms to be consistent with U.S. law; a non-self-executing-declaration, which states that no new laws would be required as a result of U.S. ratification of the CRPD.

Blanchfield and Brown (2015, pp. 6–7). The version of the treaty with these RUDs was reported out favourably to the full Senate by the Foreign Relations Committee (SFRC). The SFRC addressed these concerns by proposing additional RUDs. Ibid.

[39] Melish (2007) has argued that the federalism argument is misplaced. The CRPD itself is not self-executing. It can be implemented through the ordinary legislative process. State-elected House and Senate representatives can give expression to state interests with respect to each piece of implementing legislation.

Another issue of concern, expressed most vehemently by Senator Santorum, was the potential impact of US ratification on parental rights. Senator Santorum argued that the "best interest of the child" standard in Article 7 of the CRPD (2006) would undermine parental authority over their children (Collins 2012). Article 7—Children with Disabilities, paragraph 2, states that "in all actions concerning children with disabilities, the best interests of the child shall be a primary consideration" (CRPD 2006, Art. 7(2)). The opponents of CRPD ratification argued that this Article would change US law by requiring that the "best interest of the child" standard supersede parental interests (Blanchfield and Brown 2015). Yet courts in the US have used the "best interest of the child" standard since at least the 1970s. Therefore, the argument that this language in the CRPD represented a change from current US law with respect to parental rights was false as well. Although parental rights in the US are not absolute, the US Supreme Court has held consistently that parents have a fundamental liberty interest in the care, custody, and management of their children.[40] Such rights, therefore, cannot be undone by ratification of a treaty, including the CRPD.

In addition to an unwarranted concern about the risk to parental rights posed by the "best interests of the child" standard in the CRPD, opponents of ratification claimed that Article 24—Education of the CRPD (2006) also would undermine the rights of parents in the context of education (Petersen 2010). The Homeschooling Legal Defense Association, which previously had opposed the CRC as well as the CEDAW, argued that ratification of the CRPD would prevent parents from deciding how and where to educate their children (Farris 2012).

Article 24—Education, of the CRPD (2006) ensures the right to education for all children with disabilities.[41] Accordingly, this article is generally

---

[40] *Santosky v Kramer*, 455 US 745, 753 (1982); see also *Meyer v Nebraska*, 262 US 390, 399 (1923); *Pierce v Society of Sisters*, 268 US 510, 534 (1925); *Parham v JR*, 442 US 584, 602 (1979).

[41] Article 24—Education, in recognising the right to education, provides: "States Parties recognize the right of persons with disabilities to education. With a view to realizing this right without discrimination and on the basis of equal opportunity, States Parties shall ensure an inclusive education system at all levels and lifelong learning directed to: a. The full development of human potential and sense of dignity and self-worth, and the strengthening of respect for human rights, fundamental freedoms and human diversity; b. The development by persons with disabilities of their personality, talents and creativity, as well as their mental and physical abilities, to their fullest potential; c. Enabling persons with disabilities to participate effectively in a free society" (CRPD 2006, Art. 24(1)). For more information on Article 24 of the CRPD, see Kanter (2018).

consistent with US law since at least 1975, when Congress passed the Education for All Handicapped Children's Act (EAHCA 1975). This law, whose current version is known as the Individuals with Disabilities in Education Improvement Act (IDEIA 2004), guarantees all children with disabilities the right to a "free, appropriate public education."[42] The argument against ratification on the grounds that it would undermine the choice and control of parents over their child's education is especially spurious since, as the Senators are well aware, education is an issue for state and local law, not federal law. It is the States, and not the federal Government, that have authority over educational programmes; ratification of the CRPD would not nor could not affect the rights of students and their parents under state education laws (Blanchfield and Brown 2015).

For example, during the Senate debate on ratification, Senator Santorum argued that ratification of the CRPD would prohibit parents from choosing to homeschool their children. Yet homeschooling is an issue for state, not federal, law. Moreover, neither the CRPD nor any federal law, including the IDEIA 2004,[43] or the ADA 1990, even mention homeschooling. Although children with disabilities have the right to attend public school and to receive services pursuant to the IDEIA 2004 and the ADA 1990, states are free to decide whether or not to cover homeschooled children with disabilities under their state laws.[44] The federal Government has no say whatsoever regarding a parent's decision to homeschool their child. Therefore, Senator Santorum's argument that ratification of the CRPD would somehow interfere with a parent's right to decide to homeschool their child was again, simply wrong. Neither the CRPD, nor any treaty, can overturn state laws, including state laws governing homeschooling (Blanchfield and Brown 2015).

---

[42] The EAHCA was enacted in 1975, following two court decisions, in Pennsylvania and Washington, D.C. which established the right of children with disabilities to attend public school. *PARC v Commonwealth*, 343 F Supp 279 (ED Pa 1972); *Mills v Board of Education, DC*, 348 F Supp 866 (D DC 1972). In 1990, the EAHCA 1975 was amended and renamed the IDEA 1990, and in 2004 it was amended and renamed again, the IDEIA (2004).

[43] The law was originally enacted in 1975 as the EAHCA 1975 and was later amended and renamed the IDEA 1990. In 2004, it was renamed the IDEIA. 20 USC 1400 *et seq*.

[44] See, for example, *Hooks v Clark Cnty Sch Dist*, 228 F 3d 1036 (9th Cir 2000) and Knickerbocker (2001).

This homeschooling claim provoked a sharp rebuke by supporters of the CRPD. For example, during the 2013 hearing on the CRPD, Senator Robert Menendez stated that he was "dumbfounded" at how [the Senate Republicans] could take noncontroversial language and "twist it into something that's rather sinister" (Menendez.gov. 2014). In response to the specific assertion that the CRPD would threaten parental rights and the ability of parents to homeschool their children, Senator Menendez stated emphatically that "[t]he text says nothing about the state stepping into the shoes of the parents. In fact, Article 23 describes in detail, protecting parental rights and the rights of the extended family to care for and to make decisions for children with disabilities" (Menendez. gov. 2014).

Former Attorney General of the US, Richard Thornburgh, a Republican, who served in the Bush Administration, also addressed the homeschooling issue during the Senate hearing. He stated that "[n]othing in this treaty prevents parents from homeschooling or making other decisions about their children's education" (Menendez.gov. 2014). Moreover, the former Attorney General also noted that the CRPD "embraces the principles of the Individuals with Disabilities Education Act …, which emphasizes the importance of the role of parents of children with disabilities in making decisions on behalf of their children" (Menendez.gov. 2014).

In addition to the specious homeschooling argument, some Republican lawmakers raised concerns about the CRPD's possible impact on access to healthcare, and the extent to which the CRPD would affect existing laws related to family planning, reproduction and abortion.[45] Indeed, the

---

[45] Article 10—Right to Life, of the CRPD (2006) provides that "States Parties reaffirm that every human being has the inherent right to life and shall take all necessary measures to ensure its effective enjoyment by persons with disabilities on an equal basis with others" (CRPD 2006, Art. 10). Article 25—Health, requires state parties to "Provide persons with disabilities with the same range, quality and standard of free or affordable health care and programmes as provided to other persons, including in the area of sexual and reproductive health and population-based public health programmes" (CRPD 2006, Art. 25). During the negations on the CRPD, one of the attorneys from the US Department of Justice stated, it was the understanding of the US that the phrase "reproductive health" in Article 25(a) "does not include abortion, and its use in that Article does not create

right to reproductive health is an important issue, particularly for women with disabilities (Kanter and Villarreall Lopez 2018; Frohmader and Ortoleva 2013, p. 2). Women with disabilities face insurmountable barriers to accessing health care in the US and elsewhere (NCD.gov. Undated). Arguably, "no group has ever been as severely restricted, or negatively treated, in respect of their reproductive rights, as women with disabilities" (Frohmader and Ortoleva 2013, p. 4). As recently as July 2017, the UN Special Rapporteur on the Rights of Persons with Disabilities condemned the violence, abuse and harmful practices which women with disabilities face, including forced sterilisation, forced abortion and forced contraception (UN Special Rapporteur on the Rights of Persons with Disabilities 2017). Because of the importance of the issue of access to health, including reproductive health care, the CRPD (2006) includes Article 23—Respect for and the family and Article 25—Health, which, together, ensure equal access to health, including reproductive health and family planning services, for men and women with disabilities. The drafters of the CRPD specifically noted, however, that the CRPD does not take a position on the issue of abortion.[46] Thus the Republicans' claim that the CRPD would create a new right to abortion was wrong not only because the CRPD does not even mention abortion but because women with and without disabilities in the US enjoy a constitutional right to abortion.

In short, the claims by Senate Republicans, led by Senator Santorum and the Homeschooling Legal Defense Association, regarding the alleged risks associated with US ratification of the CRPD, had no basis in fact. Not only does the CRPD generally comply with existing US laws, but if there was any lingering concerns about the risk to US sovereignty posed

any abortion rights, and cannot be interpreted to constitute support, endorsement, or promotion of abortion. We stated this understanding at the time of adoption of the Convention in the Ad Hoc Committee, and note that no other delegation suggested a different understanding of this term" (UN 2006).

[46] In fact, if the CRPD had explicitly supported abortion, the Editors of the *America Magazine: The National Catholic Review*, a Catholic journal, would likely not have endorsed the ratification of the CRPD as strongly as it did. In response to the Senate's failure to ratify the CRPD, the Review stated that the ratification of the CRPD is "an ecumenical opportunity for the leadership of many faiths to call for justice with one voice. It deserves broad public support" (America Magazine 2013). See also, Shaffer (2013) and Silecchia (2013).

by ratification of the CRPD, the "federalism reservation" attached to the CRPD made it clear that US law supersedes the CRPD, and not the other way around. Yet even with this reservation, the Senate refused to ratify the CRPD in 2012 and in 2014. On September 17, 2014, Senator Harkin, citing the "false claims of those who object to this treaty," asked for a unanimous consent vote on the CRPD (Harkin 2014). The Senate refused the vote, and Senator Harkin responded by stating that it was "another sad, irresponsible day in the history of the US Senate" (Harkin 2014). Since 2014, the Senate has failed to bring the CRPD to another vote. Moreover, given the current composition of the US Senate, it is unlikely that the ratification of the CRPD will be considered again during the current Congress.

5 The Failure of the United States to Ratify the CRPD: Where We Go from Here

Although the proposed Bricker Amendment to the US Constitution limiting the role of international law in the US legal system failed to win Congressional approval in the 1950s, its legacy continues to play a role in the failure of the US to ratify human rights treaties, including the CRPD. Most recently, the US has witnessed an assault on human rights. Within just two months of assuming office, the Trump Administration reduced funding to the UN, reneged on the US commitment to internationally negotiated trade and environmental agreements, and provoked actions towards other countries in the name of "America First," to name a few examples. Accordingly, the failure of the CRPD to muster the necessary votes for ratification may be seen as harkening the beginning of a new period of US antipathy towards international human rights law.

Yet even before the last presidential election, in December 2013, the Pew Research Center reported that 52 per cent of respondents in the national poll said that the US "should mind its own business internationally and let other countries get along the best they can on their own" (Healy.com. 2013).[47] Only about a third of respondents felt this way a

[47] This was the most people to answer that question this way in the history of the question, one which pollsters began asking in 1964.

decade ago (Lindsay and Kauss 2013). In fact, simply citing international law in US court decisions has become so controversial that Republicans in Congress have introduced legislation to prohibit federal courts from referring to foreign laws or rulings in cases involving interpretation of the US Constitution (Mears 2006). In addition, two of our Supreme Court justices, Justice Ruth Bader Ginsburg and now-retired Justice Sandra Day O'Connor, have reported receiving anonymous death threats for simply citing international law in their opinions (Mears 2006; Mauro.com. 2006).[48] Nonetheless, CRPD supporters have not given up hope that the Senate will eventually ratify the CRPD. As Senator Harkin has stated, "[w]e will succeed in ratifying this treaty. We will restore America's stature as the world leader on disability rights, and we will continue to fight for justice and a fair shake for people with disabilities, not just here in America but around the world" (Harkin 2014). Similarly, Obama Administration officials have observed that ratification of the CRPD would put the US in the best possible position to influence the international community on disability rights, and that non-ratification makes it "difficult" to advance such interests (Heumann 2012). In addition, as one scholar has observed:

> Ratification will allow us simultaneously to serve as a model for the rest of the world, projecting our commitment to the rights of persons with disabilities outward, while ensuring that we are in fact living up to that projection as a nation and social community of equals at home. In doing so, we make ourselves a stronger democracy; there is no excuse not to ratify. (Melish 2007, p. 37)

Other countries in Europe as well as Australia, Canada, and Israel, which also have strong domestic disability laws, have already ratified the CRPD, as have numerous other countries in the Americas, Asia, and

[48] After citing foreign law in their decisions, Justices Ginsberg and O'Connor became targets of online death threats, including one that is quoted as saying: "Okay commandoes, here is your first patriotic assignment…This is a huge threat to our Republic and constitutional freedom ... If you are what you say you are, and NOT armchair patriots, then those two justices will not live another week" (Mauro.com. 2006).

Africa.[49] As one of the only countries that has not ratified the CRPD, the US risks losing its credibility abroad, as other countries would have no reason to listen to the US, at least about the treatment of people with disabilities, since the US has not bothered to ratify a treaty that is modelled after its own domestic law.

By ratifying the CRPD, the US will show the world that to be a global leader in disability law means supporting international efforts to advance the rights of people with disabilities worldwide. By not ratifying the CRPD, which now joins the list of the many other human rights treaties that the US has not ratified, the US will remain an outlier in the monitoring and enforcement of human rights laws worldwide.

References

Ability Magazine. (Undated). *The signing of the United Nations convention on the rights of persons with disabilities*. Retrieved May 5, 2019, from http://ability-magazine.com/un-ada.html.

ADA (Americans with Disabilities Act). (1990). 42 USC §§12101–12213.

ADA.gov. (Undated). *Introduction to the ADA*. Retrieved May 5, 2019, from https://www.ada.gov/ada_intro.htm.

Americans with Disabilities Amendment Act. (2008). ADA Amendments Act of 2008, Pub. L. No. 110-325, 122 Stat. 3553.

Alston, P. (2009). *Putting economic social and cultural rights back on the agenda of the United States*. Working paper No 5, NYU Center for Human Rights and Global Justice, New York University, New York.

Alston, P., & Goodman, R. (2012). *International human rights*. Oxford: Oxford University Press.

America Magazine. (2013, January 7–14). Missed opportunity to lead. *America Magazine: The National Catholic Review*. Retrieved May 5, 2019, from https://www.americamagazine.org/issue/missed-opportunity-lead.

American Convention on Human Rights. (1969). Organization of American States, November 22, 1969, O.A.S.T.S. No. 36, 1144 U.N.T.S. 123.

[49] In the United Kingdom, the Disability Discrimination Act 1995 resulted from a campaign to adopted the language of the anti-discrimination civil rights approach of the ADA 1990 (Fletcher and O'Brien 2008; Kanter 2015b).

Blanchfield, L., & Brown, C. (2015). *'The United Nations convention on the rights of persons with disabilities:' Issues in the U.S. ratification debate congressional research service* (pp. 17–18). Retrieved May 5, 2018, from https://fas.org/sgp/crs/misc/R42749.pdf.

Boyd, R. F., Jr. (2003). *Second session of the ad hoc committee on a comprehensive and integral international convention on protection and promotion of the rights of persons with disabilities*. Retrieved May 5, 2019, from http://www.un.org/esa/socdev/enable/rights/contrib-us.htm.

Bradley, C. A. (1992). US reservations, declarations, and understandings, international covenant on civil and political rights. *International Law in the US Legal System, 138*, 83–84.

Bradley, C. A. (2000). The treaty power and American federalism, part II. *Michigan Law Review, 99*, 123.

Bradley, C. A. (2010). The United States and human rights treaties: Race relations, the cold war, and constitutionalism. *Chicago Journal of International Law, 9*, 321.

Bradley, C. A. (2015). *International law in the US legal system. Oxford scholarly authorities on international law*. Oxford: Oxford University Press.

Convention Against Torture and Other Cruel, Inhuman and Degrading Treatment or Punishment (1984, December 10). A. Res. 39/46, Convention Against Torture and Other Cruel, Inhuman or Degrading Treatment or Punishment, art. 27(1).

Convention on the Elimination of Discrimination Against Women. (1979, December 18). G.A. Res. 34/180, Convention on the Elimination of All Forms of Discrimination against Women, art. 10(f).

Chaffin, S. (2015). Challenging the United States position on a United Nations convention on disability. *Temple Political and Civil Rights Law Review, 15*, 129.

Chayes, A., & Chayes, A. H. (1995). *The new sovereignty*. Cambridge, MA: Harvard University Press.

Ciment, J. (2015). *Postwar America: An encyclopedia of social, political, cultural, and economic history*. New York: Routledge.

Cole, W. S. (1962). *Senator Gerald P nye and American foreign relations*. Minneapolis, MN: University of Minnesota Press.

Cole, W. S. (1983). *Roosevelt and the non-interventionists, 1932–1945*. Lincoln Nebraska: University of Nebraska Press.

Collins, G. (2012, December 5). Santorum strikes again. *New York Times*. Retrieved May 5, 2019, from http://www.nytimes.com/2012/12/06/opinion/collins-santorum-strikes-again.html.

Committee on Foreign Affairs. (1974). *Human rights in the world community: A call for US leadership*. Washington, DC: US House of Representatives.
Congress.gov. (2012a). *Convention on the rights of persons with disabilities: Senate consideration of treaty document 112–7*. Retrieved May 5, 2019, from https://www.congress.gov/treaty-document/112th-congress/7.
Congress.gov. (2012b). *Senate executive report 112–6 convention on the rights of persons with disabilities (treaty doc. 112–7)* (p. 14). Retrieved May 5, 2019, from https://www.congress.gov/congressional-report/112th-congress/executive-report/6.
Congress.gov. (2014). *Senate executive report 113–12 convention on the rights of persons with disabilities (treaty doc. 112–7)* (p. 23). Retrieved November 29, 2017, from https://www.congress.gov/congressional-report/113th-congress/executive-report/12.
Convention Against Transnational Organized Crime. (2000, November 15). Adopted by the UN general assembly, by resolution 55/25.
Convention on Cluster Munitions. (2010). May 30, 2008, 2688 U.N.T.S. 39.
Convention Relating to the Status of Refugees. (1951). G.A. Res. 429 (V), art. 43, December 14, 1950.
Cook, R. (1990). Reservations to the convention on the elimination of all forms of discrimination against women. *Virginia Journal of International Law, 30*, 648.
Convention on the Rights of the Child. (1989, November 20). G.A. Res. 44/25, Convention on the Rights of the Child, art. 49.
Convention on the Rights of Persons with Disabilities. (2006, December 13). U.N. GAOR, 61st Sess., 76th plen. mtg., U.N. Res. A/RES/61/106, 2515 U.N.T.S. 3.
Dale, K. (2009, July 9). *Valerie Jarrett and ambassador rice at the us signing of the UN convention on the rights of persons*. White House Blog. Retrieved May 5, 2019, from https://obamawhitehouse.archives.gov/blog/2009/07/30/valerie-jarrett-ambassador-rice-us-signing-un-convention-rights-persons.
Diament, M. (2012). *Senate rejects UN disability treaty*. DisabilityScoop. Retrieved November 27, 2017, from http://www.disabilityscoop.com/2012/12/04/senate-rejects-treaty/16887/.
Disability Discrimination Act. (1995). c. 50 (UK).
EAHCA. (1975). Education for All Handicapped Children's Act, Pub. L. No. 94-142, 89 Stat. 773.
Farris, M. P. (2012). *The UN convention on the rights of persons with disabilities: A danger to homeschool families*. Purcellville, VA: HSLDA. Retrieved May 5, 2019, from https://hslda.org/content/docs/news/2014/201407180.asp.

Fletcher, A., & O'Brien, N. (2008). Disability rights commission: From civil rights to social rights. *Journal of Law and Society, 35*, 523.

Frohmader, C., & Ortoleva, S. (2013). *The sexual and reproductive rights of women and girls with disabilities: Issues paper*. ICPD beyond 2014: International conference on human rights. Retrieved May 5, 2019, from http://wwda.org.au/wp-content/uploads/2013/12/issues_paper_srr_women_and_girls_with_disabilities_final.pdf.

Convention on the Prevention and Punishment of the Crime of Genocide. (1948, December 9). G.A. Res. 260 A (III), art. XIII.

Hafner-Burton, E. M., & Tsutsui, K. (2005). Human rights in a globalizing world: The paradox of empty promises. *The American Journal of Sociology, 110*(5), 1373–1411.

Hafner-Burton, E. M., Tsutsui, K., & Meyer, J. W. (2008). International human rights law and the politics of legitimation: Repressive states and human rights treaties. *International Sociology, 23*, 115.

Harkin, T. (2014). *Senator Harkin on disabled persons treaty*. C-SPAN. Retrieved May 5, 2019, from http://www.c-span.org/video/?321544-7/senator-harkin-disabled-persons-treaty.

Hathaway, O. (2002). *Do human rights treaties make a difference* (Yale Law School Faculty Scholarship Series 839). New Haven, CT: Yale Law School.

Healy, G. (2013, December 10). *It's not Isolationist for America to Mind its own business*. Washington Examiner. Retrieved May 5, 2019, from http://www.washingtonexaminer.com/its-not-isolationist-for-america-to-mind-its-own-business/article/2540441.

Henkin, L. (1995). US ratification of human rights conventions: The ghost of Senator Bricker. *American Journal of International Law, 89*, 341.

Heumann, J. (2012). *Statement of Judith Heumann, special adviser for international disability rights*. Washington DC: US Department of State. At SFRC Hearing "convention on the rights of persons with disabilities" (treaty zhearing-convention-on-the-rights-of-persons-with-disabilities-treaty-doc-112-7

Holmes, K. R. (2004, June 3). *Assistant secretary of state for international organization affairs*. United States Department of State, Letter to Lex Frieden, Chairperson, National Council on Disability. Retrieved from http://www.usicd.org/StateDept_Letter_to_NCD.pdf.

House of Representatives. (2012). 158 cong. rec. S7365-79 executive session. Retrieved from https://www.congress.gov/crec/2012/12/04/CREC-2012-12-04.pdf.

HSLDA (Homeschooling Legal Defense Association). (2017). *Our mission*. Purcellville, VA: HSLDA. Retrieved May 5, 2019, from https://www.hslda.org/about/mission.asp.

Human Rights First. (Undated). *Senate report on CIA torture*. Retrieved May 5, 2019, from https://www.humanrightsfirst.org/senate-report-cia-torture.

Human Rights Watch. (2009). *United States ratification of international human rights treaties*. New York: Human Rights Watch. Retrieved May 5, 2019, from http://www.hrw.org/news/2009/07/24/united-states-ratification-international-human-rights-treaties.

International Covenant on Civil and Political Rights. (1966, December 16). G.A. Res. 2200A (XXI), art. 2(1) and (2).

International Convention on the Elimination of all Forms of Racial Discrimination. (1965, December 21). 660 U.N.T.S. 195.

International Covenant on Economic, Social and Cultural Rights. (1966, December 16). G.A. Res. 2200A (XXI), art. 2(1).

IDEA (Individuals with Disabilities in Education Act). (1990). (Otherwise Known as Education of the Handicapped Act Amendments of 1990). (1990, October 30). Pub. L. No. 101-476, 104 Stat. 1103.

IDEIA (Individuals with Disabilities in Education Improvement Act). (2004, December 3). Individuals with Disabilities in Education Improvement Act of 2004, Pub. L. No. 108-446, 118 Stat. 2647.

ICPPED (International Convention for the Protection of all Persons from Enforced Disappearance). Adopted in 2006 by the United Nations general assembly.

International Convention on the Protection of the Rights of All Migrant Workers and Members of their Families. (1990, December 18). G.A. Res. 45/158.

International Court of Justice. (1951). *Advisory opinion concerning reservations to the convention on the prevention and punishment of the crime of genocide* (p. 51). International Court of Justice Report, The Hague. Retrieved May 5, 2019, from https://www.refworld.org/cases,ICJ,4023a7644.html.

International Law Commission. (2011). *Guide to practice on reservations to treaties*. 63d Sess A/66/10. Retrieved May 5, 2019, from http://legal.un.org/ilc/texts/instruments/english/draft_articles/1_8_2011.pdf.

Jacoby, T. (1986). The Reagan turnaround on human rights, foreign affairs. *Council on Foreign Relations, 64*(5), 1066–1086.

Kanter, A. S. (2015a). *The development of disability rights under law: From charity to human rights*. New York: Routledge. (Paperback edition in 2017).

Kanter, A. S. (2015b). The Americans with disabilities act at 25 years: Lessons to learn from the UN convention on the rights of people with disabilities. *Drake Law Review, 63*, 819.

Kanter, A. S. (2018). The right to inclusive education under international human rights law. In G. de Beco, S. Quinlivan, & J. Lord (Eds.), *The right to inclusive education under international human rights law*. Cambridge: Cambridge University Press.

Kanter, A. S., & Villarreal Lopez, C. (2018). A call for an end to violence against women and girls with disabilities under international and regional human rights law. *Northeastern Law Review, 10*, 583.

Kanter, A. S. (2019a). Do human rights treaties matter: The case for the United Nations convention on the rights of people with disabilities. *Vanderbilt Journal of Transnational Law, 52*, 577.

Kanter, A. S. (2019b). Why the U.S. should ratify the United Nations convention on the rights of people with disabilities. *Touro Law Review, 35*, 301.

Kaufman, N. H. (1990). *Human rights treaties and the senate*. Chapel Hill, NC: University of North Carolina Press.

Kaye, D. (2013). *Stealth multilateralism: US foreign policy without treaties—Or the senate*. New York: Council on Foreign Relations Inc. Retrieved May 5, 2019, from http://cf.linnbenton.edu/artcom/social_science/clarkd/upload/David%20Kaye,%20Stealth%20Multilateralism.pdf.

Knickerbocker, L. R. (2001). The education of all children with disabilities: Integrating home-schooled children into the individuals with disabilities education act. *Ohio State Law Journal, 62*, 15.

Koh, H. H. (2002). A United States human rights policy for the 21st century. *Saint Louis University Law Journal, 46*, 293.

Landmine Ban Treaty. (1999, September 18). Convention on the Prohibition of the Use, Stockpiling, Production and Transfer of Anti-Personnel Mines and on their Destruction. 2056 U.N.T.S. 211.

Lindsay, J. M., & Kauss, R. (2013, December 3). *The public's mixed message on America's role in the world*. Pew Research Center for People and the Press. Retrieved May 5, 2019, from http://www.people-press.org/2013/12/03/commentary-by-james-m-lindsay-and-rachael-kauss-of-the-council-on-foreign-relations/.

Lobe, J. (2012). UN disabilities treaty rejected by US senate. In *International press service: Global issues*. Retrieved May 5, 2019, from http://www.globalissues.org/news/2012/12/05/15441

Lord, J. E., & Stein, M. A. (2009). *Ratify the UN disability treaty*. Foreign Policy in Focus. Retrieved May 5, 2019, from http://fpif.org/ratify_the_un_disability_treaty.

Lowe, D. (Undated). *Idea to reality: NED at 30*. Washington, DC: National Endowment for Democracy. Retrieved May 5, 2017, from https://www.ned.org/about/history/.

Marcus, V. K. (2013). *US can lead on rights for those with disabilities*. LegalNews.com. Retrieved May 4, 2019, from http://www.legalnews.com/detroit/1379870./.

Mauro, T. (2006, March 16). *Justice ginsburg says death threat fueled by dispute over international law*. California Supreme Court Monitor. Retrieved May 5, 2019, from https://www.law.com/almID/900005449284/?slreturn=20181028203059.

Mears, W. (2006). *Justice Ginsburg details death threat*. CNN.com. Retrieved May 5, 2019, from http://www.cnn.com/2006/LAW/03/15/scotus.threat/.

Melish, T. J. (2007). The UN disability convention: Historic process, strong prospects, and why the US should ratify. *Human Rights Brief, 14*, 37–47.

Menendez, R. (2014). *Convention on the rights of persons with disabilities (treaty doc 112–6)*. Retrieved November 29, 2017, from http://www.gpo.gov/fdsys/pkg/CRPT-113erpt12/html/CRPT-113erpt12.htm.

NCD (National Council on Disability). (2008). *Finding the gaps: A comparative analysis of Disability Laws in the United States to the United Nations convention on the rights of persons with disabilities*. Washington DC: National Council on Disability. Retrieved May 5, 2019, from http://www.ncd.gov/newsroom/publications/2008/pdf/ncd_crpd_analysis.pdf.

NCD (National Council on Disability). (2012). *NCD statement on failed CRPD ratification vote in the senate*. Washington, DC: National Council on Disability. Retrieved May 5, 2019, from http://www.ncd.gov/newsroom/2012/120512.

NCD (National Council on Disability). (Undated). *Reports on health and disability*. Retrieved from http://www.ncd.gov/policy/health_care.

Optional Protocol to the Convention on the Rights of Persons with Disabilities. (2006). *United Nations treaty collection 15a*. Retrieved May 5, 2019, from https://treaties.un.org/Pages/ViewDetails.aspx?src=TREATY&mtdsg_no=IV-15-a&chapter=4&clang=_en.

Palmer, J. S. (2013). The convention on the rights of persons with disabilities: Will ratification lead to a holistic approach to postsecondary education for persons with disabilities. *Seton Hall Law Review, 43*, 551.

Petersen, C. J. (2010). Inclusive education and conflict resolution: Building a model to implement article 24 of the convention on the rights of persons with disabilities in the Asia pacific. *Hong Kong Law Journal, 40*, 481.

Presidential Proclamation. (2012). *International day of persons with disabilities 2012*. Washington, DC: The White House. Retrieved May 21, 2019, from https://obamawhitehouse.archives.gov/the-press-office/2012/12/03/presidential-proclamation-international-day-persons-disabilities-2012.

Protocol to Prevent, Suppress and Punish Trafficking in Persons Especially Women and Children, supplementing the United Nations Convention against Transnational Organized Crime, Adopted and opened for signature, ratification and accession by General Assembly resolution 55/25 of 15 November 2000.

SFRC (Senate Committee on Foreign Relations) Hearing. (Undated). *Convention on the rights of persons with disabilities (treaty doc 112–7)*. Retrieved May 5, 2019, from https://www.foreign.senate.gov/hearings/hearing-convention-on-the-rights-of-persons-with-disabilities-treaty-doc-112-7.

Shaffer, B. (2013). The right to life, the convention on the rights of persons with disabilities, and abortion. *Pennsylvania State International Law Review, 28*, 265.

Sikkink, K. (2017). *Evidence for hope: Making human rights treaties work in the 21st century*. Princeton, NJ: Princeton University Press.

Silecchia, L. A. (2013). The convention on the rights of persons with disabilities: Reflections on four flaws that tarnish its promise. *The Journal of Contemporary Health Law and Policy, 30*, 96.

Simmons, B. A. (2009). *Mobilizing for human rights: International law in domestic politics*. Cambridge: Cambridge University Press.

Stein, M. A., & Lord, J. E. (2009). Ratify the UN disability treaty. *Popular Media*, p. 33. Retrieved May 5, 2012, from https://scholarship.law.wm.edu/popular_media/33.

UN (United Nations). (2006). *Press release*. United States mission to the United Nations. Retrieved from http://www.usunnewyork.usmission.gov/06_396.htm.

UN (United Nations). (Undated-a). *History of the document*. Retrieved May 21, 2019, from https://www.un.org/en/sections/universal-declaration/history-document/index.html.

UN (United Nations). (Undated-b). *Member states*. Retrieved May 5, 2019, from http://www.un.org/en/members.

UN General Assembly. (2006). *Sixty-first session 76th plenary meeting*. A/61/PV.76. Retrieved May 5, 2019, from https://www.un.org/en/ga/search/view_doc.asp?symbol=A/61/PV.76&Lang=E.

UN OHCHR (Office of the High Commissioner for Human Rights). (Undated-a). *Elected members of the committee on the rights of persons with disabilities*. Retrieved May 5, 2019, from http://www.ohchr.org/EN/HRBodies/CRPD/Pages/Membership.aspx.

UN OHCHR (Office of the High Commissioner for Human Rights). (Undated-b). *View ratification status by country or by treaty*. Retrieved May 5, 2019, from http://tbinternet.ohchr.org/_layouts/TreatyBodyExternal/Treaty.aspx.

UN Special Rapporteur on the Rights of Persons with Disabilities. (2017, July 14). *Report of the special rapporteur on the rights of persons with disabilities in relation to their sexual and reproductive health and rights*. UN Doc A/72/133. Retrieved May 5, 2019, from https://www.google.com/url?sa=t&rct=j&q=&esrc=s&source=web&cd=2&ved=2ahUKEwjM3JG2uuTfAhWIMo8KHZTLBkMQFjABegQIAxAC&url=https%3A%2F%2Fwww.ohchr.org%2FDocuments%2FIssues%2FDisability%2FA_72_133_EN.docx&usg=AOvVaw36eW2V135EyVH92Cag_JNJ.

UN Vienna Convention on the Law of Treaties. (1969). *United Nations treaty collection*. Retrieved May 5, 2019, from https://treaties.un.org/pages/ViewDetailsIII.aspx?src=TREATY&mtdsg_no=XXIII-1&chapter=23&Temp=mtdsg3&clang=_en.

US Department of State. (1977–1981). *Carter and human rights, 1977–1981*. Office of Historian. Retrieved May 5, 2019, from https://history.state.gov/milestones/1977-1980/human-rights.

US International Council on Disabilities. (2015). *The convention on the rights of persons with disabilities*. Retrieved May 5, 2019, from http://usicd.org/initiatives/advocacy/convention-on-the-rights-of-persons-with-disabilities-crpd/.

US International Council on Disabilities. (Undated). *TimeLine of CRPD in the US senate*. Retrieved from http://usicd.org/index.cfm/archive-of-crpd-in-the-112th-congress.

US Senate. (2012). *Roll call vote 112th congress—2nd session*. Retrieved November 17, 2017, from http://www.senate.gov/legislative/LIS/roll_call_lists/roll_call_vote_cfm.cfm?congress=112&session=2&vote=00219.

Venetis, P. (2011). Making human rights treaty law actionable in the United States: The case for universal implementing legislation. *Alabama Law Review, 63*, 97.

Vreeland, J. R. (2008). Political institutions and human rights: Why dictatorships enter into the United Nations convention against torture. *International Organization, 62*(1), 65–101.

Wotipka, C. M., & Tsutsui, K. (2008). Global human rights and state sovereignty: State ratification of international human rights treaties, 1965–2001. *Sociological Forum, 23*(4), 724–754.

7

The Long Road to Ratification: Ireland and the CRPD

Eilionóir Flynn

1 Introduction

Ireland was among the first countries to sign the United Nations (UN) Convention on the Rights of Persons with Disabilities (CRPD/ Convention 2006) when it opened for signature in March 2007. However, it was another decade before Ireland ratified the Convention, making it the last European Union (EU) Member State to do so, in March 2018. This chapter will consider the domestic cultural context—in terms of the legal and political landscape, which shaped the process of ratification in Ireland and will help to contextualise and understand the reason for the lengthy gap between signature and ratification. It will also consider some of the issues that have emerged during the domestic process of ratification, which have been identified as priorities or concerns by the Irish disability community.

E. Flynn (✉)
CDLP, National University of Ireland (NUI), Galway, Ireland
e-mail: eilionoir.flynn@nuigalway.ie

E. J. Kakoullis, K. Johnson (eds.), *Recognising Human Rights in Different Cultural Contexts*, https://doi.org/10.1007/978-981-15-0786-1_7

2 The Legal Context for Ratification: Ireland's Approach to International Law

In order to understand the legal context of ratification, it is important to first set out Ireland's approach to International Law. Ireland has a common law legal system with a written Constitution which adopts a dualist approach to International Law. This means that international treaties do not automatically become part of Irish law unless they are incorporated into legislation (Constitution of Ireland 1937, Art. 29.6). At the time of writing, the CRPD, although ratified by Ireland, has not been incorporated into domestic law. Without incorporation, international treaties cannot be relied upon directly in the Irish courts. Therefore, ratification of international human rights treaties, such as the CRPD, does not mean in practice that disabled people in Ireland can rely on the Convention to seek enforcement of their rights.

In Ireland, the usual procedure when signing or ratifying international agreements is that the Minister for Foreign Affairs brings a proposal to Government.[1] The Minister, or the Government, will generally seek legal advice from the Attorney General as to any legal or Constitutional impediments to ratification. In the case of UN treaties, once the proposal for ratification by the Minister for Foreign Affairs has been approved by the Government under Article 29.4 (Constitution of Ireland 1937), Ireland's representatives at the UN can deposit the instruments of ratification.

Therefore, the legal consequences of Ireland's ratification of an international human rights treaty, such as the CRPD, are relatively limited. Such instruments can be used as an interpretative aid in cases taken in the Irish courts, but are considered persuasive, rather than legally binding, unless they have been incorporated into domestic Irish legislation. If and when Ireland ratifies the Optional Protocol, individual complaints can be made to the UN Committee on the Rights of Persons with Disabilities (CRPD Committee) (OP-CRPD 2006). Until this time, the main legal consequence of ratification is that Ireland is obliged to report periodically to

[1] This is a convention and not a process explicitly provided for in the Constitution.

the CRPD Committee (CRPD 2006, Art. 35), establish a national focal point within Government on disability rights and designate an independent monitoring framework at national level (CRPD 2006, Art. 33). The State Report to the CRPD Committee presents an opportunity for civil society organisations to develop shadow reports and provide insight to Committee members on the real issues facing disabled people in Ireland—with a view to ultimately influencing the Committee's recommendations, known as 'Concluding Observations' to the Irish Government for better implementation of the Convention.

3 The Political Context for Ratification: Ireland's Record on Human Rights Treaties

Given that Ireland's journey from signature to ratification of the CRPD took over a decade, it is worth considering the political context which shaped this process with reference to Ireland's track record on ratifying other UN human rights treaties. In the past, Ireland has tended to sign many UN human rights treaties shortly after their adoption, but in most cases, Ireland has not speedily ratified these Conventions. For example, the International Covenant on Civil and Political Rights (ICCPR 1966) and the International Covenant on Economic, Social and Cultural Rights (ICESCR 1966) were adopted by the UN in 1966, signed by Ireland in 1973, but not ratified until 1990 (United Nations, *Treaty Series*, vol. 999, p. 171 and vol. 1057, p. 407; United Nations, *Treaty Series*, vol. 993, p. 3). The Convention on the Elimination of All Forms of Racial Discrimination (CERD 1965) was adopted by the UN in 1965, and signed by Ireland in 1968, but not ratified until 2001 (United Nations, *Treaty Series*, vol. 660, p. 195). The Convention on the Elimination of All Forms of Discrimination Against Women (CEDAW 1979) was adopted by the UN in 1979 and was ratified by Ireland in 1986—but the Optional Protocol to this convention was not ratified by Ireland until 2000 (United Nations, *Treaty Series*, vol. 1249, p. 13). The Convention Against Torture and Other Cruel, Inhuman or Degrading Treatment or Punishment (CAT 1984) was adopted by the UN in 1984, signed by Ireland in 1992, but not ratified by Ireland until

2002 (United Nations, *Treaty Series*, vol. 1465, p. 85). Finally, the Convention on the Rights of the Child (CRC 1989), which was adopted by the UN in 1989, was signed by Ireland in 1990, and ratified in 1992 (United Nations, *Treaty Series*, vol. 1577, p. 3). To date, therefore, the CRC remains the UN human rights convention which Ireland was quickest to ratify—the entire process from signature to ratification taking only 2 years, while Ireland took longest to ratify CERD—the gap between signature and ratification being 31 years. Within this context it is hardly surprising, then, that Ireland signed the CRPD in 2007 but did not ratify it until 2018.

From this brief analysis however, it seems that most treaties were ratified by Ireland between 1990 and 2002—and that this decade was the most prolific in terms of Ireland's ratification of international human rights conventions. This in part might be attributed to a growing awareness of human rights in Ireland during the 1990s and early 2000s, including with Ireland's incorporation of the European Convention on Human Rights (ECHR 1950) into domestic law (ECHR Act 2003). Therefore, while some of the older human rights conventions from the 1960s and 1970s took Ireland longer to ratify, the current climate of human rights awareness within the Irish State means that ratification of newer UN human rights conventions should be smoother, and also speedier.

While it is up to each individual State to determine when it is ready to ratify a particular human rights convention, Ireland has taken the approach that "it does not become party to treaties until it is first in a position to comply with the obligations imposed by the treaty in question, including by amending domestic law as necessary" (Dáil Éireann 2014, p. 22). However, the determination of whether or not Ireland is 'in a position to comply with the obligations imposed by the treaty' tends to vary. For example, when Ireland ratified CEDAW in 1986, rape within marriage was not prohibited by the criminal law (Criminal Law [Rape Amendment] Act 1990). Nevertheless, Ireland ratified the convention without any reservations. Similarly, Ireland ratified the CRC long before the 31st amendment to the Constitution, which now explicitly recognises the rights of the child. The following section will consider how decisions were made about the laws that needed to be reformed in order to 'comply with the obligations imposed' by the CRPD prior to ratification.

4 The Legislative Framework: A Programme of Reform

With specific reference to the ratification of the CRPD, the UN Office of the High Commissioner for Human Rights (OHCHR/Office) has recommended that "States considering ratification should review national legislation and policies for compliance with the Convention" (OHCHR 2009, p. 5). The Office also clarifies that "any pre-ratification review should be part of a process that continues in the implementation phase to review existing and proposed legislation" (OHCHR 2009, p. 6). From these statements it seems clear that the expectation is that not all issues of compliance will be resolved prior to ratification—and that the process of ensuring compliance is an ongoing one.

The OHCHR also strongly urges States to engage in a meaningful consultation process in order to prepare for ratification, stating that 'Adequate consultation should take place at the level of government departments and agencies ... Non-governmental stakeholders and in particular civil society and organizations of persons with disabilities should also be integrated in such national consultations' (OHCHR 2009, p. 6). Similarly, the OHCHR asks that States "publicly launch the process of ratification, make publicly available a plan that includes timelines and opportunities for consultation, and invite civil society and organizations of persons with disabilities to make submissions presenting their views on the opportunities, implications and challenges of ratification" (OHCHR 2009, p. 6).

Following the procedure recommended by the OHCHR, the Irish Government formed an interdepartmental committee to review legislation and policy on disability and to develop a work programme of reforms necessary to ratify the Convention. This committee included representatives from the following departments: Department of Justice, Equality and Defence; Department of Social Protection; Department of Foreign Affairs; Department of Education and Skills; Department of Jobs, Enterprise and Innovation; Department of Communications, Energy and Natural Resources; Department of the Environment, Community and Local Government; Department of Health and Department of Transport,

Tourism and Sport (Dáil Éireann 2014). The Office of Public Works was the only public body which is not a Government department to be represented on the committee. The committee did not have any members who are persons with disabilities nor any representation from civil society. Its meetings were not open to the public and minutes of meetings were not made available to the public. The existence of the committee and the nature of its work only emerged in response to parliamentary questions on Ireland's preparations to ratify the CRPD. Both the Minister for Justice and the Minister of State for Disability responded to these questions as follows:

> The Government intends to proceed to ratification of the convention as quickly as possible, taking into account the need to ensure all necessary legislative and administrative requirements under the convention are met … An interdepartmental committee on the convention is monitoring the remaining legislative and administrative actions required to enable ratification. As part of its work programme, the committee has identified issues to be considered by various Departments. It is a matter for these Departments to determine whether any actions are required to address the issues in advance of ratification and report back to the committee. This work is ongoing in all Departments. At the request of the committee, the National Disability Authority, the lead statutory agency for the sector, is also assisting in assessing remaining requirements for ratification to ensure that all outstanding issues will be comprehensively addressed. … [O]ne of the key requirements is the enactment of capacity legislation. … The enactment of this legislation is one of the core elements of the remaining work to be completed to enable ratification by the State of the UN convention. (Dáil Éireann 2014, p. 22)

In April 2015, the Department of Foreign Affairs published some further information on the work of the interdepartmental committee—and identified other areas beyond the capacity bill which, in its view, needed to be addressed prior to Ireland's ratification of CRPD (Department of Foreign Affairs 2015). Three other key issues were identified by the Department—sexual offences legislation, mental health law and various miscellaneous amendments, including a Constitutional issue with respect to the CRPD's definition of 'reasonable accommodation'. A commitment was also made at this time to publish a roadmap to ratification once all departments with responsibility in these areas reverted with information on how they intended to progress actions required under their remits to enable ratification, and Government had approved the actions to be taken. As the main legislative obstacle to ratification that was consistently identified was the need to reform Ireland's law on legal capacity, the following section will provide an overview of how that reform progressed and its impact on ratification.

5 The Main Barrier: Law Reform on Legal Capacity

From the very first responses to parliamentary questions, successive Irish Ministers with responsibilities for disability and justice identified that Ireland's substituted decision-making regime, the ward of court system, was in need of reform, prior to ratification of the CRPD. As described by Doyle and Flynn (2013), a proposal for reform of this system had been made by the Law Reform Commission in 2006, although this proposal did not take account of new ideas about legal capacity which had emerged from the drafting of Article 12 CRPD (2006). A General Scheme of the Mental Capacity Bill was published by Government in 2008, which largely reflected the recommendations of the Law Reform Commission. However, given the subsequent economic crisis, this issue was not prioritised in the Governments' legislative reform programmes, and the Assisted Decision-Making Capacity Bill was not published until five years later (Oireachtas 2013). While this delay was frequently criticised by civil society and opposition politicians, it also meant that civil society had greater opportunities to influence and shape the drafting of the resulting Bill, which is in many respects is much closer to compliance with Article 12 CRPD (2006) than either the 2008 General Scheme or the original Law Reform Proposal.

The Bill (Oireachtas 2013) proposed the abolition of the existing ward of court system—in which a person 'of unsound mind incapable of governing [themselves] or [their] property' (Regulation of Lunacy (Ireland) Act 1871) was deemed, on the basis of medical evidence, to lack all capacity to make decisions through a procedure of the High Court (O'Neill 2004). To replace this, the Bill (Oireachtas 2013) set out a three-tiered system, within which a person could access support to exercise capacity or have decisions made on their behalf. The support options were provided through the appointment of a decision-making assistant or co-decision-maker. Where a person was deemed to lack capacity by the Circuit Court, a substitute decision-maker known as the decision-making representative could be appointed. The Bill (Oireachtas 2013) also proposed some reforms to enduring powers of attorney which were already provided for in Irish law, and at the Committee stage debates, provisions on advance healthcare directives were added into the legislative Bill.

Two major innovations of the Bill were its recognition of formal supported decision-making options, and the decision to prohibit substitute decision-makers from applying the best interests test (Oireachtas 2013, s.8). Rather, the Bill recognised 'respect for will and preferences', drawn from the text of Article 12 CRPD (2006), as a core guiding principle. However, the Bill also defined 'capacity' according to a functional test of mental capacity, which could trigger a restriction of the individual's legal capacity. At the time of its publication, the functional test of mental capacity had begun to be criticised in international human rights law discourse, and during the course of the Bill's progression through parliament, the UN CRPD Committee adopted General Comment 1, which clarified that such an approach was contrary to the Committee's interpretation of Article 12 CRPD (CRPD Committee 2014).

Throughout the development of the legislative Bill, a civil society coalition on legal capacity reform emerged. This was co-ordinated by the Centre for Disability Law and Policy (CDLP) at the National University of Ireland Galway and Amnesty Ireland's Mental Health Campaign, and member organisations represented persons with disabilities, people with experience of the mental health services and older people. The coalition sought to influence the drafting and development of the legislation, and once the Bill was published, it issued a response, outlining eight issues which required further reform in the legislation (CDLP 2013). These included expanding the provision of supported decision-making, changing the definition of capacity, significantly restricting provisions on informal substitute decision-making, providing opportunities for people to challenge decisions made under the new law, ensuring the legislation interacted with other key areas of law such as the Mental Health Act, addressing deprivation of liberty, enhancing the review process for the legislation and changing the name and functions of the proposed Office of Public Guardian, which was to oversee implementation of the Bill (CDLP 2013, pp. 3–7).

Significant changes were made during the subsequent parliamentary debates on the Bill, including the removal of the provisions on informal substitute decision-making, and the introduction of a specific legal aid scheme for persons whose capacity would be determined by the courts. However, the final Act adopted maintained the Bill's definition of mental capacity based on the functional test, despite the arguments of advocates that to comply with the CRPD this should be changed to a universal recognition of legal capacity (Flynn and Gooding 2015). Similarly, despite the objections of the civil society coalition on legal capacity reform, the final Act continued to provide that advance healthcare directives would no longer be legally binding if the person was detained under the Mental Health Act (ADMC Act 2015, s. 85[7]; Morrissey 2015).

The Bill's original proposal for an Office of Public Guardian was reframed as a 'Decision Support Service' and given a broader remit including raising awareness of the CRPD. However, in the final stages, the Decision Support Service was relocated away from the Courts Service into the Mental Health Commission. This change in location was purportedly to address the concerns of families of existing wards of court who felt that keeping the office in the courts service might not lead to a sufficiently new approach. However, the move to the Mental Health Commission was also criticised (Flynn and Gooding 2015), due to the potential confusion this might cause with respect to the remit of the Decision Support Service, which aimed to serve all groups who might use the legislation—including persons with disabilities, those with experience of the mental health services and older people.

Although the Act was adopted in December 2015, very few of its provisions have entered into force at the time of writing. In October 2017, a Director of the Decision Support Service was appointed to the Mental Health Commission, and one year later, further roles within the Service have been advertised. However, the Service only received an allocation of €3 m in the 2018 Budget, compared to the €20 m it had requested to scale up the full implementation of the legislation. The Director of the

Decision Support Service has stated that her target is for full implementation of the legislation to occur by Spring 2020 in the most recent report from the Mental Health Commission (2018, p. 8).

Those involved in efforts to influence the legislation might well question now whether it was indeed worth the wait, but it seems clear that there would not have been a shift away from 'best interests' to 'respect for will and preferences' if the legislation had been developed following the ratification of the CRPD. If Ireland had ratified the CRPD earlier, for example, in 2007 or 2008, when there were few Concluding Observations on Article 12 issued by the CRPD Committee, and no General Comment, then Ireland might simply have introduced the kind of adult guardianship reform envisaged in the 2008 General Scheme, which was based on a 'best interests' framework. It could also be argued that if ratification had occurred earlier, there is no guarantee that any reform of the ward of court system would have included a recognition of formal mechanisms for supported decision-making, such as the role of the decision-making assistant set out in the Assisted Decision-Making (Capacity) Act 2015. The following section will put this legislative reform in a broader context, by discussing efforts which were underway simultaneously during the drafting and negotiation of the Bill to maintain pressure on Ireland to ratify the CRPD.

6 A Decade of Delays: Civil Society Strategies and the Role of the Courts

As a result of the significant delays in the development of the Capacity Bill, civil society had to employ different strategies to maintain pressure on Government to ensure ratification of the CRPD. These included posing parliamentary questions to the relevant Ministers for Justice and Disability,[2] using the existing treaty body monitoring processes within

[2] Ireland has appointed junior ministers (also known as Ministers of State) with responsibility for disability since 2008. In 2016, the Minister for Disability was changed to a super-junior role, which gives the minister voting rights at Cabinet (junior ministers are normally not granted such voting rights). See Department of An Taoiseach 2016. *List of Ministers and Ministers of State*. Available at https://www.taoiseach.gov.ie/eng/Taoiseach_and_Government/List_of_Ministers_Ministers_of_State/ (accessed 11 January 2019).

the UN (and the Universal Periodic Review) to ensure questions were regularly posed on CRPD ratification. Attempts to raise CRPD compliance issues through the courts have also been made (Flynn 2018). References to CRPD rights have been made in various direct actions undertaken by disabled activists, including a protest outside the Dáil in 2012 which resulted in Government reversal of a significant cut proposed to the personal assistance funding scheme (Hyland 2012).

At various times during the 11 years from Ireland's signature to ratification of the CRPD, civil society questioned whether it was worth continuing to push for legislative reform prior to ratification. This issue was first aired publicly at an Inclusion Ireland conference in 2011, during which its CEO, Deirdre Carroll, strongly criticised Ireland for its delay, and argued that Government should press ahead with ratification rather than waiting for the Capacity Bill to be finalised (Carroll 2011). At the same event, Professor Gerard Quinn urged caution, noting that if ratification was completed without the called-for legislative reform, the impetus to introduce such reform would dissipate, and the impact on the lives of disabled people on the ground would not change significantly following Ireland's ratification without additional domestic law reform (Quinn 2011). Quinn also noted that the disability community should not wait indefinitely for legislative reform, but that it should give Government some time to 'get it right' in the development of CRPD-compliant capacity legislation (Quinn 2011).

During the long delay on ratification, a number of cases before the Irish courts on issues related to the rights of persons with disabilities and mental health service users referenced the CRPD (Flynn 2018). As noted above, the CRPD at best can only have persuasive force in the Irish courts, even following ratification, unless it is subsequently incorporated into domestic law. Nevertheless, various strategies were employed by lawyers in these cases to rely on the CRPD as an interpretative aid. One argument which frequently surfaced in these cases concerned the EU's accession to the CRPD, which entered into force in 2011 (European Council 2009). In one such case, *MX v HSE* (2012 IEHC 491), the plaintiff's counsel argued that the CRPD should have direct effect in the Irish legal system by virtue of Ireland's membership of the EU, and the EU's accession to the CRPD. The plaintiff's counsel in this case argued that the treatment permitted under the Mental Health Act (2001) failed to properly reflect the changes in international human rights norms reflected by the CRPD. The judge in this case, MacMenamin J held that:

> the broader range of constitutional 'personal capacity rights' now fall to be informed by the United Nations Convention on the Rights of Persons with Disabilities, as well as the principles enunciated in the judgments of the European Court of Human Rights. (MX v HSE 2012, para. 33)

This finding is particularly remarkable in light of the fact that Ireland had not, at the time, ratified the CRPD. More specifically, in his final judgment in the case, MacMenamin J found that there was a Constitutional duty to ensure that the views of a person treated under the Mental Health Act (2001) are heard, if necessary, through a representative in the form of 'assisted' decision-making (MX v HSE 2012). MacMenamin J explained that this could be achieved, for example, "through the help of carers, social workers or, perhaps most appropriately, family members" (MX v HSE 2012, para. 75). It is important to note that at the time this judgment was written in 2012, the Irish Government had not yet published its Assisted Decision-Making (Capacity) Bill (Oireachtas 2013) and so there was no link to a clear legislative framework, or even Government intention to introduce legal recognition for 'assisted decision-making' as a less restrictive alternative to involuntary treatment without the person's consent. Therefore, this decision was significant, in maintaining pressure on Government to publish its proposals for reform of capacity law.

However, ultimately, MacMenamin J remained unconvinced by the arguments made by MX's counsel that the CRPD should have direct effect in the Irish legal system by virtue of Ireland's membership of the EU, and the EU's accession to the Convention. As the judgment notes:

> In order to establish her case, the plaintiff would be required to establish (a) that the relevant provision of the UNCRPD falls within a community competence which had been exercised to a "large degree" or was an "integral part of Community law"; and, also, (b) that the provision sought to be enforced is sufficiently clear, concise and unconditional as to be capable of itself directly regulating the legal position of individuals. (MX v HSE 2012, para. 33)

A more direct link to the CRPD via EU law has been made in subsequent cases before the Irish courts, such as the case of *Marie Daly v Nano Nagle School* (2018 IECA 11). This case originated before the Equality Tribunal and Labour Court, and appeals have now been heard in both the High Court and Court of Appeal. The case was initiated by an employee working in a special school for children with disabilities, who had been deemed incapable of performing her duties after she acquired a physical disability. She claimed that this decision constituted disability-based discrimination on the grounds that no effort to reasonably accommodate her had been made by the school.

As part of this claim, she argued that existing Irish employment discrimination law should be interpreted through the lens of the CRPD by virtue of the EU's 'approval' of the Convention, relying on the decision of the Court of Justice of the European Union in HK Danmark (Ring and Skouboe Werge) (2013 2 CMLR 21). While the complainant lost her case before the Equality Tribunal, she won an action in the Labour Court. The Labour Court found that although Ms Daly may not have been competent to carry out the duties of a special needs assistant at the school, the school was in breach of its statutory duties for its failure to consider a re-allocation of Ms Daly's tasks as a special needs assistant. This decision was upheld by the High Court on appeal but overturned by the most recent Court of Appeal decision in February 2018 (2018 IECA 11). The Court of Appeal judgment returned to the earlier Equality Tribunal reasoning, focusing on section 16(1) of the Employment Equality Act 1998. That section provides that nothing in the Act shall be construed as requiring an employer to retain an individual who is no longer fully capable of performing their duties. The decision of the Court of Appeal in this case is currently under appeal to the Supreme Court. Since the jurisprudence in this case occurred both prior to and following Ireland's ratification of the CRPD, it is worth continuing to track how the Irish courts rely on, and interpret the CRPD, as it applies to Irish law, including where Irish law has been developed based on Ireland's obligations as a Member State of the EU.

It is worth noting that overall, the disability community in Ireland has not had significant success to date in recognising or enforcing rights through strategic litigation, with some notable exceptions such as *Sinnott v Minister for Education* (2001 2 IR 505), establishing a right to appropriate education for children with disabilities, and *Sinnott v Minister for Environment* (2017 IEHC 214), recognising the need for adaptation to voting procedures to maintain the right to a secret ballot for blind people and those with low vision. Nevertheless, this avenue for reform may continue to expand in future, and it will be interesting to track the extent to which the courts engage with arguments concerning the rights contained in the CRPD, now that Ireland has finally ratified the Convention.

7 The Final Steps: Roadmap, Ratification and Reservations

In October 2015, following sustained pressure from civil society to commit to a timeline for completion of the legislative reforms necessary to ratify the CRPD, the Department of Justice published a 'Roadmap to Ratification' (Department of Justice 2015). This document provided an article-by-article overview of the Convention and relevant legislative reforms, with an estimated timeline for completion of each. The roadmap confirmed the four major areas of legislative reform outlined by the Department of Foreign Affairs in its April 2015 memo, and added further detail on the proposed declarations and reservations Ireland planned to enter upon ratification. It further committed that Ireland would ratify the Optional Protocol at the same time as the CRPD (Department of Justice 2015).

An omnibus Disability Equality Bill (2016) was proposed in the Roadmap to address all remaining miscellaneous issues concerning compliance with the CRPD. These included 'those needed to update outmoded, unsuitable and sometimes archaic language and provisions' (Department of Foreign Affairs 2015, p. 1). It was also proposed that this Bill would attempt to reconcile the Irish Supreme Court's position on the constitutionality of 'reasonable accommodation' provisions in anti-discrimination law, with the definition of 'reasonable accommodation' in the CRPD (Department of Justice 2015). In a 1996 case, Ireland's Supreme Court held that the requirement on employers to provide 'reasonable accommodation' to employees with disabilities (unless to do so would constitute an undue hardship), was a disproportionate interference with the constitutional right to private property (Re Article 26 and the Employment Equality Bill 1996). As a result, the Employment Equality Bill (Oireachtas 1996) was deemed unconstitutional, and the legislature subsequently enacted a much lower threshold which required employers to reasonably accommodate disabled employees if to do so would not exceed a 'nominal cost' (Employment Equality Act 1998). Following the entry into force of the European Community (EC) Employment Equality Framework Directive (2000/78/EC) on non-discrimination in employment, Ireland was obliged to amend its equality legislation to impose a higher threshold of 'disproportionate burden' on employers' obligations to reasonably accommodate.[3]

This change was made possible due to Article 29.6 of the Constitution, which states that "No provision of this Constitution invalidates laws enacted, acts done or measures adopted by the State … that are necessitated by the obligations of membership of the European Union" (Bunreacht na hÉireann 1937, Art. 29(6)). However, since the EU has not introduced a directive on non-discrimination in respect of access to goods and services for people with disabilities, the lower threshold of 'nominal cost' continues to exist in Ireland's Equal Status Act (2000) with respect to these matters. Since the CRPD defines 'reasonable accommodation' as requiring measures "not imposing a disproportionate or undue burden" (2006, Art. 2), the Roadmap acknowledged that Ireland's existing anti-discrimination legislation presents a challenge for compliance with the CRPD. The Roadmap also clarified that:

> The Supreme Court decision hinges on the private property protection provisions of the Constitution. Clearly, these do not arise in relation to provision of public services. We also have legal advice that the State can impose a higher obligation on commercial bodies whose activities are regulated for quality of service, such as banks, insurance companies, telecommunications providers, and so on. We are then left with a range of smaller businesses, such as shops and restaurants. In the case of such service providers we need to find a solution. (Department of Justice and Equality 2015, p. 14)

[3] This was incorporated into Irish law by section 9 of the Equality Act 2004, amending section 16, Employment Equality Act 1998.

The solution ultimately proposed in the Bill was to delineate which types of service providers would be required to adhere to the higher standard of disproportionate burden, as discussed further below.

Subsequently, in 2016, the Minister for Disability introduced the Disability (Miscellaneous Provisions) Bill (Oireachtas 2016) in the Dáil. This Bill proposed extending the requirement to reasonably accommodate where such accommodation would not impose a 'disproportionate burden' on certain categories of service providers, including public bodies, financial institutions and credit unions, insurance providers, communication service providers and public transport operators (Oireachtas 2016, S. 4). The Bill (Oireachtas 2016) also reformed the eligibility of persons with disabilities for jury service—recognising that deaf people should not be excluded from jury service by virtue of requiring a sign language interpreter. Similarly, it proposed the deletion of a provision of the electoral acts providing that a person of 'unsound mind' was disqualified from membership of the Dáil (Oireachtas 2016, S. 2). Finally, the Bill (Oireachtas 2016) designated the Irish Human Rights and Equality Commission, with assistance from the National Disability Authority, as the independent monitoring mechanism under Article 33 CRPD. Despite commitments in the Roadmap to introduce legislative reform on deprivation of liberty through this Bill, no provisions on this matter appeared in the Bill as published, although the Minister noted in his speech that these would be introduced as amendments to the Bill at Committee Stage. The second stage debate on the Bill took place in February 2017, and since then, there has been no further development on the legislative Bill. A public consultation on deprivation of liberty was undertaken by the Department of Health in March 2018; however, at the time of writing, no legislative proposals have been brought forward on this matter.

The Programme for Partnership Government contained a commitment to ratify the CRPD by the end of 2016 (Department of An Taoiseach 2016). In introducing the Disability (Miscellaneous Provisions) Bill to parliament in February 2017, the Minister for Disability noted his regret that the legislative reforms required to enable ratification were taking longer than planned, and that it had not been possible to adhere to this commitment. The Criminal Law (Sexual Offences) Act 2017, which included a change of existing sexual offences involving persons with disabilities, was passed by both houses of parliament in February 2017, which meant that the main remaining legislative reform identified in the Roadmap was the Disability (Miscellaneous Provisions) Bill (Oireachtas 2016). In response to further parliamentary questions regarding ratification and delays in April, September, October and December 2017 (Dáil Éireann 2017), the Minister for Disability continued to state that the remaining obstacle to ratification was the Disability (Miscellaneous Provisions) Bill and in particular the need for legislative clarity on deprivation of liberty of persons with disabilities.

Increased media attention and sustained protest by the disability community in the final months of 2017 resulted in a statement from the Minister for Disability on the 3rd December, the international day of persons with disabilities, that he would submit draft legislation to cabinet the following week "which is a very significant milestone in Ireland's process for ratifying the UN Convention on the Rights of People with Disabilities" (McGrath 2017). This referred to the Draft Heads of Bill on Deprivation of Liberty, which were published for public consultation on 11 December 2017. In January 2018, the Taoiseach (Prime Minister), Leo Varadkar, announced that Ireland would ratify the CRPD "early in the new year" (Barry 2018). The Minister for Disability subsequently confirmed that a political decision was made by Cabinet in January to ratify by the end of February, without completion of the outstanding legislative reforms, and that he would then bring the remaining relevant legislation through the Houses of the Oireachtas (Parliament) (Ní Aodha 2018). This was followed by the tabling of a motion on the CRPD in the Dáil by the Minister for Disability on the ratification of CRPD, in March 2018.

During the debates on this motion, the Minister stated that "The necessary legislation will be in place before the first phase of reporting under the convention" (Dáil Éireann 2018, p. 464). Since Ireland will be obliged to report to the UN CRPD Committee by April 2020, in practice, this means that completion of the outstanding legislative reforms is not to be expected before then. The Minister also responded to criticism from other parliamentarians regarding the inclusion of reservations and declarations on Articles 12, 14 and 27 of the CRPD (2006). He noted that:

> In each of these areas, it is the Government's view that there is a reason to make a declaration or issue a reservation to allow for compulsory care and treatment under the Mental Health Act to permit substitute decision-

> making in limited circumstances as a last resort where there are considerable capacity issues and to deal with specific occupational requirements for employment in the Defence Forces or emergency services. (Dáil Éireann 2018, p. 464)

Following the debate, it became clear that Government would not ratify the CRPD's Optional Protocol at the same time as the CRPD, breaking the commitment that had previously been made in the Roadmap to Ratification. This decision again led to outcry within the disability movement (Holland 2018). The Minister for Disability was asked to respond to this issue at a meeting of the Oireachtas Committee on Justice and Equality in June 2018. He noted that:

> the Convention and the Optional Protocol cover a broad range of commitments some of which require substantive cultural change. Indeed an analysis of the some 14 complaints brought under the Optional Protocol since 2010, indicates a range of areas that we are actively working hard on to address such as deprivation of liberty, and the right of deaf persons to participate in jury duty. Work is continuing on the final reforms needed for Ireland's compliance with the Convention's requirements. For this reason, a phased approach is seen as the most practical and realistic way of moving ahead. (Joint Oireachtas Committee on Justice and Equality 2018, p. 4)

This statement demonstrates that the decision not to ratify the Optional Protocol (2006) has been influenced by knowledge of the existing jurisprudence of the CRPD Committee on individual complaints, and a recognition that Ireland has not yet completed the promised legislative reforms which Government believes would bring it into closer alignment with the rights set out in CRPD.

8 Final Reflections on Ratification Without Completion of Reforms

After 11 years, the decision of the Irish Government to ratify without completing the promised legislative reforms seems to be a strange one at first glance. Why spend over a decade claiming that Ireland could not ratify without first changing its laws, only to reverse that decision at the last minute? There are several possible explanations that should be considered here as part of the cultural context which shaped what appears to be a sharp political turn-about. Perhaps the most significant of these is the increasing political pressure on Ireland, both at home, and abroad, to ratify. Ireland was the last EU member state to ratify, a fact that was repeatedly emphasised in media reports on this subject (Power 2018). The Irish Government had also been repeatedly called upon by other states and international bodies to complete the ratification process. Further, disability activists in Ireland had maintained pressure on Government to ratify, briefing opposition politicians and preparing parliamentary questions for Government ministers, engaging in campaigns using print, broadcast and social media, using direct action, and generally raising the failure to ratify at every possible opportunity for public consultation or engagement with Government.

Ireland's ratification of CRPD must be acknowledged as a positive step, and it provides civil society and disabled people's organisations (DPOs) in particular with opportunities to engage with the CRPD Committee on the completion of Ireland's first report, due in April 2020. However, a number of significant challenges for the disability community in Ireland remain. The laws that were passed purportedly to achieve compliance with the CRPD, for example, the Assisted Decision-Making (Capacity) Act (2015) and the Criminal Law (Sexual Offences) Act (2017), have been criticised by several commentators for their failure to adhere to the CRPD's standards (Flynn and Gooding 2015; Inclusive Research Network 2018). Ireland has also entered reservations and declarations which make clear that this is deliberate, and that Ireland does not intend to change its laws regarding legal capacity and deprivation of liberty to become fully compliant with the interpretations issued by the CRPD Committee. Since ratification, as Quinn warned back in 2011, no further progress has been made on the outstanding legislative reforms, despite the Minister's commitment to enact the Disability (Miscellaneous Provisions) Bill by the end of 2018. However, one positive recent development is that the Irish Human Rights and Equality Commission (IHREC), which will ultimately be designated as Ireland's independent monitoring mechanism for the

CRPD at the domestic level, has called for applications for its Disability Advisory Committee, which is mandated to include a majority of persons with disabilities among its membership. According to IHREC, this Committee will "advise the Commission on the fulfilment of its CRPD Article 33 independent monitoring role" (IHREC 2018, p. 3). As we move into the first reporting period for Ireland under the CRPD, the disability community must therefore continue to maintain pressure on the State and associated duty-bearers to respect, protect and defend the rights of persons with disabilities, in law, policy and practice. The forthcoming reporting process and dialogue between Ireland and the CRPD Committee should provide interesting opportunities for civil society to continue to highlight the disparity between the commitments in the CRPD, and the lived realities of disabled people in Ireland. The lessons learned from the ratification process clearly demonstrate the need to use all possible avenues to generate the necessary political will to advance the rights of persons with disabilities.

References

ADMC Act (Assisted Decision-Making (Capacity) Act). (2015). Enacted in 2003 by the Oireachtas.

Barry, A. (2018). After 10 years, Ireland is to finally ratify the UN Convention on rights of people with disabilities. *theJournal*.ie [online]. Retrieved November 23, 2018, fromhttps://www.thejournal.ie/ireland-ratify-rights-people-disabilities-3775103-Jan2018/.

Bunreacht na hÉireann (Constitution of Ireland, enacted in 1937), Article 29.4 (International Relations).

Carroll, D. 'Introductory Remarks' at Inclusion Ireland 'The Law and People with an Intellectual Disability' Conference 19 October 2011. The Law Society Dublin.

CAT (Convention Against Torture and Other Cruel, Inhuman or Degrading Treatment or Punishment). (1984). Adopted in 1984 by the United Nations general assembly.

CDLP (Centre for Disability Law and Policy). (2013, September 1). *Equality, dignity and human rights, does the assisted decision-making (Capacity) bill 2013 fulfil Ireland's human rights obligations under the Convention on the Rights of Persons with Disabilities?* National University of Ireland Galway.

CEDAW (Convention on the Elimination of All Forms of Discrimination Against Women). (1979). Adopted in 1979 by the United Nations general assembly.

CERD (Convention on the Elimination of All Forms of Racial Discrimination). (1965). Adopted in 1965 by the United Nations general assembly.

CRC (Convention on the Rights of the Child). (1989). Adopted in 1989 by the United Nations general assembly.

Department of An Taoiseach. (2016). *Programme for Partnership Government* [online]. Retrieved Nov 23, 2018, from https://www.merrionstreet.ie/MerrionStreet/en/ImageLibrary/Programme_for_Partnership_Government.pdf.

Department of Foreign Affairs. (2015). *Ratification of UN Convention on the Rights of Persons with Disabilities (CRPD) by Ireland.* Dublin.

Department of Justice and Equality. (2015). *Roadmap to ratification of the United Nations convention on the rights of persons with disabilities (UN CRPD)* [online]. Retrieved November 23, 2018, from http://www.justice.ie/en/JELR/Roadmap%20to%20Ratification%20of%20CRPD.pdf/Files/Roadmap%20to%20Ratification%20of%20CRPD.pdf.

Doyle, S., & Flynn, E. (2013). Ireland's ratification of the UN convention on the rights of persons with disabilities: Challenges and opportunities. *British Journal of Learning Disabilities, 41*(3), 171–180.

ECHR (European Convention on Human Rights). (1950). Adopted in 1950 by the Council of Europe.

ECHR Act (European Convention on Human Rights Act). (2003). Enacted in 2003 by the Oireachtas.

Equal Status Act. (2000). Enacted in 2000 by the Oireachtas.

European Council. (2009). Council Decision 2010/48/EC of 26 November 2009 concerning the conclusion, by the European Community, of the UN CRPD. OJ L 23, 27.1.2010, pp. 35–61.

European Council Decision 2010/48/EC of 26 November 2009 concerning the conclusion, by the European Community, of the United Nations Convention on the Rights of Persons with Disabilities OJ L 23/35, 27/01/2010.

European Council Directive 2000/78/EC of 27 November 2000 establishing a general framework for equal treatment in employment and occupation OJ L 303, 02/12/2000, Article 5.

Flynn, E. (2018). Ireland. In L. Waddington & A. Lawson (Eds.), *The UN convention on the rights of persons with disabilities in practice: A comparative analysis of the role of courts* (pp. 220–244). Oxford: Oxford University Press.

Flynn, E., & Gooding, P. (2015). Warning over 'assisted decision-making' plans in new Bill. *Irish Times* [online]. Retrieved November 23, 2018, from https://www.irishtimes.com/opinion/warning-over-assisted-decision-making-plans-in-new-bill-1.2254880.
HK Danmark (Ring and Skouboe Werge) Case C-335/11 [2013] 2 CMLR 21.
Holland, K. (2018). Ratifying UN laws on disability without appeal option 'ridiculous'. *Irish Times* [online]. Retrieved November 23, 2018, from https://www.irishtimes.com/news/social-affairs/ratifying-un-laws-on-disability-without-appeal-option-ridiculous-1.3425282.
Hyland, P. (2012). Cuts to personal assistant services will NOT take place. 2012. *theJournal.ie* [online]. Retrieved November 23, 2018, from https://www.thejournal.ie/personal-assistant-cuts-hse-disabilities-584573-Sep2012/.
ICCPR (International Covenant on Civil and Political Rights). (1966). Adopted in 1966 by the United Nations general assembly.
ICESCR (International Covenant on Economic, Social and Cultural Rights). (1966). Adopted in 1966 by the United Nations general assembly.
In Re Article 26 and the Employment Equality Bill 1996 [1997] 2 I.R. 321.
Inclusive Research Network. (2018). *Response to UN CRPD* [online]. Retrieved November 23, 2018, from http://www.fedvol.ie/_fileupload/Inclusive%20Research%20Network/IRN%20Response%20to%20Ireland%20UNCRPD%20-%20press%20release.pdf.
Dáil Éireann (Ireland) (2014). *Debates, 832*(3), 22.
Dáil Éireann (Ireland) (2017). *Debates, 936*(3), 81–99.
Dáil Éireann (Ireland) (2018). *Debates, 966*(4), 435–464.
Joint Oireachtas Committee on Justice and Equality Meeting (Ireland). (2018, June 27). (p. 4).
Irish Human Rights and Equality Commission. (2018). *Disability advisory committee applicant information booklet* [online]. Retrieved November 23, 2018, from https://www.ihrec.ie/app/uploads/2018/09/IHREC_Information-Booklet_Disability-Advisory-Committee.pdf.
Lunacy Regulation (Ireland) Act. (1871). Retrieved from http://www.irishstatutebook.ie/eli/1871/act/22/enacted/en/print.html.
Marie Daly v Nano Nagle School. (2018). IECA 11.
McGrath, F. (2017). *Statement on the ratification of the UN convention on the rights of persons with disabilities* [online]. Retrieved November 23, 2018, from http://www.finianmcgrath.ie/statement-on-ratification-of-the-un-convention-on-the-rights-of-persons-with-disabilities/.
Mental Health Act. (2001). Enacted in 2001 by the Oireachtas.

Mental Health Commission. (2018). *Annual report 2017* [online] (p. 8). Retrieved November 23, 2018, from https://www.mhcirl.ie/File/2017_AR_Incl_OIMS.pdf.

Morrissey, F. (2015). *Assisted decision-making bill: Why changes are needed to current laws.* Irish Examiner [online]. Retrieved November 23, 2018, from https://www.irishexaminer.com/viewpoints/analysis/assisted-decision-making-bill-why-changes-are-needed-to-current-laws-366167.html.

MX v HSE. (2012). (IEHC) 491.

Ní Aodha, G. (2018). Ireland will ratify UN Convention on Disabilities at end of February. *theJournal.ie* [online]. Retrieved November 23, 2018, from https://www.thejournal.ie/un-convention-disabilities-3825646-Jan2018/.

Oireachtas (1996). *Employment equality bill 1996.* Published in 1996 by the Oireachtas. Retrieved from https://www.oireachtas.ie/en/bills/bill/1996/38/.

Oireachtas (2013) Assisted decision-making (capacity) bill. Published in 2013 by the Oireachtas.

Oireachtas. (2016). *Disability (miscellaneous provisions) bill.* Published in 2016 by the Oireachtas. Retrieved from https://www.oireachtas.ie/en/bills/bill/2016/119/.

O'Neill, Wards of Court in Ireland. (First Law, 2004).

OP-CRPD (United Nations Optional Protocol to the Convention on the Rights of Persons with Disabilities). (2006). Adopted in 2006 by the United Nations general assembly.

Power, J. (2018). 'No legal grounds' for State not to ratify UN disability rights convention. *Irish Times* [online]. Retrieved November 23, 2018, from https://www.irishtimes.com/news/politics/no-legal-grounds-for-state-not-to-ratify-un-disability-rights-convention-1.3314088.

Quinn, G. (2011). *Legal capacity law reform: The revolution of the UN Convention on the rights of persons with disability.* At Inclusion Ireland 'The Law and People with an Intellectual Disability' Conference 19 October, The Law Society Dublin.

Sinnott v Minister for Education. (2001). 2 IR 505.

Sinnott v Minister for Environment. (2017). IEHC 214.

United Nations Committee on the Rights of Persons with Disabilities. (2014). General Comment No. 1. Retrieved November 23, 2018, from http://www.ohchr.org/EN/HRBodies/CRPD/Pages/CRPDIndex.aspx.

United Nations, Convention Against Torture and Other Forms of Cruel, Inhuman and Degrading Treatment, *Treaty Series*, vol. 1465, p. 85.

United Nations, Convention on the Elimination of Discrimination Against Women, *Treaty Series*, vol. 1249, p. 13.

United Nations, Convention on the Elimination of Racial Discrimination, *Treaty Series*, vol. 660, p. 195.

United Nations, Convention on the Rights of the Child, *Treaty Series*, vol. 1577, p. 3.

United Nations General Assembly, Convention on the Rights of Persons with Disabilities, 13 December 2006, A/RES/61/106.

United Nations, International Covenant on Civil and Political Rights, *Treaty Series*, vol. 999 and 1057, pp. 171 and 407.

United Nations, International Covenant on Economic, Social and Cultural Rights, *Treaty Series*, vol. 993, p. 3.

United Nations Office of the High Commissioner on Human Rights. (2007). *From exclusion to equality: Realising the rights of persons with disabilities. Handbook for parliamentarians on the convention on the rights of persons with disabilities and its optional protocol*. Geneva, HR/PUB/07/6.

United Nations Office of the High Commissioner on Human Rights. (2009). *Thematic study by the office of the United Nations high commissioner for human rights on enhancing awareness and understanding of the convention on the rights of persons with disabilities*. Geneva, A/HRC/10/48.

8

A Consultative Culture? The Ratification Process for the CRPD in Cyprus

Emily Julia Kakoullis

[T]he main reason for which the [Cypriot] Government at the time moved to sign the Convention and the Optional Protocol, was the recognition that we need to transition to a new more upgraded stage regarding the enshrinement of the rights of persons with disabilities ... the then Government ... [coupled by] the intervention and the demands of the movement of the disabled, recognised that [the Convention] was a step forwards in the field of the enshrinement of the rights of persons with disabilities (Interview with the Ministry of Labour and Social Insurance).

1 Introduction

In 2007 the Republic of Cyprus (Cyprus) was among the first 82 countries to sign the United Nations (UN) Convention on the Rights of Persons with Disabilities (Convention/CRPD 2006) at its Opening for

E. J. Kakoullis (✉)
School of Law and Politics, Cardiff University, Cardiff, UK
e-mail: KakoullisE@cardiff.ac.uk

E. J. Kakoullis, K. Johnson (eds.), *Recognising Human Rights in Different Cultural Contexts*, https://doi.org/10.1007/978-981-15-0786-1_8

Signature Ceremony. This was the first step in the journey towards ratification, the act through which Cyprus would formally establish its consent to be bound by the Convention at the international level and to implement its provisions at the domestic level (VCLT 1969; Achiron 2007; Kallehauge 2009). While signing occurred quickly, the journey to ratification was complex and it was not until four years later that Cyprus ratified the CRPD, in 2011. This chapter provides a case study of the journey towards ratification of the CRPD in Cyprus and in particular considers how the Cypriot context struggled to embrace the consultative and participatory culture that is found in the CRPD.

This issue is of particular importance because the CRPD aims to entrench more consultative and participatory political cultures for all ratifying States by embodying the Disabled People's Movement's mantra 'Nothing About Us Without Us!' (Charlton 2000), which it does through its provisions. Article 4(3) states:

> In the development and implementation of legislation and policies to implement the present Convention, and in other decision-making processes concerning issues relating to persons with disabilities, States Parties shall closely consult with and actively involve persons with disabilities, including children with disabilities, through their representative organizations. (CRPD 2006, Art. 4(3))

This participatory mantra is also woven into the CRPD's Preamble:

> Considering that persons with disabilities should have the opportunity to be actively involved in decision-making processes about policies and programmes, including those directly concerning them. (CRPD 2006, Preambular, para. o)

The CRPD also establishes a novel monitoring framework (Stein and Lord 2009), which requires the involvement of:

> Civil society, in particular persons with disabilities and their representative organizations, shall be involved and participate fully in the monitoring process. (CRPD 2006, Art. 33(3))

The Committee on the Rights of Persons with Disabilities (CRPD Committee) recently adopted a General Comment on the participation of persons with disabilities through their representative organisations in the implementation and monitoring of the Convention, setting out in further detail its own vision of a more participatory and consultative political culture around disability law and policy (CRPD Committee 2018).

This obligation to consult and involve persons with disabilities through their representative organisations was also emphasised in relation to States' ratification processes in a report by the Office of the UN High Commissioner for Human Rights (OHCHR 2009). The report focused on the legal measures required for the ratification and effective implementation of the CRPD, highlighting that a State's ratification process offers important opportunities for "awareness-raising and promoting understanding" of the CRPD (OHCHR 2009, para. 15). The ratification process is an important opportunity for persons with disabilities and their organisations to build a shared understanding of disability and human rights, to identify particular areas of concern in domestic law and policy, and to seek their Government's commitments to addressing these. Ratification is a 'testbed' for *how* the CRPD can effect change towards a more consultative and participatory culture.

The OHCHR report advises States embarking on the ratification process to carry out a screening process of their legislation and policies for compliance with the CRPD and to engage in consultation with persons with disabilities and disabled people's organisations (DPOs) (OHCHR 2009). In particular, the report states that:

> Adequate consultation should take place at the level of government departments and agencies [...]. Such consultation should enhance understanding of the Convention, contribute to ascertaining compliance of laws, policies and programmes with the Convention and identify areas for improvement. Non-governmental stakeholders and in particular civil society and organizations of persons with disabilities should also be integrated in such national consultations. Full and effective participation and inclusion in society of persons with disabilities is a general principle of the Convention, which also specifically establishes the duty on States to closely consult and

actively involve persons with disabilities in the development and implementation of policies that affect them. (OHCHR 2009, para. 17)

The report further stresses the importance of States publicly planning the process of ratification and ensuring that time and resources are available for DPOs to actively participate in consultation about ratification (OHCHR 2009).

This chapter focuses on the degree to which persons with disabilities and their DPOs were consulted and/or involved in the CRPD ratification in Cyprus. It draws from semi-structured interviews with Cypriot governmental bodies, semi-governmental organisations (also known as quasi-autonomous non-governmental organisations or 'quangos' in some English-speaking countries), political parties, civil society organisations and DPOs, as well as analysis of documents relating to the ratification process from these organisations, press releases and news media materials, which formed the basis of doctoral research on the ratification of the CRPD in Cyprus (Kakoullis 2015).

This chapter begins with a short account of the Cypriot context in which the ratification process for the CRPD took place. It then proceeds to describe the roles and activities of the key stakeholders involved in the ratification process, and their developments are traced across phases in the process showing how power moved over time. In this chapter I demonstrate that even where States designate DPOs as formal partners in consultative processes, there are still considerable dangers of missed opportunities to build the relevant shared understandings and to identify areas of concern in order to effect the consultative and participatory culture that the CRPD aims to bring about.

2 The Cypriot Context

The geographical location of Cyprus is at the south-east edge of Europe. Cyprus has only been an independent State since 1960, having been under British colonial rule from 1878 to 1960, and therefore has only 60 years' experience of governing its people and administering and developing its own legal system (ToE 1960; Faustmann 1999). Cyprus's early years of independence were far from calm and included civil violence, breakdown of the constitutional order (in 1963), a *coup d' etat* and invasions (Ker-Lindsay and Faustmann 2008; Ker-Lindsay 2011).

This history has had effects on the development of Cyprus as a State, a democracy, a legal and political system, a society and civil society organisations. It has also had an impact on the legislative and policy areas that have been granted priority and the research carried out on these, including in relation to disability (Symeonidou 2009b). It is notable that disability has not historically been an area granted priority by the Cypriot Government (Trimikliniotis and Demetriou 2008; Symeonidou 2009a). However, inspired by the UN International Year of the Disabled in 1981 DPOs representing groups with particular impairments decided to establish an 'umbrella' organisation to represent all persons with disabilities, and in 1984 the Cypriot Confederation of Organisations of the Disabled (Confederation/CCOD) was founded (Symeonidou 2005; Peters et al. 2009; Poyiadji et al. 2012). Despite internal tensions the Confederation was considered one of the strongest civil society movements in Cyprus—after the trade unions and employers' organisations (Symeonidou 2005; Trimikliniotis and Demetriou 2008).

In 2006, legislation enshrining an obligation on the Government to explicitly consult with the Confederation was enacted, the Consultation Process of State and Other Services on Matters that Concern Persons with a Disability Law of 2006 (Consultation Law/L. 143(I)/2006). This legislation reflected the dominant position the Confederation had developed and enshrined its position in the institution of law:

> Obligatory consultation with the CCOD
>
> (1) The CCOD is established as a social partner to the state on matters that concern persons with a disability.
> (2) Every Service, that is about to decide on matters or is dealing with matters that concern in any way directly or indirectly persons with a disability, consults during the discussion on these matters, with the CCOD.
> (3) For the purposes of subsection (2), the Service will ask from the CCOD to indicate its representative or its representatives on every occasion. (L. 143(I)/2006, Art. 3, my translation)

Prior to this legislation in 2006, the Cypriot Government had enacted the Persons with Disabilities Law of 2000 (L. 127(I)/2000), which created the first framework to provide potential for participatory practice with the voices of persons with disabilities to be fed into governmental decisions through the statutory creation of the Pan-Cyprian Council for Persons with Disabilities (PCPD) (L. 127(I)/2000, Art. 10). Members of the PCPD are selected by the Ministry of Labour and it has only four statutory members who are persons with disabilities. During the ratification process, members of the PCPD included representatives from five governmental ministries,[1] and 'social partners to the State' on industrial, labour and on disability matters, the latter of which was the Confederation.

Thus prior to the signing and ratification of the CRPD, Cyprus had taken some steps towards recognition of civil society organisations representing persons with disabilities, and the establishment of consultative bodies that included persons with disabilities. This laid an important foundation for the ratification process in Cyprus. However, as this chapter will demonstrate, it is by no means guaranteed that this consultative provision would include DPOs as equal partners in the ratification process.

3 Roles and Activities of the Key Stakeholders

Over 20 organisations or groups were identified as being involved in the ratification process for the CRPD in Cyprus (Kakoullis 2015). However, four of these were particularly significant and are discussed in this chapter.

3.1 The Cypriot Confederation of Organisations of the Disabled

A key stakeholder was the Cypriot Confederation of Organisations of the Disabled, which was involved in the ratification process through its

[1] These were representatives from the ministries of (1) Labour and Social Insurance, (2) Finance, (3) Education and Culture, (4) Health, and (5) the Planning Bureau (L. 127(I)/2000).

positions as both a "social partner" to the State on disability matters (L. 143(I)/2006, Art. 3(1)) and as a member of the Pan-Cyprian Council of Persons with Disabilities (PCPD) (L. 127(I)/2000). At the time the Confederation was made up of nine DPOs, some of which undertook a more active role than others during the ratification process. For example, the Pan-Cyprian Organisation of the Blind (POB) played an active role, whereas persons with intellectual disabilities were excluded.

3.2 The Ministry of Labour and Social Insurance and Its Department of Social Inclusion for Persons with Disabilities

The Ministry of Labour and Social Insurance (Ministry/MLSI) was the competent ministry for overseeing the ratification process of the CRPD, and for its subsequent implementation. In early 2009, the Ministry also created a new department, the Department of Social Inclusion for Persons with Disabilities (Department of Social Inclusion/DSIPD) (DSIPD 2015). Subsequently, the majority of the management of the ratification process was moved from the Ministry of Labour to the Department of Social Inclusion (HLGD 2009). The Ministry and its Department's roles included taking responsibility for what was referred to in the Cypriot context as 'public dialogue', that is, a consultation process, during the ratification process.

3.3 The Office of the Law Commission

The Office of the Law Commission (Law Commission) was also involved in the ratification process through its competencies concerning International Law treaties. Its role included advising the executive on signing and ratifying the CRPD and in carrying out official translations, including of the CRPD from the English language to the Greek language and the translation of the domestic incorporation law from the Greek into the English language.

3.4 Parliamentarians

Parliamentarians were involved in the ratification process through their responsibilities concerning the legislative enactment process regarding the incorporation of the CRPD into domestic law (Constitution 1960, Art. 169). In particular, Parliamentarians sitting on the Parliamentary Committee for Human Rights (PCHR) influenced the ratification process.

4 The Ratification Process in Cyprus

The research found that the Cypriot CRPD ratification process was not a single, seamless or straightforward process but rather that it was a complex cultural and political process that comprised five distinct phases of activity and involved over 20 stakeholders (Kakoullis 2015). The phases were identified in accordance with (a) the kinds of activities, events (or absence thereof) and processes that took place; and (b) the inclusion or exclusion of certain stakeholders over particular time periods. The particular processes that took place within each phase included translations of the text of the CRPD, screening of domestic legislation for compliance with the CRPD, a legislative process to incorporate the CRPD into domestic law and processes of consultation. These processes did not take place in a linear order; rather, they took place in an iterative and overlapping manner during the five phases. Table 8.1 sets out the processes that took place in each phase.

Because of the iterative nature of the phases, in this chapter I focus on the key activities that were undertaken and trace their development across the phases showing how power moved over time.

4.1 Translation of the CRPD

The Republic of Cyprus's official languages are Greek and Turkish, although since 1964 Cypriot legislation is only published in the Greek language (Constitution 1960, Art. 3(1); Interview with the Law

Table 8.1 The processes that took place during each phase of the journey towards ratification of the CRPD in Cyprus

The five phases identified:	Processes that took place within each Phase:
Phase 1: Cyprus and the CRPD 'meet' (March 2007 to February 2008)	• Translation of the CRPD
Phase 2: a translation and cooperation process (March 2008 to December 2008)	• Translation of the CRPD
Phase 3: a 'public dialogue' and screening process (January 2009 to January 2010)	• Screening of legislation for compatibility with the CRPD
Phase 4: moving towards incorporation (December 2009 to December 2010)	• Translation of the CRPD • Legislative process • Consultation process
Phase 5: incorporation and moving towards ratification (December 2010 to June 2011)	• Legislative process

Commission). The six official UN languages are Arabic, Chinese, English, French, Russian and Spanish. Therefore, translation from the English language version of the CRPD was required into the Greek language.

Following the signing of the CRPD by the Government, there was silence both in terms of activities and in the media. The Confederation saw the translation of the CRPD into the Greek language as of primary importance. Cyprus is a Member State of the European Union (EU), and although a Greek-language translation of the CRPD had been prepared by the European Commission the Confederation did not see it as adequate:

> [T]here was already a translation from the European Commission [but] with which we did not agree at all! It was rough, wrong, sloppy. It did not convey so strongly the letter of the Convention. (Interview with the POB)

Invoking the domestic Consultation Law (L. 143(I)/2006), the Confederation requested a number of times that it be involved in preparing a translation of the CRPD (CCOD 2007). However, there was no response from the Government, so the Confederation decided to prepare its own translation "because the months were passing by and nothing was happening" (Interview with the POB).

Subsequently, the Confederation's equivalent DPO in Greece, the Greek Confederation of Persons with Disabilities (Greek Confederation) and the Cypriot Confederation were in contact. The two DPOs decided to join forces concerning the CRPD's translation "… so that a unitary and uniform translation in the Greek language could be achieved …" (CCOD 2007, p. 2) and a Transnational Translation Cooperation Process (TTCP) was established. The (Cypriot) Confederation, now also involved in the TTCP, again tried to engage the Ministry of Labour in the process but failed to obtain a response. However, a change of Government in 2008 led to more involvement in the process by the Ministry of Labour and to a more collaborative approach to the translation of the CRPD. The Confederation wrote to the Minister of Labour confirming the TTCP, repeating its request "for participation and substantive cooperation … with the Ministry of Labour …" in the translation process; and also suggested the Ministry and Confederation "cooperate on the translation of the OP-CRPD" and invoked the Consultation Law (CCOD 2008b, p. 2). In contrast to the Confederation's previous requests (in Phase 1), the (new) Minister of Labour responded positively. The Minister agreed to the TTCP and affirmed that the Confederation should "participate actively in this process" (MLSI 2008, p. 1). In turn, the Ministry of Labour and the Confederation cooperated jointly on the translation of the CRPD through reciprocal correspondence. This involved the translation of certain words, terms and expressions from the English language text into the Greek language (CCOD 2008a, b, c, d; MLSI 2008). By the end of 2008, a Greek translation of the text of the CRPD (and its Optional Protocol (OP-CRPD 2006)), had been produced with the Ministry's involvement (CCOD 2008d). The Confederation considered the translation process complete and was satisfied with the cooperation it had shared with the Ministry of Labour in 2008 as it considered it had been 'allowed' to be directly involved (Phase 2) (CCOD 2008d; Interviews with the Confederation).

However, in Phase 4 of the ratification process, the translation of the CRPD again became an issue as the Law Commission became involved in the ratification process because it had competency for the final translation. In undertaking this new translation, the previous Greek translation of the CRPD was used as a basis. During this 'new' translation process, the Law Commission distinguished between what it considered and described as 'technical/disability' terms, which related specifically to persons with disabilities, and 'legal' terms, which it saw as falling within its competence and responsibility. It also consulted the Ministry of Labour, and through it but indirectly, the Confederation, on what it considered to be 'technical/disability' terms, about which it was unsure. The Law Commission did not, however, consult on 'legal' terms, which it saw as its mandate. It is noted that it was the Law Commission that made decisions about which terms were to be categorised as 'legal' and which as 'technical/disability' terms. This led to some significant changes from the earlier translations.

One categorisation issue concerned the concept of 'legal capacity', a concept which is central to the CRPD as it obligates States to recognise that all persons with disabilities are equal before the law, that they enjoy legal capacity on an equal basis with others, and to take appropriate measures to ensure access to support that people with disabilities may need in exercising their legal capacity (2006, Art. 12). The CRPD is associated with a radical 'new paradigm' approach to legal capacity, which the CRPD Committee (2014) refers to as one of 'universal legal capacity', which admits of no exceptions or limitations based directly or indirectly on a person's disability. This new paradigm of legal capacity radically departs from traditional and prevailing approaches to legal capacity (Series and Nilsson 2018). However, this new understanding of legal capacity was not familiar to the Law Commission. Accordingly, the Law Commission categorised the term as 'legal' and finalised its definition in a different and narrower way to its meaning in the CRPD:

> Capacity to contract and convey … this is … an example of a legal term for which we would not accept an intervention let's say on their part [that is, the Department of Social Inclusion and the Confederation]. (Interview with the Law Commission)

The categorisation of terms in the CRPD text also had the implication that the Ministry of Labour, its Department of Social Inclusion and the CCOD, were consulted and were listened to in relation to some terms in the translation process but not to others.

This division of terms into two categories is in contrast with the CRPD that tries to do away with such divisions. Rather, the CRPD tries to ensure that areas historically dealt with separately, are dealt with in a more holistic approach and situated within the social model of disability (CDLP Undated). Further, the division of terms had significant implications in relation to who was able to exercise power over the final translation of particular terms in the CRPD into the Greek language, including which bodies were involved in this process. Power over the final Greek CRPD translation lay with the Law Commission.

4.2 Consultation Process

The OHCHR report (2009) emphasises the importance of States engaging DPOs in adequate consultation during the ratification process, basing its arguments on Article 4(3) CRPD (2006). However, it was not until late 2008, that is, a year and a half into the ratification process, that the Ministry of Labour called a meeting of the Pan-Cyprian Council for Persons with Disabilities (PCPD) (L. 127(I)/2000, Art. 10(2); PIO 2008). The content of the CRPD was not the focus of the meeting, nor was there discussion on the CRPD's translation process (PIO 2008). It is noteworthy that no prior DPO consultation had taken place and that this was the first time all PCPD members were directly informed about the CRPD and that Cyprus had become a signatory 19 months earlier.

This meeting was the first direct opportunity for disability stakeholders to ask questions about the CRPD. Although the PCPD audience only included representatives from governmental departments, the Confederation, trade union and employers' organisations, the Ministry of Labour considered this meeting to be an avenue through which "society at large" was informed about the CRPD (DSIPD 2010; Interview with the DSIPD). During the PCPD meeting, it was decided that a 'technical committee' would be established for the purpose of "scheduling the necessary requirements for [the] ratification of the Convention" (PIO 2008, par 6). However, this proposed committee did not materialise.

Although the evidence does not show that PCPD members were consulted on the ratification process during this meeting (DSIPD 2010;

Interview with the Employers and Industrialists Federation); nevertheless, this meeting was included in the list of activities considered by the Ministry of Labour and its Department of Social Inclusion to have comprised an "Official consultation" (DSIPD 2010, p. 6). The processes of consultation with DPOs and other stakeholders in the ratification of the CRPD were therefore scant, tokenistic and did not create meaningful opportunities for participation by DPOs and society at large. This is particularly noteworthy in view of the fact that Cyprus had already given formal recognition to the Confederation, and had established the Council, for the purposes of consulting with persons with disabilities. It shows that the creation of formal structures for consultation alone are inadequate to truly embed the spirit of the mantra 'Nothing About Us Without Us!', if the governmental will is not there.

4.3 Screening of Domestic Legislation

The OHCHR report (2009) reminds States that they should carry out a screening process of domestic legislation and policies for compliance with the CRPD and should consult DPOs in this process. This is an important opportunity for persons with disabilities and their DPOs to highlight areas of concern and seek commitments from their Government to remedy domestic legislation and/or policies of concern.

In order to carry out the screening process, the Department of Social Inclusion consulted all governmental and public bodies, including ministries, services, departments, semi-governmental organisations, and municipalities through the means of a circular, which requested them to assess their legislative and/or administrative frameworks against the CRPD's provisions (DSIPD 2009; Interview with the Office of the Ombudsperson). The circular comprised:

1. A one-page summary of the human rights enshrined in the CRPD, in the Greek language
2. Texts of the CRPD (and OP-CRPD) in the original English versions with Greek-language translations

3. A short, four-question questionnaire regarding the compatibility of domestic legislation and regulations with the CRPD, and implications perceived to flow from the CRPD's implementation[2] (DSIPD 2009, 2010; Interviews with the DSIPD, MLSI and Office of the Ombudsperson)

The circular did not include an introduction to the CRPD and made no mention of the CRPD's values and principles, including no mention of its participatory provisions. The circular's aim was two-fold. First, to inform State bodies about the CRPD; and second, to seek their opinions as to the compatibility of domestic legislation with the CRPD's provisions, and the implications of the implementation of the Convention (DSIPD 2010).

The Department of Social Inclusion examined the 40 responses it received from "the main … ministries and departments which handle disability matters" and using these it assessed whether existing legislation and regulations conflicted with the CRPD (Interview with the DSIPD). The findings of the screening process were not made publicly available nor was access to the information collected granted upon request, although some of the findings were made available through various sources (HLGD 2009; DSIPD 2010; DOTCOM 2014). Significantly, the Department's overall main finding was "that there was no conflict" between domestic Cypriot law and the CRPD (Interview with the DSIPD) and "… that generally, we were, not, [far] away from the requirements … the Convention placed on us" (Interview with the MLSI). There was, however, acknowledgment that some amendments were required in the area of legal capacity legislation. The screening process resulted in confirming to the Department of Social Inclusion, the Ministry of Labour and the Cypriot Government that there was no conflict between Cypriot law and the CRPD. The findings were understood to indicate that Cyprus could proceed to ratification. It is also

[2] The questionnaire asked the recipients to assess the extent to which the legislative and/or administrative framework they worked within "related … to matters of persons with disabilities" (Interview with the Office of the Ombudsperson); the extent to which the framework complied with the CRPD's provisions; and their "opinion[s] about the implications of the application of the Convention", such as to legislative amendments (Interview with the DSIPD).

noted that evidence suggests this was the first time a screening process had taken place as part of a ratification process for an international UN human rights law convention in Cyprus (Trimikliniotis and Demetriou 2008).

In view of Article 4(3) (CRPD 2006) and the OHCHR report (2009), it is significant to note that DPOs were not consulted in the screening process.[3] It is also significant to note that the Confederation did not object to the exclusion of DPOs from the screening process but it did object to the Department of Social Inclusion undertaking a screening process. This was because the Confederation saw the screening process as unnecessary, as once ratified the CRPD would prevail over domestic legislation.[4] The Confederation was also concerned that the Government was trying to delay ratification because of concerns about the possible financial costs of its implementation—as this was during the financial crisis (CCOD 2009; Interview with the Confederation). However, participation in the screening process would have given DPOs and others the opportunity to seek commitments to reforms of problematic legislation and policies. The lack of transparency surrounding the screening process meant that opportunities were missed for DPOs to challenge the Government on areas where they felt that Cypriot legislation and policies were not compliant with the CRPD.

During Phase 3, the Confederation had grown increasingly concerned over the delay in the ratification process because by the end of Phase 2 it had understood that the translation process was complete and that the Ministry could move to submitting the CRPD to the legislature (CCOD 2008b, 2009; Interview with the Confederation).

4.4 Legislative Process

In accordance with Cypriot law, in order for an international human rights convention to be ratified at the international level, it must first be

[3] Although the circular was sent to governmental bodies, it was not sent to the State's 'social partners', including the Confederation; nor was it sent to any other disability stakeholders or DPOs.

[4] Cyprus has a Mixed Legal System and its relationship to international law 'sits' closer to the Monist doctrine.

incorporated into the Cypriot legal system (Cypriot Constitution 1960, Art. 169(2)). The task of drafting the incorporation Bill had been assigned by the Ministry of Labour to the Department of Social Inclusion (Interviews with the DSIPD and MLSI). Following from lobbying by DPOs and disability stakeholders about the slow rate of progress towards ratification of the CRPD, the Parliamentary Committee on Human Rights (Committee/PCHR) met in 2010 to discuss the need for the ratification of the CRPD and OP-CRPD (POB 2010). In addition to PCHR Parliamentarians, representatives from the Ministry of Labour and its Department of Social Inclusion and a disability stakeholder (the Committee for the Protection of Mentally Retarded Persons (CPMRP)) as well as the Confederation and one of its DPO members, the POB, attended the Committee meeting. The explicit rationale for inviting these particular disability stakeholders to the meeting is not known. However, evidence suggests that the CPMRP and POB were invited because they had lobbied members of the PCHR, in particular, the PCHR's president. They had done so as they were concerned about the delay in, and need for, the CRPD's ratification (POB 2010).

The CRPD's content was not discussed at the meeting, rather the meeting focused on the need to ratify the CRPD. The result of this meeting was that PCHR Parliamentarians exercised pressure on the Ministry of Labour and its Department of Social Inclusion to proceed to the ratification of the CRPD by submitting questions to the Ministry of Labour before the House of Representatives (Interview with Parliamentarian).

The ratification of the CRPD finally occurred when the instrument of ratification was deposited with the UN Secretary-General in New York on 27 June 2011. This was four years after Cyprus had signed the CRPD (L. 8(III)/2011).

5 Conclusion

The ratification process for the CRPD in Cyprus was a long, complex and iterative journey and reveals that the cultural understanding of the concept of 'consultation' in the Cypriot context differed to the cultural understanding of 'consultation' conceptualised in the CRPD and the OHCHR report. The 'social partner' status of the Confederation gave it legal legitimacy to be consulted in the ratification process for the CRPD as it was a matter that directly concerned persons with disabilities (L. 143(I)/2006, Art. 3(2)); however, the same legislation did not enable other non-Confederation DPO members and civil society organisations to be involved.

During the journey to ratification, the Confederation used the Consultation Law to lobby the Government to proceed with the ratification of the CRPD. For example, in relation to the translation of the CRPD, the failure of the Government to take action led not only to the Confederation taking the initiative but it also led to a collaboration with a Greek DPO. However, as the ratification process moved forward and the governmental bodies became more active, the power shifted to the Government and away from the Confederation. This was particularly the case regarding the final translation of the CRPD where the Law Commission had the final determination as to the terminology in the Greek-translated text of the CRPD, with implications as to how it would be implemented.

The active involvement of, and close consultation with, persons with disabilities and their DPOs, as set out in the CRPD (2006, Art. 4(3)) and highlighted in the OHCHR report (2009), in particular, that States should carry out a screening process of their legislation and policies for compliance with the CRPD and engage in consultation with DPOs during their ratification processes, was not practised in later processes of the ratification for the CRPD as the Confederation and other DPOs were excluded from the screening process and there was only minimal involvement in the 'public dialogue' consultation process.

However, within the Cypriot historical context of (little to no) consultation with DPOs, the Confederation was largely satisfied with its involvement in the ratification process for the CRPD, which it saw in positive contrast to previous efforts to be consulted:

> If only everything operated like the [things] moved for the Convention. If [only] everything [the Confederation] wanted to be consulted on moved as easily as with the Convention. (Interview with the Confederation)

Nevertheless, this satisfaction was not unanimous within the Disability Movement. A Confederation member DPO considered that the

Confederation's involvement had been 'passive' during the ratification process, except for its involvement in the translation process (Interview with the POB). This reveals an understanding of 'consultation' and 'active involvement' closer to that conceptualised in the CRPD.

Overall, in spite of these challenges during Cyprus's CRPD ratification journey, this was the first time the State had undertaken a screening process of its domestic legislation for compliance with a convention before ratifying it. Further, there was some change regarding the practice of consultation, in that there was explicit involvement of the Confederation in the ratification process as per the Consultation Law.

The experience of the ratification process for the CRPD in Cyprus reveals the complexity of introducing the concept of 'consultation' and 'active involvement' in the CRPD into domestic contexts, particularly when a State, such as Cyprus, did not historically have a developed culture of consultation with DPOs (although it had a well-developed culture of 'social dialogue' with trade unions and employers' organisations (Yannakourou and Soumeli 2004)). Further, the Government viewed the concept of 'disability' from within a welfare discourse, and persons were not fully cognisant of the social model of disability or of the disability human rights discourse that underpins the CRPD. Nevertheless, this chapter has shown how persons with disabilities and their DPOs, through their lobbying of the Cypriot Government, achieved the ratification of the CRPD and for the Confederation to be consulted in some of the ratification processes, such as the translation of the CRPD into the Greek language.

References

Achiron, M. (2007). *From exclusion to equality realizing the rights of persons with disabilities handbook for parliamentarians on the convention on the rights of persons with disabilities and its optional protocol.* Geneva: Secretariat for the Convention on the Rights of Persons with Disabilities, United Nations Department of Economic and Social Affairs, Office of the United Nations High Commissioner for Human Rights, and Inter-Parliamentary Union.

CCOD (Cypriot Confederation of Organisations of the Disabled). (2007, May 18). *Correspondence.* Unpublished.

CCOD (Cypriot Confederation of Organisations of the Disabled). (2008a, March 6). *Correspondence*. Unpublished.

CCOD (Cypriot Confederation of Organisations of the Disabled). (2008b, May 20). *Correspondence*. Unpublished.

CCOD (Cypriot Confederation of Organisations of the Disabled). (2008c, September 29). *Correspondence*. Unpublished.

CCOD (Cypriot Confederation of Organisations of the Disabled). (2008d, December 22). *Correspondence*. Unpublished.

CCOD (Cypriot Confederation of Organisations of the Disabled). (2009, September 30) *Correspondence*. Unpublished.

CDLP (Centre for Disability Law and Policy Galway). (Undated). *Submission on legal capacity the oireachtas committee on justice, defence and equality* (pp. 1–99). CDLP. Retrieved from http://www.nuigalway.ie/cdlp/documents/cdlp_submission_on_legal_capacity_the_oireachtas_committee_on_justice_defence_and_equality_.pdf.

Charlton, J. (2000). *Nothing about us without us disability oppression and empowerment*. Berkeley, CA: University of California Press.

CRPD Committee (Committee on the Rights of Persons with Disabilities), General comment No 1. (2014, May 19). *Article 12: Equal recognition before the law*. CRPD/C/GC/1, 2014.

CRPD Committee (Committee on the Rights of Persons with Disabilities), General comment No. 7. (2018, November 9). *On the participation of persons with disabilities, including children with disabilities, through their representative organizations, in the implementation and monitoring of the convention*. CRPD/C/GC/7, 2018.

Constitution (The Constitution of the Republic of Cyprus). (1960). Ratified on 16 August 1960.

CRPD (United Nations Convention on the Rights of Persons with Disabilities). (2006). *Adopted in 2006 by the United Nations general assembly*.

DOTCOM. (2014). *DOTCOM: The disability online tool of the commission*. ANED (Academic Network of European Disability Experts). Retrieved from http://www.disability-europe.net/dotcom.

DSIPD (Department of Social Inclusion for Persons with Disabilities). (2009) Circular. *Department for social inclusion of persons with disabilities*. Unpublished.

DSIPD (Department for Social Inclusion of Persons with Disabilities). (2010, December). *Impact assessment. Department for social inclusion of persons with disabilities*. Unpublished.

DSIPD (Department for Social Inclusion of Persons with Disabilities). (2015). *The UN convention on the rights of persons with disabilities*.

Retrieved from http://www.mlsi.gov.cy/mlsi/dsid/dsid.nsf/dsipd08_gr/dsipd08_gr?OpenDocument.

Faustmann, H. (1999). *Divide and quit? The history of British colonial rule in Cyprus 1878–1960 including a special survey of the transitional period February 1959–August 1960*. Mannheim: MATEO.

HLGD (High Level Group on Disability). (2009). *Second disability high level group report on implementation of the UN convention on the rights of persons with disabilities*. European Commission High Level Group on Disability.

Kakoullis, E. (2015). *A shift from welfare to rights: A case study of the ratification process for the convention on the rights of persons with disabilities in Cyprus*. Unpublished PhD thesis, University of Bristol.

Kallehauge, H. (2009). General themes relevant to the implementation of the UN disability convention into domestic law: Who is responsible for the implementation and how should it be performed? In G. Quinn & O. M. Arnadottir (Eds.), *The UN convention on the rights of persons with disabilities: European and Scandinavian perspectives*. Leiden: Martinus Nijhoff Publishers.

Ker-Lindsay, J. (2011). *The Cyprus problem what everyone needs to know*. Oxford: Oxford University Press.

Ker-Lindsay, J., & Faustmann, H. (2008). *The government and politics of Cyprus*. Bern: Verlag Peter Lang.

L. 127(I)/2000 'The persons with disabilities law of 2000' (my translation). Nicosia: Official Gazette of the Republic of Cyprus.

L. 143(I)/2006 'The consultation process of state and other services on matters that concern persons with a disability law of 2006' (my translation). Nicosia: Official Gazette of the Republic of Cyprus.

L. 8(III)/2011 'The convention for the rights of persons with disabilities and related matters (ratification) law of 2011' (my translation). Nicosia: Official Gazette of the Republic of Cyprus.

MLSI (Ministry of Labour and Social Insurance). (2008, July 18) *Correspondence*. Unpublished.

OHCHR (Office of the United Nations High Commissioner for Human Rights) (2009, January 26). Thematic study by the office of the united nations high commissioner for human rights on enhancing awareness and understanding of the convention on the rights of persons with disabilities (pp. 1–21). A/HRC/10/48.

Peters, S., Gabel, S., & Symeonidou, S. (2009). Resistance, transformation and the politics of hope: Imagining a way forward for the disabled people's movement. *Disability & Society, 24*, 543–556.

PIO (The Press and Information Office). (2008). Press release 07 November. Retrieved from http://www.pio.gov.cy/moi/pio/pio.nsf/All/7F820C0FCA7D0B91C22574FA00597F61?OpenDocument&highlight=07/11/2008

POB (Pan-Cyprian Organisation of the Blind). (2010, November 9). *The immediate need to ratify the United Nations Convention on the Rights of Persons with Disabilities and the relevant Optional Protocol.* My translation, Unpublished.

Poyiatzi, A., Christou, E., & Phitiaka, H. (2012, June 8–9). Financial crisis and persons with a disability in Cyprus. *12th Conference of the Cypriot Education Company Proceedings, 303*, 351–361. Retrieved from http://www.pek.org.cy/Proceedings_2012/papers/eniaia_ekpaidefsi/Poyiatzi_Christou_Phtiaka.pdf.

Series, L., & Nilsson, A. (2018). Article 12: Equal recognition before the law. In I. Bantekas, M. Stein, & D. Anastasiou (Eds.), *Commentary on UN convention on the rights of persons with disabilities*. Oxford: Oxford University Press.

Stein, M. A., & Lord, J. E. (2009). Monitoring the convention on the rights of persons with disabilities: Innovations, lost opportunities, and future potential. *Human Rights Quarterly, 32*, 689–728.

Symeonidou, S. (2005). *Understanding and theorising disability and disability politics: The case of the Cypriot disability movement.* Unpublished, Ph.D. thesis, University of Cambridge.

Symeonidou, S. (2009a). Trapped in our past: The Price we pay for our cultural disability inheritance. *International Journal of Inclusive Education, 13*, 565–579.

Symeonidou, S. (2009b). The experience of disability activism through the development of the disability movement: How do disabled activists find their way in politics? *Scandinavian Journal of Disability Research, 11*, 17–34.

ToE (Treaty of Establishment of the Republic of Cyprus). (1960). Signed in Nicosia on 16 August 1960.

Trimikliniotis, N., & Demetriou, C. (2008). Evaluating the anti-discrimination law in the Republic of Cyprus: A critical reflection. *The Cyprus Review, 20*, 79–116.

VCLT (Vienna Convention on the Law of Treaties). (1969). *Adopted in 1969 by the United Nations Conference on the Law of Treaties.*

Yannakourou, S., & Soumeli, E. (2004). *The evolving structure of Collective Bargaining in Europe 1990–2004.* Research Project Co-financed by the European Commission and the University of Florence (VS/2003/0219-SI2.359910) National Report Greece and Cyprus. Retrieved from http://adapt.it/adapt-indice-a-z/wp-content/uploads/2014/08/matina_yannakourou.pdf.

9

A Janus-Faced Affair: Sri Lanka's Ratification of the CRPD

Dinesha Samararatne

1 Introduction

This chapter examines the ratification of the United Nations (UN) Convention on the Rights of Persons with Disabilities (CRPD 2006) by Sri Lanka within the broader political and legal context of an emerging disability rights discourse in the country. Sri Lanka signed the CRPD in 2007 when the treaty was declared open for signature. It then ratified it nine years later in February 2016. It is difficult to identify any significant domestic political or legal development that led to the CRPD's ratification by Sri Lanka. Since ratification, minimal ground has been gained in the advancement of the rights of persons with disabilities to date. Even the minimal protection afforded by the relevant laws, regulations and policies largely remains ineffective, with a welfare approach dominating the State services for persons with disabilities. In the absence of concrete measures for improving respect for rights of persons with disabilities or

D. Samararatne (✉)
Faculty of Law, University of Colombo, Colombo, Sri Lanka
e-mail: d.samararatne@unimelb.edu.au

E. J. Kakoullis, K. Johnson (eds.), *Recognising Human Rights in Different Cultural Contexts*, https://doi.org/10.1007/978-981-15-0786-1_9

plans for the adoption of such measures, the reasons for Sri Lanka's initial signing of the CRPD and its subsequent ratification seem unclear. However, this ratification seems to have had a discernible and progressive impact on civil society and on advocacy for the rights of persons with disabilities. It has influenced the development of a 'rights-based approach' to disability among some stakeholders. It has also resulted in greater recognition of specific needs of persons with disabilities in the post-war island-wide consultative processes, with regard to constitutional reform and with regard to consultations for the design of mechanisms for reconciliation. Sri Lanka's experience suggests that even if ratification of the CRPD does not bring about immediate results in terms of impact on State conduct, it does contribute to the mobilisation of and advocacy for disability rights on the ground.

2 Disability Rights in Sri Lanka

Respect for the human rights of persons with disabilities in Sri Lanka is significantly weak (Department of State 2017; Jiffry and Perera 2017). The discourse on rights of persons with disabilities is a latecomer to the older and more vibrant general discourse on human rights. Sri Lanka occupies a unique place with regard to human rights and human development. Although Sri Lanka is ranked as a lower middle-income country by the World Bank (World Bank 2017), its Human Development Index is 0.766, placing Sri Lanka in the high human development category (UNDP 2016). It is evident that significant progress has been achieved at the macro-level in the economy, as well as in overall human flourishing. On the other hand, Sri Lanka has experienced two youth insurrections and an approximately 30-year-long internal armed conflict. These events have resulted in serious human rights violations with minimal accountability of perpetrators. The national indicators veil increasing inequalities in human development, as well as socio-political factors that function as barriers preventing communities from enjoying their human rights. The experiences of violence have resulted in a heavy focus on civil and political rights among civil society organisations and activists over the years. In comparison, the rights of persons with disabilities have received little, if any, attention in mainstream human rights activism or advocacy.

As per a survey carried out in 2012, 8.7% of Sri Lankans are persons with disabilities (Department of Census and Statistics 2012). More women in Sri Lanka have disabilities—57%, as opposed to men—43% (Department of Census and Statistics 2012). While Sri Lanka's literacy is 96%, only 70.9% of children with disabilities in the 5–14-year age group have been enrolled at school (Law and Society Trust 2016). Moreover, only 2.6% of university students are persons with disabilities (Law and Society Trust 2016). Access to education, therefore, is severely limited for persons with disabilities in a country in which general literacy and school enrolment levels are on par with developed countries. As per a submission made to the UN Office of the High Commissioner for Human Rights (OHCHR) by a civil society organisation in 2016, only 41.1% of persons with disabilities are employed and of that percentage approximately only 24% are women (Law and Society Trust 2016). These statistics point to the lack of enjoyment of human rights by persons with disabilities in the country.

The lack of progress that is evident through the above given statistics is matched by the lived experiences of persons with disabilities. For instance, in an interview reported in the press, a visually impaired person notes that "When traffic lights are imported to the country, there is an audible traffic system attached. Even certain buses have these systems. But they have been disabled in some places" (Ismail 2016). In the same news report, it is noted by a Disability Inclusion Specialist that currently the procedure for casting votes marginalises persons with disabilities. He observes for instance that,

> When I go to vote, I have to produce several documents at the polling station and get a person I trust to vote on my behalf. If I don't have the documents, … someone else at the polling station can vote on behalf of me. This isn't me voting. How am I assured that my vote is cast? (Ismail 2016)

Further, another prominent disability rights activist notes that "Speaking from my own personal experience, I can attest that there are no wheelchair-accessible toilets in government hospitals" (Ismail 2016). These personal accounts affirm the statistical assessment of the lack of respect for the right to equality of persons with disabilities.

Within the general community of persons with disabilities, those who are war-affected can be identified as a distinctive sub-category. War-affected persons with disabilities are concerned that they are marginalised in the post-war reconstruction and reconciliation processes (Bombi 2010). The *Ranaviru Seva* (Services for War Heroes) Authority is mandated to provide for members of the armed forces with disabilities, and to ensure that they are provided with the required medical and rehabilitation services (RSAA 1999). However, according to the submissions made to the Consultation Task Force on Reconciliation Mechanisms (CTFRM), soldiers with disabilities face difficulties in accessing the benefits that they are entitled to and some are dissatisfied with the current system for computation of compensation (CTFRM 2016).

The war-affected civilian population and ex-combatants with disabilities are reliant on the existing general services of the Ministry of Social Empowerment and Welfare. War-affected persons with disabilities have specific and urgent needs. These include medical and rehabilitation support, accountability for human rights violations, reparations and inclusion in reconstruction initiatives. Research carried out among war-affected persons with disabilities suggests that most post-armed war responses, programmes and policy developments do not recognise the specific concerns and issues of this category of persons (Samararatne and Soldatic 2018). Consequently, their needs continue to be met mostly through civil society interventions and collective mobilisation (Kandasamy et al. 2017). Furthermore, persons with disabilities have been marginalised in transitional justice processes and peace-building efforts as well as in general initiatives for strengthening the rule of law in the country. Whether it be the national policy for reconciliation (ONUR 2017), the UN Human Rights Council resolutions with regard to reconciliation (UNHRC 2015) in Sri Lanka or even civil society lobbying on these issues, disability has only been a peripheral concern. The report by the Consultation Task Force on Reconciliation Mechanisms (CTFRM 2016) is an exception to this general lack of sensitivity to disability issues, and its observations and recommendations are discussed more fully in the next section of this chapter.

The key factors that contribute to the above situation include a lack of respect for human rights of persons with disabilities in the State architecture for disability, which shapes a welfare- and charity-based approach to disability (Campbell 2009). Since the inception of welfare services, disability has been assigned exclusively to the Ministry of Social Empowerment and Welfare. Regardless of the nature of the issue, such as housing, health or children, if it relates to a person with a disability, only the Ministry of Social Empowerment and Welfare is mandated to address it. Over almost seven decades, this institutional architecture has established the view that disability has to be dealt with exclusively, and as a matter of welfare. All the services that are provided to persons with disabilities by the State are provided on that basis and are therefore dependent on the reasonable exercise of administrative discretion (Samararatne and Soldatic 2015). The Ministry offers a monthly allowance, an allowance for housing and an allowance for purchasing medicines.[1] These services though offered universally are not actually available to everyone with a disability. A recent study undertaken among 23 war-affected women with disabilities points to the lack of access to welfare services among these women regardless of their ethnicity (Samararatne et al. 2018). Restrictions by the Government on the number of grants available per administrative district, and other administrative regulations and practices often prevent many persons with disabilities from availing themselves of these services (Samararatne et al. 2018). Eligibility for these services is determined according to stipulated criteria and for a limited number of persons (Samararatne and Soldatic 2015). Research has shown that information regarding these services and accompanying restrictions is scarce. Moreover, these services are not always directly accessible to persons with disabilities, rather, they are often dependent on third parties when accessing these services. Frequently, there are delays in obtaining approvals, which in turn cause hardship and uncertainty to the recipients. Due to these factors, not all persons with disabilities are able to access these welfare services. For instance, in a preliminary identification survey on disability and women's vulnerabilities carried out in the Kilinochchi District of the Northern Province, only 32.2% were recipients of a finan-

[1] See, for instance, Circular No 1/3/2015/NSPD issued by the Ministry of Social Empowerment and Welfare on 27 April 2015; see also services provided by the Ministry of Social Empowerment and Welfare for persons with disabilities available at www.socialmwelfare.gov.lk.

cial grant scheme for low-income families (in Sinhalese: '*Samurdhi*'), while only 22.9% were recipients of a Public Assistance Monthly Allowance (PAMA) (Ministry of Health 2017).

The Sri Lankan Constitution guarantees the right to equality (8th Parliament of Sri Lanka 1978, Art. 12[1]). Although the grounds of discrimination are listed in a non-exhaustive manner, 'disability' is not listed as a prohibited ground (8th Parliament of Sri Lanka 1978, Art. 12[2]). The only mention of 'disabled persons' is with reference to 'special measures' that may be adopted as an exception to the right to equality (8th Parliament of Sri Lanka 1978, Art. 12[4]). These constitutional guarantees have not resulted in the actual improvement of the quality of life of persons with disabilities. Even when a disability rights activist filed a fundamental rights petition claiming a violation of his right to equality due to the non-implementation of the accessibility regulations, the Supreme Court made no reference to the constitutional right to equality or to the prohibition on non-discrimination in its order (*Dr. Ajith C.S. Perera v. Attorney General and Others* [2009] S.C. (FR) NO. 221/2009). Although the Court did order the full implementation of the accessibility regulations, this order has not been complied with. The non-adoption of a rights-based approach by the judiciary in this order is problematic and compounds the general lack of recognition for the rights of persons with disabilities in legislation and policy.

3 CRPD Ratification

Sri Lanka made voluntary pledges in the UN Universal Periodic Review (UPR) process in 2008 and in 2013 to ratify the CRPD, while the actual ratification only took place in 2016 (UNHRC 2017b). A few months after ratifying the CRPD, the Government of Sri Lanka went on to ratify the only other major human rights law treaty that it had not signed, that is, the UN International Convention for the Protection of All Persons from Enforced Disappearance (ICPPED 2006).[2]

[2] Ratified on 25 May 2016 by Sri Lanka.

At the first Conference of States Parties to the CRPD that Sri Lanka attended, its representative stated that the reason for the long delay in ratifying the treaty was "to ensure that … the necessary legislative and administrative framework to give full effect" to the obligations under the treaty were in place (UN 2016). However, between 2007 and 2016, there were no specific reforms or developments in terms of law reform or institutional redesign for the improvement of the rights of persons with disabilities. The National Action Plan for Disability of 2013 (Action Plan) (Ministry of Social Services and Ministry of Health 2013) was perhaps the only significant development with regard to disability rights, pre-ratification. This Action Plan mapped out actions to be taken by the State in seven thematic areas, namely empowerment, health and rehabilitation, education, work and employment, mainstreaming and enabling environments, data and research, and social and institutional cohesion. This Action Plan however remains a paper commitment with minimal impact on the ground (Ministry of Social Services and Ministry of Health 2013). Neither the signing nor the ratification of the CRPD seem to have any correlation with any of the commitments or concrete measures taken by the Government of Sri Lanka with regard to disability rights.

Also since ratification, no significant reforms or developments have yet taken place with regard to improving respect for the rights of persons with disabilities. Before the CRPD there were some discussions regarding the adoption of new legislation on disability rights, this was the Protection of the Rights of Persons with Disabilities Act of 1996 (PRPDA 1996). This is the primary legislation that is specific to persons with disabilities in Sri Lanka. It establishes the National Council for Persons with Disabilities (NCPD). This Council has the mandate to "ensure the promotion, advancement and protection of the rights of persons with disabilities" (PRPDA 1996, s. 12). However, it recognises only two rights: the right to be free from discrimination in recruitment or in admission to an educational institution, and accessibility in the built environment (PRPDA 1996, s.23). As discussed in the previous section in this chapter, these rights have not been implemented effectively. Over the last few years, disability rights activists have lobbied for new legislation that would recognise a broader range of disability rights and provide an effective mechanism for their enforcement. Drafts of bills have been proposed and discussed, but with little progress in terms of reaching a consensus on the mechanism for enforcement. There is significant disagreement as to the new institutional mechanism that should be introduced for the monitoring, protection and promotion of the CRPD. As a result, the drafting process has not moved forward.

One exception to this general lack of progress in the advancement of the rights of persons with disabilities during the post-ratification period was the budget proposals for 2018. For the first time in Sri Lanka's history, the guidelines issued by the Department of National Budget (2017) for preparing estimates for 2018 included the empowerment of 'Differently Abled People'. The guidelines refer to the Action Plan (Ministry of Social Services and Ministry of Health 2013) and note that "all spending agencies are required to identify focus areas and relevant activities on empowering the differently abled community and mobilising them as an equally useful segment of the society" (National Budget Department 2017, para 3.1). The other two items referred to in the guidelines were the 'Sustainable Development Goals' and 'Gender Response Budgeting'. These guidelines are significant in that they suggest that the Government is responding positively to the call for mainstreaming disability and is making a commitment by way of budgetary allocations.

For the first time in Sri Lanka's post-war history, the budget proposals of 2018 gave due weight to national reconciliation and to social inclusion. Accordingly, the proposals included "the construction of a special home for differently abled women in the North" (Minister of Finance 2017, p. 265). It includes an 'Enterprise Sri Lanka Credit Scheme' for which the "differently abled" are to be eligible, and which will provide them with an interest subsidy of 15% extra (Minister of Finance 2017, p. 79). Furthermore, the proposals permit an additional 15% above the norm from the incentives and support for Small and Medium Enterprises if it is headed by "differently abled" persons (Minister of Finance 2017, p. 93). These proposals are indicative of a change of direction in Government policy to the subject of disability. The fiscal commitment to recognising persons with disabilities as a distinctive category and to providing special incentives for their business, as well as in post-war reconstruction efforts, will have a normative impact and provide the momentum that is much needed for the shift to a rights-based approach to disability.

It is evident that in terms of domestic legal enforcement, the ratification of the CRPD has had minimal impact on State behaviour. However, the collateral consequences among the non-State actors in the Sri Lankan experience have been qualitatively different (Hathaway 2007) and are discussed in the following section.

4 The CRPD and Civil Society Activism

The increased mobilisation of disability rights activists and greater visibility for disability rights are probably two positive outcomes from the ratification of the CRPD. Soon after the ratification of the CRPD, several civil society disability rights organisations and disability rights activists came together as the 'February 8th Movement', this being the date on which Sri Lanka ratified the CRPD. As per newspaper reports and press statements, one of the main goals of the Disability Movement is to lobby the Government for the establishment of a new high-level coordination and monitoring mechanism for disability rights and to push for the passage of suitable legislation for guaranteeing these rights (Nafeel 2016). The Disability Movement called for the mainstreaming of disability and for disability to cease to be an exclusive subject handled by the Ministry of Social Empowerment and Welfare (Nafeel 2016).

During the same time, several disability rights organisations collectively made submissions to the Public Representations Committee on Constitutional Reforms (PRC 2016). Detailed proposals were submitted by disability rights activists to the Committee including proposed constitutional provisions. In addition to proposing the inclusion of specific rights for persons with disabilities, such as the inclusion of disability as a prohibited ground of discrimination, it included a proposal for an independent disability rights commission (PRC 2016). These submissions were well-received by the Committee and were included in their recommendations to the Government (PRC 2016). The Report notes that persons with disabilities suffer from multiple forms of discrimination and recommends the recognition of several specific rights (PRC 2016). They include the right to equal opportunities, the right to dignity and autonomy and the right to be free from exploitation. The Committee recommended the establishment of a Disability Commission as an independent body that would supervise the enforcement of these rights (PRC 2016).

The visibility for disability rights increased with these interventions by civil society. The Ministry of Foreign Affairs convened for the first time, a drafting committee on the rights of persons with disabilities to contribute a specific section on disability to the National Action Plan for the Protection and Promotion of Human Rights 2017–2021 (Ministry of Foreign Affairs 2017). This action plan covered a wide range of disability rights including the right to autonomy, right to decent work, social protection, political and public participation, access to justice and freedom from violence.

The recommendations of the PRC were presented to the Constitutional Assembly that had been established in 2016 to draft a new constitution for Sri Lanka (PRC 2016). The Sub-Committee on Fundamental Rights appointed under the Steering Committee of this Assembly presented a draft Fundamental Rights chapter as its proposal to the Assembly (Sub-Committee on Fundamental Rights 2017). This draft includes a specific section on disability rights and recognises, among other rights, the right to dignity, accessibility rights and the right to information of persons with disability (Sub-Committee on Fundamental Rights 2017). This is the first time that the rights of persons with disabilities have been proposed for inclusion in a fundamental rights chapter in Sri Lanka's constitutional history.

In January 2016, another body was appointed to undertake consultations regarding reconciliation mechanisms, the Consultation Task Force on Reconciliation Mechanisms (CTFRM 2016). It carried out island-wide consultations during which several submissions relating to disability were received. The report of this Task Force documents these submissions and makes several recommendations to the Government with the purpose of addressing the human rights violations experienced by war-affected persons with disabilities (CTFRM 2016). For the first time since the end of the war in May 2009, this report documents in some detail the issues that are faced by war-affected persons with disabilities. The issues that were identified include issues related to accessibility in the built environment, as well as in systems and processes, a lack of opportunity to participate in initiatives for transitional justice, and the lack of psychosocial support to deal with the impact of disability. The report recognises the intersectionality of discrimination that is experienced by war-affected persons with disabilities (CTFRM 2016). Further, it identifies ex-combatants with disabilities as a specific category of persons who require targeted support and interventions. The report recommends that the computation of reparations takes due account of disability and the introduction of supportive structures for reconciliation that would be inclusive of persons with disabilities (CTFRM 2016). The Government has not taken any measures yet to implement the recommendations of the Task Force. Nevertheless, the report represents a significant milestone in the official recognition of the rights of war-affected persons with disabilities in Sri Lanka's post-war period.

The two consultation processes, the National Action Plan for the Protection and Promotion of Human Rights (Ministry of Foreign Affairs 2017) and the report of the Sub-Committee on Fundamental Rights (Sub-Committee on Fundamental Rights 2017), are instances of official and progressive recognition of the rights of persons with disabilities. These outcomes are a direct result of the mobilisation of disability rights activists and their advocacy. This period appears to mark the emergence of disability rights activism into the 'mainstream' of human rights advocacy among Sri Lankan civil society.

Sri Lanka's civil society activism gained momentum in the 1970s (Asian Development Bank 2013) and has played a key role in seeking greater respect for human rights since then. However, civil society organisations that work on disability rights have by and large been distinctive from other organisations that work in general on human rights concerns. Consequently, the rights of persons with disabilities have not been flagged with due weight among human rights activists and activism, while human rights issues related to the armed conflict and human rights issues related to governance have not been taken up by disability rights activists or organisations. This bifurcation has been to the disadvantage of civil society activism in Sri Lanka.

More recently however, two Colombo-based and long-standing non-governmental organisations (NGOs) have included disability rights in their work (ICES 2017; Law and Society Trust 2018). Several other regional organisations too have either included disability in their human rights work or begun to partner with disability rights organisations in working on the rights of persons with disabilities. In doing so these organisations have been able to bridge the gap between disability rights organisations and activists, and other activists and organisations working in human rights. The research and projects undertaken by these organisations have included rights of war-affected women with disabilities, constitutional or legal reform for the recognition of disability rights and engagement with the UN OHCHR on disability rights (Law and Society Trust 2018).

5 Impact of Human Rights Treaty Ratification in Sri Lanka's Legal System

Sri Lanka is a State Party to all of the major UN human rights law treaties and has not submitted any reservations to these.[3] Respective Governments have been diligent in their State reporting to these treaty bodies. However, the implementation of the recommendations made by respective UN human rights committees has been selective and has been primarily in the form of law reform, national action plans and programmatic design. The *à la carte* approach to fulfilling Sri Lanka's human rights obligations under multilateral treaties has led to inconsistencies in domestic law, including in the Constitution, in policy and in the implementation of programmes. The selective inclusion of six human rights in the domestic

[3] Convention Against Torture and Other Cruel Inhuman or Degrading Treatment or Punishment—03 January 1994, Optional Protocol of the Convention against Torture—05 December 2017; Convention for the Protection of All Persons from Enforced Disappearance—25 May 2016; Convention on the Elimination of All Forms of Discrimination against Women—05 October 1981; International Convention on the Elimination of All Forms of Racial Discrimination—18 February 1982; International Covenant on Economic, Social and Cultural Right—11 June 1980; International Convention on the Protection of the Rights of All Migrant Workers and Members of Their Families—11 March 1996; Convention on the Rights of the Child—12 July 1991; Optional Protocol to the Convention on the Rights of the Child on the Involvement of Children in Armed Conflict—08 September 2000; Optional Protocol to the Convention on the Rights of the Child on the Sale of Children, Child Prostitution and Child Pornography—22 September 2006; Convention on the Rights of Persons with Disabilities—08 February 2016.

International Covenant on Civil and Political Rights Act of 2007 (ICCPRA 2007) is a case in point.

This state of affairs can be partly explained by the 'dualist' nature of the Sri Lankan legal system. In the absence of specific constitutional provisions for the automatic inclusion of treaty obligations into the domestic law, Sri Lanka has been designated as 'dualist'.[4] Accordingly, legislation to incorporate treaties is deemed essential for the enforcement of treaties at the domestic level. The domestic ICCPR Act (2007) and the Convention Against Torture and Other Cruel, Inhuman or Degrading Treatment or Punishment Act of 1994 (CATA 1994) are two examples of such legislation. However, there are also a few instances in which judges have relied on Sri Lanka's international treaty obligations in the interpretation of constitutional and legislative provisions. The latest example of direct judicial incorporation of treaty law is the *Manohari Pelaketiya v. H. M. Gunesekera Secretary, Ministry of Education and Others* (SC/FR/No. 76/2012) in which the Supreme Court referred to the Convention for the Elimination of All Forms of Discrimination Against Women (CEDAW 1979) in holding that sexual harassment in the workplace is a violation of the right to equality (8th Parliament of Sri Lanka 1978, Art.12[1]). Another example is *Ceylon Tobacco Company PLC v. Minister of Health* (2012) CA 336/2012 (Writ), where the Court of Appeal relied on the Framework Convention on Tobacco in interpreting the *National Authority on Tobacco Control Act*. In comparison however, as discussed earlier, when a disability rights issue was petitioned, the Court did not refer to or acknowledge relevant international human rights law.

In general, the State continues to go through the rituals of state reporting and to engage actively in the UPR. Regarding disability, though voluntary pledges were made in the first cycle itself in 2008, the actual ratification only took place in 2016. The UPR State Report of 2017 deals with disability under a separate heading and several observations are made. For instance, the State declares that enabling legislation for the implementation of the CRPD is to be presented to the Cabinet by the end of September 2017 (UNHRC 2017b) and it refers to a website through which persons with disabilities can register and seek employ-

[4] See, for instance, the case of *Nallaratnam Singarasa v Attorney General* 2013.

ment opportunities. Furthermore, reference is made to the quota of 3% allocated to recruitment in the public service and the regulations mandating accessibility for all public buildings (UNHRC 2017a). However, as pointed out in the summary of stakeholder submissions and in several research studies, neither employment nor physical accessibility satisfies the standards laid down in these regulations (UNHRC 2017b). This view is further affirmed in the UN Compilation for the UPR in 2017 (UNHRC 2017c). Often these engagements at the international level translate into domestic efforts that are ad hoc and lacking in sustainability.

Sri Lanka is due to submit its State Report in May 2018 to the UN CRPD Committee and will be required to explain its progress or lack of progress regarding disability rights to the Committee. The opportunity for shadow reporting however is bound to provide further momentum to the civil society activism that seems to have been generated through the state ratification of the CRPD.

6 Human Rights Treaties' Impact on the Framing of Freedoms

The 'positivist' explanation or justification for a human rights treaty regime is twofold. First, it is a method of crystallising consensus at the level of the international community on universally recognised human rights (Alston and Goodman 2013). Second, it is presented as an effective method of holding a State accountable at the international level for the way in which it respects its obligations under the treaty (Alston and Goodman 2013). A rational view of this process assumes that States give due consideration to the treaty provisions and ratify a treaty only when it is politically committed to respecting those provisions. Accordingly, States are required to allocate the required resources for the implementation of the treaty.

The Sri Lankan experience thus far in acceding to the CRPD as discussed in this chapter challenges this positivist and linear account. It is evident that Sri Lanka did not have any clear plans for fulfilling its obligations under the CRPD when it chose to ratify it in February 2016. No significant efforts were made between signing the treaty in 2007 and in ratifying it in 2016 to 'prepare' for the implementation of this treaty. The actual political reasons for ratification of the CRPD therefore remain unclear. Thus, following ratification, no concrete steps have been taken for law reform, policy development or programme implementation for the fulfilment of Sri Lanka's obligations under the CRPD.

The analysis undertaken in this chapter suggests that even though the State structures, processes and practices seem to be by and large unaffected by the ratification of the CRPD, the same cannot be said of civil society. Considerable mobilisation was evident among disability rights activists and organisations with regard to drafting legislation, making proposals for constitutional reform and in lobbying the government for institutional reform. Furthermore, new partnerships have emerged across a long-standing divide between civil society actors and organisations that focus on general human rights and governance issues on the one hand, and civil society actors and organisations that have been working on issues related to disability on the other hand.

It seems then that even when the State ratifies a human rights treaty with minimal political will to ensure respect for its provision, such ratification can nevertheless have a positive and progressive impact. That impact is achieved by empowering and thereby mobilising civil society actors and organisations. They in turn lobby the State, mobilise other stakeholders and can potentially generate some momentum around the human rights recognised in the treaty. It is necessary therefore to broaden the scope of analysis in evaluating the impact of the ratification of human rights treaties. Treaty ratification seems to influence non-state actors much more than the State, at the very least, in the immediate aftermath of ratification.

It must be noted however that the gathering of momentum in seeking greater respect for disability rights is by and large confined to civil society actors and organisations that are located close to the centre of political power. Especially in the case of disability rights, this almost always means geographical proximity to political power as well. This activism therefore was mostly evident in and around Sri Lanka's capital. In the study that was carried out among 23 women with disabilities who were war-affected, it was clear that none of them were aware of the CRPD or its general content (Samararatne et al. 2018). These women were from rural Sri Lanka and represented different provinces. Within a general context of poor literacy and minimal legal literacy among persons with disabilities, a lack of knowledge regarding human rights is to be expected. The positive and progressive impact of the ratification of the CRPD therefore seems to be confined to the more privileged sectors of civil society. These actors use the CRPD as a platform to lobby the State. However, other stakeholders who are spread out across Sri Lanka are not 'reached out' to in this process. That process will probably unfold in time to come.

In that unfolding however, it would be helpful for civil society actors and the State to adopt a cautious strategy. Generating awareness regarding the ratification of the CRPD, its contents and the implications of the ratification for persons with disabilities in Sri Lanka should be undertaken as a dialogue. Research undertaken among rural and war-affected women with disabilities in Sri Lanka has shown that they do not demonstrate or articulate a consciousness of human rights (Samararatne and Soldatic 2015). They do however articulate an appreciation for freedom that goes beyond a libertarian account of freedom and autonomy. Early research into these ideas suggests that this articulation of 'freedom' and 'autonomy' is intermeshed with ideas of justice, resilience and adaptability. Further research is necessary to develop a better understanding of such localised approaches to freedom, autonomy and justice. In promoting literacy and awareness around the CRPD, it is necessary that these accounts of freedom are acknowledged and included rather than be forced out of the discourse on disability rights in Sri Lanka.

7 The Janus-Faced Approach

The analysis of the ratification of the CRPD and State practice post-ratification reveals a 'Janus-faced' approach by the State. To the international community, Sri Lanka expresses political will and commitment to respect the provisions of the CRPD, while at the domestic level the State takes no concrete measures to meet that commitment. At the international level, strong language is used by the State to commit to the fulfilment of its obligations under the treaty. However, it is evident that treaty ratification is seen merely in symbolic and aspirational terms by the State at the domestic level. Civil society activism is one factor which can disrupt this status quo and demand some measure of accountability from the State. Disability rights activists have made the most of the consultation processes undertaken by the State and made in-depth representations regarding the status of persons with disabilities to the two State appointed consultation bodies. Both bodies have given due consideration to these submissions and made several detailed recommendations regarding disability rights—the substantive guarantees, procedural guarantees, for institutional design and for the recognition of the rights of specific categories of persons with disabilities. In the Sri Lankan context, civil society activism has additionally resulted in partnerships among those working exclusively on disability rights issues with those working more generally on human rights issues.

These experiences suggest that in understanding the ratification of human rights law treaties, it would be misleading to focus exclusively on the behaviour and reactions of the State. Although treaty ratification takes place at the international level where individuals have no legal standing, its immediate consequences are felt by individuals and organisations at the domestic level. These influences of State action at the international level point to the need to broaden the scope of analysis when accounting for the effects of treaty ratification.

Clearly, the CRPD presents a critical moment and an essential platform for civil society in developing a rights-based approach to disability. This impact of the CRPD is greater in contexts where welfare and charity have dominated approaches to disability for over seven decades. However, the promotion of the human rights language articulated in the CRPD should not be at the cost of already existing approaches to framing autonomy, freedom and justice by persons with disability. Promoting the CRPD among wider society should therefore be approached as a dialogue in which the universalist human rights language is interpreted through a local lens. The development of such an approach calls for more intense and consistent engagement with persons with disabilities.

8 Conclusion

This chapter has carried out an analysis of the national impact of the ratification of the CRPD by Sri Lanka. Through the analysis of State action (or inaction) and developments in civil society, it has been argued that the State has a 'Janus-Faced Approach' to treaty ratification. A significant gap is evident in the political and legal commitments made at the international level on the one hand, and State action at the domestic level on the other hand. However, Sri Lanka's experience suggests that the transformation of State action at the domestic level is perhaps not to be expected immediately but rather would only follow after advocacy and lobbying by civil society. Lobbying and advocacy around the ratification of the CRPD by civil society organisations and individuals working on disability was evident in the aftermath. These events suggest that human rights treaty ratification, though carried out by States, depends largely on responses of civil society for actual transformations on the ground.

Acknowledgements The author wishes to acknowledge the assistance provided by Ms Sajini Wickramasinghe, Undergraduate of the Faculty of Law, University of Colombo, Sri Lanka, in writing this chapter. The research for this chapter was undertaken November 2017–February 2018.

References

8th Parliament of Sri Lanka. (1978). Constitution of the Democratic Socialist Republic of Sri Lanka.

Alston, P., & Goodman, R. (2013). *International human rights*. Oxford: Oxford University Press.

Asian Development Bank. (2013). *Sri Lanka civil society briefs*.

Bombi, F. (2010). Disability and displacement—Perception and protection in Sri Lanka. *Forced Migration Review, 35*, 14–15.

Campbell, F. K. (2009). Disability, legal mobilisation and the challenges of capacity building in Sri Lanka. In C. E. Marshall, E. Kendall, & R. Gover (Eds.), *Insights from across fields and around the world* (Vol. III, pp. 111–128). Westport, CT: Praeger Press.

CATA (Convention Against Torture And Other Cruel, Inhuman Or Degrading Treatment Or Punishment Act of 1994). (1994). *Sri Lankan government.*

CEDAW (Convention for the Elimination of All forms of Discrimination Against Women). (1979).

Ceylon Tobacco Company PLC v. Minister of Health. (2012). CA 336/2012 (Writ).

CRPD (United Nations Convention on the Rights of Persons with Disabilities). (2006). Adopted in 2006 by the United Nations general assembly.

CTFRM (Consultation Task Force on Reconciliation Mechanisms). (2016). *Final report of the consultation task force on reconciliation mechanisms.* V 1 and V2. Retrieved from http://war-victims-map.org/wp-content/uploads/2017/02/CTF-Final-Report-Volume-I-Nov-16.pdf.

Department of Census & Statistics. (2012). *Census of population and housing.* Sri Lanka: Ministry of Policy Planning and Economic Affairs. Retrieved from http://www.statistics.gov.lk/PopHouSat/CPH2011/Pages/Activities/Reports/FinalReport/FinalReportE.pdf.

Department of National Budget. (2017, July 31). *Letter issued to all secretaries to ministries, chief secretaries of provincial councils, heads of departments, and chairmen of corporations and statutory boards.* Director General of the Department of National Budget Sri Lanka. http://www.treasury.gov.lk/documents/10181/31346/NBD-addendum-II-2018-20170731E_1.PDF/af142196-d757-46fb-8761-a3102039e465?version=1.0.

Department of State (United States). (2017). 2016 Country Reports on Human Rights Practices - Sri Lanka, 3 March 2017. Retrieved from https://www.state.gov/documents/organization/265760.pdf.

Dr. Ajith C.S. Perera v. Attorney General and Others. (2009). S.C. (FR) NO. 221/2009.

Hathaway, O. A. (2007). Why do countries commit to human rights treaties? *Journal of Conflict Resolution, 51*(4), 588–621.

ICCPR Act (International Covenant on Civil and Political Rights) Act No 56 of 2007. *Sri Lankan Government.*

ICES (International Centre for Ethnic Studies). (2017). *Forgotten Voices: Women with disabilities in post-war Sri Lanka's development and peace building agenda.*

ICPPED (International Convention for the Protection of All Persons from Enforced Disappearance). (2006).

Ismail, A. (2016, December 6). Disability is not inability. *Daily Mirror.* Retrieved from http://www.dailymirror.lk/article/Disability-Is-Not-Inability-120267.html.

Jiffry, A., & Perera, B. (2017). *Status of persons with disabilities in Sri Lanka.* Sri Lanka: State of Human *Rights 2017.* Law and Society Trust.

Kandasamy, N., Soldatic, K., & Samararatne, D. (2017). Peace, justice and disabled women's advocacy: Tamil women with disabilities in rural post-conflict Sri Lanka. *Medicine, Conflict, and Survival, 33*(1), 41–59.

Law and Society Trust (Law and Society Trust and University of Western Sydney). (2018). *'Out of the Shadows': War-Affected Women with Disabilities in Sri Lanka.*

Law and Society Trust (Law and Society Trust in Consultation with Persons with Disabilities, Activists and Researchers). (2016, October 21). *Response to request for information from the special rapporteur on the rights of the persons with disabilities Sri Lanka.* Retrieved from http://www.ohchr.org/Documents/Issues/Disability/ProvisionSupport/NGOs/Law%20and%20Society%20Trust%20Sri%20Lanka.docx.

Manohari Pelaketiya v. H. M. Gunesekera Secretary, Ministry of Education and Others. (2012). SC/FR/No. 76/2012.

Minister of Finance. (2017, November 9). *Budget speech.* Parliament of Sri Lanka.

Ministry of Foreign Affairs. (2017). *National action plan for the protection and promotion of human rights 2017–2021.* Sri Lanka. Retrieved from http://www.pmoffice.gov.lk/download/press/D00000000063_EN.pdf.

Ministry of Health (Ministry of Health, Indigenous Medicine and Probation & Childcare Services, Northern Province). (2017, October 20). *Preliminary identification survey for disabilities & women vulnerabilities in Northern Province.* Killinochchi: Government of Sri Lanka. Retrieved from https://www.np.gov.lk/pdf/publications/Preliminary%20Report%20for%20DS-2016.pdf.

Ministry of Social Services & Ministry of Health. (2013). *National action plan for disability.* Adopted by the Sri Lankan Cabinet on 16th December 2013.

Nafeel, N. (2016, December 19). Disability does not disable but discrimination does. *Daily News.* Retrieved from http://www.dailynews.lk/2016/12/19/features/102276.

Nallaratnam Singarasa v Attorney General. (2013). 1 Sri LR 245.

ONUR (Office for National Unity & Reconciliation). (2017). National policy on reconciliation and coexistence Sri Lanka.

PRC (Public Representations Committee on Constitutional Reforms). (2016, March 4). *Constitutional reforms—Submission by civil society organizations and individuals advocating for the rights of persons with disabilities in Sri Lanka.* Retrieved from http://ices.lk/wp-content/uploads/2016/03/Disability-Constitutional-Reform-Mar4.pdf.

PRPDA (Protection of the Rights of Persons with Disabilities Act of 1996). (1996). *Sri Lankan government.*

RSAA (Ranaviru Sewa Authority Act of 1999 No. 54). (1999). *Sri Lankan government.*

Samararatne, D. W., & Soldatic, K. (2015). Inclusions and exclusions in law: Experiences of women with disability in rural and war-affected areas in Sri Lanka. *Disability & Society, 30*(5), 759–772.

Samararatne, D., & Soldatic, K. (2018). Transitioning with disability: Justice for women with disabilities in post-war Sri Lanka. In L. Fiske & R. Shackel (Eds.), *Rethinking transitional gender justice: Transformative approaches in post-conflict settings*. Cham: Palgrave.

Samararatne, D., & Soldatic, K., & Perera, B. (2018). *A study of war-affected women with disabilities in Sri Lanka: Pre-consultation report 2018*. Penrith: Western Sydney University. Retrieved from https://www.westernsydney.edu.au/__data/assets/pdf_file/0011/1345583/a_study_of_war_affected_women_with_disabilities_in_sri_lanka.pdf.

Sub-Committee on Fundamental Rights. (2017). *Report of the sub-committee on fundamental rights.*

UN (United Nations). (2016). *Statement by the permanent representative of Sri Lanka to the United Nations.*

UNDP (Human Development Report Office—United Nations Development Programme). (2016). *Human development report—Human development for everyone.* Retrieved from http://hdr.undp.org/sites/default/files/2016_human_development_report.pdf.

UNHRC (United Nations Human Rights Council). (2015, October 14). *Promoting reconciliation, accountability and human rights in Sri Lanka: Resolution/adopted by the Human Rights Council.* A/HRC/RES/30/1.

UNHRC (United Nations Human Rights Council). (2017a). *National report submitted in accordance with paragraph 5 of the annex to human rights council resolution 16/21annex*. Sri Lanka. A/HRC/WG.6/28/LKA/1.

UNHRC (United Nations Human Rights Council—Working Group on the Universal Periodic Review). (2017b). *Summary of stakeholders' submissions on Sri Lanka—Report of the Office of the United Nations High Commissioner for Human Rights*. A/HRC/WG.6/28/LKA/3.

UNHRC (United Nations Human Rights Council—Working Group on the Universal Periodic Review). (2017c, August 28). *Compilation on Sri Lanka—Report of the office of the United Nations high commissioner for human rights*. A/HRC/WG.6/28/LKA/2.

World Bank. (2017). *Sri Lanka development update, November 2017: Creating opportunities and managing risks for sustained growth*. Washington, DC: World Bank. Retrieved from https://openknowledge.worldbank.org/handle/10986/28826.

Part III

Making Disability Human Rights Happen? Cultural Challenges to Implementing the CRPD

10

The 'Transposition' of Article 12 of the CRPD in China and Its Potential Impact on Chinese Legal Capacity Law and Culture

Huang Yi

1 Introduction

This chapter focuses on the implementation of Article 12—Equal recognition before the law, of the United Nations (UN) Convention on the Rights of Persons with Disabilities (CRPD 2006) in China. Based on an in-depth understanding of Article 12 of the CRPD (2006) and empirical research regarding relevant Chinese cultural contexts, this chapter will identify and examine the key cultural issues to be considered in the implementation of Article 12 in China. The analysis in this chapter is limited to the scope of adults' rights to equal recognition before the law in civil law in China. Section 2 will start with a brief analysis of the theoretical framework and methodology that are used in this chapter. Article 12 CRPD (2006) will be discussed in Sect. 3. Section 4 examines the gap between current Chinese civil law and Article 12 of the CRPD (2006) and identifies the areas that are in need of reform in order to meet with

H. Yi (✉)
Shenzhen University, Shenzhen, China

E. J. Kakoullis, K. Johnson (eds.), *Recognising Human Rights in Different Cultural Contexts*, https://doi.org/10.1007/978-981-15-0786-1_10

the requirements of Article 12. Based on empirical data collected in China regarding the practice of legal capacity and guardianship, the chapter concludes by analysing key cultural issues that need to be taken into account in the implementation process of Article 12 CRPD in China.

2 Theoretical Framework and Methodology

This section will introduce the theoretical framework and methodology that are used in this chapter. In order to achieve the full and effective implementation of Article 12 of the CRPD (2006), at the national level, requires much more than using it as a 'model law' or template and copying it into domestic law (Stein and Lord 2008). The implementation of Article 12 will foster changes in domestic law, which should be brought about in a way that is compatible with the given legal system and culture (Stein and Lord 2008). To explore the implementation of Article 12 at the national level in China, this chapter will proceed by applying the argument raised in comparative law scholarship that the relationship between law and cultural context of a jurisdiction is an intricate interrelationship (see, Teubner 1998; Esin Örücü 2010; Mertus 1999). Culture may have an influence on how the law is understood and applied (Lord Hoffmann 1999; Kroncke 2012), and at the same time, the law may bring about 'simultaneous and complementary change' (Teubner 1998, p. 12) to relevant cultural contexts and social fields (Merry 2009). Such an interrelationship offers the possibility for law to be moved from one context to another (Esin Örücü 2010; Teubner 1998; Esin Örücü 2002), and thus the possibility for the implementation of international human rights law at the national level (Merry 2009; Mertus 1999).

Esin Örücü (2002) developed the metaphor of 'transposition' to describe the transnational or cross-border spread of law. According to Örücü, when the law 'travels' from one system to another, it should go through "a process of transposition, tuning and fitting" (Esin Örücü 2002, p. 205). The social and cultural context of the recipient of the law should be comprehensively understood and considered to determine an appropriate 'tuning'; that is, the law should be transposed to suit the particular socio-legal culture and needs of the recipient (Esin Örücü 2002). The purpose of 'transposition, tuning, and fitting' is to enable the content of the law; that is, not only its text but also its meaning, implications and values, to successfully find its way from one system to another (Esin Örücü 2002). If this is not done, only the text of the law is copied, while the meaning, implications and values, which should be embedded in the text, get lost.

Sally Engle Merry (2009) investigates how human rights law, developed at the international level, may have had an influence on gender violence and women's rights in five different jurisdictions, each with different cultural contexts, namely, India, mainland China, Fiji, Hong Kong and the United States. Her research findings show a more specific view of the role played by the social and cultural context in the implementation of international human rights law at the national level. Based on her empirical research in these five jurisdictions, she points out that whether human rights law is codified into local law and documents is only half of the question, and that it should also be asked whether the law can really be used by local people, as well as whether those who are most vulnerable and in need of rights protection recognise their entitlements and assert their rights. Accordingly, when international human rights law is implemented at the local level, the local culture should be comprehensively understood, and based on such an understanding, human rights law and values should be translated into the version that grassroots local people can understand, accept and use.

While Merry (2009) recognises the important role played by cultural context in the implementation of international human rights law at the national level, she also demonstrates a circumspect view to the degree of cultural variations. In her study of human rights and gender violence, she disaggregates human rights law into three levels, namely, human rights value, the rights framework and the expression of human rights ideas (Merry 2009). Her study illuminates her strong position that cultural variations happen only at the level of the expression of human rights law ideas. A typical example of such cultural variation given by Merry is that when a women's group in mainland China worked on the issue of gender violence, they delivered international human rights ideas to local people, and such international ideas, themes and values were presented and expressed through local language, Cantonese and local symbols (Merry 2009). The culture should not influence what kind of value is implemented, but only how to enable people to understand, accept and use these values. Human rights law may be elaborated and presented in familiar cultural terms when it is implemented at the national level; however, it should retain its fundamental grounding, and this should not be challenged by the local conditions (Donoho 2001; Merry 2009; Renteln 1988).

Applying the metaphor of 'transposition' and Merry's analysis of 'cultural variation' to the current chapter, it is argued that the full and effective implementation of Article 12 of the CRPD (2006) should be based on a comprehensive understanding of both Article 12 and the relevant Chinese social and cultural context. When Article 12 'travels' from the international human rights law system to China's domestic law system, its fundamental meaning, implications and values should be maintained, and at the same time, go through a process of transposition to be 'repackaged' in culturally resonant 'wrappings', to enable local people to understand, accept and use the provision. This is the theoretical framework used in this chapter.

As a relatively practical issue, Teubner (1998) pointed out that cultural factors may be too abstract to be operationalised. The term 'culture' can be understood in different ways. In this chapter, culture is understood in a broad sense, as referring to not only beliefs and values but also practices, habits, commonsensical ways of doing things, institutional arrangements, political structures and legal regulations (Merry 2010). Based on this broader understanding of culture, however, it is not possible in one chapter to investigate the whole culture of a country. In view of that, the cultural aspect discussed in this chapter for the purpose of implementing Article 12 of the CRPD in China and carrying out law reform focuses on investigating China's legal culture.

Merry (2010) has developed an anthropological approach in order to study legal culture. According to Merry, legal culture can be broken down into four analysable dimensions, namely, the practice and ideologies within the legal system; public's attitude towards the law; legal mobilisation, that is, the extent to which people are willing to define their problems in legal terms and resort to law for help or settlement; and legal consciousness, which is the degree to which people see themselves as entitled to legal protection. Merry (2010) argues that disaggregating legal culture into these four dimensions makes it more amenable to empirical study. This anthropological approach to legal culture forms the framework for my empirical study of legal culture in China.

I conducted empirical research of legal culture in China in 2015, with six groups of people who are involved in legal capacity and guardianship issues: 23 persons with disabilities, 16 people who define themselves as having the roles of guardians of persons with disabilities, four lawyers with experience of providing legal services on disability issues, four judges with experience of legal capacity and guardianship cases, 11 social workers with experience of providing services for persons with disabilities and 15 members of neighbourhood committees with authority to assign guardianship. I collected data through semi-structured interviews and focus groups. My empirical research design, data processing and analysis were based on the anthropological approach to legal culture.

3 Article 12 of the CRPD: Equal Recognition Before the Law

3.1 Normative Content of Article 12

Article 12 of the CRPD (2006) affirms that the right to equal recognition before the law should be enjoyed by all persons with disabilities. Article 12(1) reaffirms the right of persons with disabilities to be recognised as persons before the law.[1] As explained in the General Comment No. 1 of the Committee on the Rights of Persons with Disabilities, recognition as a person before the law is the precondition for an individual to be recognised as having legal capacity (CoRPD 2014). Article 12(2) recognises right to legal capacity of persons with disabilities on an equal basis with others in all areas of life.[2] According to General Comment No.1, the term 'legal capacity' has two components. The first is the legal capacity to be a rights holder, which entitles a person to the full protection of his or her

[1] Article 12 (1): States Parties reaffirm that persons with disabilities have the right to recognition everywhere as persons before the law (CRPD 2006, Art. 12[1]).

[2] Article 12 (2): States Parties shall recognize that persons with disabilities enjoy legal capacity on an equal basis with others in all aspects of life (CRPD 2006, Art. 12[2]).

rights. The second is the legal capacity to be an actor under the law, which recognises the person as having the power to engage in transactions and create, modify or end legal relationships (CoRPD 2014). Additionally, 'legal capacity' should be distinguished from 'mental capacity', which refers to the decision-making skills of a person (CoRPD 2014). It is not an "objective, scientific and naturally occurring phenomenon" (CoRPD 2014, para. 14), but is highly controversial and contingent on the social and political context. Under Article 12, perceived or actual deficits in mental capacity can never justify the denial of legal capacity (CoRPD 2014). Article 12(3)[3] places an obligation on State Parties to take appropriate measures to provide support that may be needed by persons with disabilities in exercising their legal capacity. The CRPD Committee recognises support as "a broad term that encompasses both informal and formal support arrangements of varying types and intensity" (CoRPD 2014, para. 17). It also recognises that the support measures provided for different individuals may differ significantly because of the diversity of the needs and situations of persons with disabilities, and that some people may not be willing to have support in the exercise of their legal capacity (CoRPD 2014, para. 19). Article 12(4)[4] outlines safeguards that must be present in a system of support for the exercise of legal capacity. General Comment No. 1 indicates that central to the safeguards is ensuring that the support respects persons with disabilities' "rights, will, and preferences" (CoRPD 2014, para. 17). The CRPD Committee has emphasised that in order to ensure rights to legal capacity of persons with disabilities on an equal basis with others, the 'will and preferences' paradigm must replace the 'best interests' paradigm (CoRPD 2014). It is further clarified in the General Comment No. 1

[3] Article 12(3): States Parties shall take appropriate measures to provide access by persons with disabilities to the support they may require in exercising their legal capacity (CRPD 2006, Art. 12[3]).

[4] Article 12(4): States Parties shall ensure that all measures that relate to the exercise of legal capacity provide for appropriate and effective safeguards to prevent abuse in accordance with international human rights law. Such safeguards shall ensure that measures relating to the exercise of legal capacity respect the rights, will and preferences of the person, are free of conflict of interest and undue influence, are proportional and tailored to the person's circumstances, apply for the shortest time possible and are subject to regular review by a competent, independent and impartial authority or judicial body. The safeguards shall be proportional to the degree to which such measures affect the person's rights and interests (CRPD 2006, Art. 12[4]).

that the support and safeguards to the exercise of legal capacity should not amount to allowing substituted decision-making, and that all regimes of substituted decision-making should be abolished (CoRPD 2014). Lastly, Article 12(5)[5] deals with rights of persons with disabilities specifically concerning financial and economic affairs. It places an obligation on State Parties to take measures to ensure that persons with disabilities can exercise legal capacity in financial and economic matters on an equal basis with others.

3.2 Obligations of States Parties

Based on Article 12 of the CRPD (2006), States Parties have an obligation to respect, protect and fulfil the right of all persons with disabilities to equal recognition before the law. According to the Committee's General Comment No. 1, the right set out in Article 12 should be regarded as a civil and political right, and therefore, upon ratification, State Parties must immediately begin taking steps to achieve the realisation of Article 12 (CoRPD 2014). States parties are obliged, first, to abolish denials of legal capacity that are discriminatory on the basis of disability in purpose or effect. In particular, the Committee has emphasised that laws which allow for guardianship, trusteeship, and other forms of substitute decision-making should be scrutinised (CoRPD 2014). Substitute decision-making that is not based on the will and preference of persons with disabilities should not be allowed, as it constitutes a form of denying the person's full legal capacity (CoRPD 2014). In addition, States Parties are obliged to take actions, for example, to develop the regime of supported decision-making and to provide access to support needed by persons with disabilities in their exercise of legal capacity (CoRPD 2014).

---

[5] Article 12(5): Subject to the provisions of this article, States Parties shall take all appropriate and effective measures to ensure the equal right of persons with disabilities to own or inherit property, to control their own financial affairs and to have equal access to bank loans, mortgages and other forms of financial credit, and shall ensure that persons with disabilities are not arbitrarily deprived of their property (CRPD 2006, Art. 12[5]).

4 Current Chinese Civil Law Relevant to the Implementation of Article 12 CRPD

China ratified the CRPD in 2008, and therefore is legally obligated to take measures to achieve the full realisation of Article 12 at the national level. As an essential step to the full realisation of Article 12, the relevant domestic laws should be reviewed and those that are in conflict with Article 12 should be abolished or modified. The most relevant area of domestic law to be scrutinised in the light of Article 12 is the law on legal capacity and adult guardianship (CoRPD 2012). According to Chinese law on legal capacity (General Provisions of the Civil Law of the People's Republic of China 2017), citizens have legal capacity as rights holders from birth until death (General Provisions of the Civil Law of the People's Republic of China 2017, Art. 13), and all citizens are recognised as rights holders before the law on an equal basis (General Provisions of the Civil Law of the People's Republic of China 2017, Art. 14). An individual aged 18 or over is an adult and is recognised by law as a person with full legal capacity to act under the law (General Provisions of the Civil Law of the People's Republic of China 2017, Art. 18). However, there is also a provision that states:

> An adult incapable of discerning his or her conduct is a person without capacity for civil conduct, who shall be represented by his or her statutory agent in performing juridical acts. (General Provisions of the Civil Law of the People's Republic of China 2017, Art. 21)

In Chinese law, in order to determine the degree to which a person is capable of discerning his/her own conduct, the factors that are to be considered include, for example, whether he/she can understand their own conduct and foresee the consequence, of an act and the degree to which he/she has the ability of 'judgement' and 'self-protection' (Opinions of the Supreme People's Court on Several Issues concerning the Implementation of the General Principles of the Civil Law of the People's Republic of China 1988). Domestic law provides the ground for denying an individual's legal capacity for disability-related reasons and conflates 'legal capacity' with 'mental capacity'. This is a material conflict between domestic law and Article 12 of the CRPD (2006). Moreover, in relation to denying an individual's legal capacity for disability-related reasons, it is not clear in the current law whether the recognition of one's legal capacity, especially the legal capacity to act under the law, is an individual's right protected by the law, or whether it is closer to a legal standard with the purpose of excluding some individuals from exercising legal capacity. This is one of the fundamental gaps between Chinese law on legal capacity and Article 12 of the CRPD.

Furthermore, according to Chinese law on adult guardianship, once a person is denied full legal capacity, he/she shall be placed under guardianship (General Provisions of the Civil Law of the People's Republic of China 2017, Art. 23). Among other guardian's rights and obligations, the guardian is authorised by law to make a wide range of decisions, including financial and medical decisions for the person under guardianship (General Provisions of the Civil Law of the People's Republic of China 2017, Art. 34, 35). Together with the authorisation given to the guardian, the current law imposes a large number of restrictions on the rights of the person under guardianship, including, for example, the right to enter into contracts (Contract Law of the People's Republic of China 1999, 2012 Amendment, Art. 9) and the right to apply for legal aid (State Council 2003, Art. 16). The legal mechanism of guardianship, in most cases, has the characteristics of substitute decision-making, and therefore, is in conflict with the requirements of Article 12. In addition, as has been noted by the CRPD Committee in its Concluding Observation on China's initial state report, there is no system of support in the exercise of legal capacity under current Chinese law (CoRPD 2012).

5 Culturally Related Issues to Be Considered in the Implementation of Article 12 CRPD in China

The above analysis shows that Article 12 of the CRPD (2006) presents challenges to current Chinese law in many significant ways. In view of China's obligations under the CRPD, domestic law, especially the regulations on legal capacity and guardianship in the General Provisions of the Civil Law of the People's Republic of China 2017, should be reformed in order to meet with the requirements of Article 12. It is here argued that when Article 12 'travelled' from the international human rights law system to the Chinese domestic law system, it should have been 'repackaged' in a culturally resonant 'wrapping', so to enable local people to understand, accept and use it. The full implementation of Article 12 in China, and the relevant domestic law reform, should be based on an understanding of the relevant social and cultural context in China. My empirical research of legal culture in China revealed many cultural issues that should be considered in the implementation of Article 12 of the CRPD in China. In this chapter, I discuss the four key cultural issues which emerged from the research.

5.1 A Low Legal Consciousness of Right to Legal Capacity of Persons with Disabilities

As discussed in the previous section, current Chinese law leaves ambiguities regarding whether the recognition of one's full legal capacity is a legal right. My research found that such ambiguities in law, in many ways, lead to or reinforce the practice of relatively arbitrary and discriminatory interference in the exercise of legal capacity of persons with disabilities. According to the current law, the denial of legal capacity should be applied only by a court, and only to people with a mental or intellectual impairment. However, my research found that people with non-cognitive-related impairments, such as deaf people and blind people, may also be regarded as not having full legal capacity and be prevented from exercising legal capacity in practice. In addition to such a gap between law and practice, I also found that in practice, being recognised as having full legal capacity is seldom understood as a legal right. The judges I interviewed showed a similar understanding, that the legal capacity prescribed in the current law, especially legal capacity to act, is a kind of standard or a sort of qualification, to determine whether an individual can exercise civil juristic acts; rather than a right that should be enjoyed by all people on an equal basis.

The majority of the persons with disabilities I interviewed understood legal capacity in a vague and imprecise way. Most of them, to a large extent, conflated disability or impairment with the lack of legal capacity. They seldom associated legal capacity with their legal right. Instead, terms such as 'restrictions', 'limitations', 'not allow' and 'prevent' were frequently used by interviewees' talking about legal capacity:

> [M]y mother and our tutor said that the law does not allow me to marry Kaka … is this law relevant to what you called 'legal capacity'? (Female, 23 years old, with Down's syndrome)

> [T]he bank does not allow deaf people to purchase funds on our own, I think this is relevant to denying … the word you use … my 'legal capacity'. (Female, 26 years old, deaf)

My findings also indicated that some of the persons with disabilities interviewed obtain their knowledge or understanding of legal capacity, not from reading legal documents or professional legal advice, but from their experiences. In particular, when their legal capacity is denied by someone with authority or power, they may tend to be convinced that what they experienced is in accordance with the law, even though it is in fact an arbitrary and discriminatory deprivation of legal capacity of persons with disabilities and contrary to international human rights law:

> I have not found any law saying that people like me cannot do something, but restrictions are everywhere, the bank, the post office, the housing agency … and these are not some private business, you know … these are all state-owned (in Mandarin: "guoyou de"). So, I think, if all of them can have such restrictions on me, the restrictions must be legal, because the state-owned bank, the state-owned post office will not violate the law. (Female, 27 years old, blind)

Moreover, my findings revealed that even when a person with a disability is aware of an infringement to his/her right to equal recognition before the law, it may be very difficult for them to challenge such infringements:

> [W]e all felt that this is unfair, however, we are not sure whether such practice is authorised by some other pieces of law that we do not know … one of my friends tried to find some lawyers for help, but it seems that lawyers are not very helpful to deaf people especially when you want to have face to face communication with the help of a sign language interpreter. (Female, 22 years old, deaf)

> I called the legal aid center and a law firm. When they knew that I had been diagnosed as with mental illness, they both refused to help me. The lawyers in the legal aid centre explained to me that according to the law, people with mental illness do not have legal capacity, and thus cannot apply for legal aid on their own. (Male, 44 years old, diagnosed with depression, but he does not agree with the diagnosis)

The legal and practical obstacles for persons with disabilities to defend their exercise of legal capacity may further influence their awareness of their legal rights and willingness to use the law to defend their rights:

> [Y]ou might know that deaf people, just like other persons with disabilities, have our own communities … So, when some of us find out that turning to the law cannot solve our problems, the rest of us may not be willing to take the same approach. (Female, 22 years old, deaf)

When arbitrary intervention of exercise of legal capacity in persons with disabilities becomes common practice without being challenged by the law, persons with disabilities and other social actors may come to the view that persons with disabilities can be legitimately prevented from exercising legal capacity. Therefore the prejudicial presumption that all persons with disabilities are without legal capacity might also be reinforced in practice.

My research findings indicate that the failure to define the recognition of one's full legal capacity as a legal right in Chinese law is a factor that results in the low consciousness of the right to legal capacity of persons with disabilities and is therefore a barrier to the realisation of the right to equal recognition before the law. To remove this barrier, domestic law reform in the light of Article 12 of the CRPD should include a definite affirmation in domestic law that individuals have the legal right to be recognised as persons before the law with full legal capacity on an equal basis with others.

5.2 The Driving Force for the Interference of Exercise of Legal Capacity in Persons with Disabilities

According to the CRPD Committee's General Comment No. 1, the conflation between 'mental capacity' and 'legal capacity' is highlighted as one of the important factors that drives the denial of legal capacity of persons with disabilities (CoRPD 2014). Section 4 also showed that the legal standard of legal capacity is, to a large degree, conflated with mental and intellectual capacity in Chinese law on legal capacity. However, I found that in practice, concern about mental or intellectual capacity of persons with disabilities may not necessarily be the only factor behind interference of exercise of legal capacity in persons with disabilities. This is particularly evident in cases where persons with disabilities with non-cognitive-related impairments are discriminatorily prevented from exercising legal capacity. For example, some deaf people and blind people I interviewed talked about their experience of being prevented from exercising legal capacity to open a bank account because of their impairments. Such practice further suggests that distinguishing mental capacity and legal capacity in law, as required by Article 12 of the CRPD (2006), may not be sufficient to completely abolish the denial of legal capacity on the grounds of disability in practice. Rather, it is necessary to also identify further factors that drive the practice of preventing persons with disabilities from exercising legal capacity on an equal basis with others.

My research revealed that apart from the persons with disabilities interviewed, the majority of the other research participants were concerned that persons with disabilities may not be able to be responsible for their actions or decisions. This led to the concern that exercise of legal capacity of persons with disabilities may consequently expose the rights and interests of themselves, or others, to disproportionate and unnecessary risks. For example, in the focus group with guardians, one of the participants explained why she thought her husband with a mental disability should not have full legal capacity:

> My husband, for example, does not have a decent job and therefore has no income. I can foresee that he is, at least, financially incapable of being responsible for some of his decisions, and I will not let him make those kinds of decisions … I think the purpose of the law on legal capacity is not to forbid mentally disabled people to do anything, but to ensure that people who have the right to do whatever he/she wants have the capability to be responsible about what he/she has done … If a person is given the rights to do whatever he/she wants but cannot be responsible, it may do harm to both him/herself and others. (Female, her husband has a psycho-social disability)

Only a few of the research participants explicitly associated the possible negative consequences of exercise of legal capacity of persons with disabilities with concerns that persons with disabilities may lack the cognitive ability to, for example, understand and balance information, or communicate a decision. The majority of the other participants associated their concerns about an exercise of legal capacity of persons with disabilities with, for example, the experience of negative consequences of an exercise of legal capacity of persons with disabilities, financial decision-making capacities and social class. These factors may, directly or indirectly, constitute the driving forces for discriminatory interference of exercise of legal capacity in persons with disabilities. Such driving forces should not be oversimplified or completely attributed to the prejudice against persons with disabilities, the conflation of mental capacity with legal capacity, or that some of them are arguably grounded in, or interact with structural disadvantages or oppression suffered by persons with disabilities. For example, relatively limited financial capabilities of persons with disabilities may be grounded in, or interact with discrimination in employment, and discrimination in childhood education. These factors do not initially appear relevant to the right to legal capacity, but, as I found in the research, they may be linked with interference of exercise of legal capacity in persons with disabilities.

The implementation of Article 12 of the CRPD should recognise and take into consideration the complexity of the factors that drive the discriminatory denial of full legal capacity of persons with disabilities in practice in China. The domestic law reform in the light of Article 12 of the CRPD should provide the legal mechanism to deal with such driving forces. Although some of them cannot be completely removed with the implementation of Article 12, especially those rooted in the structural disadvantages and oppression that persons with disabilities experience, the domestic law reform in the light of Article 12 should, at least, refrain from underpinning the existing disadvantages and oppression or imposing new disadvantages on persons with disabilities.

5.3 The Moral Context of Adult Guardianship and Substitute Decision-Making

As discussed in Sect. 4, adult guardianship in current Chinese law is a typical form of substitute decision-making, which conflicts with the requirements of Article 12 of the CRPD (2006). Therefore, as an important step to the implementation of Article 12 in China, adult guardianship should be abolished and replaced by the regime of supported decision-making in the exercise of legal capacity in the light of Article 12 (CoRPD 2012, 2014). In my research, I found that the practice of guardianship and substitute decision-making to a large degree goes beyond the boundaries of legal guardianship. While adult guardianship provided in domestic law is applied only to people who have been denied full legal capacity by a court, the practice of guardianship and substitute decision-making is applied to persons with disabilities regardless of whether or not they have legally been denied full legal capacity. In such situations, the family members of the person with disability always hold the role of 'guardian', and are recognised as the 'guardian' by others in practice, even where they are not legally appointed as the person's guardian.

My findings also illustrate that the legal status of guardian, and the moral status of family members, may be conflated in practice. The moral context, especially the context of family relationships, arguably plays a more significant role in the practice of guardianship and substitute decision-making. Accordingly, in order to abolish guardianship, as a form of substitute decision-making, in both law and in practice as required by Article 12, it is necessary to understand the moral context of the practice of 'guardianship'. Two important points of the moral context of guardianship are here analysed.

5.3.1 The Driving Force for Substitute Decision-Making in Practice

An important research finding was that the guardians, based on the moral context, were not only the substitute decision-makers but also the people who took most of the responsibility for the person with a disability and his/her behaviour. Such responsibilities included, for example, protecting and taking care of the person with a disability, supporting the person with a disability's development, and deciding whether the person with a disability's decisions or actions should be recognised as having legal effect. In cases where the person with a disability caused damage and could not compensate for it, his/her family may have had to compensate for it on his/her behalf. My findings revealed that even though persons with disabilities' families may not necessarily have had a legal obligation to take such responsibility, the moral and cultural understanding of the family relationship may have made them feel morally obliged to take on this responsibility:

> I don't think we have to be appointed by someone to be the guardian. I am the guardian of my brother because he is my brother. (Male, with a brother with a psycho-social disability)

> I agreed that all we discussed before are the guardian's obligations, but I don't think they are a legal obligation. I think all of us will do all these things for our daughter, or son, or brother, or mother … even if we are not the guardian … because all these are our moral obligation as a part of the family. (Female, with a son with Down's syndrome)

> I know that the law provides a list of guardian's legal obligations, but we, as the guardian, in fact, have much much more obligations ... Most of these are moral obligations. (Female, with a daughter with mental impairments)

The responsibilities based on the moral context influenced the attitudes of guardians or families of persons with disabilities towards their exercise of legal capacity. The focus group discussions with guardians showed that based on either their legal or moral responsibilities, families of persons with disabilities had concerns about not only the immediate consequences of their exercise of legal capacity, for example, whether it will cause damage, but also the consequences in a long-term sense. A typical example was that when discussing a person with a disability's exercise of legal capacity to get married, the main concern of most of the guardians in the group discussion was the possible influence of the marriage on the person with a disability's future life.

> When my son said he wants to marry his girlfriend, I knew that getting married may be in his best interest for now because it will make him happy. However, I have to think about whether it is in his best interest in the future. What if they have a baby? They will not be able to raise the child, so, am I able to raise the child for them? I can foresee that the marriage will add a burden to his life and our family. The law does not give me the power to require others to share such a burden with my family. So, I have to prevent such a burden at the beginning for my son's good. It makes him sad now, but is good for him in the future ... the law does not oblige me to consider these issues, but since I am both a mother and a guardian, I have to. (Female, with a son with an intellectual disability)

As the quote suggests, the mother's worries about her son's exercise of legal capacity to get married were not rooted in her son's impairments alone. Rather, such worries were rooted in the complicated interaction between persons with impairments and different social barriers, disadvantages and inequalities, such as the lack of social support.

The concerns about exercise of legal capacity of persons with disabilities further led their guardians or families to make substitute decisions to guarantee what they thought were the best interests of the persons with disabilities. The focus group discussion with guardians revealed that more than half of the participants were aware that what they consider to be in the best interests of the person with a disability might conflict with the person's own will and preferences. However, such awareness did not necessarily lead them to be more supportive of autonomous decision-making of persons with disabilities. The barriers, disadvantages and inequalities that were already faced by persons with disabilities seemed to be one of the main factors driving families of persons with disabilities to make substitute decisions, in order to avoid further disadvantages. Guardians or families of persons with disabilities regarded substitute decision-making, for the purpose of guaranteeing their best interests, as the major approach to fulfilling their legal or moral responsibilities for the person with a disability and his/her behaviour.

The findings from this research revealed that substitute decision-making in practice was driven by the complex interaction between the concerns about impairments, the culturally based understanding and practice regarding the responsibility of families of persons with disabilities, and the social barriers and disadvantages faced by persons with disabilities. Accordingly, abolishing the legal status and authorisation of substitute decision-maker in law may not be sufficient to abolish substitute decision-making in practice. The complexity of the driving forces behind substitute decision-making in practice should be recognised and carefully taken into account in the implementation of Article 12 of the CRPD.

5.3.2 The Role Played by Family Members

Another important point of the moral context of guardianship is that it suggests a possible dilemma that should be considered in developing the legal regime of support in line with Article 12 of the CRPD, at the national level. On the one hand, in view of the current practice of guardianship, when families of persons with disabilities hold the role of the 'guardian', it may be very difficult to monitor the 'guardianship' as it is always outside the legal context. The engagement of families of persons with disabilities in the 'guardianship' practice may also result in different degrees of paternalism and undue influence. It can be argued that these issues are, to a certain extent, rooted in the cultural and moral understanding of the family relationship. Therefore, it is very likely that such matters may remain when the guardianship mechanism is replaced by support in the exercise of legal capacity where families of persons with disabilities are engaged in the support arrangements. This may be a further barrier to ensuring that all of the support provided for persons with disabilities is based on their will and preferences, as required by Article 12 of the CRPD. On the other hand, I found, in interviews with persons with disabilities, that the cultural and moral understanding of family relationships and their emotional bond with their families or guardians may influence their view towards their autonomous decision-making and the role played by their guardians:

> I was disappointed when I knew that my mum refused my job offer without asking me. I also know that I have the legal right to work and to earn money … But I cannot blame my mum … Because of my illness, my mum sacrificed a lot for me … she is nearly the only one that stands by my side … Maybe I can also make some sacrifice, for example, not go to work. (Female, 33 years old, with bipolar disorder)

Considering the cultural and moral understanding of the family relationship, as revealed by my research, it may be culturally and emotionally unacceptable to persons with disabilities, and perhaps against their will and preferences, if their family members are completely excluded from the legal regime of support in the exercise of legal capacity. Therefore, some degree of conflation between the moral context of the family relationship and the legal regime of support may be inevitable.

Given such a dilemma, a key issue to be considered in developing the legal regime of support in the light of Article 12 of the CRPD at the national level is to balance the interaction between the moral context of the family relationship and the legal regime of support. It should ensure that, on the one hand, autonomous decision-making of persons with disabilities can benefit from the trust, faith and intimacy rooted in the moral context of the family relationship; and on the other hand, that the engagement of families of persons with disabilities in the support regime does not undermine their rights, will, preferences and autonomy.

5.4 Narrow Social Network of Persons with Disabilities

I also found that under the current law and practice, persons with disabilities may live with a relatively narrow social network. This may result in various difficulties for persons with disabilities to access support in the exercise of legal capacity. In cases where the person with a disability concerned had a very narrow social network, for example, a limited number of family members, it might be difficult for others, including the potential supporter, to approach the person with a disability because the family might restrict the contact between them and others. It might also be very difficult for others to know the real will and preferences of a person with a disability with narrow social networks because others can get information about the persons with disabilities only from very limited sources. In addition, my research indicates that in comparison with individuals with broader social networks, persons with disabilities with narrow social networks might have less opportunity to get support or help from different people. Therefore, they might be at higher risk of experiencing fear and deception caused by people within their narrow social networks. Further, losing their social network per se can be a kind of threat to persons with disabilities with a narrow social network. It may, to some degree, force persons with disabilities to defer to the influences of the people within their narrow social network:

> [M]y family treats me as a troublemaker … especially my father, he is also my guardian on the disability card … he has thrown me to the mental hospital many times … Someone I know told me that my father was wrong and I should defend my rights … so what? I have no money, no job, no friend … and if they throw me out of the family, I will have no place to live. (Female, 24 years old, with bipolar disorder)

Moreover, several participants in my research pointed out an even worse possibility is that narrow social network of persons with disabilities may disappear. A specific category of cases were highlighted in which people with mental or intellectual disabilities were cared for by their parents, and their parents represented their only social relationship. The main concern raised by this was that if the person with disability's parents died before them, the person concerned may find themselves in a very isolated situation and have no-one else familiar around him/her. In such a case, it may be very difficult to develop support for either exercise of legal capacity of persons with disabilities or other more informal daily activities.

Based on these findings, it is argued that the degree to which a person with a disability has a broad, flexible and sustainable social network may be an important factor that influences the effectiveness of the support provided for them in their exercise of legal capacity. Given such influences, the implementation of Article 12 of the CRPD (2006) should take into account two issues. One is that, given that narrow social networks of some persons with disabilities is to some degree, a current social reality, it may cause difficulties in providing support for persons with disabilities in their exercise of legal capacity. Therefore, in the implementation of Article 12 of the CRPD, how to address such pre-existing difficulties and remedy the pre-existing disadvantages faced by persons with disabilities should be considered. The second issue to be considered is that to ensure the effectiveness of support in the exercise of legal capacity, the implementation of Article 12 should entail a legal regime of support that is built on diverse, flexible and sustainable social networks. Depending on the individual's will and preferences, the legal regime of support should offer the possibility of broadening social networks of persons with disabilities, which can then provide persons with disabilities with more options and further advance their autonomy. Otherwise, the legal regime of support in the exercise of legal capacity might not be able to respect and effectively promote will, preferences and autonomy of persons with disabilities.

6 Conclusion

This chapter has explored the implementation of Article 12 of the CRPD (2006) at the national level in China from a cultural perspective. Section 2 set out the theoretical framework and methodology used in this chapter to explore the implementation of international human rights law, in particular Article 12 CRPD (2006), at the national level. Analysis of research findings revealed that the full implementation of Article 12 in China should be based on both a comprehensive understanding of both Article 12 and the social and cultural context in China. Four key cultural issues that need be considered in the implementation of Article 12 have been identified. Following from both the legal and theoretical analysis, this chapter reflected on the symbiotic relationship between the implementation of Article 12 (CRPD 2006) and the relevant social and cultural context in China, on the one hand, and the importance of implementing Article 12 of the CRPD in China in a culturally sensitive way with the culturally related issues to be considered, on the other hand. This chapter demonstrates that the implementation process for Article 12 CRPD (2006) requires changes to both the relevant domestic Chinese law, and to the socio-cultural context.

References

CoRPD (Committee on the Rights of Persons with Disabilities). (2012, October 15). *Concluding observations on the initial report of China, adopted by the Committee at its eighth session (17–28 September 2012).* CRPD/C/CHN/CO/1.

CoRPD (Committee on the Rights of Persons with Disabilities). (2014, May 19). *Convention on the rights of persons with disabilities general comment no. 1 (2014): Article 12: Equal recognition before the law.* CRPD/C/GC/1.

CRPD (United Nations Convention on the Rights of Persons with Disabilities). (2006). Adopted in 2006 by the United Nations general assembly.

Donoho, D. L. (2001). Autonomy, self-governance, and the margin of appreciation: Developing a jurisprudence of diversity within universal human rights. *Emory International Law Review, 15*, 391.

Esin Örücü. (2002). Law as transposition. *The International and Comparative Law Quarterly, 51*(2), 205–223.

Esin Örücü. (2010). *Legal culture and legal transplants. Legal culture and legal transplants.* Washington, DC: XVIIIth INTERNATIONAL CONGRESS of Comparative Law.

Kroncke, J. (2012). Law and development as anti-comparative law. *Vanderbilt Journal of Transnational Law, 45*, 477.

Lord Hoffmann. (1999). Human rights and the house of lords. *Modern Law Review, 62*(2), 159–166.
Merry, S. E. (2009). *Human rights and gender violence: Translating international law into local justice*. Chicago and London: University of Chicago Press.
Merry, S. E. (2010). What is legal culture? An anthropological perspective. *Special Issue of Journal of Comparative Law, 5*(2), 40.
Mertus, J. (1999). From legal transplants to transformative justice: Human rights and the promise of transnational civil society. *American University International Law Review, 14*(5).
National People's Congress. (1999). *Contract law of the People's Republic of China (2012 Amendment)*. Order [1999] No.15 of the President of the People's Republic of China.
National People's Congress. (2017). *General provisions of the civil law of the People's Republic of China.*
Renteln, A. D. (1988). Relativism and the search for human rights. *American Anthropologist, 90*(1), 56–72. https://doi.org/10.1525/aa.1988.90.1.02a00040.
State Council. (2003). Regulation on Legal Aid.
Stein, M., & Lord, J. (2008). The domestic incorporation of human rights law and the United Nations convention on the rights of persons with disabilities. *Washington Law Review, 83*, 449.
Supreme People's Court. (1988). *Opinions of the Supreme People's Court on several issues concerning the implementation of the general principles of the civil law of the People's Republic of China* (For Trial Implementation).
Teubner, G. (1998). Legal irritants: Good faith in British law or how unifying law ends up in new divergences. *Modern Law Review, 61*(1), 11–32. https://doi.org/10.1111/1468-2230.00125.

11

Implementation of Article 19 of the CRPD in Hungary and Its Impact on the Deinstitutionalisation Process So Far

Magdi Birtha

1 Introduction

This chapter discusses the implementation of Article 19—Living independently and being included in the community, of the United Nations (UN) Convention on the Rights of Persons with Disabilities (CRPD/Convention 2006), in the context of the deinstitutionalisation process in Hungary. A decade ago, Hungary was one of the first States that ratified the CRPD along with its Optional Protocol; therefore, it is timely to assess the state of play of the implementation process and the impact of the Convention so far on the quality of life of persons with disabilities. The chapter will build on the findings of research funded by the Open Society Foundation, which studied the spending of European Union (EU) funds in Hungary, and the implementation of the first six deinsti-

M. Birtha (✉)
CDLP, National University of Ireland (NUI), Galway, Ireland

E. J. Kakoullis, K. Johnson (eds.), *Recognising Human Rights in Different Cultural Contexts*, https://doi.org/10.1007/978-981-15-0786-1_11

tutionalisation projects (Kozma et al. 2016). The author of this chapter was one of the four researchers who carried out the research project between 2015 and 2016. To some extent, the chapter will take into account the experiences of the people moving out of institutions. It will take a socio-historical-cultural approach to understand why institutions are still present in Hungary and the challenges encountered in the first projects to close them. These challenges included collective versus individual solutions, the vested interest by rural communities in keeping the institutions open, the isolation and lack of choice experienced by people living in institutions, the lack of training of staff as well as the limited provision of appropriate community services.

2 Article 19 CRPD and Its Implications at National Level

2.1 Obligations Under Article 19 CRPD

Throughout history, persons with disabilities have been denied choice and control over their lives (Quinn and Stein 2009). Most lived in isolation as mere recipients of care, either in large totalitarian institutions, or hidden in families (Quinn and Stein 2009). Quinn and Stein (2009) argue that one of the central motivations for the adoption of the CRPD was the removal of the 'invisibility' of persons with disabilities from both international law and their communities. Article 19 of the CRPD (2006) recognises the equal right of persons with disabilities to live independently and to be included in the community. It calls on States Parties to the CRPD to take effective and appropriate measures to facilitate the full inclusion and participation of persons with disabilities in the community, by ensuring that:

(a) Persons with disabilities have the opportunity to choose their place of residence and where and with whom they live on an equal basis with others, and are not obliged to live in a particular living arrangement.

(b) Persons with disabilities have access to a range of in-home, residential and other community support services, including personal assistance necessary to support living and inclusion in the community, and to prevent isolation or segregation from the community.
(c) Community services and facilities for the general population are available on an equal basis to persons with disabilities and are responsive to their needs (CRPD 2006, Art. 19).

As Quinn and Doyle (2012) argue, Article 19 builds on a more general trend towards restoring the voice and power of the individual to determine where she/he wishes to live and with whom. It interlinks with Article 12—Equal recognition before the law, of the CRPD (2006) and its requirements to reform traditional legal capacity laws and ensure that the will and preferences of persons with disabilities will be predominant. The wording of Article 19 leaves no doubt that 'choice' and 'autonomy' are the central components of its provisions, and that as an equal right, it applies to all persons with disabilities regardless of their impairment. Through the 'prism' of Article 19, 'choice' is understood in a way that empowers persons with disabilities to have a realistic prospect of a home they can afford in the community; however, financial and other constraints will naturally limit people's choices on where to live.

Article 19(b) CRPD calls for some specific support services that enable individuals to live in the community, including personal assistance and a range of in-home services. 'Personal assistance' is a relatively new concept, which derives from the Independent Living Movement,[1] and is probably the most adequate way, in line with Article 19 CRPD, to respect personal choices and provide individualised social services at the same time (Kanter 2014). However, personal assistance alone is not enough to achieve social inclusion of all persons with disabilities in the community. Article 19(c) CRPD (2006) outlines that mainstream community services and facilities, including housing, public libraries, hospitals, schools, transport, shops, markets, museums, the Internet, and social media, should be accessible and available to persons with disabilities.

[1] The term 'independent living' is derived from the Independent Living Movement, which started in the late 1960s in Berkeley, California, as a grassroots movement.

2.2 Interpretation of Article 19 CRPD and Its Implications at National Level

Article 19 regards persons with disabilities as citizens, who can actively participate in the community, and it is a key provision towards the realisation of the 'paradigm shift' from the medical to the social model of disability (Quinn and Doyle 2012). Quinn and Doyle (2012) emphasise that independent living is critically important to the intellectual and political structure of the CRPD, and is an important element through which the effect the Convention has on the everyday life of persons with disabilities can be measured. Article 19 is about empowering people to live dignified lives in the community by removing physical and social barriers, as well as providing them with adequate community-based support.

Article 19 is an example of the interrelation, interdependence and indivisibility of all human rights and entails civil and political, as well as economic, social and cultural rights. In other words, the right to independent living and being included in the community can only be realised if all civil, political, economic, social and cultural rights enshrined in this norm are fulfilled. As Degener (2014) argues, Article 19 is one of the most challenging substantive provisions of the CRPD, which brings new challenges to conventional human rights theory and jurisprudence, as it does not have a clear equivalent in binding pre-treaty law.

While Article 19 does not specifically mention institutions, the provision on the right to independent living and being included in the community is in response to the systemic institutionalisation and exclusion of persons with disabilities from society. The concept of 'independent living' has its roots in the disability rights movement and other social movements, such as the deinstitutionalisation movement that arose in the 1960s and 1970s in the United States, as well as in Scandinavia and other countries.

Institutional care has been a common living arrangement for persons with disabilities in the Western world, especially for those with intellectual or psychosocial disabilities (Quinn and Doyle 2012). In Europe, there are still over one million people living in institutions, many of them are children and adults with complex needs, intellectual, or psychosocial disabilities (Ad-Hoc Expert Group on the Transition from Institutional to Community Care 2009). Therefore, the implementation of Article 19 requires two parallel processes to take place: the process of closing down of large-scale residential institutions; and the process of investing available resources in the transition from institutional to community-based care and support services for all persons with disabilities and their families.

In different languages and cultures, many definitions exist on what constitutes 'institutional care'.[2] In this chapter, the Common European Guidelines on the Transition from Institutional to Community-based Care are used, which define an 'institution' as any residential care where:

residents are isolated from the broader community and/or compelled to live together;
residents do not have sufficient control over their lives and over decisions which affect them; and
the requirements of the organisation itself tend to take precedence over the residents' individual needs (Common European Guidelines 2012, p. 25).

While this definition does not mention the number of residents, size is an important factor for policy makers when they develop new services in the community. Although smaller and more personalised living arrangements are more likely, they do not necessarily ensure the choice and self-determination of service users (Health Service Executive 2011). Institutional characteristics can be easily reproduced even in small living arrangements of group homes for five or six people. If persons with disabilities are not seen as rights holders, their choices as service users are extremely limited, or they are coerced into using certain services in the community (Szmukler and Appelbaum 2008). When developing strategies for the transition from institutional to community-based care provision, 30 or more places in a residential facility can be considered as an 'institution', regardless of the quality of

[2] For example, in the French language, the word 'institution' means the structure, or the establishment; therefore, the English word 'deinstitutionalisation' connotes the breaking down of social structures and the system as such.

service provided there (Ad-Hoc Expert Group on the Transition from Institutional to Community Care 2009).

'Independent living' does not mean living alone, rather it means having choice and control over one's own life and lifestyle, through the combination of various environmental and individual factors, including the built environment, services, transport, or information.[3] The European Guidelines define 'community-based services' as a spectrum of services that enable individuals to live in the community, and in the case of children, to grow up in a family environment, as opposed to an institution (Common European Guidelines 2012). It encompasses early childhood care and education, in-home services, personal assistance, housing support services and other mainstream and specialised services to support the autonomy of persons with care, or support needs.

In 2017, the UN Committee on the Rights of Persons with Disabilities (Committee) issued a General Comment on Article 19 of the CRPD to clarify its interpretation, and to suggest approaches States Parties could follow on how to best implement its provisions (CRPD/C/GC/52017). The General Comment clarifies that the transition from institutional to community-based care is underpinned by the right of being included in the community, which means "living a full social life and having access to all services offered to the public and to support services offered to persons with disabilities to enable them to be fully included and participate in all spheres of social life" (CRPD/C/GC/52017, para. 16b). Deinstitutionalisation, therefore, must be accompanied by comprehensive service and community development programmes to decrease the dependency on disability-specific programmes and to ensure independent living in more rural areas. These services can, among others, relate to housing, transport, shopping, education, employment, recreational activities and all other facilities and services offered to the public, including social media (CRPD/C/GC/52017). Community-based services are ideally complemented by preventative measures, for instance, family support, income support or anti-poverty measures to eliminate the need for institutionalisation.

---

[3] Definition of the European Network on Independent Living, see at: http://enil.eu/independent-living/definitions/ (accessed 20 August 2017).

3 The CRPD in Hungary and the Role of the EU in the Implementation of Article 19 CRPD

3.1 Socio-Historical-Cultural Context: Persons with Disabilities in Hungary

Hungary is a medium-sized Member State of the EU, situated in Central-Eastern Europe with a population of 9,937,628 according to the 2011 census (KSH 2014). After the Second World War, Hungary became a satellite state of the Soviet Union, which contributed to the establishment of a socialist republic between 1947 and 1989. In 1989, it became a democratic parliamentary republic and joined the EU in 2004.

According to the 2011 census in Hungary, the total number of persons with disabilities is 456,638, which is 4.59% of the population, and the number of persons with psychosocial disabilities is 46,265.[4] In 2014, the Hungarian Central Statistical Office reported that altogether about 25,000 persons lived in institutional care, of which 16,516 were persons with intellectual, or physical disabilities and 8783 persons with psychosocial disabilities (KSH 2014). There are significant geographical differences in the prevalence of institutions, with more institutions concentrated in North-East and in South-West Hungary, than elsewhere (KSH 2014). In fact, there are fewer institutions in regions with a healthier economy and better employment statistics, which suggests that one of the main functions of institutions is to fill the local employment gaps.[5]

Hungary has a long-established practice of placing persons with disabilities in long-stay residential institutions, often against their will (Verdes 2009). The first institution was established in 1875 and similarly to other European countries, the growing number of institutions served the purpose of educating young persons with intellectual disabilities

[4] Due to the definition of 'disability' in the Hungarian Disability Law, persons with psychosocial disabilities were not counted under the category 'persons with disabilities', but separately.

[5] In 2007, altogether 85,283 persons lived in institutions in Hungary and the total number of staff employed in these institutions was not less than 22,584 people (KSH 2008), See: Verdes, T. (2009), 'A ház az intézet tulajdona', in Esély 2009/4, pp. 92–112.

(Ruzsics 2013). During the Communist era, social policy placed thousands of persons with intellectual and psychosocial disabilities in newly created institutions in old mansion buildings, mostly in rural economically deprived areas. Besides, removing from public sight a group of socially excluded people, they were also able to absorb a large part of the unskilled labour in traditionally agricultural areas that fell outside of the realm of industrial investments.

As Verdes (2009) points out, the persistent existence of institutions in Hungary is not the result of their internal coherence, but rather derives from the social structure that became stabilised by the end of the democratic transition. Institutions provided a simple and comforting answer to some elements of the post-socialist crisis, including on the one hand, the increasing unemployment rate, especially in areas where industrialisation was dismantled after the transition; and on the other hand, individualisation and decreasing solidarity in local communities (Verdes 2009). The latter trend was worsened by the lack of support services available in the community and by the fact that the vast majority of care provision to disabled or other vulnerable people fell completely back upon their families. However, by the early 1990s, family structures had changed significantly, and in nuclear families, a disabled relative residing at home had the implication that one earner, usually the woman, had to give up employment to become a full-time family carer. Family carers in Hungary face particular challenges in terms of the lack of social and financial recognition, lack of access to social rights, benefits, respite, as well as isolation and social exclusion (Verdes 2009). The lack of income and adequate work-life balance measures that would support at least taking up part-time paid occupation, resulted in an increasing risk of poverty and social deprivation for thousands of families. Once families could not bear long-term unemployment, poverty and social exclusion anymore, there was a demand coming from families to place persons with disabilities in institutional care. While institutions are not a preferred solution, but always a last resort for families, the lack of alternative services in the social care sector, for example, personal assistance, in-home nursing, day care centres and vocational training, created an urgent need and long waiting lists for institutional placements.

3.2 Hungary and the CRPD

Hungary was the first Member State of the EU and one of the first countries worldwide to ratify the CRPD on 30 March 2007, as well as its Optional Protocol on 20 July 2007. The act of ratification indicates to the international community a country's commitment to improve the human rights situation of a marginalised group. The prompt ratification of the CRPD was a good sign that Hungary was ready to promote and protect the rights of persons with disabilities. However, the early ratification of a UN human rights treaty does not necessarily result in designing a comprehensive strategy and implementing it through concrete actions. For example, some countries, such as the Netherlands and Finland, chose to first make their legal system compliant with the CRPD and then to proceed with its ratification.

The implementation of UN human rights treaties does not happen overnight and requires States Parties to align all laws, policies and programmes with the treaty's provisions (Quinn 2009). States Parties are therefore expected to demonstrate a clear understanding of their obligations and to plan the implementation in an ambitious way, taking into account whether certain provisions require immediate (civil and political rights), or progressive realisation (economic, social and cultural rights). Yet, the progressive nature of some provisions does not release States Parties from using the available resources in a treaty compliant way, as soon as possible (Quinn 2009). This chapter is unable to provide a comprehensive overview of the implementation of the CRPD in Hungary, but it will focus on what efforts have been made to implement Article 19 and to what extent they can be considered, as successful.

In view of Article 35—Reports by States Parties, of the CRPD (2006), all States Parties have to submit regular reports to the Committee, initially within two years of ratifying the CRPD and, thereafter, every four years, on how the rights enshrined in the Convention are being implemented. The Hungarian Government submitted its first report to the Committee in 2010. The Constructive Dialogue between the Hungarian Government's delegation and the Committee took place in 2012. The Committee questioned the Hungarian Government over the fact that about 25,000 persons with disabilities were still living in isolated, large-scale residential institutions, deprived of their human rights and freedoms (Birtha 2013).

In response to the Committee's remarks, the Hungarian delegation presented its plan to launch a deinstitutionalisation strategy, which would close down institutions within the next 30 years and move persons with disabilities to smaller living facilities, including group homes and so-called residential centres accommodating up to 50 people. A lengthy part of the Committee's Concluding Observations is dedicated to Article 19 CRPD, its concerns about the lengthy time frame to carry out the deinstitutionalisation process, as well as the spending of "disproportionally large resources, including regional European Union funds, on the reconstruction of large institutions, which will lead to continued segregation, in comparison with the resources allocated for setting up community-based support service networks" (CRPD/C/HUN/CO/12012, para 33). Furthermore, the Committee noted with concern that Hungary failed to provide sufficient and adequate support services in the local communities to enable persons with disabilities to live independently outside an institutional setting. The Committee specifically called on the Hungarian Government to enable persons with disabilities to:

enjoy the freedom to choose their residence on an equal basis with others;
access a full range of in-home, residential and other community services for daily life, including personal assistance; and
to enjoy reasonable accommodation with a view to supporting their inclusion in their local communities (CRPD/C/HUN/CO/12012)

Finally, the Committee also called upon Hungary to re-examine the allocation of EU funds, including the EU Regional Development Funds, and to ensure that they are spent on community-based support services in line with Article 19 of the CRPD.

3.3 Legal and Policy Context for the Deinstitutionalisation Process in Hungary

In 2012, the Hungarian government centralised its social system; therefore, social services for children and persons with disabilities were no longer managed by local authorities (Bugarszki et al. 2013). As a result of this structural change, the newly created Directorate General of Social Affairs and Child Protection now plays a central role in the Hungarian deinstitutionalisation process, as it is the managing authority for most institutions.

The Hungarian Government adopted a Deinstitutionalisation Strategy 2011–2036, which targets persons living in large-scale residential institutions, where there are more than 50 people living in one institution (1257/2011 VII.21.). Verdes (2009) argues that the initiators of the Hungarian Deinstitutionalisation Strategy were keen to adapt Western European solutions which involved moving persons with disabilities from larger to smaller living arrangements, however, they did so without reflecting on the broader human rights context in which persons with disabilities have equal citizenship rights, and can take part in the mainstream education system and labour market, just like anyone else. Furthermore, the Deinstitutionalisation Strategy lacked a vision for transforming the social sector towards a more person-centred and community-based one, which would support the autonomy and community living of a broad range of people, including older or homeless people.

Another important prerequisite to the enjoyment of the right to living independently and being included in the community is Article 12—Equal recognition before the law, of the CRPD (2006). As Lewis (2011) highlights:

> incapacity and institutionalisation are the two main mechanisms which have resulted in the segregation and isolation of persons with disabilities from society. In many European jurisdictions, the vast majority of residents in long-term institutions have been deprived of their legal capacity, with some managers of residential institutions going so far as to make deprivation of legal capacity a prerequisite for admission. (Lewis 2011, p. 175)

Since the transition in 1989, the number of persons under guardianship has doubled, and in 2011, 53,830 persons were affected, showing a steady increase.[6] Despite a few recent positive changes to the regulations

[6] Almost half of the people under guardianship are placed under plenary guardianship, which affect all aspects of their life. The other common type removes decision-making rights in certain areas

in the Hungarian Civil Code in 2014, such as the introduction of the concept of 'supported decision-making' and advance directives,[7] persons with disabilities may continue to be deprived of their legal capacity and can be placed under guardianship.[8] According to the analysis of the Hungarian Civil Liberties Union, the new Civil Code maintains a paternalistic approach towards persons with disabilities by allowing deprivation of their legal capacity (plenary, or partial guardianship), instead of providing them with adequate support that would facilitate their equal participation in society (TASZ 2014). The Guardianship Office will remain responsible for organising supported decision-making and it will be within its competence to designate a maximum of two guardians for each person with support needs in decision-making. Unfortunately, this element will prevent persons with disabilities from building a support network around them composed of both formal and informal supporters, whom they can choose from their immediate circles in line with Article 12 (CRPD 2006). While the new law moves towards a slightly more diversified and individualised assessment of the areas in which a person needs support; in practice, persons with intellectual and psychosocial disabilities may still be deprived of their legal capacity (fully, or partially), if the court deems that they lack the ability to make decisions. As a consequence, supported decision-making is only available for people with less complex support needs. The effect of the changes in the Hungarian regulations is that despite persons with disabilities being able to enjoy certain social rights, those rights are not accompanied with civil and political rights on an equal basis with others (Verdes 2009).

(e.g. healthcare or finances) is known as partial guardianship. See more Gurbai Sándor et al. (2013): Legal Capacity in Europe. A Call to Action to Governments and to the EU. Budapest, Mental Disability Advocacy Center.

[7] By 'advance directives', any person, including a person with a disability, can stipulate how major life decisions and especially treatment decisions are to be made about his or her life, at any time when he or she is unable to communicate such decisions. To date, this instrument has been primarily utilised to make advance decisions about treatment; however, its scope goes beyond this. See: Joint written comments by the International Disability Alliance, the World Network of Users and Survivors of Psychiatry, the European Disability Forum, and the European Network of (ex-) Users and Survivors of Psychiatry on Mihailovs v Latvia (Application no 35939/10).

[8] 2013. évi CLV törvény a támogatott döntéshozatalról.

3.4 The Role of the EU in the Hungarian Deinstitutionalisation Process

Hungary became a Member State of the EU in 2004 and subsequently accessed EU Funds under the Cohesion Policy, including the European Structural and Investment Funds (ESIF). To provide an indication, over the period of 2014–2020, with a national contribution of 4.63 billion Euros, Hungary has received a total budget of 29.63 billion Euros to invest in various areas, ranging from infrastructure networks to employment measures, as well as social inclusion and education.[9] While the EU does not have competence in the area of social policy, as that belongs to the Member States, the ESIF can be directed to projects supporting the labour market and social inclusion pathways (under the European Social Fund), and supporting community-based social, health and housing infrastructure, in line with deinstitutionalisation principles (under the European Regional Development Fund). These EU funds, coupled with national funding schemes, can therefore indirectly have an impact on how social protection is organised in the Member States, and are instrumental in financing the transition towards twenty-first-century solutions in the social sector. Given that along with 27 EU Member States, the EU itself also ratified the CRPD in 2010, EU legislation, policies and investments should be carried out in line with the obligations under the CRPD. Nevertheless, there is no overarching strategy for the implementation of the Convention at EU level,[10] and the realisation of Article 19 (CRPD 2006) is happening through encouraging Member States to allocate funding for the transition from institutional to community-based care services.

Moreover, in the EU's 2014–2020 programming period, the European Commission introduced some important conditions in its funding

---

[9] See at: http://ec.europa.eu/regional_policy/en/information/publications/factsheets/2016/european-structural-and-investment-funds-country-factsheet-hungary (last accessed 13 January 2019).

[10] The European Disability Strategy 2010–2020 was adopted before the EU ratified the UN CRPD and it covers only eight policy areas, but not all matters that are included in the UN CRPD. For instance, independent living is not one of the eight areas, but somehow covered under participation. See: https://eur-lex.europa.eu/LexUriServ/LexUriServ.do?uri=COM:2010:0636:FIN:en:PDF (last accessed 10 January 2019).

regulation,[11] the so-called ex-ante conditionalities,[12] to ensure that the ESIF will support the shift from institutional care to community-based support services (Quinn and Doyle 2012). This includes measures that prevent institutional care and investment in building or renovating long-stay residential institutions, from EU funding.[13] The European Commission identified 12 Member States,[14] including Hungary, where concrete measures on deinstitutionalisation must be included in the National Strategic Policy Framework, as a prerequisite for spending EU funding. This is a good example of how the EU, although with its limited competence, can still generate positive changes in the area of human rights and social inclusion in its Member States.

In 2015, the CRPD Committee in the Concluding Observations to the EU noted that "despite changes in regulations, the European Structural and Investment Funds continue to be used in different Member States for the maintenance of residential institutions rather than for the development of support services for persons with disabilities in local communities" (CRPD/C/EU/CO/12015, para. 50). The Committee furthermore recommended that the EU strengthen its monitoring of the use of the funds to ensure that they are used strictly for the development of support services for persons with disabilities in local communities, and not for the renovation, or expansion of institutions (CRPD/C/EU/

[11] Regulation (EU) No 1303/2013 of the European Parliament and the Council of 17 December 2013 laying down common provisions on the European Regional Development Fund, the European Social Fund, the Cohesion Fund, the European Agricultural Fund for Rural Development and the European Maritime and Fisheries Fund and laying down general provisions on the European Regional Development Fund, the European Social Fund, the Cohesion Fund and the European Maritime and Fisheries Fund and repealing Council Regulation (EC) No 1083/2006. Available at: https://eur-lex.europa.eu/legal-content/EN/TXT/HTML/?uri=CELEX:32013R1303&from=EN (last accessed 10 January 2019).

[12] Ex-ante conditionalities are one of the key elements of the cohesion policy reform for 2014–2020. They were introduced for the European Structural and Investment Funds (ESI Funds) to ensure that all necessary institutional and strategic policy arrangements for the effective and efficient use of ESI Funds are in place at national level, before funding is released to the Member States. See: https://ec.europa.eu/regional_policy/en/policy/what/glossary/e/ex-ante-conditionalities (last accessed 10 January 2019).

[13] More information on the ex-ante conditionalities is available at: https://communitylivingforeurope.org/exanteconditionality/ (last accessed 30 September 2017).

[14] The 12 Member States are Bulgaria, Czech Republic, Estonia, Greece, Hungary, Lithuania, Latvia, Poland, Romania, Slovenia, Slovakia and Croatia.

CO/12015). It also recommended that in the case of misuse, the EU should withdraw payments. In practice, after the agreement on the general direction and framework for investment (the so-called Operational Programmes), the European Commission has limited competence to closely monitor the implementation of projects at national level. Similar to the realisation of international human rights treaties, it is up to the countries to monitor rigorously and ensure full compliance with different international obligations and regulations. In summary, the EU plays an important role in facilitating the deinstitutionalisation process and independent living of persons with disabilities in Hungary, by providing a large amount of funding mainly through the Regional Development Fund and Social Fund; however, it is up to Hungary to guarantee that the funds are indeed used in a CRPD compliant way.

4 Experiences from the First Deinstitutionalisation Projects Financed by the EU in Hungary

The research that serves as a primary reference in this chapter was carried out between December 2014 and March 2016, by a research team, including the author of this chapter. The aim of the research was to provide information and expand knowledge of advocacy work in the 2014–2020 programming period. The research report consisted of three methodologically distinct studies:

Study 1 discussed whether EU funding in the 2007–2013 programming period facilitated deinstitutionalisation and the development of community living in Hungary, using a structured analysis of publicly available documents and information obtained from the relevant organisations, as well as interviews with stakeholders;

Study 2 analysed the experiences of the implementation of the six deinstitutionalisation projects;

Study 3 focused on the narratives of persons with disabilities who are moving out of the institutions as a result of the deinstitutionalisation projects.

The purpose in regard to the first deinstitutionalisation project was to assess the implementation process, especially by addressing the positive and negative aspects of the process. We relied on three main sources of information: the implementation plans; the final reports and other relevant documents; as well as field trips and interviews with the management of the institutions and other stakeholders.

It is important to note that while Hungary had already accessed EU funds in the 2007–2013 funding period, the preparation for this period had been completed before Hungary had ratified the CRPD. As the findings from the research discussed below show, despite the Operational Programme's mention of 'deinstitutionalisation' as a primary goal, there was no guarantee in the text of the programmes that only investments that support the closing of institutions would be financed (Kozma et al. 2016). Due to the lack of adequate indicators and benchmarks, 40% of the total funding supported large-scale institutions. During the 2007–2013 funding period, both the European Commission and the Hungarian Government used the CRPD as a reference framework, rather than a solid guideline to finance deinstitutionalisation projects (Kozma et al. 2016). Nevertheless, there were some important projects that contributed positively to the implementation of Article 19 (CRPD 2006) and created community-based support services for persons with autism and their families, and improved accessibility for persons with visual or physical impairments (Kozma et al. 2016).

This part of the chapter will build on the findings of the research[15] that studied the role of EU funding in the deinstitutionalisation process in Hungary and the experiences of the first six deinstitutionalisation projects so far (Kozma et al. 2016). The aim of the research was to study to what extent the projects that received funding for deinstitutionalisation and community living had been in line with the CRPD. The scope of the study covered the 2007–2013 programming period and the planning and preparatory work for the 2014–2020 programming period. Initially, the research aimed to cover in detail the experiences of persons with disabilities upon leaving the institutions, but due to significant delays in the

[15] The research was carried out between December 2014 and March 2016, commissioned by the Hungarian Civil Liberties Union and financed by the Open Society Foundation.

project's implementation, this was not feasible. In general, the implementation of the CRPD and the distribution of EU funding presented a challenge for both the Hungarian public administration and the social and disability policy sector.

4.1 The Selection of Deinstitutionalisation Projects

In 2012, the Hungarian National Development Agency put out a call for proposals[16] for deinstitutionalisation projects, and decided to support six projects. The first residents were supposed to leave the institutions in January 2015, but there was about a year-long delay due to different bureaucratic barriers. Most of these institutions are located in remote villages in economically disadvantaged parts of the country. The table below summarises the distribution of the roughly 700 people who were to be deinstitutionalised, but apparently, the projects did not target everyone living in these institutions (Kozma et al. 2016). In three institutions (Berzence, Mérk, Bélapátfalva), about 100 people, mostly older people and persons with profound intellectual disabilities, were not considered as 'able to live outside of the institution' (Table 11.1).

In the application form to take part in the first round of deinstitutionalisation projects, managers of the institutions described their commitment to improve the inhuman living conditions of the residents, as institutions were in overcrowded, outdated and ecologically unsustainable buildings. For example, there were 12–15 people in a room, a lack of insulation and inadequate heating. It is important to acknowledge that there was no willingness from other institutions to apply to the project call and these six institutions were indeed pioneers in starting the deinstitutionalisation process in Hungary. There was also a lack of coordination in the deinstitutionalisation process, as the National Committee for the Coordination of the Replacement of Institutions emerged to be a weak body, lacking both in resources and mandate, to be a strong actor in the deinstitutionalisation process (Kozma et al. 2016).

[16] Under project call TIOP 3.4.1.-A-11/1.

Table 11.1 The six participating institutions in the deinstitutionalisation process and the number of people leaving institutions

Name of the institution	Location (Hungary)	Residents	Number of beds in the institution	Number of people leaving the institution
Szent Lukács Görögkatolikus Szeretetszolgálat Ápoló-Gondozó Otthon[a]	Szakoly[b]	Persons with disabilities	150	150
Kalocsa Város Önkormányzat Egyesített Szociális Intézménye Értelmi Fogyatékosok Otthona	Kalocsa[c]	Persons with disabilities	60	60
Aranysziget Otthon Szentesi Otthona	Szentes[d]	Persons with psychosocial disabilities	90	90
Somogy Megyei Szeretet Szociális Otthon	Berzence[e]	Persons with psychosocial disabilities	150 (144 filled)	120
Bélapátfalvi Idősek, Fogyatékosok Otthona és Módszertani Intézete[f]	Bélapátfalva[g]	Persons with disabilities	200	150
Szabolcs-Szatmár-Bereg-Megyei Önkormányzat Ápoló-Gondozó Otthona	Mérk[h]	Persons with disabilities	120	102
Total			770	672

[a]St. Lukács Greek Catholic Large-Scale Residential Institution
[b]Population: 2917
[c]Population: 17,008
[d]Population: 28,444
[e]Population: 2704
[f]Bélapátfalva Large-Scale Institution and Methodology Center for Older People and Persons with Disabilities
[g]Population: 3187
[h]Population: 2266

4.2 Preparation for the Deinstitutionalisation Process

The Hungarian deinstitutionalisation projects were supposed to be initiated and carried out by the very same people who had been running institutional care services for decades. These are managers and staff of institutions, including nurses, carers, social workers and others, who have viewed persons with disabilities for a very long time as care recipients and not necessarily as rights holders. One of the common characteristics of institutional care is the tendency to give preference to the organisation's requirements over the residents' individual needs, and to subsequently neglect the personal choices, will and preferences of those living there. This is why large-scale institutions can hardly function in a way that respects the rights of persons with disabilities.[17]

4.2.1 Preparing the Staff of the Institutions

A unique element in the Hungarian deinstitutionalisation process was the creation of a 'mentor system' to provide a professional support network available to the institutions for the preparation and implementation of the deinstitutionalisation project.[18] The role of the mentors was to support the management in carrying out the large-scale organisational change, as well as the staff and residents in coping with the transition. In these terms, despite some structural problems, such as the selection of mentors, preparation of mentors, timing, and the number of mentors per institutions that were reported by both mentors and the institutions; the mentor system had the potential to better oversee the human side of the deinstitutionalisation process and look beyond an investment project of purchasing land and building houses. However, the main problem with the mentor system was that the management and staff of the institutions had different expectations of the outcome of mentoring, namely that the mentors would provide

[17] For instance, violation of the right to liberty will occur whenever people are denied to leave the institution without assistance.

[18] Under project call TÁMOP 5.4.5-11-1.

guidance on how to carry out the deinstitutionalisation. Although the mentors were not experts on deinstitutionalisation, they were able to coach the institutions through a difficult and stressful transition process. According to interviews with mentors, the greatest challenge was to convince the staff of the institutions that deinstitutionalisation is a realistic and feasible process, and to change their attitude towards persons with disabilities. While the staff in all of the six institutions eventually became more positive about the deinstitutionalisation process, it is still questionable whether everyone who provided nursing care in institutional care settings is able to adapt to the new professional challenges and to become personal assistants in supported living facilities.

4.2.2 Involvement of Persons with Disabilities Who Moved Out of the Institutions

The involvement of persons with disabilities in the deinstitutionalisation process happened through two main channels: by preparing them to move out and live independently, and by their involvement in some of the decisions about the project's implementation. According to the research report, there was no person-centred planning tool available to ensure the meaningful involvement of all persons who were affected by the projects, and the complex needs assessment tool was too limited for this purpose (Kozma et al. 2016). Interestingly, the projects wanted to make people to become 'capable' of living independently with as little support as possible, and they even determined the project's success on the basis of individuals' abilities to 'live independently'. First of all, it is impossible to fully prepare people who have spent most of their lives in institutional care to live independently while they are still living in institutions. Preparation and most importantly counselling should be available for the transition period, but the real support should be provided when persons with disabilities settle into their new life and learn how to cope with everyday life situations outside of the walls of the institution. Second, this approach showed that the concept of 'independent living' was misinterpreted by the management of the institutions, as in practice anyone can live 'independently' with as little, or as much support as is necessary (Kozma et al. 2016).

As mentioned earlier, the research aimed to explore the experiences of people after they moved out of the institution, however, this was not possible due to the delays in the project's implementation. However, by using a participatory research method, 'Photovoice' (Booth and Booth 2003), the voices of persons with disabilities from one of the institutions (Szakoly) were channelled to a certain degree into the research.[19] The core of the Photovoice method is that participants from a marginalised group make a photo-documentation in order to explain fundamental changes in their lives that otherwise would be difficult to share by using merely verbal communication tools, for example, during interviews.

According to the photographs and the information that the residents shared, it seemed that they took part in the deinstitutionalisation process from the planning stage and were looking forward to moving out.[20] This included deciding with whom they wanted to live, or about the colour of their bedroom in their new home. Although furniture was purchased through public procurement, those who had personal belongings, including furniture, could take them to the new apartments to make the space more personal. The research found that the residents mostly expected improvement in the quality of their living arrangements, but also in their quality of life, after moving to smaller group homes or flats, including more security, or less conflict with fellow residents, despite the fact that they did not have a choice about where they lived.

4.2.3 Preparing the Local Community for the Deinstitutionalisation Process

In Hungary, wherever there is an institution, most people in the local community have been employed by, or linked to, the institution in one way or another. These people often have first-hand experiences and know the residents of the institutions by name; therefore, they do not necessar-

[19] Seven people took place in the Photovoice data collection between October 2015 and February 2016.

[20] From mentor interviews the researchers knew that it was not the case in other institutions.

ily hold the same fears and stereotypes as other members of society who have never had personal contact due to the long-standing segregation, for instance, in the education system or labour market (Bugarszki et al. 2013). This factor may have had an impact on the attitude of the entire community when persons with disabilities were moving out of institutions. For example, some institutions organised public events with the local community to improve their attitude towards persons with disabilities. In two cases, there was an objection by the local city council against allowing persons with disabilities to move into supported living facilities as part of the deinstitutionalisation process.[21] Residents and members of the city council strongly opposed the idea to create group homes in Bélapátfalva and Szilvásvárad, arguing that as a result estate prices would drop, and that persons with disabilities may disturb others in the community or misbehave in public and their presence would have a negative impact on tourism. Initially, the mayor shared these prejudices, but due to the increasing pressure from the media and civil society organisations, he made a public statement that persons with disabilities have a constitutional right to live in these towns and that the purchasing of group homes should not depend on public attitudes. Unfortunately, the voices of persons with disabilities were completely missing from the discourse. This incident shows that local communities need awareness training, information and face-to-face meetings with persons with disabilities to make the deinstitutionalisation process smooth and to protect persons with disabilities from potential hate crimes.

4.3 Compliance of the First Deinstitutionalisation Projects with the CRPD?

Overall, the research found that the implementation plans for the first six deinstitutionalisation projects were not in line with the provisions of the CRPD (2006). First, only a minority of the residents had the opportunity to move to flats; the majority were placed in smaller residential institutions housing up to 25–30 people. In line with the recommendations

[21] See: http://ataszjelenti.blog.hu/2013/09/20/belapatfalva_es_szilvasvarad (last accessed 25 February 2018).

issued by the CRPD Committee, these so-called residential centres are to be considered as 'mini institutions' and are unable to ensure 'independent living' for persons with disabilities (CRPD/C/HUN/CO/1). Second, it is against the CRPD's provisions to leave older people and persons with complex support needs in institutional care, and to carry out the deinstitutionalisation process in a selective way (CRPD/C/HUN/CO/1). Lastly, the implementation plans did not clarify the number of living arrangements and their capacity, thus it was difficult to see how many people would actually be able to move to supported living facilities. As the Open Society Foundation (OSF) funded research concludes, the "closure of institutions is not part of a comprehensive reform strategy that would challenge the circumstances that have perpetuated the institutionalisation of persons with disabilities, but rather has been a piecemeal process" (Kozma et al. 2016, p. 12).

5 Main Barriers to Carrying Out Successful Deinstitutionalisation in Hungary

The following part of the chapter includes a reflection of the main challenges towards successful deinstitutionalisation in Hungary. The aspects outlined below derive from existing literature (Bass (2008), Bulic et al. (2009), Degener (2016), Degener and Koster-Dreese (1995), Kálmán and Könczei (2002), Kozma (2008), Parker and Clements (2012), Walmsley and Johnson (2003), Wang and Burris (1997)), reports and analysis available on the Hungarian deinstitutionalisation process. This list of concerns is not exhaustive, but refers to some key barriers to making the transition from institutional to community living and social inclusion of persons with disabilities a reality. Ultimately, Article 19 (CRPD 2006) is about supporting persons with disabilities to be included in society and to make choices about their own life, like anyone else. As mentioned above, the deprivation of legal capacity and existing substituted decision-making via guardianship present a great legal barrier towards the independent living of persons with disabilities in Hungary.

5.1 Local Interest in Keeping the Institutions Alive

As Bugarszki et al. (2013) pointed out, local city councils in Hungary have a vested interest in keeping institutions alive, and more specifically in keeping jobs in place, as institutions are often the main employers in economically less developed areas. It is important to note that many large-scale institutions in Hungary are situated in rural areas and thus represent an important economic factor for the community. As the manager of one institution explained:

> Everyone in this town has already worked in the institution, or is currently working in the institution, or will be working in the institution at some point. (Bugarszki et al. 2013, p. 20)

Local governments are no longer responsible for the running and maintenance of institutions in Hungary, but they are still powerful actors when it comes to political lobbying at national level (Bugarszki et al. 2013). Moreover, they are interested in spending the available public funding for the deinstitutionalisation processes locally, for example, by purchasing estates or residential units within the territory of their own municipality, or organising different support services themselves, such as catering, day care, health and rehabilitation services. From their perspective, deinstitutionalisation is a threatening process that may result in financial loss and increased unemployment. The local economic concern may easily pave the way to centralised deinstitutionalisation projects with the aim of keeping persons with disabilities in place along with jobs in the social services sector. This potentially also prevents persons with disabilities from choosing the place where they want to live after leaving the institution. This approach does not reflect Article 19 of the Convention and its main purpose, which is to include persons with disabilities in the community and to respect their choice on where and with whom they want to live. As the implementation of the first completed deinstitutionalisation projects show, the Hungarian deinstitutionalisation process is very much dominated by an 'institutional logic', which is based on the view that for economic reasons it is better to keep persons with support needs close to the old institution.

Building on international examples, it is also questionable whether the management team of large-scale institutions is able to successfully lead the transition process from institutional to community-based care services. In Hungary, it is the institution that has to apply for the available grant to carry out the deinstitutionalisation process. As described above, the deinstitutionalisation process requires a complete change in attitude both in terms of the perception of persons with disabilities, as well as regarding how social care services should be provided. Bugarszki et al. (2013) notes that managers of large-scale institutions are not well placed to lead on the closure of institutions, in view of their conflict of interest.

5.2 Lack of a 'Paradigm Shift' in the Perception of Persons with Disabilities

Unlike in some Western European countries, the deinstitutionalisation process in Hungary has not emerged as a grass-root civil rights movement led by persons with disabilities themselves, but has been motivated by various external factors. The ratification of the CRPD has indeed been the main driver behind the adoption of the Hungarian Deinstitutionalisation Strategy and the revision of the relevant legal and policy framework. Unfortunately however, persons with lived experience of institutional care were not involved in the preparation or implementation of the deinstitutionalisation projects so far. It is a positive element that some civil society organisations, which represent persons with disabilities, may have had some influence on the process through their membership in the National Committee for the Coordination of the Replacement of Institutions; nevertheless, this does not release the State from its obligations under Article 4(3) of the CRPD to involve the voices of self-advocates more directly in the whole process.[22] Social care and special education professionals who contributed to advancing the deinstitution-

[22] Article 4(3) of the CRPD states that 'In the development and implementation of legislation and policies to implement the present Convention, and in other decision-making processes concerning issues relating to persons with disabilities, States Parties shall closely consult with and actively involve persons with disabilities, including children with disabilities, through their representative organizations' (UN CRPD).

alisation agenda did not necessarily embrace a holistic approach, and their assessment of the success factors from Western countries was also limited to the moving of people out of institutions. In Hungary, persons with disabilities are still seen by policy makers as 'recipients' of social services, and not as 'active citizens'.

Furthermore, the deinstitutionalisation projects in Hungary were considered as 'investment projects' to be carried out by the institutions' management. The management centrally organised the purchasing of land or houses, and was obligated by rules on public funding, to use public procurement to purchase furniture and other goods. Despite some ad-hoc training sessions provided by the centrally appointed mentors, the management and staff of the institutions were not adequately prepared to change their perceptions of persons with disabilities from dependents in receipt of care towards rights holders who are able to live independently in the community with support and make decisions over their own lives. Further, the negative effect of applying a medical model of disability by carers and service providers who are working in institutions should not be underestimated. The 'paradigm shift' from the medical to the social model of disability does not happen overnight, and it may be personal attitudes of professionals in their immediate circle that undermine the enjoyment of the rights of persons with disabilities.

5.3 The Persistence of Institutional Care Following Deinstitutionalisation

One of the recurring questions in the implementation plans of the Hungarian deinstitutionalisation projects was how to use the old buildings after the residents leave. The implementation plans proposed to create so-called resource centres in the old buildings that could function as a day care centre, medical centre or even a common kitchen to cater for the new group homes. These ideas all point to the same outcome: keeping people with support needs close to the old institution. Despite moving people to a different living arrangement, they would remain dependent on the myriad of social and healthcare services offered by the very same institution that once deprived them of their liberty on a day-to-day basis.

Even if the deinstitutionalisation process continues to advance in Hungary, persons with disabilities will continue to depend on institutional support, unless the State starts developing person-centred, individualised and community-based support systems. Only these types of services would allow persons with disabilities to choose and purchase the social services they want to use. Bagenstos (2012) argues that in the 1970s and 1980s, the first attempts in the United States to deinstitutionalise people failed due to the lack of attention to community-based facilities and services. The European Social Fund and European Regional Development Fund have been made available to cover the costs of transition towards more modern, community-based services; however, the use of EU funding in Hungary so far has not led to the development of country-wide, individualised budget schemes, personal assistance, or other empowering forms of service provision.

6 Conclusion

Building on the experiences of the last couple of years in Hungary, there have been some important positive steps to start the deinstitutionalisation process and to close down large-scale institutional care settings, in which persons with intellectual and psychosocial disabilities have been routinely placed for decades. Hungary began to use significant amounts of EU funding to move investments towards community-based solutions that are more in line with Article 19 of the CRPD (2006). Nevertheless, this chapter has shown that these investment projects are not underpinned by an overarching vision to create wide-ranging person-centred support services (such as personal budgets and personal assistance), which would support and enable people to make decisions about where and with whom they want to live. This further raises concerns about the potential re-institutionalisation, in the newly established supported living facilities, to which the Hungarian deinstitutionalisation process does not offer any possible solutions. This could happen for instance through the persistent institutional culture in the smaller living facilities.

The centrally organised, top-down approach that dominates the deinstitutionalisation process in Hungary cannot result in solutions that are fully compliant with Article 19 of the CRPD. Concurrently however, the deinstitutionalisation projects so far may undoubtedly bring positive changes to the quality of life and freedom of persons who had lived for decades isolated in overcrowded institutions. Nevertheless, one should not forget that the CRPD calls for more than merely improving inhuman living conditions for persons with disabilities; rather, it envisions a society in which persons with disabilities are rights holders and participate fully in all spheres of life on an equal basis with others. All States Parties to the CRPD should keep that in mind and implement its provisions in an ambitious way.

References

Bagenstos, S. R. (2012). *The past and future of deinstitutionalization litigation*. Law & economics working papers.

Bass, L. (Ed.). (2008). *Amit tudunk és amit nem … Az értelmi fogyatékos emberek helyzetéről Magyarországon*. Budapest: Kézenfogva Alapítvány.

Birtha, M. (2013). *Mennyire lehet konstruktív egy párbeszéd?—Az ENSZ CRPD Bizottságának felülvizsgálata a Fogyatékosjogi Egyezmény magyarországi végrehajtásáról*. Fundamentum (Hung Hum Rights J) (in Hungarian).

Booth, T., & Booth, W. (2003). In the frame: Photovoice ad mothers with learning difficulties. *Disability & Society, 18*(4), 431–442.

Bugarszki, Z., Eszik, O., & Kondor, Z. (2013). *Az intézményi férőhely kiváltás alakulása Magyarországon 2012–2013*. ELTE-TÁTK.

Bulic, I., Evans, J., Parker, C., Quinn, G., & Stein, M. (2009). *Focus on article 19 of the UN convention on the rights of persons with disabilities*. ECCL.

Common European Guidelines on the Transition from Institutional to Community-based Care. (2012). European expert group on the transition from institutional to community-BASED care. Online publication. Retrieved from https://deinstitutionalisationdotcom.files.wordpress.com/2017/07/guidelines-final-english.pdf.

Concluding observations on the initial periodic report of Hungary, adopted by the Committee at its eighth session (2012, September 17–28). CRPD/C/HUN/CO/1.

Concluding observations on the initial report of the European Union. (2015). CRPD/C/EU/CO/1.

Degener, T. (2014). *A human rights model of disability*. Retrieved February 25, 2018, from https://www.researchgate.net/publication/283713863_A_human_rights_model_of_disability.

Degener, T. (2016). Disability in a human rights context. *Laws, 2016*(5), 35.

Degener, T., & Koster-Dreese, Y. (1995). *Human rights and disabled persons: Essays and relevant human rights instruments*. Dordrecht and Boston: M. Nijhoff.

European Network on Independent Living. (2015). *Report on personal assistance services in Europe*.

Fundamental Rights Agency. (2012). *Choice and control: The right to independent living Experiences of persons with intellectual disabilities and persons with mental health problems in nine EU Member States*.

General comment No. 5. (2017). On living independently and being included in the community, CRPD/C/GC/5.

Gurbai, S., et al. (2013). *Legal capacity in Europe. A call to action to governments and to the EU*. Budapest: Mental Disability Advocacy Center.

Health Service Executive. (2011). *Time to move on from congregated settings: A strategy for community inclusion*. Report of the Working Group on Congregated Settings.

Kálmán, Z., & Könczei, G. (2002). *A Taigetosztól az esélyegyenlőségig*. Osiris kiadó.

Kanter, A. S. (2014). *The development of disability rights under international law: From charity to human rights*. Abingdon: Routledge.

Kozma, Á. (2008). Az intézetben élő értelmi fogyatékos emberek helyzete. In L. Bass (Ed.), *Amit tudunk és amit nem ... Az értelmi fogyatékos emberek helyzetéről Magyarországon* (pp. 157–177). Budapest: Kézenfogva Alapítvány.

Kozma, A., Petri, G., Balogh, A., & Birtha, M. (2016). *The role of EU funding in deinstitutionalisation (DI) in Hungary and the experiences of the DI programme so far*. TASZ

KSH. (2008). *Szociális statisztikai évkönyv, 2007*. Budapest: Központi Statisztikai Hivatal.

KSH. (2014). *2011. évi Népszámlálás. 11. Fogyatékossággal élők*. Budapest: KSH. Retrieved from http://www.ksh.hu/docs/hun/xftp/idoszaki/nepsz2011/nepsz_11_2011.pdf.

Lewis, O. (2011). Advancing legal capacity jurisprudence. *European Human Rights Law Review, 6*, 700–706.

Parker, C., & Clements, L. (2012). *The European Union and the right to community living*. New York: Open Society Foundations.

Quinn, G. (2009). Resisting the "temptation of elegance": Can the convention on the rights of persons with disabilities socialise states to right behaviour? In O. M. Arnadóttir & G. Quinn (Eds.), *The UN convention on the rights of persons with disabilities* (pp. 215–256). Leiden: Martinus Nijhoff Publishers.
Quinn, G., & Doyle, S. (2012). *'Getting a life'—Living independently and being included in the community*. UN OHCHR.
Quinn, G., & Stein, M. (2009). Challenges in realizing the right to live in the community, in focus on article 19 of the UN convention on the rights of persons with disabilities. In *European coalition for community living*.
Report of the Ad-Hoc Expert Group on the Transition from Institutional to Community Care. (2009).
Ruzsics, I. (2013). *A kitagolás folyamatai Európában és Magyarországon*. Mentor(h)áló 2.0 Program, TÁMOP-4.1.2.B.2-13/1-2013-0008 projekt.
Szmukler, G., & Appelbaum, P. (2008). Treatment pressures, leverage, coercion, and compulsion in mental health care. *Journal of Mental Health, 17*(3), 233–244.
TASZ. (2014). *Joghalál a törvényben: A fogyatékos személyek bármikor megfoszthatók önrendelkezési joguktól.*
United Nations Convention on the Rights of Persons with Disabilities and Its Optional Protocol.
Verdes, T. (2009). A ház az intézet tulajdona. *Esély, 2009*(4), 92–112.
Walmsley, J., & Johnson, K. (2003). *Inclusive research with people with learning disabilities: Past, present, and futures*. London: Jessica Kingsley Publishers.
Wang, C., & Burris, M. A. (1997). Photovoice: Concept, methodology, and use for participatory needs assessment. *Health Education & Behavior, 24*(3), 369–387.

12

Implementing Article 19 of the CRPD in Nordic Welfare States: The Culture of Welfare and the CRPD

Ciara Brennan and Rannveig Traustadóttir

1 Introduction

The Nordic countries are internationally known for their generous welfare policies and services. This is true of welfare policies and provisions in general (Kangas and Kvist 2013) as well as disability policy and disability services (Goodley 2010). In this chapter we discuss the implementation of the United Nations (UN) Convention on the Rights of Persons with Disabilities (Convention/CRPD 2006) in three Nordic welfare states: Iceland, Norway and Sweden. Our focus is primarily on Article 19—Living independently and being included in the community (CRPD 2006). The Nordic countries were European pioneers in deinstitutionalisation and have made significantly more progress in community-based services than most other countries. Since the 1970s, law and policy reforms have prohibited large institutions and offered access to community services, including personal assistance. In the early 1990s, "Norway

C. Brennan • R. Traustadóttir (✉)
Centre for Disability Studies, University of Iceland, Reykjavík, Iceland
e-mail: csb1@hi.is; rannvt@hi.is

E. J. Kakoullis, K. Johnson (eds.), *Recognising Human Rights in Different Cultural Contexts*, https://doi.org/10.1007/978-981-15-0786-1_12

and Sweden, decided to close all institutions as a matter of public policy" (Tøssebro et al. 2012, p. 135). As a result, disability human rights scholars and activists have looked to the Nordic countries for promising examples of deinstitutionalisation and community-based services (Brennan et al. 2018). Referring to the implementation of the CRPD in Europe, Quinn and Arnardóttir suggest that the Nordic model of reshaping social services "to support independent living and in ensuring adequate community support to hasten deinstitutionalization is worthy of study in its own right" (2009, p. xv).

All five Nordic countries have signed and ratified the CRPD and thereby obligated themselves to implement its requirements. Considering all the above, it is logical to assume that implementing Article 19 of the CRPD (2006) would be smooth and non-problematic in the Nordic countries. Yet, recent studies have highlighted an increase in the size of institutions and retrenchment of personal assistance services in the two most advanced Nordic countries, Norway and Sweden, since their respective governments ratified the Convention in 2011 and 2008 respectively (Askheim et al. 2014; Brennan et al. 2018; Rice et al. 2015). The chapter draws on qualitative research carried out in Iceland, Norway and Sweden. It examines the barriers to implement some of the core rights of the Convention, such as independent living and personal assistance, in three Nordic countries. In essence it asks how the human rights approach of the CRPD 'fits' within the culture of the Nordic welfare states. Culture is a challenging term to define, and scholars have presented multiple ways to understand culture (Spencer-Oatey 2012). When referring the 'culture' of the Nordic welfare states in this chapter, we refer broadly to an understanding of culture as the characteristics and knowledge of a particular group of people, culture as a way of life, including values, beliefs, customs, language and traditions.

2 The Nordic Context

Many of the general principles of the CRPD (2006) are reflected in the laws and policies that regulate Nordic disability service provisions including deinstitutionalisation, community-based services, independent living and personal assistance (Brennan et al. 2018; Hvinden 2013). Esping-Andersen (1990, 2002) has suggested that a key goal of the Nordic welfare states is to "strive for greater individual independence" (Esping-Andersen 2002, p. 13). This emphasis is evident in laws and policies in all three countries. For instance, the Swedish Act Concerning Support and Service Provision for Persons with Certain Functional Impairments (LSS: 1993: 387) contains a right to access personal assistance and requires that services are tailored to meet "the individual needs of the recipient and be framed in such a way that they are easily accessible for those who need them and enhance the ability of the latter to live an independent life". Swedish law recognises "the right to be independent and the welfare state has a responsibility to lift the care burden from the closest persons" (Lewin et al. 2008, p. 244). Likewise, the Icelandic Act on services for disabled people with long-term support needs (38/2018) emphasises individual independence and tailor-made service provision. Article 1 of the Act, which came into force in October 2018, states that the services outlined in this act "shall aim at providing disabled people with the necessary support so that they can enjoy full human rights equal to others and create the conditions for independent life on their own terms. In implementing services for disabled people, respect for human dignity, autonomy and independence should be respected". These and many other Nordic laws and policies are regularly referenced as 'best practice' in comparative European studies. Nordic researchers, however, have highlighted the gaps between the policies and the reality on the ground. For instance, a study of services for persons with intellectual disabilities (ID) in the Nordic countries acknowledged "the gap between the national policy ideals and the practical realities confronting people with ID. It appears as if national government ideals evaporate on their way to implementation" (Tøssebro et al. 2012, p. 141).

In discussing the Nordic context, it is important to note that the values and ideologies that drove the Nordic deinstitutionalisation reforms were quite different from the human rights principles of the CRPD (Degener 2016). Deinstitutionalisation had its roots in the principle of normalisation, first conceptualised by Nordic scholars in the 1960s (Nirje 1969). In line with the principles of normalisation, the Nordic countries closed large institutions and established an extensive system of community-based services originally mostly focused on people with intellectual disabilities, who had been the majority of those living in the institutions. The emphasis was on making it possible for people with intellectual disabilities to lead an existence as normal as possible and take part in everyday community life (Flynn and Nitsch 1980). In the beginning the focus was on residential services, and the first wave of group homes were established in the 1970s followed by community-based sheltered workshops and other 'integrated' services. These were indeed revolutionary ideas in the 1970s and 1980s. The emphasis, however, was on training and rehabilitation, care and protection. Combined with the basic Nordic welfare values of equality through universal benefits and services, which aimed to address a wide range of social inequalities and ensure active citizenship, this formed the basis for the current disability service system which has become an integral part of Nordic welfare services (Christiansen and Markkola 2005; Hvinden 2013). Looking back, the disability services developed in the Nordic countries had, and still possess, many characteristics of being paternalistic in that the professionals and staff within the services were expected to act in a manner that often limited the person's or group's liberty or autonomy but which was intended to promote their own good or prevent harm to that person (Dworkin 2010; Löve et al. 2018; Sandvin and Lichtwarck 2005).

3 The Research

The chapter draws on qualitative research carried out in Iceland, Norway and Sweden between 2012 and 2014. The overall aim of the research was to explore the meaning of independent living and personal assistance as well as the implementation of Article 19 of the CRPD (2006). In-depth interviews were carried out with multiple stakeholders who were involved in the implementation of Article 19 in all three countries. The data that form the basis for the chapter include interviews with 29 leaders of Centers for Independent Living and 12 policymakers. The data was analysed according to the constant comparative method of grounded theory which involves interpreting the data though coding, creating analytic memos during the data collection process and searching for central themes (Creswell 2007). The findings reported here are primarily based on the perspectives of a group of leaders in the Disability Movement who had extensive knowledge of the Convention and the laws and policies for independent living in their home country. We believe that understanding the views and perspectives of persons with disabilities and their representative organisations is vital for assessing the implementation of the CRPD (2006). The qualitative approach enabled us to gain an in-depth understanding of the meanings and implementations of human rights principles of the CRPD from the research participants' perspectives. This chapter is one of several publications based on this research (see Brennan 2017; Brennan et al. 2016a, b, 2017, 2018).

4 Findings

The findings suggest that the reputation of the Nordic welfare states as leaders in deinstitutionalisation, community-based services, independent living and personal assistance has, in part, served to hide some of the problems in implementing the CRPD (2006) within the current Nordic welfare disability services. Our research shows a service system that is inflexible with an imbalance of power where the control is mostly with the professionals and the service system. We found that efforts to preserve the existing services were hindering the development of new and innovative services, especially those which arose from grassroots disability activism and those that moved the control to disabled service users. Interviews with activists from the independent living movement and policymakers revealed a widespread resistance to implementing personal assistance at local government level and within the existing services. Attempts to preserve the status quo and the existing service system were evident in all three countries. An Icelandic policymaker who was involved in designing the law for personal assistance feared that there was too much resistance to new ideas within the local governments and within the traditional services:

> They are afraid, they are afraid to change. They don't know about empowerment and they don't know how to do that. Some people think it's dangerous to give disabled people the control. I think that may be the problem.

Policymakers tried to maintain the existing services that were on offer. Most of them emphasised the positive aspects and values of well-established services and supports as an alternative to providing personal assistance. Many of these services had been available for decades prior to the ratification of the CRPD. These included serviced apartments, respite and municipal-run social programmes. For example, a Norwegian municipal policymaker wanted to improve municipal-serviced apartments to deter people from applying for personal assistance:

> I'm trying to organise the service so that people are not that keen to get BPA (personal assistance). There will be some people that should have it, probably. But I think also there should be an alternative (to personal assistance).

Persons who were already using some existing municipal services, such as group homes or home nursing, could not apply for personal assistance unless they switched from one to the other. Many of the policymakers recognised the potential cost savings of replacing the established services with personal assistance. Yet, the cost of meeting the demand for new services was one of the key barriers to introducing tailor-made services at local government level. This was not because personal assistance was necessarily more expensive than the existing services, but because of the anticipation of a high demand for personal assistance. Policymakers were honest about their fears regarding an increased cost as a result of the significant demand for personal assistance. An Icelandic policymaker suggested that the local governments were fearful of the costs of providing personal assistance services for people who were not using the traditional municipal services:

> If the ones who apply for personal assistance are not using some [existing] services when they apply there will be no cost reduction but only additional cost. Even though in the long term you will see cost reduction

because of less need to build more special homes and special government services.

The efforts to preserve the current service system annoyed many of the disability activists in the independent living movement. They regarded the policymakers as arrogant and uninterested in improving the quality of services because they believed that the existing services already met the requirements of the Convention prior to ratification. An activist from Sweden described the stagnation in implementing the Convention:

> The Government ordered a review of the ways in which Swedish law have to be changed. Low and behold they found out that absolutely nothing had to be changed because we in Sweden had already fulfilled the Convention or were very close to completing (our obligations). So the Convention as such has really left no impact on the Swedish population.

Interviews with policymakers reflected this attitude. For instance, when asked about a new law for personal assistance, a Norwegian municipal policymaker explained that "In [this municipality] we are better than the new law. The way we practice, I think it's better. It won't make a difference in [this municipality]". Another Norwegian policymaker shared this perspective. "Hopefully for us [the Convention] will not make much of a difference. I believe that we are doing the right things, not all things right but a lot of them".

There were also concerns that the Nordic welfare state was a difficult environment for introducing key principles of the Convention. Some of the activists complained that the paternalistic nature of the Nordic welfare state encouraged a culture of complacency among persons with disabilities and prevented the kinds of activism that would otherwise advance human rights reforms. For instance, an Icelandic activist in the independent living movement argued that:

> In institutions people had to fight for their rights, they had to stick together and find ways to get better services ... Now things have changed, now we have service up to some level and instead of keeping on fighting people sit back and then they just sit back and complain.

Similarly, another Icelandic activist suggested that the welfare state encourages passivity among some persons with disabilities:

> The goal of the Scandinavian welfare system is to take care of you. It takes the power from people and you take the responsibility from the people. There's a danger of you becoming passive. You get your money, you get your money from the social system, but if you do something on your own they don't support you anymore.

Others criticised the ways in which the service system dictates the quality of life of the service users. One Swedish activist stated: "My friends live in group homes and the personnel at a group home think 'well it's enough if you go dancing once a year and go to Stockholm once a year.' They (the service staff) think that's enough, that's a good enough life."

Although the Nordic countries have been praised for their deinstitutionalisation efforts, the disabled activists in this study strongly criticised the services that replaced large-scale institutions. There was a general consensus that most services, especially residential services and group-based activities, were stagnant and did not go far enough in addressing the needs of a diverse range of persons with disabilities or meet the human rights demands of the CRPD (2006).

5 Conclusion: Human Rights and the Culture of Welfare

At the beginning of this chapter we asked how the human rights approach of the CRPD 'fits' within the culture of the Nordic welfare states. As stated at the outset, our understanding of culture refers broadly to an understanding of it as the characteristics and knowledge of a particular group of people and as a way of life, including values, beliefs, customs, language and traditions. The Nordic welfare states have been singled out as a special 'model' of welfare state since the 1930s with particular characteristics: practices, policies, customs and values (Christiansen and Markkola 2005). This approach to examine the implementation of the

CRPD within three Nordic countries reveals a disaccord between some of the key aspects of the human rights approach and the culture of the Nordic welfare services. Our study sheds light on some of the problems that arise when new services, based on the ideological underpinnings of the human rights principles of the CRPD, are introduced into the pre-existing service system and culture of the welfare state. What we observed was a rigid Nordic welfare culture that was inflexible in implementing new, tailor-made services, particularly those that arose from grassroots disability activism. This rigidity and resistance to change was widely criticised by activists in the independent living movement, whereas the policymakers defended and protected the established services. Disability activists also pointed to the arrogance among policymakers because of the Nordic reputation for generous welfare policies and feared that policymakers would rely on this reputation of 'being number one' (Brennan et al. 2018) to help them resist the changes required by the CRPD.

Article 19 of the CRPD (2006) requires that a range of individualised and flexible community-based services are available to ensure that persons with disabilities can live independently in the community on an equal basis with other citizens. Our study highlights a range of barriers in implementing disability human rights and independent living in Nordic welfare states. Ironically one of these barriers is the reputation of the Nordic welfare states as 'the best' when it comes to welfare policies and services. In the light of the glowing reputation of the Nordic welfare states, criticism does not seem credible by the international community and tends to be rejected by Nordic governments as unreasonable. 'We are the best! What more can be asked for?' The lesson, among others, is that introducing new and innovative policies and practices is problematic if the basic underlying ideologies and systems are not compatible with the proposed innovations. Another important lesson is that violations of disability and other human rights should not be overlooked in countries that appear to be progressive leaders in welfare provisions and equality of its citizens. In closing we express our disappointment with the culture of the Nordic welfare states, which we found to be in many aspects incompatible with the human rights demands of the CRPD.

Acknowledgements This research was supported by the FP7 Marie Curie Initial Training Network (ITN) DREAM, Disability Rights Expanding Accessible Markets (DREAM). Project ID: 265057.

References

Act Concerning Support and Service Provision for Persons with Certain Functional Impairments. (LSS: 1993: 387). (In Swedish: Lag (1993:387) om stöd och service till vissa funktionshindrade.) Retrieved from https://www.riksdagen.se/sv/dokument-lagar/dokument/svensk-forfattningssamling/lag-1993387-om-stod-och-service-till-vissa_sfs-1993-387.

Act on services for disabled people with long-term support needs no. 38/2018. (In Icelandic: Lög um þjónustu við fatlað fólk með langvarandi stuðningsþarfir 38/2018). Retrieved from https://www.althingi.is/altext/stjt/2018.038.html.

Askheim, O. P., Bengtsson, H., & Bjelke, B. R. (2014). Personal assistance in a Scandinavian context: Similarities, differences and developmental traits. *Scandinavian Journal of Disability Research, 16*(1), 3–18.

Brennan, C. (2017). Article 19 and the Nordic experience of independent living and personal assistance. In P. Blanck, E. Flynn, & G. Quinn (Eds.), *A research companion to disability law* (pp. 156–165). Oxford: Ashgate.

Brennan, C., Traustadóttir, R., Anderberg, P., & Rice, J. (2016a). Are cutbacks to personal assistance violating Sweden's obligations under the UN convention on the rights of persons with disabilities? *Laws, 5*(23), 85–99. https://doi.org/10.3390/laws5020023.

Brennan, C., Traustadóttir, R., Rice, J., & Anderberg, P. (2016b). Negotiating independence, choice and autonomy: Experiences of parents who coordinate personal assistance on behalf of their adult son or daughter. *Disability & Society, 31*(5), 604–621. https://doi.org/10.1080/09687599.2016.1188768.

Brennan, C., Rice, J., Traustadóttir, R., & Anderberg, P. (2017). How can states ensure access to personal assistance when service delivery is decentralized? A multi-level analysis of Iceland Norway and Sweden. *Scandinavian Journal of Disability Research, 19*(4), 334–346. https://doi.org/10.1080/15017419.2016.1261737.

Brennan, C., Traustadóttir, R., Rice, J., & Anderberg, P. (2018). "Being number one is the biggest obstacle": Implementing the UN convention on the rights of persons with disabilities within Nordic welfare services. *Nordic Welfare*

Research, 3(1), 18–32. https://doi.org/10.18261/ISSN.2464-4161-2018-01-03.

Christiansen, N. F., & Markkola, P. (2005). Introduction. In N. F. Crhistiansen, K. Petersen, N. Edling, & P. Haave (Eds.), *The Nordic model of welfare: A historical reappraisal* (pp. 9–29). Copenhagen: Museum Tusculanum Press.

Creswell, J. (2007). *Qualitative inquiry and research design: Choosing among five approaches* (2nd ed.). London: SAGE.

CRPD. (2006). *Convention on the rights of persons with disabilities.* Retrieved from http://www.un.org/disabilities/documents/convention/convoptprot-e.pdf.

Degener, T. (2016). Disability in the human rights context. *Laws, 5*(35), 1–24.

Dworkin, G. (2010). Paternalism. In E. N. Zalta (Ed.), *The Stanford Encyclopedia of philosophy*. Stanford: Stanford University.

Esping-Andersen, G. (1990). *The three worlds of welfare capitalism.* Princeton, NJ: Princeton University Press.

Esping-Andersen, G. (2002). *Why we need a new welfare state.* Oxford: Oxford University Press.

Flynn, R. J., & Nitsch, K. E. (Eds.). (1980). *Normalization, social integration and community services.* Baltimore: University Park Press.

Goodley, D. (2010). *Disability studies: An intersectional introduction.* London: SAGE.

Hvinden, B. (2013). Disability. In B. Greve (Ed.), *The Routledge handbook of the welfare state* (pp. 371–180). London: Routledge.

Kangas, O., & Kvist, J. (2013). Nordic welfare states. In B. Greve (Ed.), *The Routledge handbook of the welfare state* (pp. 148–160). London: Routledge.

Lewin, B., Westin, L., & Lewin, L. (2008). Needs and ambitions in Swedish disability care. *Scandinavian Journal of Disability Research, 10*(4), 237–257. https://doi.org/10.1080/15017410802410068.

Löve, L., Traustadóttir, R., & Rice, J. G. (2018). Trading autonomy for services: Perceptions of users and providers of services for disabled people in Iceland. *ALTER: European Journal of Disability Research, 12*, 193–207. https://doi.org/10.1016/j.alter.2018.04.008.

Nirje, B. (1969). The normalizational principle and its human management implications. In R. B. Kugel & W. Wolfensberger (Eds.), *Changing patterns in residential services for the mentally retarded.* Washington, DC: President's Committee on Mental Retardation.

Quinn, B., & Arnardóttir, O. M. (2009). *The UN convention on the rights of persons with disabilities: European and Scandinavian perspectives*. Boston: Martinus Nijhoff.

Rice, J., Björnsdóttir, K., & Smith, E. (2015). Spaces of indifference: Bureaucratic governance and disability rights in Iceland. In T. Shakespeare (Ed.), *Disability research today: International perspectives* (pp. 135–148). London: Routledge.

Sandvin, J. T., & Lichtwarck, W. (2005). Gradual improvement or deterioration in disguise? In A. Gustavsson, J. Sandvin, R. Traustadóttir, & J. Tøssebro (Eds.), *Resistance, reflection and change: Nordic disability research* (pp. 59–73). Lund: Studentlitteratur.

Spencer-Oatey, H. (2012). *What is culture? A compilation of quotation*. GlobalPAD Core Concepts. Available at Global PAD Open House. Retrieved from http://www.warwick.ac.uk/globalpadintercultural.

Tøssebro, J., Bonfils, I. S., Teittinen, A., Tideman, M., Traustadóttir, R., & Vesala, T. (2012). Normalization fifty years beyond: Current trends in the Nordic countries. *Journal of Policy and Practice in Intellectual Disabilities, 9*(2), 134–146.

13

Article 30 of the CRPD as a Vehicle for Social Transformation: Harnessing the CRPD's Potential for Persons with Intellectual Disabilities

Matthew S. Smith and Michael Ashley Stein

1 Introduction

The United Nations (UN) Convention on the Rights of Persons with Disabilities (CRPD/Convention 2006) requires States Parties to affirmatively engage in attitudinal changes as part of its broad vision of societal transformation. To this end, several of the CRPD's substantive provisions—and especially prominently Article 8—Awareness-raising—recognise the centrality of altering cultural biases to implementing the treaty's mandates. At the same time, the CRPD's potential for social transformation depends heavily on whether local human rights activists with disabilities can leverage mechanisms for triggering social belief changes independently of pursuing prescriptive legal compliance.

M. S. Smith (✉) • M. A. Stein
Harvard Law School, Harvard University, Cambridge, USA
e-mail: mastein@law.harvard.edu

E. J. Kakoullis, K. Johnson (eds.), *Recognising Human Rights in Different Cultural Contexts*, https://doi.org/10.1007/978-981-15-0786-1_13

Enter Article 30—Participation in cultural life, recreation, leisure and sport (CRPD 2006). Theatre is a time-tested vehicle for facilitating belief changes and can therefore be central to the CRPD's transformative project. This is especially true for self-advocates with intellectual disabilities who have historically been marginalised—even within the broader disability rights movement—and who thus face significant barriers to participating in formal processes. Although theatre has traditionally been performed *on* persons with intellectual disabilities as a form of therapy rather than performed *by* them on their own terms (Ineland and Sauer 2007; Perring 2005), theatre provides unique opportunities for (re)negotiating their rights-holder status with society at large.

Excitingly, the CRPD has come into force at a time when some theatre programmes around the world have shifted from therapeutic interventions to expressive and countercultural outlets (Hargrave 2015; Hall 2013; Ineland and Sauer 2007). Moreover, regardless of whether theatrical productions aspire to convey political messages consistent with the CRPD or wish to foreground the aesthetic dimensions of their productions, theatre provides an avenue for persons with intellectual disabilities to act as belief-change agents. Whether by creating constitutive processes that facilitate stakeholder engagement or by altering the "social meaning" of conduct that contributes to marginalisation, participation in theatre by persons with intellectual disabilities can help ensure that they partake equally in the CRPD's promised social renovation.

This chapter draws timely attention to how persons with intellectual disabilities and their allies can leverage the right "to develop and utilize their creative, artistic and intellectual potential, not only for their own benefit, but also for the enrichment of society" (CRPD 2006, Art. 30(2)). We begin by explicating two ways in which the CRPD effects belief changes with respect to persons with disabilities. The first of these ways requires duty-bearers to closely consult and engage with persons with disabilities in mutually constitutive processes, which alter unstated rules and expectations for their interactions. The second involves redefining previously innocuous-seeming behaviour in terms of its implications for persons with disabilities' inherent dignity. Third, we describe how theatre programmes and companies involving persons with intellectual disabilities increasingly eschew the therapeutic origins of such programmes in favour of either embracing theatre as a forum for either conveying political messages about themselves and their rights or showcasing the unique aesthetic contributions of actors with intellectual disabilities that call into question traditional theatrical conventions. Based on the CRPD's mechanisms of belief change and the nascent trajectory of progressive theatre programmes and companies, we argue for an interpretation of Article 30(2) that captures the CRPD's broad transformative vision more fully than a narrow textual reading. Such an understanding enables persons with intellectual disabilities and their supporters to harness Article 30 as a vehicle for attitudinal reconstruction.

2 The CRPD and Changing Beliefs About Persons with Intellectual Disabilities

The CRPD's drafters "attempted to build a framework within which the Convention's eventual domestic incorporation would evolve beyond current human rights practice toward a broader transformative vision" (Lord and Stein 2008, p. 456). Specifically, the drafters aspired for both the process by which the CRPD was created and the substance of its provisions, to catalyse normative restructuring and trigger concomitant social change. Trenchantly, by modelling and calling for mutually constitutive processes but also maximising law's expressive effects on individuals' behaviour,[1] the CRPD can help change beliefs about persons with intellectual disabilities, a precursor to their full enjoyment and exercise of CRPD rights.

2.1 Constitutive Processes

Human rights treaties are most commonly implemented through constitutive processes—whereby stakeholders develop normative content through iterative dialogue—that can both accelerate their domestic incorporation and "form the backbone of lasting social change" (Lord and Stein 2008, pp. 454–455). Specifically, through the processes of

[1] One of the ways in which the CRPD seeks to maximize law's expressive effects is by expressly mandating disability rights education and awareness-raising activities (CRPD 2006, Art. 4(1)(i), 8, 9(2)(c), 13(2), 24(4), 25(d), and 32(1)(b)) which go above and "beyond monitoring and reporting on violations or top-down law-reform efforts" (Lord and Stein 2008, p. 457).

'persuasion' and 'acculturation' human rights change agents can actively engage duty-bearers to 'internalise' the normative content of treaties.[2] When either the State or private individuals internalise the content of treaty obligations, the obligations become self-executing: enforcement occurs independently of external controls, and triggers a self-perpetuating culture shift. "The most effective legal regulation thus aims to be constitutive, in the sense of seeking to shape and *transform* the personal identity" of actors, because "self-enforcement is widely recognized as both more effective and more efficient than third-party controls" (Koh 1998, pp. 627–628, emphasis in original). Empirical studies bear this out: for example, the act of publicly making an unenforceable promise can change a government's behaviour (Woods 2010).

Despite the potential of constitutive processes, and that the CRPD negotiations modelled a constitutive process, CRPD commentators have largely focused on the programmatic implications of the CRPD's provisions through formal processes, such as constitutional or legislative reforms.[3] Throughout the negotiations, persons with disabilities demanded and earned the respect of State representatives as subject matter experts (Stein and Lord 2008). Citing one example, Lord and Stein note that at the outset of negotiations, the Nigerian delegation distinguished between persons with disabilities and "normal people," whereas at a later session the South African delegation "called on delegates to

[2] Gonzalez (2016) helpfully explains these processes. Persuasion denotes when individuals "actively assess the content of a particular message—a norm, practice, or belief—and change their minds." Acculturation, by contrast, occurs when individuals "adopt the beliefs and behavior patterns of the surrounding culture without actively assessing either the merits of those beliefs and behaviors or the materials costs and benefits of conforming to them." For example, persuasion occurs when a training participant comes to believe that persons with disabilities have a right to inclusive education by virtue of the trainer's explanation, whereas acculturation occurs when the same participant reaches an identical conclusion because she attended a school with inclusive classrooms. In other words, people may internalize the normative content of the CRPD either because of its intrinsic logic or because they have witnesses similar effects. Although a given activity may simultaneously utilize techniques of both persuasion and acculturation (e.g., a module led by a trainer with a disability as part of an inclusive education curriculum), persuasion depends on the substance of the activity's underlying message whereas acculturation relies on the relationship between the target audience and another group. These processes describe macro-level mechanisms yet make intuitive sense when applied to individuals.

[3] Illustrative examples include Flynn and Arstein-Kerslake (2014) on European legislative reforms relating to legal capacity and Harpur and Bales (2010) on CRPD-inspired reforms among Pacific Island countries.

refrain from using inappropriate language when referencing persons with disabilities" (Lord and Stein 2008, p. 476). The ensuing "linguistic shift ... among States representatives ... from medical and charity-model terminology toward a social model of rights-based taxonomy" likely belied a deeper reconstitution of social norms (Lord and Stein 2008, p. 476). Constituent participation caused duty-bearers to adjust their language in a way intimating underlying attitudinal shifts about persons with disabilities' inherent dignity. Indeed, States representatives' "internalization" of new codes of conduct (Stein and Geisinger 2016, p. 1065), paved the way for marshalling consensus on some of the CRPD's more progressive provisions. Consequently, both the object of the negotiations and the participants in them exited the process transformed by it.

Unsurprisingly, the CRPD expressly militates for "the participation of people with disabilities (along with other stakeholders) in the process of societal reconstruction so that they may claim their rights" (Stein and Stein 2007, p. 1240). Constituent participation facilitated a course correction in the evolution of the human rights movement, which many disability rights advocates viewed as having historically failed persons with disabilities (Lord and Stein 2008). At the same time, persons with disabilities' participation in all life activities can similarly change perceptions of social norms.[4] Because increased social participation makes persons with disabilities more visible (Lord and Stein 2009), the CRPD helps to normalise disability as a naturally occurring hallmark of human diversity by requiring persons with disabilities' involvement, both in the design and in the execution of programmes, processes, and activities that affect their full and effective participation in society. Thus, the CRPD calls for interactions that trigger belief changes integral to vindicating the inherent dignity of persons with disabilities at the core of the CRPD's purpose.

[4] For example, the benefits of persons with disabilities' participation in the workplace—including increased profitability, competitive advantage, inclusive work culture—are well documented (Lindsay et al. 2018).

2.2 Expressive Effects

The CRPD also effects belief changes through law's expressive effects on how individuals perceive their conduct and adjust their behaviour accordingly.[5] Traditionally, scholars have explained the effects of law on behaviour primarily in terms of opportunity costs, that is, increases or decreases in the utility of undertaking a certain activity due to the consequences of running afoul of the law (Geisinger 2002). Under this view, the spectre of sanctions, whether vis-à-vis formal state coercion (e.g., fines), or informal social opprobrium (e.g., public shaming), drives individuals' behaviour (Geisinger 2002).

More recently, scholars have identified law's expressive effects as an independent means of affecting behaviour (Sunstein 1996; Lessig 1995). This view posits that, alongside or even in the absence of sanctions, law can affect individuals' behaviour by reshaping their attitudes about undertaking a certain activity (Stein and Geisinger 2016). Laws may, for example, create new 'focal points' that cause individuals to adjust their strategies for coordinating with others who have competing interests (McAdams 2000), or convey to individuals new information about activities affecting perceived payoffs (Stein 2004; Geisinger 2002). New "focal points" and new information trigger belief changes, which in turn alter the "social meaning" of conduct (Geisinger 2002, p. 72). These phenomena invite comparisons with theatre's similar belief-changing potential.

To illustrate law's effects on 'social meaning', Lessig describes nineteenth-century efforts to deter duels in the American South (1995). Outright bans on duelling proved ineffectual, in contrast to laws barring duellers from holding public office. Lessig posits that the latter laws changed would-be duellers' beliefs about declining a challenge: instead of cowardice, it meant civic duty.[6] Similarly, even without sanctions,

---

[5] Although not framed in terms of expressive law, Louise Arbour, then UN High Commissioner for Human Rights, announced the CRPD's belief-change potential, averring "the Convention enshrines a 'paradigm shift' in attitudes" (Arbour 2006).

[6] Other examples are also instructive. Sunstein, for one, hypothesizes that restaurant owners backed passage of the United States' 1964 Civil Rights Act because the law promised to convert refusals to discriminate on the basis of race into mere acts of lawfulness rather than provocative statements about racial equality, which would open them to retaliation from racists (Sunstein 1996). The sudden lawfulness of non-discrimination would legitimize it for citizens who "intrinsically value obeying the law" irrespective of its content (Cooter 2000, p. 1600).

disability-based discrimination bans may induce employers to hire disabled workers, if the laws can change employers' beliefs such that they perceive engaging disabled workers not as an act of charitable deference to so-called better angels but one exemplifying civic-mindedness (Stein 2003).[7] For example, the Americans with Disabilities Act (ADA 1990) sought to maximise expressive effects by attributing social exclusion to artificial barriers not inherent to impairment, and prescribing accommodations as non-discrimination, rather than as 'special' measures; thereby inducing members of society to embrace a duty to remove barriers (Stein 2003).

The CRPDs' drafters intuited that the treaty would work similarly.[8] The CRPD catalyses behaviour-altering belief changes, by imputing social exclusion to human rights violations that infringe persons with disabilities' inherent dignity as rights-holders. By couching barriers to social participation in human rights terms, the CRPD induces both duty-bearers and society at large, to reconsider whether formerly lawful, justified conduct impinges on persons with disabilities' newly formulated dignity interests. To cite just one example from the post-CRPD landscape, a housing association in Mexico exercised a statutory right to cut off a disabled tenant's electricity due to years of missed payments, and consequently her accessibility via a private elevator. The Mexican Supreme Court held that this situation impermissibly undercut the dignity inherent in the tenant's countervailing interest in freely entering and leaving her condominium[9] (Smith and Stein 2018). The CRPD thereby endowed barrier elimination with legal as well as superseding moral imperatives,

---

[7] Of course, laws may just as easily have unintended expressive effects. For example, the Americans with Disabilities Act may have changed parents' attitudes about children with Down syndrome, triggering a decline in birthrates of children with Down syndrome not otherwise explained by other technological, demographic, or cultural variables.

[8] Indicia of this intuition pervade the treaty text. However, Article 8 stands out as evidence of the drafters' understanding of belief change's behavioural ramifications. It specifically exhorts States Parties to engage actively in belief-changing activities, including by combatting negative stereotypes and promoting awareness of persons with disabilities' capabilities and contributions.

[9] Amparo Directo en Revisión 989/2014, Primera Sala de la Suprema Corte de Justicia de la Nación (Mexico). Without opining as to whether the Mexican Supreme Court reached a "correct" result, its general shift away from its traditional non-discrimination heuristics towards less formulaic, morality-tinged criteria (e.g., stigma) suggests the CRPD's expressive effects at work (Smith and Stein 2018).

and forcefully precipitated a belief change about previously unquestioned conduct.

2.3 Towards Belief Changes

The CRPD operates to facilitate belief changes by encouraging constitutive processes and law's expressive effects. These twin mechanisms for effecting belief changes are critical for persons with intellectual disabilities, who often experience marginalisation due to exclusion from normative formation processes, and who frequently lack effective means to regulate their daily interactions with the general population. Constructivist and expressive law theories, if applied to the day-to-day interactions between persons with and without intellectual disabilities, yield insights into how the CRPD works to counter these micro-processes that contribute to marginalisation.

Belief change, an effective means of upholding human rights in general, is critical for ensuring the rights of persons with intellectual disabilities who often lead highly regimented lives and depend on third parties to attend basic needs or engage in common activities. Consequently, they must regularly negotiate preferences for activities with family members, guardians, caregivers, service providers, or community members that surround them and impose their own countervailing priorities. This is particularly true for persons with intellectual disabilities living in 'supported' settings such as group homes with prescribed formal relationships with caregivers or providers. They often must expend enormous and unnecessary energy, to enjoy the most basic freedoms and engage in rudimentary activities, which the general population assumes as a matter of course. For example, over what recreational activity to pursue.

Imagine a person with an intellectual disability negotiating with a staff worker, employed by the person's group home, over a leisure interest. The person with an intellectual disability prefers going out to a concert, while the staff worker prefers staying in to watch television. Influenced by prevalent stereotypes, ableist attitudes, or narcissistic desire, the staff compels in-home television viewing.[10] Yet both in its general provisions and in specific articles,[11] the CRPD urges mutually constitutive processes. To illustrate: CRPD-consistent conduct manifests when staff workers support persons with intellectual disabilities by jointly plotting out a schedule of activities predicated on the latter's preferences. Such processes afford persons with intellectual disabilities opportunities to develop and express their own preferences, thereby making them visible in the eyes of others. Additionally, because Article 30 of the CRPD (2006) recognises a right to access cultural performances or services, it helps to recast the staff's insistence on his or her own preferences as a human rights violation impinging on the dignity of the person with an intellectual disability, because it erects an artificial barrier to that person participating on an equal basis with others in cultural life. It is especially in such everyday situations, where persons with intellectual disabilities cannot access coercive mechanisms, that the CRPD's potential to alter behaviour depends on its potential for triggering a belief change in the staff worker.

3 Theatre, Changing Beliefs, and Persons with Intellectual Disabilities

The CRPD provides clues on how to change beliefs about persons with intellectual disabilities by engendering mutually constitutive processes through day-to-day interactions.[12] It also leverages law's expressive functions by projecting messages that reshape attitudes. The ways in which some groups are using theatre to change beliefs about themselves as

---

[10] Similarly, artificial scenarios involving men and women have shown that men more inclined to insist on their preferred outcomes when told that the other scenario's participants were women, suggesting how unstated, stereotypical assumptions operate in real-world situations (McAdams 2009).

[11] For example, the decision-making processes latent in Articles 12 and 19 CRPD, which require that persons with intellectual disabilities receive support to make decisions and decide on where and how they live, respectively, mandate some form of dialogue in order to establish persons with intellectual disabilities' baseline preferences.

[12] Specifically, the CRPD's global inclusion mandate not only guarantees persons with disabilities access to equal opportunities to travel, vote, earn, and learn, but also positions them to affect the beliefs of the others they encounter while doing so.

persons with intellectual disabilities, mirror the constructivist and expressive law theories of belief change underpinning the CRPD's promise of social transformation. This may come as little surprise: theatre has long been used to empower marginalised groups to challenge existing power structures and break down societal barriers (Boon and Plastow 2004; Cohen-Cruz 2006). Yet, despite the promise of theatre as an agent of social change, theatre activities involving persons with intellectual disabilities historically have been anything but politically inspiring.

Theatre has often been performed *on* persons with intellectual disabilities rather than performed *by* them. Theatre programmes organised in the confines of institutions, sheltered workshops or other segregated facilities more often than not are palliative—striving to soothe or distract persons with intellectual disabilities from the tensions, tedium, or even abuses inherent to segregated settings (Goodley and Moore 2002; Parr 2006). In segregated settings, theatre programmes also serve as a ready and convenient substitute for meaningful social engagement outside of segregated congregate care, including employment or other socially rewarding activities (Ineland and Sauer 2007). More benignly, theatre programmes may aim to further habilitative goals, such as developing the adaptive functioning skills of persons with intellectual disabilities (Hall 2013), or simply pursue a version of the good life (Goodley and Moore 2002). Whether to soothe, distract, or habilitate, these adulterated theatre programmes adhere closely to outmoded biomedical notions of disability, which predicate therapeutic or rehabilitative interventions to repair segregated and "broken" bodies or minds (Ignagni and Church 2008). And, although theatre programmes with expressly non-therapeutic aims are on the rise—notably, those involving persons with intellectual disabilities who explicitly pursue self-expression and excellence—they inevitably have to contend with an inherited therapeutic discourse (Hargrave 2015).

In addition, many theatre programmes fall under the purview of state-funded disability services, which not only hold them to regulatory constraints but also impose competing agendas. For example, in order to continue to receive state funding, the Swedish theatre group Olla must demonstrate that its performances contribute to normalising the actors with intellectual disabilities, while also aspiring to critical acclaim and legitimacy within the mainstream arts community. Moreover, means-tested public benefits programmes can discourage persons with intellectual disabilities' professionalisation by creating barriers to pursuing remunerative work (Hargrave 2015). Nevertheless, even theatre programmes with therapeutic origins have progressed. To wit: the Australian troupe Back to Back, "today an internationally acclaimed, professional company of actors with disabilities, emerged as a subversive collaboration among staff and volunteers at a disability services agency" (Johnston 2016, pp. 27–28).

In documenting the tectonic shift of theatre for persons with intellectual disabilities from a palliative and therapeutic model to a scheme of self-empowerment and expression, Giles Perring (2005) distinguishes between productions that "challenge[] mainstream cultural and aesthetic precepts and views about disability" by "addressing their marginalization and institutionalization" and those that aim to "bring[] performers with learning disabilities into mainstream performance discourse" without foregrounding their disabilities or thematising disability in the way that consciously "disability arts" do (Perring 2005, pp. 185–186). Similarly, Hargrave (2015) signals a second-order shift away from expressly political theatre to performances that emphasise aesthetic dimensions. Contextualising this shift in terms of the CRPD's mechanisms for belief change; post-therapeutic theatre groups create spaces for constitutive dialogue between rights-holders and the general population, and also empower persons with intellectual disabilities to convey political messages, overtly or inferentially, and persuade their audiences of them. Even avowedly apolitical groups, by challenging established conventions for theatrical performance, can contribute to belief changes by causing spectators to re-evaluate conventions much in the way that law's expressive effects can help alter the social meaning of normalised conduct.

3.1 Constitutive Processes

The Theater of the Oppressed, attributed to the Brazilian theatre activist Augusto Boal's eponymous polemic published in 1974, denotes a collection of techniques designed to transform the non-actor into the protagonist in his or her own life, and thus not be usurped as a subject in someone else's story (Cohen-Cruz and Schutzman 1994; Wheeler 2015). More than merely a technical heuristic to theatre, the Theatre of the Oppressed assumes that latent power structures impede marginalised participants' full self-realisation and encourages participants to subvert those structures (Spry 1994). Given how systems professing to support persons with intellectual disabilities, instead at times impede them—for example, limiting their spontaneous participation in cultural, social, or other events by obliging them to arrange transportation or staff assignments in advance—the Theater of the Oppressed equips persons with intellectual disabilities with tools to deconstruct tessellated systems of service and control. For example, Lynd describes how two Theatre of the Oppressed-infused productions by a popular theatre group of persons with intellectual disabilities in western Massachusetts empowered them to describe their service system as a "chain of oppression" (1992, p. 110).

Outside Voices Theater Company (Outside Voices) has been utilising Theater of the Oppressed heuristics since 2011. Although a programme offered by a not-for-profit agency in New York City that is supported by public funds for habilitative services to promote adults with intellectual disabilities' community integration,[13] the group has adopted a countercultural agenda that empowers its members by enabling them to subvert latent power structures affecting their social participation. In contrast with many professional theatre companies, almost every weekly session begins with the group's facilitator, or another member, going around the room and checking in with each person to celebrate achievements or give support in rough times. The group's approach is consciously Boalian,[14] and it employs various quintessentially Theater of the Oppressed methods.[15]

[13] Ineland and Sauer analyse a similar tension experienced by members of Olla, where workers play dual roles as both "artistic leaders" and "care givers" responsible for actors' skills development (Ineland and Sauer 2007, p. 52).

[14] The eponymic "Boalian" denotes the vast, rhizomatic body of work inspired by the Brazilian Augusto Boal's subversive and emancipatory pedagogy, first set out in Boal (1974), that delivers human rights education to marginalised groups through popular theatre.

[15] Participants' stories "do not necessarily address oppression; they are as likely about cultural celebration and individual affirmation" (Cohen-Cruz 2006, p. 104).

In one Boalian exercise, the facilitator assists a single actor to position other group members in *tableaux vivants*,[16] which physically portray the actor's relationships to various individuals and entities. Thus, an actor might ask two other members to stand close beside the other, with one's hand on the other's shoulder, to represent the relationship with a staff worker, while positioning another pair far away with their backs turned, to represent the relationship with policymakers in the state's capital. A crucial expressive act for persons with intellectual disabilities—some of whom might have difficulty exploring latent power dynamics or may prefer not to do so verbally—this scaffolding exercise enables them both to model complex social strata and also to express how they view their role in these systems. Through these exercises, they consciously explore the power structures that shape their environments and generate productions based on the insights they gain through engaging in these exercises. Put another way, theatre allows them to understand the mechanisms of the marginalisation they feel in their day-to-day interactions.[17]

One such Outside Voices production, *What If I Were Whole?* (2015), challenges deficit models of intellectual disability and portrays disability as a joint enterprise that "implicates everyone" (Hargrave 2015, p. 75), a touchstone message of "disability theater."[18] Throughout the performance, the actors with intellectual disabilities deliver disparaging remarks and re-enact deprecatory interactions based on their lived experiences,

[16] A *tableau vivant*, is the French term for a silent and motionless group of people arranged to represent a scene or incident.

[17] Other exercises allow persons with intellectual disabilities to develop strategies for combating the exclusion they experience. For example, in another Boal-inspired activity, the facilitator helps an actor confront prejudices she encounters in her daily life. Three group members are asked to deliver hurtful lines the actor herself has heard others say to her. She then selects a fourth group member whom she considers brave to play the role of "warrior." The warrior confronts each of the three offending group members one by one and improvises a retort for each one. While the warrior confronts each one, the actor has her hand on the warrior's shoulder. Then, the actor and warrior change places: the actor herself confronts each offending group member and repeats verbatim the retorts developed by the warrior, while the warrior follows her with his hand on her shoulder.

[18] Disability studies scholars differentiate between theatre that involves persons with disabilities and "disability theater" which consciously channels "impulses for social justice in the face of ableist ideologies and practices as well as a profound recognition of disabled lives and experiences as inherently valuable" (Johnston 2016, p. 25). "Disability theater" thus embraces a political and emancipatory agenda as "a cultural weapon to be wielded against the twin oppressions of mainstream culture and therapeutically aligned art" (Hargrave 2015, p. 27).

which in Boalian fashion, serve as "the point of departure for collective problem-solving around oppression" (Cohen-Cruz 2006, p. 103). These scenes are interspersed with soliloquies that engage critically with those words and actions. The disjointed pastiche of vignettes and asides—when portrayed by actors who identify as persons with intellectual disabilities and in the absence of a cohesive narrative thread—both undermines the coherence of societal expectations and emphasises the absurdity of the views the actors regularly encounter as persons with intellectual disabilities. At the same time, the actors' deliveries forcefully convey that persons with intellectual disabilities fully understand those words and actions, thereby confronting head-on prevailing misconceptions about what persons with intellectual disabilities are capable of understanding. In addition to the political content of the production, immediately following the performance the company invites its audience into a dialogue, thereby allowing the audience to respond to and engage with the performance's message, and creating a space for the audience to share, exploring and developing the production's layers of meaning. In this way, Outside Voices engages its audience in a mutually constitutive process, albeit informal and micro-level, towards developing an alternative normative framework for eliminating barriers to persons with intellectual disabilities participating fully in society.

Though not steeped in the Boalian tradition, SEID (the Society for the Education and Inclusion of the Disabled) Trust—a Bangladeshi Dhaka-based not-for-profit organisation that relies on private funds to provide special education and related services to children with intellectual disabilities—has supported a self-advocacy group since 2010 to use theatre as a means of educating audiences about their CRPD (2006) Article 24 right to education Oporajeyo (2011).[19] The self-advocates, following a series of trainings on the CRPD, arranged by the Harvard Law School Project on Disability (HPOD), intuitively chose theatre as their preferred vehicle for engaging peers in a dialogue about inclusive education. They instructed the SEID Trust staff and

[19] And more recently, the Article 12 and 16 CRPD rights to make decisions and to be free from violence, respectively (SEID Trust 2017).

HPOD trainer to develop a script that they would then workshop and refine.[20]

The resultant *Education, My Right*, is a didactic play that models how self-advocates can support children with intellectual disabilities to educate duty-bearers and society at large, including a hypothetical public school headmaster, about their right to go to school together with their non-disabled peers (SEID Trust 2011). The play dramatises adult conversations that the SEID Trust self-advocates have themselves overheard regarding how their intellectual disabilities render them unfit for mainstream schooling.[21] Rather than merely represent a rights denial, the actors demonstrate how self-advocates can come to the aid of a peer, transmit knowledge about the CRPD right to education to that peer, and then assist the peer in respectfully confronting the duty-bearer responsible for the denial and making him aware of his CRPD obligations. In this play, the headmaster, after learning about the CRPD from self-advocates, agrees to admit the child with an intellectual disability despite his earlier refusal. Although aesthetically less complex than *What If I Were Whole?*, the SEID Trust self-advocates' *Education, My Right* provides an explicit roadmap for belief change, vis-à-vis educating duty-bearers about the CRPD, and articulates a precise vision for how self-advocates can become belief-change agents by leveraging the CRPD's expressive effects. Moreover, *Education, My Right* frames CRPD implementation as the result of constitutive processes of rights-holder/duty-bearer engagement. To thematise and model this theory of change, the SEID Trust actors engage audience members in a dialogue immediately after each performance.[22] Although the self-advocates did not intentionally follow Boal's methodology, their activities nevertheless evince a similar conviction in the power of theatre to convey political messages in furtherance of

[20] The original Bengali-language script is reproduced as an appendix to SEID Trust and HPOD's 2013 self-advocacy manual, on file with the authors.

[21] Despite Bangladesh's 2007 ratification of the CRPD and subsequent positive ministerial directives and policies, the state's 1990 primary education law still deems some children with disabilities as "unfit" for mainstream schooling. Compulsory Primary Education Act 1990 (Bangladesh). Available from http://bdlaws.minlaw.gov.bd/pdf/738____.pdf.

[22] Some audience members' impressions are documented in the short film *Oporajeyo*, available at: https://www.youtube.com/watch?v=a23Qvb7Ah1A&t=7s.

fostering belief changes in an economic, social, and cultural context far removed from that of their New York City peers.

3.2 Expressive Effects

Whereas the actions of Outside Voices and SEID Trust actors illustrate how actors with intellectual disabilities can channel the CRPD's belief-change mechanisms into theatrical performance, other theatre groups aim to resist a perceived emerging stereotype—that the value of their productions inheres to the content of their political messages and not their aesthetic merits. By emphasising the aesthetic dimensions of their craft as independent of disability politics, these aesthetics-oriented groups seek recognition first and foremost as artists in their own right, rather than as activists employing theatre for political ends. Thus, whereas Boalian practitioners use theatre to "blur false boundaries" between "politics, art, and therapy" (Cohen-Cruz and Schutzman 1994, p. 1), others seek to accentuate those boundaries in order to invite attention to their aesthetic innovations. Nevertheless, in emphasising aesthetics, these productions call into question the meaning of performance itself by staging scenes that undermine theatrical conventions, thereby mirroring the CRPD's expressive effects.

Indeed, the capacity of persons with intellectual disabilities to produce theatre is frequently underestimated (Hargrave 2015), explaining why persons with disabilities in general have only recently gained access to this medium despite a long history of theatre either thematising disability or using it as a trope (Johnston 2016). For this reason, the unique contributions that persons with intellectual disabilities can make to theatre are underexplored, despite compelling accounts of their work stirring aesthetic pots. In working with actors with intellectual disabilities, theatre scholar Fran Leighton found herself subconsciously imposing on the actors received wisdom about what constitutes "recognisable … theatre practice" (Leighton 2009, p. 106). Ultimately, she dispensed with these conventions and adopted a "more fluid, flexible, spontaneous way of working" (Leighton 2009, p. 106).

Similarly, the choreographer Jérôme Bel found that he had to adapt his own preconceived notions of theatre practice in developing a production with the Swiss company, Theatre HORA. What Perring dubs "intuitive anti-performance" (2005, p. 181), induced Bel to stage a production that broke with theatrical conventions by asking the actors to step forward one by one to state their names, disabilities, and opinions about the work before performing an unchoreographed dance set to music they chose. By Bel's own account, his aesthetic choices were dictated by his inability to direct the actors in a conventional way over four weeks of rehearsal (Kourlas 2013). As a collection of probing essays explores in great detail, by employing actors with limited technical proficiency, by not requiring them to perform identically from night to night, and by instructing the actors to "play" themselves, the production poses existential questions about the nature of performance, prompting spectators to re-evaluate received wisdom (Umathum and Wihstutz 2015).

Such performances evidence the complex questions actors with intellectual disabilities may be uniquely qualified to elicit. Indeed, this under-explored terrain may necessitate "a new critical space in which the work of learning disabled artists and their collaborators can be evaluated and appreciated as art, rather than advocacy or therapy" (Hargrave 2015, p. 6). But for all the aesthetic avenues opened by casting actors with intellectual disabilities, Hargrave's pursuit of an apolitical aesthetic appreciation of intellectual disability theatre may prove impractical in the shadow of the myriad manifestations of marginalisation experienced offstage by persons with intellectual disabilities. Against this backdrop, audiences foreground the actors' political identities rather than concurrent aesthetic partitions, such as the primordial division between performers and spectators (Lepecki 2015). Indeed, once onstage, persons with intellectual disabilities enter into a novel power relation with non-disabled audience members (Siegmund 2015)—literally and figuratively repositioning them as actors both in the theatrical sense and as the term is used in human rights discourse. The political implications of this repositioning as subjects with agency inevitably reverberate artistically too, as "aesthetic equality collides with social inequality" (Wihstutz 2015, p. 50). Thus, "Does the director exploit or instrumentalize the actors for aesthetic ends, or do the actors use the director for political ends?" echoes the real-life question, "Do staff support persons with intellectual disabilities (by assisting them to live independently) or do persons with disabilities support staff (by supplying jobs)?" (Boal 1974, p. ix). For oppressed groups, perhaps "all theater is necessarily political" (Boal 1974, p. ix).

Whatever the precise contours of the rapidly changing landscape of persons with intellectual disabilities' theatre activities, the opportunities to engage this medium are both increasing and diversifying. At bottom, these emerging theatre activities-cum-belief-change catalysts reflect the underlying mechanisms on which the CRPD's vision of social transformation depends. As such, theatre empowers persons with intellectual disabilities to participate directly in and accelerate the operation of these mechanisms, and consequently persons with intellectual disabilities have strong incentives to exploit to the fullest their Article 30 right to participate on an equal basis in cultural activities (CRPD 2006).

4 (Re)Interpreting Article 30's Transformative Role

If fully harnessed, Article 30(2) CRPD (2006) will afford powerful opportunities for persons with intellectual disabilities to "[c]onfront[] the passivity that paternalistic and non-participatory models of disability typically evoke" (Lord and Stein 2009, p. 179). But in order to align Article 30(2) with the CRPD's transformative vision, persons with intellectual disabilities must maximise theatre's potential to do what the CRPD's drafters intuited, namely: engage duty-bearers and members of society at large in mutually constitutive processes and change their beliefs about conduct contributing to marginalisation.

Few of the CRPD's specific Articles better embody mutually constitutive processes than Article 30's right to participation in cultural life, recreation, leisure and sport. "For members of the disability community, participation in cultural life and sporting activities serves as a vital channel of engagement with society when such participation is embraced by the community" (Lord and Stein 2009, p. 182). For example, facilitating persons with disabilities' participation in sport and recreation helps to increase their self-reliance and empowerment, while denying them those opportunities can undermine their autonomy (Lord and Stein 2009). "Isolation from culturally enriching activities can reinforce internalized oppression and disconnection from community" (Lord and Stein 2009, p. 182). Thus, Article 30's implementation plays a vital role in furthering the CRPD's transformative vision of persons with disabilities' full-fledged membership in an inclusive society.

The CRPD's drafters were keenly aware of the high stakes of Article 30's implementation: the final text incorporates important innovations to the existing right to participation in cultural life, recreation, leisure, and sport frameworks. Notably, Article 30(3) (CRPD 2006) recognises prominently that intellectual property rights can obstruct persons with disabilities' access to cultural materials and it paved the way for the Marrakesh Treaty to Facilitate Access to Published Works for Persons Who Are Blind, Visually Impaired or Otherwise Print Disabled (2013), which imposes specific obligations on States Parties to carve out exceptions to national copyright laws for reproducing and distributing materials in accessible formats (Fruchterman 2017). Article 30(4) urges respect for the unique "cultural and linguistic identit[ies]" of persons with disabilities, a matter of special importance for D/deaf and signing communities (CRPD 2006, Art. 30(4)).[23] Article 30(5) (CRPD 2006) helps to bring persons with disabilities' participation in sports programmes in from the sidelines of the global human rights agenda (Lord and Stein 2009).

Consistent with the CRPD's larger project to delegitimise segregation in all spheres of life (Kayess and French 2008), Article 30(2) helpfully acknowledges and rebuts outmoded notions about the creative and artistic activities of persons with intellectual disabilities. States Parties cannot fulfil their obligations under Article 30(2) by organising segregated creative and artistic programmes. Rather, persons with intellectual disabilities must have creative and artistic outlets that showcase their talents to the general public. In so doing, States Parties help foster greater awareness

[23] Such recognition is of particular importance to these communities because some express their identity as members of a discrete cultural or linguistic minority—as "Deaf"—rather than as persons with disabilities, and all the connotations that inhere (Stein and Lord 2008, p. 180).

of "the valued existing and potential contributions made by persons with disabilities to the overall well-being and diversity of their communities" (CRPD 2006, Preamble, para. m).

Section 2 of Article 30, however, did not receive much attention during the CRPD negotiations.[24] Indeed, it largely tracks Rule 10(1) of the Standard Rules for the Equalization of Opportunities for Persons with Disabilities (UNGA 1993).[25] Its final form—"States Parties shall take appropriate measures to enable persons with disabilities to have the opportunity to develop and utilize their creative, artistic and intellectual potential, not only for their own benefit, but also for the enrichment of society" (CRPD 2006, Art. 30[2])—did not change significantly from the Chair's initial draft text.[26] The CRPD, a negotiated text, reflects numerous compromises, some of which have drawn significant criticism.[27] At the same time, the Standard Rules had already been "heavily criticised by disability activists for its failure to accept disability as part of human diversity, and to respect the inherent dignity of persons with disability" (Kayess and French 2008, p. 16). In the light of the rigorous debate that forged some of the CRPD's most controversial provisions and omissions, and discontent with the shortcomings of the CRPD's forerunner instruments, Article 30(2) CRPD stands out as a largely consensus provision.

Predictably, in reproducing pre-CRPD provisions, Article 30(2) CRPD on its face, falls short of the transformative intent otherwise manifest in the CRPD. Specifically, Article 30(2) does not promote inclusion as forthrightly as other CRPD articles. For example, Article 19—Living independently and being included in the community, provides that

---

[24] The implications of Article 30(2) CRPD have also been underexplored even within the literature on Article 30 CRPD.

[25] Rule 10(1) provides in part: "States should ensure that persons with disabilities have the opportunity to utilize their creative, artistic and intellectual potential, not only for their own benefit, but also for the enrichment of their community, be they in urban or rural areas" (UNGA 1993, Rule 10(1)).

[26] Article 27(1)(a) of the Chair's initial draft text provided: "States Parties recognize the right of all persons with disabilities to take part in cultural life and shall take all necessary measures to ensure that persons with disabilities … have the opportunity to utilise their creative, artistic and intellectual potential, not only for their own benefit, but also for the enrichment of their community[.]" Available from http://www.un.org/esa/socdev/enable/rights/wgcontrib-chair1.htm#27.

[27] Including the conceptualisation of 'disability' itself (Kayess and French 2008).

persons with disabilities may not be "obliged to live in a particular living arrangement," and asserts a preference for "living and inclusion in the community" (CRPD 2006, Art. 19). Article 24—Education, establishes a right to inclusive education at the same time that it accommodates alternative settings, so long as they "maximize academic and social development" and accord "with the goal of full inclusion" (CRPD 2006, Art. 24(2)(e)). Article 25 affirmatively prescribes health service delivery "as close as possible to people's own communities" (CRPD 2006, Art. 25(c)). Article 30(2), by contrast, features a subdued version of the CRPD's inclusion mandate. It does not assert a preference for inclusive theatre activities, and its disjunctive "not only ... but also" construction appears to give States Parties latitude to implement Article 30(2) through segregated theatre activities (CRPD 2006). Failing to convey that non-inclusive theatre activities may constitute discrimination and impinge upon persons with disabilities' inherent dignity, mutes Article 30(2)'s potential for effectuating belief changes vis-à-vis expressive effects.

More importantly, Article 30(2) fails to recognise theatre's potential to marshal persons with disabilities' talents to convey the CRPD's transformative vision to members of society at large. In other words, Article 30(2) alludes to theatre's traditional therapeutic or entertainment functions to the exclusion of its potential as a tool for confronting and subverting systemic power structures that contribute to marginalising the group it intends to empower. Especially for persons with intellectual disabilities, whose capacity to produce meaningful creative and artistic work is frequently questioned, Article 30(2)'s apparent dichotomy between therapeutic and mainstream theatre activities overlooks how persons with intellectual disabilities today are using theatre as a vehicle for contributing to the realisation of the CRPD's transformative vision.

Indeed, notwithstanding Article 30(2)'s surface limitations, actors with intellectual disabilities across the globe—from the United States to Bangladesh to Switzerland—are using theatre to change beliefs and alter exclusionary conduct. Just as state representatives learned from persons with disabilities participating in the CRPD negotiations, so too should human rights actors learn from the practice of actors with intellectual disabilities that Article 30(2) should be reinterpreted more broadly in the light of the CRPD's belief-change bent. Properly contextualised, Article

30(2) both describes how persons with intellectual disabilities might play the role of belief-change agents essential to the CRPD's mission and also enshrines their right to do so.

5 Conclusion

Article 30(2) articulates the right of persons with disabilities to participate in cultural activities as an end in itself, not as a means for achieving the CRPD's promise in other areas. Yet, understanding the ways in which the CRPD writ large can affect belief changes about persons with disabilities, highlights Article 30(2)'s potential and critical contributions to the CRPD's broad, transformative project. Indeed, the extent to which persons with intellectual disabilities partake of the CRPD's transformative vision will depend in part on their ability to use theatre as a forum for staging micro-level mutually constitutive processes and as a vehicle for changing beliefs and to subvert existing conventions that have contributed to historic marginalisation. The trails actively being blazed by some theatre groups involving persons with intellectual disabilities epitomise the CRPD's aim to drastically recast persons with intellectual disabilities in the role of rights-holders entitled to fully and effectively participate in society on an equal basis with others. Human rights practitioners would do well to follow these groups' lead and direct greater attention to these novel but under-the-radar contributions to CRPD implementation.

Acknowledgements Many thanks to Alex Geisinger for cogent insights into the workings of law's expressive effects, Juliet Bowler for constructive feedback on the practice of Theater of the Oppressed, and Cathy James for incisive suggestions regarding Outside Voices Theater Company's application of Theater of the Oppressed techniques.

References

Americans with Disabilities Act (ADA). (1990). Public Law No. 101-336, codified at 42 U.S.C. Sec. 12101.

Arbour, L. (2006). *Statement to the resumed 8th session of the ad hoc committee on the convention on the rights of persons with disabilities*. [Online]. Retrieved November 22, 2017, from http://www.un.org/esa/socdev/enable/rights/ahc8hrcmsg.htm.

Boal, A. (1974). *Theater of the oppressed* (1st ed.). New York: Urizen Books, Inc.

Boon, R., & Plastow, J. (Eds.). (2004). *Theatre and empowerment: Community Drama on the world stage* (1st ed.). Cambridge: Cambridge UP.

Cohen-Cruz, J. (2006). Redefining the private: From personal storytelling to political act. In J. Cohen-Cruz & M. Schutzman (Eds.), *A Boal companion: Dialogues on theatre and cultural politics* (pp. 103–113). New York: Routledge.

Cohen-Cruz, J., & Schutzman, M. (1994). Introduction. In J. Cohen-Cruz & M. Schutzman (Eds.), *Playing Boal: Theatre, therapy, activism* (1st ed., pp. 1–16). London: Routledge.

Cooter, R. (2000). Do good laws make good citizens: An economic analysis of internalized norms. *Virginia Law Review, 86*, 1577–1601.

CRPD (United Nations Convention on the Rights of Persons with Disabilities). (2006). 999 UNTS 3, opened for signature on 30 March 2007, entered into force on 3 May 2008.

Flynn, E., & Arstein-Kerslake, A. (2014). The support model of legal capacity: Fact, fiction, or fantasy? *Berkeley Journal of International Law, 32*, 134–153.

Fruchterman, J. (2017). E-books and human rights. In J. Lazar & M. A. Stein (Eds.), *Disability, human rights, and information technology* (pp. 143–157). Philadelphia: University of Pennsylvania Press.

Geisinger, A. (2002). A belief change theory of expressive law. *Iowa Law Review, 88*, 35–73.

Gonzalez, T. (2016). From global to local: Domestic human rights norms in theory and practice. *Howard Law Journal, 59*, 373.

Goodley, D., & Moore, M. (2002). *Disability arts against exclusion: People with learning difficulties and their performing arts*. Kidderminster: BILD.

Hall, E. (2013). Making and gifting belonging: Creative arts and people with learning disabilities. *Environment and Planning, 45*, 244–262.

Hargrave, M. (2015). *Theatres of learning disability: Good, bad, or plain ugly?* (1st ed.). London: Palgrave Macmillan.

Harpur, P., & Bales, R. (2010). The positive impact of the convention on the rights of persons with disabilities: A case study on the South Pacific and lessons from the U.S. experience. *Northern Kentucky Law Review, 37*, 363–388.

Ignagni, E., & Church, K. (2008). Disability studies and the ties and tensions with arts-informed inquiry: One more reason to look away? In J. Knowles & A. Cole (Eds.), *Handbook of the arts in qualitative research: Perspectives, methodologies, examples and issues* (pp. 625–638). Los Angeles: Sage Publications.

Ineland, J., & Sauer, L. (2007). Institutional environments and sub-cultural belonging: Theatre and intellectual disabilities. *Scandinavian Journal of Disability Research, 9*(1), 46–57.

Johnston, K. (2016). *Disability theatre and modern Drama: Recasting modernism* (1st ed.). New York: Bloomsbury Methuen Drama.

Kayess, R., & French, P. (2008). Out of darkness into light? Introducing the convention on the rights of persons with disabilities. *Human Rights Law Review, 8*(1), 1–34.

Koh, H. K. (1998). The 1998 Frankel lecture: Bringing international law home. *Houston Law Review, 35*, 623–681.

Kourlas, G. (2013). *Jérôme Bel talks about Disabled Theater*. [Online]. Retrieved November 5, 2017, from https://www.timeout.com/newyork/dance/jerome-bel-talks-about-disabled-theater.

Leighton, F. (2009). Accountability: The ethics of devising a practice-as-research performance with learning-disabled performers. *Research in Drama Education, 14*(1), 97–113.

Lepecki, A. (2015). Yes, now, It's good Theater. In S. Umathum & B. Wihstutz (Eds.), *Disabled Theater* (1st ed., pp. 163–174). Berlin: diaphanes.

Lessig, L. (1995). The regulation of social meaning. *The University of Chicago Law Review, 62*, 943–1045.

Lindsay, S., et al. (2018). A systematic review of the benefits of hiring people with disabilities. *Journal of Occupational Rehabilitation, 28*(4), 634–655.

Lord, J. E., & Stein, M. A. (2008). The domestic incorporation of human rights law and the United Nations convention on the rights of persons with disabilities. *Washington Law Review, 83*, 449–479.

Lord, J. E., & Stein, M. A. (2009). Social rights and the recreational value of the rights to participate in sport, recreation, and play. *Boston University International Law Journal, 27*, 252–281.

Lynd, M. (1992). Creating knowledge through theater: A case study with developmentally disabled adults. *The American Sociologist, 23*(4), 100–115.

McAdams, R. (2000). The legal construction of norms: A focal point theory of expressive law. *Virginia Law Review, 86*, 1649–1728.

McAdams, R. (2009). Beyond the Prisoners' dilemma: Coordination, game theory, and law. *Southern California Law Review, 82*, 209–258.

Oporajeyo. (2011). *[Film] Bangladesh: SEID Trust; Harvard law school project on disability; Steps toward development*. Retrieved November 22, 2017, from https://www.youtube.com/watch?v=a23Qvb7Ah1A&t=12s.

Outside Voices Theater Company. (2015). *What if I were whole?*. New York (script on file with authors).

Parr, H. (2006). Mental health, the arts and belongings. *Transactions of the Institute of British Geographers, 31*, 150–166.

Perring, G. (2005). The facilitation of learning-disabled arts: A cultural perspective. In C. Sandahl & P. Auslander (Eds.), *Bodies in commotion: Disability and performance* (1st ed., pp. 175–189). Ann Arbor: University of Michigan Press.

SEID Trust. (2011). Education, my right. In D. S. Mitu (Ed.), *I Will Raise My Own Voice*. Retrieved January 14, 2010, from https://www.seidtrustbd.org/assets/uploads/upload/Self_Advocacy_on_Promoting_Rights_of_Persons_with_Intellectual_Disability.pdf.

SEID Trust. (2017). My life, my decisions. Dhaka: SEID Trust (video recording on file with authors).

Siegmund, G. (2015). What difference does it make? Or: From difference to in-difference. In S. Umanthum & B. Wihstutz (Eds.), *Disabled Theater* (1st ed., pp. 13–30). Berlin: diaphanes.

Smith, M. S., & Stein, M. A. (2018). Mexico. In L. Waddington & A. Lawson (Eds.), *The UN convention on the rights of persons with disabilities in practice: A comparative analysis of the role of courts*. London: Oxford University Press.

Spry, L. (1994). Structures of power: Towards a theatre of liberation. In J. Cohen-Cruz & M. Schutzman (Eds.), *Playing Boal: Theatre, therapy, activism* (pp. 171–184). London: Routledge.

Stein, M. A. (2003). The law and economics of disability accommodations. *Duke Law Review, 53*, 79–191.

Stein, M. A. (2004). Under the empirical radar: An initial expressive law analysis of the ADA. *Virginia Law Review, 90*, 1151–1191.

Stein, M. A., & Geisinger, A. (2016). Expressive law and the Americans with disabilities act (book review). *Michigan Law Review, 114*, 1061–1079.

Stein, M. A., & Lord, J. E. (2008). Jacobus tenBroek, participatory justice, and the UN convention on the rights of persons with disabilities. *Texas Journal on Constitutional Law and Constitutional Rights, 13*, 167–185.

Stein, M. A., & Stein, P. J. (2007). Beyond disability civil rights. *Hastings Law Journal, 58*, 1203–1240.

Sunstein, C. (1996). On the expressive function of law. *University of Pennsylvania Law Review, 144*, 2021–2053.

Umathum, S., & Wihstutz, B. E. (2015). *Disabled Theater* (1st ed.). Berlin: diaphanes.

United Nations General Assembly (UNGA). (1993). Standard rules for the equalization of opportunities for persons with disabilities, resolution/adopted by the General Assembly, 20 December 1993, A/RES/48/96.

Wheeler, T. (2015). Foreword. In *Theatres of learning disability: Good, bad, or plain ugly?* (pp. x–xiii). London: Palgrave Macmillan.

Wihstutz, B. (2015). … and I am an actor. In S. Umathum & B. Wihstutz (Eds.), *Disabled theater* (1st ed.). Berlin: diaphanes.

Woods, A. K. (2010). A Behavioral approach to human rights. *Harvard International Law Journal, 51*, 51–112.

Part IV

Monitoring the CRPD: Resolving Conflicting Interests?

14

Was Ratification of the CRPD the High Watermark for United Kingdom Disability Rights? Ten Years of Monitoring Implementation of the CRPD

Neil Crowther and Liz Sayce OBE

1 Introduction

In 2007, the disability non-governmental organisation (NGO) Scope hosted a live streaming, from New York, of the then Minister for Disabled People, Anne McGuire, member of parliament (MP) signing the United Nations (UN) Convention on the Rights of Persons with Disabilities (Convention/CRPD 2006) on behalf of the United Kingdom (UK) Government. A mood of celebration prevailed amongst the assembled disability rights activists, officials, and charities: at the moment of signing applause rang out. Andy Rickell, then a Director at Scope, said: "This

N. Crowther (✉)
Independent Expert, London, UK

L. Sayce OBE
International Inequalities Institute, London School of Economics (LSE), London, UK

E. J. Kakoullis, K. Johnson (eds.), *Recognising Human Rights in Different Cultural Contexts*, https://doi.org/10.1007/978-981-15-0786-1_14

marks a watershed in the history of disability rights and highlights how disability is fundamentally a human rights issue" (Ives 2007). In 2009, the UK Government ratified the Convention with cross-party support (Adams-Spink 2009).[1] It seemed that a degree of harmony had broken out—between different political parties and, unusually, between disability advocates and Government.

Eight years later, during a press conference following the examination of the UK by the Committee on the Rights of Persons with Disabilities (CRPD Committee) in August 2017, the Chair of the CRPD Committee, Theresia Degener, described the impact of austerity measures on the rights of persons with disabilities in the UK as a "human catastrophe" (Kentish 2017). Following the examination, which gave rise to an extensive range of critical findings, a number of disabled people's organisations (DPOs) felt moved to adopt a position of non-engagement with the UK Government, believing it to have misled the CRPD Committee concerning the extent of their involvement in policy formulation (DNS 2017). By 2017, the position of the different political parties and the relationship between DPOs and the Government was fractious.

Looking back over the period since 2009, it sometimes appears that ratification of the CRPD (2006) represented the high watermark for UK disability rights. Rather than a springboard for the next stage in its development, ratification may instead be considered only to have underlined all that had been achieved up until that point, adding a full stop. But how far would this be an accurate account of the impact the CRPD has had on disability rights in the UK?

In this chapter we provide an overview of activities in the UK to monitor implementation of the CRPD since it was ratified by the UK Government in 2009 and consider what the outputs and outcome of these activities tell us about the direction of travel for disability rights.

[1] The Shadow Conservative Minister for Disabled People Mark Harper MP described the delay in ratifying the Convention as 'staggering', arguing that "The government needs to be honest where reservations are required but then to get a move on and ratify the convention with the necessary reservations in place" (Adams-Spink 2009).

2 What Does 'Monitoring' the CRPD Mean?

The CRPD does not provide detailed guidance as to what is meant by 'promoting', 'protecting' and 'monitoring', and the CRPD Committee has yet to issue guidance on the matter. However, a useful starting point is the note prepared by the Secretariat for the CRPD on 'National implementation and monitoring', which suggests that monitoring:

> can be approached in a number of ways, including through the assessment of progress, stagnation or retrogression in the enjoyment of rights over a certain period of time. The development of indicators and benchmarks is a particularly effective way to monitor implementation, particularly with regard to the progressive realization of economic, social and cultural rights, as set out in the Convention.
>
> Another approach with which many human rights institutions are familiar is that of monitoring human rights violations, a common methodology of which is to collect or maintain records of the complaints filed by alleged victims before relevant judicial or quasi-judicial complaints mechanisms. Considering the specific barriers persons with disabilities have traditionally faced in accessing justice, such data can be integrated with information on violations provided by other sources, such as civil society organizations and organizations of persons with disabilities participating in the framework. (CRPD/CSP/2014/3, para. 38–39)

Monitoring can also be understood as 'eternal vigilance', with the Convention (2006) providing a frame through which to continually interpret and evaluate the past, present and future. Thought of this way, some of the usual distinctions between 'promotion', 'protection' and 'monitoring' begin to break down. For example, monitoring developing jurisprudence, might involve amicus submissions to the courts to promote adherence to the Convention. Monitoring evolving policies, laws and programmes, might involve responding to consultations and advancing Convention-compliant proposals. Such 'active' monitoring is an ongoing process of embedding the Convention, rather than a more 'passive' and periodic process of post hoc evaluation and reporting. In this chapter we take this broader 'active' view of monitoring.

3 Disability Rights in the UK Before the CRPD

Ratification of the Convention (2006) came at the end of a period mainly characterised by progress on disability rights legislation and implementation in the UK. Conservative Prime Minister John Major's Government introduced the Disability Living Allowance (DLA 1991), a social security benefit conceived to address the 'extra costs' of disability; the Disability Discrimination Act (DDA 1995), outlawing discrimination on disability grounds for the first time in Britain, and the Direct Payments Act (DPA 1996), which enabled persons with disabilities to use resources for support to lead the lives they chose—rather than accept the (often institutional) support on offer from the State.

The Labour Government led by Tony Blair from 1997, set up a Ministerial Disability Rights Task Force (1997–99) made up of activists, businesses, charities, and service providers. It published an agenda for legislation and policy for the next decade (DRTF 1999). Over the 2000s, the scope and scale of protection was expanded starting with establishing the Disability Rights Commission (DRC), with enforcement powers, to replace the purely educational National Disability Council of the 1990s (Disability Rights Commission Act [DRA 1999 Repealed]). There followed a series of extensions to disability rights law in the fields of education (Special Educational Needs and Disability Act 2001), physical access to premises and facilities (DDA 1995, Part III) and an extension of who was protected from disability discrimination.[2] The Disability Discrimination Act (DDA) 2005 also introduced a public sector duty requiring public organisations to have 'due regard' to positively promoting disability equality—rather than expecting individuals to seek redress after the event of discrimination, as was the case with original race and gender equality law (DDA 2005, S. 3). Crucially, in implementing the disability equality duty, public bodies were required to involve persons with disabilities, anticipating the requirements of Article 4(3) of the CRPD (2006), to have in place methods for assessing the potential

[2] For instance better coverage of people with Multiple Sclerosis, cancer and HIV (DDA 1995; EA 2010).

impact of policies on disability equality and to make arrangements for gathering information to appraise performance. For these reasons, the disability equality duty, and its successor the public sector equality duty, was regarded as the principal vehicle via which the CRPD would be implemented (JCHR 2012).

The Mental Capacity Act (MCA) 2005 strengthened the rights of people facing challenges in decision-making: services, ranging from medicine to banks, were no longer to assume people lacked capacity but had to first assume capacity, and offer support to enable decision-making. Although this law still falls short of CRPD (2006) compliance—since it allows substitute, rather than supported, decision-making, on grounds of 'best interests', rather than 'will and preferences' (CRPD 2006, Art. 12)—it did signal a shift to improved rights (MCA 2005). The last of the Task Force's 1999 legislative proposals was finally passed into law in 2010, when the Equality Act in effect debarred employers from asking about health conditions before making a job offer (EA 2010, S. 60).

Non-legislative policy, developed by Government with DPOs and other stakeholders, added depth to disability planning. This included the Improving Life Chances of Disabled People White Paper, published by the Prime Minister's Strategy Unit in 2005, with its aim of disability equality by 2025 (PMSU 2005) and the Independent Living Strategy 2008, which outlined plans to remove barriers to independent living in areas including housing, accessibility and social care (ODI 2008). Both were widely welcomed by DPOs (O'Hara 2008).

Nevertheless, policy is only as good as its implementation and outcomes. The 2000s saw some progress on key measures such as employment, education, and self-directed support of persons with disabilities. For example, the Office for Disability Issues (ODI 2013) found that—whilst there were entrenched inequalities across life domains—the disability employment gap had shrunk by about 10% over a decade; that educational attainment of children and young people with Special Educational Needs (SEN) or disability had improved; that disabled graduates were nearly as likely to be in graduate-level employment as non-disabled graduates; that numbers of disabled people using self-directed support, and direct payments, had increased; and that the proportion of disabled people reporting difficulties accessing goods and services had gone down (DWP 2013). It is important to note that in the early 2000s, there was considerable investment in education, health and other public services. However, progress was not straightforward or linear. There were countervailing trends.

The Mental Health Act (MHA) 2007 introduced Community Treatment Orders (CTOs), against the advice of a Mental Health Alliance that included virtually all the main mental health professional, survivor and charitable organisations, from the Royal College of Psychiatrists to the National Survivor User Network (MHA 2005). The purpose of CTOs was to reduce compulsory detentions by requiring some people to take medication in the community (MHA 2007, S. 32). The outcome was continuing steep rises in compulsory detention, which were used over 63,000 times in 2015–16 (NHS Digital 2016), plus more CTOs than predicted, therefore a significant net increase in compulsion, particularly for black people who made up 18% of people on CTOs. Also, as an evaluation by an original proponent of CTOs, Professor Tom Burns, found—no clinical benefit, but infringements of people's human rights (Burns et al. 2013). CTOs can be seen as an example of the increase in pre-emptive legal powers identified by Newton-Howes et al. (2014), introduced to prevent street drinking and anti-social behaviour, or to curtail migrant rights. Thus some persons with disabilities were caught up in a wider trend of constraint of rights in the 2000s.

Further, the Welfare Reform Act (WRA) 2007 replaced the Incapacity Benefit with Employment and Support Allowance, drawing on American rhetoric, a hand-up not a hand-out, and policy—conditionality as a lever to incentivise persons with disabilities to work (WRA 2007, Part 1). The WRA introduced provisions enabling sanctions to be applied to people who did not comply with work-related activity. This set the groundwork for the work capability assessment (WCA), benefit reductions and significant use of sanctions introduced by subsequent Governments in the 2010s. After the 2008 financial crash, public spending cuts started to impact on DPOs, social care and other public services.

One final danger in the 2000s was a belief amongst policy makers that, with legislation on the statute book, disability rights had been 'done'. Sir Bert Massie, then Chair of the DRC, warned in a speech in January 2006 of the 'lazy fatalism' of still seeing needs of persons with disabilities as an 'add-on', rather than integral to policy across Government (Massie 2006). Massie also noted how, as a result of under-investment and declining availability of the supports that some persons with disabilities required to lead their daily lives, that the introduction of equality legislation had amounted to "some disabled people being invited to look up to the stars while having the rug pulled from beneath them" (Massie 2006).

4 'Full Civil Rights', Not Human Rights

The demands of persons with disabilities during this period were overwhelmingly framed as being for 'full civil rights' or 'Disability Equality'. The language of 'human rights' was rarely deployed while domestic or International Human Rights Law or standards were only rarely drawn upon, despite the Human Rights Act (1998) having come into force in 2000. This was not unique to disability activism in the UK. Writing in 2005 Sarah Spencer reflected how:

> in contrast to common practice abroad, equality and human rights work in Britain has operated in almost entirely different spheres. (Spencer 2005, p. 29)

Sandra Fredman explained the origin of this separation, noting how:

> in most jurisdictions, equality is firmly embedded within human rights law. By contrast, anti-discrimination law in Britain has emerged from labour law, and pre-dates human rights law by a long way .... (Fredman quoted in EDF 2015, p. 88)

The absence of a comprehensive 'human rights' perspective arguably led to a 'structural deficit' in UK disability rights activism that would become starkly apparent as austerity measures began to be implemented. As Theresia Degener, the present chair of the CRPD Committee has argued:

> while the social model supports anti-discrimination policy civil rights reforms, the human rights model of disability is more comprehensive in that it encompasses both sets of human rights, civil and political as well as economic, social and cultural rights. The social model of disability served as a stepping-stone in struggles for civil rights reform and anti-discrimination laws in many countries ….. To demand anti-discrimination legislation was a logical consequence of analyzing disability as the product of inequality and discrimination …. The focus on rights was perceived as an alternative to needs based social policy which portrayed disabled persons as dependent welfare recipients. …. The shift from welfare legislation to civil rights legislation in disability policy became the focus of disability movements in many countries. 'We want rights not charity' was and still is a slogan to be heard around the world from disability rights activists. However, anti-discrimination law can only be seen as a partial solution to the problem. Even in a society without barriers and other forms of discrimination, people need social, economic and cultural rights. People need shelter, education, employment or cultural participation. This is true for all human beings, and thus for disabled persons. However, because impairment often leads to needs for assistance, it is especially true that disabled persons need more than civil and political rights. (Degener 2014, pp. 35–36)

It might be speculated that, had the UK's disability sector embraced human rights, rather than relying primarily on equality law, threats such as benefit sanctions and CTOs might possibly, though by no means certainly, have been seen off sooner. DPOs and the DRC promoted standalone campaigns on independent living, and mental health groups on CTOs—but this was without a comprehensive human rights approach and without the whole disability sector embracing human rights for everyone living with disability/health conditions. The ground could have been laid for a more powerful and effective challenge to reduced social care and social security after the financial crash. For example, the DRC's Mental Health Advisory Group published two documents aimed at building bridges with the wider disability community and increasing impact (DRC 2003, 2006); however, it would be several more years before human rights—and the Convention (2006)—came to occupy centre stage in UK disability rights discourse, activism and legal action.

5 The UK Framework for Monitoring Implementation

The UK was among the first States to sign the CRPD in March 2007 but it took over two further years to ratify the Convention and its Optional Protocol in 2009 (CRPD 2006; OP-CRPD 2006). Reflecting the UK's devolved settlement, there are three national human rights institutions (NHRIs) in the UK: the Equality and Human Rights Commission (EHRC), which is also Britain's national equality body; the Scottish Human Rights Commission (SHRC); and the Northern Ireland Human Rights Commission (NIHC). There is additionally a national equality body for Northern Ireland, the Equality Commission for Northern Ireland (ECNI). The bodies were collectively designated as the UK's 'independent mechanism'[3] (UKIM) in the Explanatory Memorandum laid before Parliament on 3 March 2009. Additionally, as a condition of the bodies being awarded 'A' status in accordance with the 'Paris Principles' by the then sub-committee on accreditation of the International Coordinating Committee of NHRIs, the three NHRIs are required to coordinate their activities on UK level matters. The bodies have met regularly since 2009 and coordinated monitoring and reporting activities, acting as a single entity in their representations to the CRPD Committee. However, while some modest additional resources were made available by the UK Government to the bodies in Scotland and Northern Ireland for promotional work post-ratification, all the bodies have endured a significant reduction in resources since 2009, with the EHRC also losing some of its powers and functions, such as operating a helpline, arranging conciliation and making grants to civil society. The EHRC was at the time of its opening in 2007 required to establish a statutory Disability Committee for a period of at least five years, half the members of which were required to be persons with personal experience of disability (EA 2006, Part 5). The Disability Committee had decision-making powers on matters such as use of the EHRC's enforcement powers as they related to disability

[3] CRPD 2006, Art. 33(2).

discrimination. This was disbanded however in 2017 and has been replaced by a non-statutory Disability Advisory Committee.

At the time that the CRPD was ratified by the UK, the Government had been pioneering new approaches to involving persons with disabilities in policy formulation, including via Equality 2025, a non-departmental public body established to advise ministers on achieving the Government's goal of equality for persons with disabilities by 2025 (ODI 2006); through a co-productive approach to developing an Independent Living Strategy in 2008 and scrutiny group to monitor its implementation (ODI 2009), and via groups established across national and local government and the public sector to support implementation of the Disability Equality Duty (ODI 2009). The Government did not however formally recognise any DPO as having a particular role in monitoring implementation, or take steps to strengthen DPO capacity to do so. Since 2009, the bodies and groups referred to above have been replaced by more ad hoc engagement on specific policy proposals and by a shallower mode of stakeholder consultation concerning implementation of the post 2010 Government's 'Fulfilling Potential' strategy (DNS 2018). Further, the public sector equality duty that replaced the disability equality duty in 2010 was less explicit in its expectation of involvement than its predecessor.

6 The UK's Initial Report to the CRPD Committee

All States Parties are required to submit an initial 'State Report' to the CRPD Committee within two years of ratification (CRPD 2006, Art. 35(1)). The UK Government's ODI set about this task in late 2010, assisted by a new Working Group comprising members of DPOs and disability charities and chaired by the UK Disabled Persons Coalition.[4] The ODI consulted on a draft initial report in 2011 and received criticism from UKIM that the report offered only a description of law and

[4] UN Convention on the Rights of Persons with Disabilities Working Group. See ODI (2011) p. 121.

policy, and lacked information concerning the current context of persons with disabilities or trends across key life domains. In response, the ODI added annexes detailing issues raised by the Working Group and outcome indicators offering some statistical data concerning the UK's performance in relation to the Articles of the CRPD (ODI 2011). As useful a report as this eventually became, it largely proved obsolete in terms of its primary purpose of informing the UK's first examination by the CRPD Committee. This is because much of the content concerned the legal and policy framework and life situation of persons with disabilities prior to the impact of the 2008 financial crash, the 2010 General Election, and the substantial reforms and spending cuts instituted by the 2010 and 2015 Conservative-led Governments. By the time of the examination in 2017, the initial State Report offered a poor guide to the state of disability rights in the UK.

7 The CRPD in Action in the UK

The profile of the CRPD (2006), and of human rights as a frame for disability rights advocacy, has risen considerably since 2007. This includes at law, in disability academia, in the advocacy of DPOs, in Parliament and in the media. The Convention (2006) has arguably been employed mostly as a 'bulwark' to challenge regressive and damaging reforms and spending decisions. However, there is also evidence of the Convention providing a 'lodestar', catalysing and guiding progressive thinking and policy proposals. For example, in 2011 the JCHR launched an inquiry into the implementation of right to independent living of persons with disabilities (JCHR 2011). The inquiry employed Article 19—Living independently and being included in the community, of the CRPD (2006), as its analytical framework (JCHR 2012). It received over 100 pieces of written and oral evidence and concluded that the right to independent living was inadequately protected in domestic law, that the cumulative impact of planned reforms and spending cuts risked leading to retrogression, and that the UK Government was systematically failing to have due regard to the CRPD when developing policy and taking decisions (JCHR 2012). This was the first time the CRPD had been used to critique the implementation of austerity measures. It presaged a number of legal cases challenging legislation, policies and individual decisions in the areas of social security and social care, including in relation to the reform of rules concerning support with housing costs, the closure of the Independent Living Fund and cuts to individual social care packages—as well as repeated calls for Government to conduct a 'cumulative impact assessment'—each of which cited Article 19 of the CRPD (2006).

Further, in 2013 disability activists, led by the campaign coalition Disabled People Against Cuts, petitioned the CRPD Committee on the impact of austerity measures on the right to live independently and on an adequate standard of living and social protection. In 2015, the CRPD Committee launched its own inquiry into whether various policies independently and cumulatively amounted to 'grave and systemic violations' of human rights of persons with disabilities. While in theory a confidential exercise, this 'worst kept secret' involved extensive engagement with disability activists and others, including UKIM and Parliamentarians via a country visit by the CRPD Committee. According to the Committee's Rules of Procedure, even the final report and State Party's response are a confidential matter (CRPD/C/1 2014). Nevertheless, the reports were leaked to the newspaper the *Mail on Sunday* (Owen 2016) and—a day later—published on the Office for the High Commissioner for Human Rights website (OHCHR 2016). The findings revealed the CRPD Committee's conclusion that the cumulative effects of various reforms and spending decisions had met the threshold of "grave or systemic violations" of human rights (CRPD/C/15/R.2/Rev.1 2016, par. 5, 13), a finding that the UK Government strongly disputed. The then Secretary of State for Work and Pensions, Damien Green MP, described the Committee's findings as "an outdated view of disability which is patronising and offensive", focusing on "the amount of money poured into the system, rather than the work and health outcomes for disabled people" (BBC News 2016). Some thought the Government may have leaked the report to the Mail on Sunday, as the article included a colourful critique of both the report and the CRPD Committee, including stating that one of the Committee members "has called for state funding for disabled people to visit prostitutes" (Owen 2016). It is noted that the UK Government did nothing in response to the Inquiry.

In contrast and more positively, policy makers and advisers in relation to the reform of social care, mental capacity law and deprivation of liberty safeguards have considered the Convention (2006). For example, in preparing its advice to the UK Government on reform of social care legislation, the Law Commission received numerous representations arguing that 'independent living' should be included as a 'statutory principle' taking account of Article 19 of the CRPD (2006) (Law Commission 2011). The Law Commission judged that 'independent living' was too vague a principle and 'too biased' towards home-based care to include (Law Commission 2011). In the end, the Care Act 2014 (CA 2014) included 'well-being principles', a number of which aligned strongly with Article 19 (CRPD 2006), such as control over day-to-day life and participation in the community (CA 2014, Part 1). However, the principles are not independently enforceable and disabled people in the UK continue not to enjoy a freestanding right to independent living (Collingbourne 2014).

Furthermore, with the support of the Ministry of Justice, the Essex Autonomy Project explored the degree to which existing or proposed law across the UK complied with Article 12—Equal recognition before the law, of the CRPD (2006). The project concluded that UK law did not comply, while at the same time challenging the CRPD Committee's interpretation of Article 12 in its General Comment (Martin et al. 2017). Following the Supreme Court judgment in *P v Cheshire West*, concerning deprivation of liberty, which took account of the CRPD (2006), the Government asked the Law Commission to prepare advice on reform of Deprivation of Liberty safeguards (Law Commission 2017). The Law Commission subsequently took account of the CRPD in developing its proposals, in particular, to propose legislation on supported decision-making. Importantly however, it concluded that "it is not on its face possible to comply with both Article 5(1)(e) of the European Convention on Human Rights and this (the UNCRPD Committee's) interpretation of Article 14 of the CRPD" (Law Commission 2017, Appendix B).

The CRPD (2006) has also been employed by national and devolved government to frame or inform overarching disability strategies; including the UK Government's 'Fulfilling Potential' strategy (ODI 2013), the Scottish Government (2016) and Scottish local government's (COSLA

2015), CRPD implementation plans and the Welsh Government's Independent Living Action Plan (2014). While these employ the Convention as a touchstone or overarching framework, it is not always clear that their content is deeply rooted in the principles and content of the Convention. For example, a 2013 report on the UK's Fulfilling Potential plans and actions focuses more on disabled role models than on strategic policy change to further the Convention's aims (ODI 2013).

Despite the developments discussed above, the decade since the Convention (2006) was signed by the UK has been marked overwhelmingly by a lack of progress, and in some cases retrogression, on disability rights.

8 A Decade of Stagnation: After the CRPD's Ratification

By 2017, reports to the CRPD Committee from UKIM[5] and civil society organisations paint a picture of retrogression or stasis on a whole series of significant human rights dimensions. There have been intensifying constraints on independent living, resulting from cuts to spending on social care. As the British 'alternative report' to the CRPD Committee from DPOs put it:

> With respect to the obligation to *progressively realise* the economic and social elements of Article 19, there has been a sharp decline in both spending on and the availability of adult social care in England and Wales. This has impacted on the overall quantum of care and the degree to which disabled people are able to exercise choice and control. We have heard personal testimony from people living with people they do not choose to live with and being forced to move home when their support needs change. (Disability Rights UK and Disability Wales 2017, p. 33)

[5] The UK Independent Mechanism (UKIM) is made up of the Equality and Human Rights Commission, the Scottish Human Rights Commission, the Northern Ireland Human Rights Commission and the Equality Commission for Northern Ireland.

A series of reforms to social security have resulted in negative impacts on an adequate standard of living and social protection, with particular impacts on disabled women. The CRPD Committee concluded that the UK Government's own equality impact assessment had foreseen that a large number of disabled people would be adversely affected by the tightening of eligibility criteria and policies designed to reduce expenditure. Further, in education, the proportion of disabled children attending segregated special schools has increased, while the numbers attending state-funded secondary schools in England,[6] Wales,[7] and Scotland[8] declined over the past decade. Furthermore, regarding the scope of 'Article 14—Liberty and security of the person' (CRPD 2006), there has been rising use of compulsion in relation to people with psycho-social impairments. In England, powers of compulsory detention were used 21,897 times in 1987–1988, 44,093 in 2007–2008, but 63,622 in 2015–2016 (NHS Digital 2016).

It has become more difficult for persons with disabilities to secure redress for discrimination and rights violations. The Legal Aid, Sentencing and Punishment of Offenders Act (LASPO 2012), removed numerous areas of law from the scope of civil legal aid, including employment cases (with the exception of discrimination) and most housing, debt and social security benefit cases. Persons with disabilities relied more on legal aid services and are likely to be disproportionately affected by the reforms (House of Commons Justice Committee 2011). Not-for-profit advice agencies relied on by many persons with disabilities when seeking advice or help to challenge decisions have also faced significant cuts.[9] At the

[6] Between 2010 and 2016 the percentage of children in England with a statement of special educational needs or Education Health and Care Plan attending maintained special schools increased from 38.2% to 42.9% while those attending State-funded secondary schools declined from 28.8% to 23.5% (Department for Education 2016).

[7] In Wales, the number of children attending special schools also rose from 4040 pupils in 2006–2007 to 4542 in 2015–2016 (Stats Wales 2017/18).

[8] In 2015 there were 15,899 pupils assessed as or declared disabled in Scotland, with 6920 in Special Schools—a 2.4% rise since 2008 (Scottish Government 2015).

[9] The Low Commission (January 2014) found that: 'reductions in local authority funding of advice and legal support [are] estimated to be at least £40 m by 2015' (p. vii); Shelter has had to close nine of its advice centres as a result of a £3 m cut in its legal aid funding; ASA has had its grant from the (then) LSC cut, reducing their ability to perform a coordinating and representative role (Low Commission 2014).

same time, the EHRC was subject to a 75% budgetary cut (contrasted with average real cuts to Government department spending of 9.7% 2010/11–2015/16) and in 2017 was required to implement a further 25% cut to its budget (Disability Rights UK and Disability Wales 2017). The Enterprise and Regulatory Reform Act 2013 removed the duties and powers of the EHRC to promote good relations and to arrange conciliation, and narrowed the scope of the Commission's duties to report on progress towards equality and human rights (S. 64).

In other areas, while there was no regression there was little progress either. For example, while the overall number of persons with disabilities in employment has increased in line with numbers in employment overall, the gap in the employment rate between disabled and non-disabled people remained static at around 30% over the last decade (Scope 2017); the gap narrowed slightly after 2015, but it is as yet unclear whether this represents the start of a trend (Powell 2018).

Nevertheless, there have been some countervailing positive trends and initiatives. For example, Coleman and Sykes (2016) note that the incidence of disability-related hate crime has declined slightly, and that the reporting of disability hate crime has increased. This follows a decade in which action has been started by DPOs, the Crown Prosecution Service, the police, the DRC and the EHRC (EHRC 2011). The Mental Health (Discrimination) Act (MHA 2013) removed the bar on people who have been 'sectioned' under the Mental Health Act 2007 from serving as members of Parliament, and the bar on people receiving mental health treatment from serving as jurors or company directors. This is an example of campaigners and politicians focusing on rights-based law with relatively minor resource implications in a time of cost constraint, and securing its passage. As noted above, the Care Act (2014) introduced some potentially helpful developments, including a duty on local authorities to consider the physical, mental, and emotional wellbeing of the individual needing care. However, without resolution of social care financing impact is limited.[10]

[10] In November 2017 the UK Government announced that it would publish a Green Paper on the funding of social care for older persons and conduct a parallel process concerning the funding of social care for persons of working age (UK Government 2017).

Following a Task Force chaired by Paul Maynard MP, apprenticeships were made more inclusive (Paul Maynard Taskforce 2016), leading to an increase in disabled apprentices in 2015–2016. Another example is the extension of peer support for employment, as advocated by DPOs (Disability Rights UK 2016), to 71 areas in 2017. Furthermore, there are also numerous examples of good practice pursued by organisations and individuals, which merit recognition—ranging from companies showing leadership in employing disabled people at all levels and influencing and supporting their supply chains, to National Health Service (NHS) Trusts adopting human rights frameworks and leading the way in non-institutional, non-coercive approaches to supporting people with learning disabilities, dementia or mental health challenges.[11]

Nevertheless, the overall picture is one of decline. In 2017, a new EHRC report, Being Disabled in Britain, concluded that disabled people remained second class citizens (EHRC 2017a).

9 The 2017 UK Examination by the CRPD Committee

It was against this backdrop that the first examination of the UK by the CRPD Committee took place in 2017. With financial support from the EHRC in 2016–2017, the organisations, Disability Rights UK, Disability Wales, and Inclusion Scotland (who had additionally received resources from the Scottish Human Rights Commission) began work on 'alternative reports' to the CRPD Committee. The organisations employed a mixed methodology to gather evidence and identify the priorities of persons with disabilities. This included establishing advisory groups made up of diverse persons with disabilities and persons with specific expertise, for example, in mental capacity and mental health law, conducting desk research, running online surveys, and holding 18 engagement events

[11] See for instance Merseycare's award-winning 'no force first' initiative, that places relationships within services at the heart of a successful approach to reducing restraint (NHS Mersey Care n.d.).

attended by over 400 people.[12] The DPOs also met with specific groups to ensure breadth of engagement. For instance, CHANGE, which is made up of people with learning disabilities, the Dementia Engagement and Empowerment Project (DEEP), which is the UK network of dementia voices, and the organisation Freedom from Torture that share the experience of disabled refugees and asylum seekers published a report on England and Wales, one on Scotland, and a combined report on Great Britain as a whole, in February 2017. These reports were then submitted to the CRPD Committee (Disability Rights UK 2017b).

This report writing involved fine judgements. It was felt important to root the testimony of persons with disabilities in an analysis of available evidence: for instance, to show that individual experiences of social care cuts were illustrative of national trends, not isolated instances. Decisions were made about which analyses and issues raised by individual persons with disabilities (in roadshows and surveys) to include, depending on the range of evidence. For example, the reports did not include reference to the view, sometimes expressed, that disability hate crime had grown as a result of 'benefit scrounger' rhetoric from the media or Government, because no empirical evidence could be found to sustain this claim. The aim was to produce a report that both drew on the current experience of persons with disabilities and was authoritative in order to leave no scope for the UK's Governments to dismiss the report's conclusions.

An issue that occasioned considerable debate was whether to include evidence that loss of benefit entitlement following a work capability assessment (WCA) was leading to suicide in reference to Article 10—Right to Life (CRPD 2006). There is worrying, emerging evidence suggestive of a potential link, but the evidence is contested. Insofar as such evidence was robust, informal legal advice suggested it was unlikely to meet the threshold of being regarded as a violation of the right to life. The report strongly included the wider detrimental impacts of benefit loss that impacted on large numbers of people, and referenced the emerging evidence on suicide in its section on the right to life. However, it did not rely mainly on suicide impact in its discussion of benefit cut impacts. The

[12] These events took place in London, Manchester, Leeds, Newcastle, Plymouth, Southampton, Birmingham, Cardiff, Wrexham, Llanelli, Edinburgh, Glasgow and Inverness.

authors did not want the whole issue of impact of benefit cuts on people's lives to be lost because decision-makers chose to contest the particular evidence on suicide. This point was a source of considerable disagreement amongst DPOs. Some took the view that emphasising the most severe impact was the most powerful way to confront Government, and the Disability News Service ran a couple of articles criticising the reports for not majoring on the issue of suicides when discussing the impact of social security reforms.[13]

Other DPOs and charities also submitted reports to the CRPD Committee including Disability Action Northern Ireland, Reclaiming our Futures Alliance (ROFA), made up of grassroots DPOs and anti-austerity campaigners, including Disabled People Against Cuts, Black Triangle and the British Deaf Association (BDA; ROFA 2017b). The UKIM also submitted a report in February 2017 (EHRC 2017b). There was considerable overlap between all the alternative reports and on many points they reinforced each other from slightly different perspectives. There were also a few important differences. For instance, the BDA and ROFA disagreed fundamentally on whether there was any role for separate rather than inclusive schooling and there were different views amongst DPOs on the WCA and suicide, which were perhaps indicative of different strategies for influence. Views ranged from the idea that it was better to be as oppositional as possible, building up the pressure following the CRPD Committee's inquiry report that had already found 'grave or systematic violations' of the CRPD by the UK Government and encouraging the Committee to up the pressure, to the idea that it was better to encourage the Committee to present solutions to the UK Government, leaving space for DPOs to have dialogue with Government in order to influence them to implement at least some of the final recommendations of the Committee.

A risk of the first approach was that Government would simply dismiss the CRPD Committee's conclusions. There was precedent for this when the 'grave or systematic' violations were found. The risk of the second

[13] The debate was not helped by omission of a point on this in one part of the report, through an oversight.

approach was that DPOs might achieve one or two solutions but not necessarily those most significant to lives of persons with disabilities.

This debate was further complicated by political considerations. Some DPOs and campaigning organisations were politically aligned (Black Triangle Campaign n.d.). Others were neutral, committed to working with and influencing whoever was in Government (Spectrum 2017). The Government for its part was signalling an open door for dialogue: it convened its own engagement with DPOs and even overcame a rule that no events should take place in pre-election Purdah to hold an engagement event (suitably re-badged to make it permissible).[14] Disability Rights UK liaised with officials and the Minister for Disabled People, aiming to keep open the possibility of constructive dialogue. With this backdrop, the DPOs planned to travel to Geneva to present to the CRPD Committee. A consensus grew that it would be important to present as united a front as possible. A report launch was held in Parliament in March 2017, hosted by Baroness Jane Campbell who encouraged the different organisations to unite.[15] The DPOs held meetings and teleconferences and agreed on seven top issues to present to the CRPD Committee, with different organisations leading on different parts of the presentation. By March they were planning together in Geneva, and despite an element of chaos—with organisations that had not been part of any of the discussions turning up on the day—the evidence session was effective and united.

The next step in the process was publication by the CRPD Committee of its 'list of issues' (LOIs). This presented few surprises, picking up on the key issues, which the DPOs and UKIM had raised—including access to justice, rights to independent living, involuntary detention, restraint, the disability pay gap and cumulative impact of welfare reform policies (CRPD 2017b). The Committee also asked the Government when it planned to withdraw its reservation on inclusive education.

The Government's response to the LOIs (ODI 2017) opened promisingly with a statement welcoming the examination as an opportunity for constructive discussion on the continued progression of rights of persons with disabilities. The responses to the Committee's issues tended to be

[14] Meeting hosted by Office for Disability Issues 2017.

[15] Meeting hosted by Baroness Jane Campbell, House of Lords, 9 March 2017.

re-statements of existing policies, or general statements of commitment, for example, "the UK Government is committed to supporting disabled people to live independently and be included in the community, including upholding the right to choice and control of residence" (ODI 2017, para. 62b), without however fully explaining how this is achieved. Further there were statements about strategies and plans that have been or will be developed—with no evidence provided as to the outcomes of such plans or how exactly they would be tracked. For instance, on the continuing institutionalisation of people with learning disabilities the response states that NHS England and partners' Building the Right Support (2015) plan, proposes developing community services and closing inpatient facilities for people with a learning disability or autism (and challenging behaviour) to reduce by between 35% and 50% the number of people in inpatient settings by 2019 (ODI 2017). Nevertheless, it does not state what has been done, with what effect. A report from DPOs in response to the Government, dated July 2017, states:

> The UKG response is notably poor in quality. In numerous places policy intent is described without evidence about how those policies are working in practice. (ROFA 2017a)

This DPO report makes many recommendations, ranging from a statutory right to independent living to strengthening the ODI and moving it out of the DWP, so to improve cross-government work to embed human rights. It also re-iterated the DPO's concern at the Government's response to the 2016 CRPD Committee Inquiry that found 'grave or systematic' violations.

In August 2017, the actual examination of the UK took place in Geneva. The ODI hosted live streaming in London, continuing their plan to encourage dialogue. UK officials responded to numerous detailed questions. Some questions stood out: for instance, a question on whether the UK will withdraw reservations given the message it sends to other countries if the UK (seen as a leader) holds on to them. Some responses also stood out: in response to questions on benefit cuts and the high levels of persons with disabilities subject to benefit sanctions, the UK Government stated that it 'stands by' the changes made to the benefit system; and when UK Government officials were challenged to explain why they were using monthly figures of the percentages of persons with disabilities sanctioned, it was pointed out that annual figures would give a fuller picture. The session ended with the EHRC commenting on a 'disconnect' between Government responses and the experience reported by persons with disabilities; and with the ODI re-iterating the Government's commitment to being a world leader, welcoming the scrutiny and inviting civil society and UKIM to join them in taking the next steps.

The CRPD Committee finally produced its concluding observations in August 2017. Its recommendations included to:

> ensure that new and existing legislation incorporates the human rights model of disability across all policy areas and all levels and regions of all devolved governments and jurisdictions and/or territories under its control;
>
> Expedite the process to develop a measurable strategic framework and plan of action, with sufficient financial resources aimed at abolishing laws, regulations, customs and practices that constitute discrimination against persons with disabilities and to ensure the equal protection of persons with disabilities; and
>
> Prevent any negative consequences for persons with disabilities by the decision of the triggering article 50 of the Treaty on European Union, in close consultation with organizations of persons with disabilities. (CRPD 2017b)

These reflect many of the specific issues that had been raised by DPOs and UKIM, for instance:

- The need for an enforceable standalone right to independent living and for adequate funding to ensure its implementation.
- To withdraw the reservation and interpretive declaration concerning inclusive education and to develop a plan for the progressive realisation of inclusive education.

- To carry out a cumulative impact assessment concerning the effect of social security reforms and to repeal social security regulations that are inconsistent with the human rights model of disability.
- To repeal legislation and practices that authorise non-consensual involuntary, compulsory treatment and detention of persons with disabilities on the basis of actual or perceived impairment.

The CRPD Committee praised some developments in devolved Scotland and Wales, but notably none in England or under the control of the UK Government (CRPD). This is a conclusion that if one looked only at evidence of action and outcomes, might not be fully merited. For instance, on devolved matters such as social care, the lack of a right to independent living pertains in Scotland as much as in England; and some English devolution deal areas have produced frameworks for action akin to those praised by the Committee in Scotland and Wales. This may reflect a lack of full analysis of devolution in all its forms, including in England, by the Committee.

The CRPD Committee's Concluding Observations were welcomed by DPOs. Disability Rights UK noted the attention given by the Committee to social security and to mental health law and said:

> The UK government should now cut the rhetoric and start delivering on these excellent recommendations. (Disability Rights UK 2017a)

Disability Wales expressed that:

> It is a relief to see that the UK Government's appalling treatment of disabled people has been called out by the UN Committee. The Concluding Observations give a clear sense of direction for the UK and devolved Governments. (Disability Wales 2017)

The 'calling out' of the UK Government took the form of a headline statement from the CRPD Committee, which said that spending cuts had caused a 'human catastrophe' with total neglect of the vulnerable situations that persons with disabilities find themselves in (CRPD 2017a). This headline statement received huge national news media coverage.[16]

10 Conclusion: What Does the Future Hold?

It is worth asking where this monitoring of implementation process leaves the alignment of the different players and the likelihood of progress on human rights of persons with disabilities in the UK. The UK Government responded to the CRPD Committee's Concluding Observations by saying that they were "disappointed that this report fails to recognise all the progress we've made to empower disabled people in all aspects of their lives" (Butler 2017). It cited the recent growth in the number of persons with disabilities in employment,[17] the strength of the Equality Act (2010) as "some of the strongest equalities legislation in the world", and a repeated claim that the UK is recognised globally as a leader in disability rights (Butler 2017). Some DPOs, meanwhile, took to the offensive, stating that they may boycott any discussion with Government until they change their approach. Tracey Lazard, chief executive officer (CEO) of Inclusion London, said "How can we work with a government whose policies are catastrophic and who deny there is anything wrong?" (Disability News Service, 7 September 2017) and Ellen Clifford, from Disabled People Against Cuts, said they were seeking a shared platform of non-engagement until the Government could be trusted to engage in good faith, rather than using discussions with DPOs to "validate policies that are actively harming disabled people and retrogressing our rights" (Pring 2017).

In 2018, the Government reported on progress, re-iterating that the UK has been at the forefront of developments in equality and disability rights (ODI 2018). Also in 2018, a review of the Mental Health Act in England and Wales produced an interim report (UK Government 2018a), which was strongly criticised by mental health and disability rights

[16] For example, the story featured as the second headline story on the BBC Ten O'clock News and was an extended feature on BBC's Newsnight.

[17] In line with overall increases in the employment rate—that is, not a measure of the disability employment gap.

advocates (Pring 2018) for seeming to pay no attention to the recommendations of the CRPD Committee to "Repeal legislation and practices that authorize non-consensual involuntary, compulsory treatment and detention of persons with disabilities on the basis of actual or perceived impairment" (CRPD 2017a, para. 35a).[18]

The examination of the UK Government in 2017 by the CRPD Committee revealed interesting dynamics, with a disability sector achieving unity in order to present a coherent picture to the Committee. This influenced Concluding Observations that are strong, coherent, far-reaching and reflect both the experience reported by persons with disabilities and the research carried out by DPOs and UKIM. This is an agenda that could help the UK develop a much more substantive structure of human rights both short and longer term, which would benefit persons with disabilities and the wider society through policies of inclusion. However, the reliance by the Government on iterations of actions already taken, rather than forward plans for change, and the disagreements between DPOs on methods to make progress, could risk stalemate. There is the risk that the unity achieved for the sake of effective presentation to the CRPD Committee could fracture again. One learning point is a need for increased dialogue not on what needs to change—on which consensus is high—but on how best to influence that change. That could result in mutual respect for different methods designed to reach the same ends, in a context of commitment to ongoing honest debate. Only then will the unity that helped stimulate the Concluding Observations generate the strength of sector needed to influence the significant changes in Government policy required for persons with disabilities to enjoy human rights in the UK.

[18] The final Mental Health Act Review was published in December 2018. It is valuable to note here that final report of the review says: "some will point out that we have not gone as far as to recommend fully implementing the UN Convention on Rights of Persons with Disabilities (CRPD), or to be precise, how that is interpreted by the Committee charged with its implementation. And they are right. We haven't … Implementing our proposals will go a substantial part of the way to addressing the concerns motivating the CRPD Committee. But in rejecting the last steps that they propose—the abolition of all mental health legislation, whether a Mental Health or Mental Capacity Act, I wish to be clear. It is true that we do not currently have the legislative space that would be required for such a radical step. But to use this as a reason would be disingenuous. The reason is simpler—I don't agree with it, and I am far from sure that is what most service users want either, as well as many others" (UK Government 2018b, p. 12).

As for opportunities to move disability rights forward, the implications of Brexit remain unclear, making predictions about the future difficult. Certainly, with the UK outside the legal framework of the EU, yet (rhetorically at least) keen to be seen as 'Global Britain', the various international human rights treaties to which the UK is party, including the CRPD (2006), may come to assume greater prominence as a framework for law and policy. On the other hand, if the 2015–17 Government's response to the CRPD Committee's Inquiry and Concluding Observations offer a guide, the status of the CRPD could equally be shaped by attitudes to British 'sovereignty' and a dislike of 'meddling foreigners' in domestic UK affairs that partially prompted Brexit and lie behind long-standing hostility to the European Court of Human Rights (1950).

There also seems little possibility that the UK's economy and public finances will see significant improvements in the short to medium term. While this does not automatically mean permanent austerity, it seems improbable, especially given the UK's ageing population, that those areas that have been particularly hard hit since the financial crash of 2008 (social security and social care) will enjoy levels of investment sufficient to significantly reverse the effects of cuts made to date. This is especially so given the generally low public support for more generous spending on social security and a lack of public salience concerning social care, save with respect to whether people are required to use the equity in their homes to pay for care in older age. However, there are strong signs following the 2019 General Election, which saw a Conservative Party victory, that austerity as a political project that has enjoyed public consent for the past three general elections may be falling out of favour.[19]

Furthermore, as we have noted, the fight against austerity has witnessed a shift in disability activism from 'civil rights' to 'human rights', in particular to begin cultivating a discourse around economic, social, and cultural rights. This shift has seen new voices enter the debate, in particular people with 'chronic health conditions', hitherto at the margins of

[19] The British Social Attitudes Survey (2017) found that "after 7 years of government austerity, public opinion shows signs of moving back in favour of wanting more tax and spend and greater redistribution of income" (NatCen 2017).

disability activism.[20] There does however seem a risk, given the unenforceable nature of economic and social rights in the UK context, that people may become disillusioned by human rights as a lever for change. The Labour Party has said that it would "incorporate the UNCRPD" if it wins power and forms a future government (Labour Party Election Manifesto 2019, p. 74), though their precise intentions to these ends continue to be unclear. Further, a wholesale shift in focus to economic and social rights risks undermining any gains that might be made for disability rights as a whole by reinforcing the 'welfare dependency' frame of disability those earlier 'civil rights' campaigners fought so hard to overcome. If human rights are to provide a progressive framing for disability rights activism in the UK, then it needs to embrace civil and political rights as readily as economic and social rights within a unified vision of social inclusion. To these ends, immediate opportunities do exist to institute more effective methods to increase the employment participation of persons with disabilities, to propose alternative ways to support working age persons with disabilities to live independently, to reduce mental health detention, and to reform mental health and deprivation of liberty law.

Since the Convention (2006) was ratified in 2009, the UK has undergone significant constitutional reform, with an extension of devolution to Scotland and Wales, and from central to local government. While much focus of debate regarding the CRPD (2006) centres on the actions and policies of the UK government in Westminster, in practice many of the decisions shaping the enjoyment of rights of persons with disabilities are no longer taken there. This is an opportunity as well as a challenge, for it offers a broader range of possibilities than policy by central diktat. A challenge for the future will be bringing the principle of 'think global, act local' to implementation of the Convention. In many ways this would be a reconnection with the origins of disability rights activism in the UK, especially in relation to independent living which grew out of local grassroots activism (Evans 2003). Nevertheless, devolution of responsibility without resources to local authorities has been criticised by the CRPD

[20] For example, the Chronic Illness Inclusion Project launched in 2017 https://inclusionproject.org.uk/about/.

Committee as a derogation of duty: central Government, they suggest, retains responsibility for safeguarding Convention rights even in a context of devolution (CRPD 2017a, para. 6(a)).

Finally, amidst the general picture of stagnation and set-backs, it is also crucial to acknowledge that while there is much more to do, for many persons with disabilities and for newer generations of persons with disabilities some things have got better than they were in the past. This has happened because disability rights activists have put forward solutions and campaigned effectively for them to be implemented. In other areas, while problems persist, they are only now recognised because disability activism has succeeded in shining a light on injustice and making the issues visible. Sometimes unforeseen developments such as digital technology, the Internet, and social media have hugely transformed the way we live, opening up myriad new possibilities for persons with disabilities, as they have for the population at large. Safeguarding against further deterioration in the living conditions of persons with disabilities will, rightly and understandably, continue to consume a great deal of the attention and energy of disability activism in the years ahead. Nevertheless, finding space to celebrate and learn from past successes, reasserting the strengths that secured them, riding the waves of new opportunities and charting out a positive agenda for inclusion are crucial steps if disability activism is to enjoy a vibrant future.

References

Adams-Spink, G. (2009, January 6). *UK "Must Ratify" Disability Pact.* BBC News. Retrieved May 3, 2019, from http://news.bbc.co.uk/1/hi/uk/7813896.stm.

BBC News. (2016, November 7). *UN: "'Grave" Disability Rights Violations under UK Reforms.* BBC News.

Black Triangle Campaign. (n.d.). *Anti-defamation campaign in defence of disability rights.* Retrieved May 4, 2019, from http://blacktrianglecampaign.org/2017/06/02/uk-general-election-why-disabled-people-oppose-the-tories-and-need-your-help/.

Burns, T., Rugkåsa, J., Molodynski, A., et al. (2013). Community treatment orders for patients with psychosis: A randomised control trial. *Lancet, 381*(9878), 1627–1633.

Butler, P. (2017, August 31). UN Panel Criticises UK Failure to Uphold Disabled Peoples Rights. *The Guardian.*

CA (Care Act). (2014).

Coleman, N., & Sykes, W. (2016). *Crime and disabled people—Measures of disability related harassment equality and human rights commission.* London: Equality and Human Rights Commission.

Collingbourne, T. (2014). The Care Act 2014: A missed opportunity? *European Journal of Legal Studies, 20*(3). Retrieved from http://webjcli.org/article/view/365/464.

COSLA. (2015). *United nations convention on the rights of persons with disabilities—Scottish local government delivery plan 2015–2018.* Edinburgh: COSLA.

CRPD (Committee on the Rights of Persons with Disabilities). (2017a). *Concluding observations on the initial report of the United Kingdom of Great Britain and Northern Ireland.* Paris: OHCHR.

CRPD (Committee on the Rights of Persons with Disabilities). (2017b). *List of issues in relation to the initial report of the United Kingdom of Great Britain and Northern Ireland.* Paris: OHCHR. Retrieved May 4, 2019, from https://tbinternet.ohchr.org/_layouts/treatybodyexternal/Download.aspx?symbolno=CRPD/C/GBR/Q/1&Lang=en.

CRPD/C/1 (Committee on the Rights of Persons with Disabilities). (2014). *Rules of procedure United Nations.* New York. Retrieved May 21, 2019, from https://documents-dds-ny.un.org/doc/UNDOC/GEN/G14/042/41/PDF/G1404241.pdf?OpenElement.

CRPD/Convention (UN Convention on the Rights of Persons with Disabilities). (2006). United Nations.

CRPD/CSP/2014/3 (Conference of States Parties to the Convention on the Rights of Persons with Disabilities Seventh Session). (2014). *National Implementation and Monitoring Note by the Secretariat.* New York: United Nations. Retrieved May 4, 2019, from.

CRPD/C/15/R.2/Rev.1 (Committee on the Rights of Persons with Disabilities). (2016). *Inquiry concerning the United Kingdom of Great Britain and Northern Ireland carried out by the committee under article 6 of the optional protocol to the convention report of the committee United Nations.* New York. Retrieved May 21, 2019, from https://www.ohchr.org/Documents/HRBodies/CRPD/CRPD.C.15.R.2.Rev.1-ENG.doc.

DDA (Disability Discrimination Act). (1995).

DDA (Disability Discrimination Act). (2005).

Degener, T. (2014). A human rights model of disability. In P. Blanck & E. Flynn (Eds.), *Routledge handbook of disability law and human rights*. London: Routledge.

Department for Education. (2016). *Special educational needs in England: January 2016. SFR 29/2016*. London: Department for Education. https://www.gov.uk/government/uploads/system/uploads/attachment_data/file/539158/SFR29_2016_Main_Text.pdf.

Disability News Service (DNS). (2017). DPOs consider boycott of government over misrepresentation at UN. Retrieved from https://www.disabilitynewsservice.com/dpos-consider-boycott-of-government-engagement-over-misrepresentation-at-un/.

Disability Rights UK. (2016). *Peer support could boost work prospects for disabled people*. London: Disability Rights UK. Retrieved May 4, 2019, from https://www.disabilityrightsuk.org/news/2016/may/peer-support-could-boost-work-prospects-disabled-people.

Disability Rights UK. (2017a). *A human catastrophe—New UN condemnation for UK human rights record*. London: Disability Rights UK. Retrieved May 4, 2019, from https://www.disabilityrightsuk.org/news/2017/august/human-catastrophe-%E2%80%93-new-un-condemnation-uk-human-rights-record.

Disability Rights UK. (2017b). *Reports to the UN committee 2017*. London: Disability Rights UK. Retrieved May 4, 2019, from https://www.disabilityrightsuk.org/news/2017/january/disabled-people-tell-un-committee-uk-failing-international-rights-convention.

Disability Rights UK and Disability Wales. (2017). *Implementation of the United Nations convention on the rights of persons with disabilities in England and Wales: Shadow report*. London and Caerphilly: Disability Rights UK and Disability Wales.

Disability Wales. (2017). *UN committee concluding observations—UK going backwards on rights*. Caerphilly: Disability Wales. Retrieved May 4, 2019, from http://www.disabilitywales.org/un-committee-concluding-observations-uk-going-backwards-on-rights/.

DLA (Disability Living Allowance and Disability Working Allowance Act). (1991).

DNS (Disability News Service). (2018, April 12). *Network neglect leaves government "closer to coercion than co-production"*. Retrieved May 3, 2019, from https://www.disabilitynewsservice.com/network-neglect-leaves-government-closer-to-coercion-than-co-production/.

DPA (Direct Payments Act). (1996).

DRC (Disability Rights Commission). (2003). *Coming together—Mental health service users and disability rights.*
DRC (Disability Rights Commission). (2006). *Coming together—Mental health service users and human rights.*
DRTF (Disability Rights Task Force). (1999). *From Exclusion to Inclusion: A report of the disability rights task force on civil rights for disabled people.* London: Department for Education and Employment.
EA (Amended to EA). (2006). Equality Act 2006, Section 5.
EA (Equality Act). (2010).
EDF (Equality and Diversity Forum). (2015). *Shaping the future of equality, human rights and social justice.* London: EDF.
EHRC (Equality and Human Rights Commission). (2017a). *Being disabled in Britain.* Manchester: EHRC.
EHRC (Equality and Human Rights Commission). (2017b). *Disability rights in the UK: UK independent mechanism.* Manchester: EHRC. Retrieved May 3, 2019, from https://www.equalityhumanrights.com/en/publication-download/disability-rights-uk-updated-submission-un-committee-rights-persons.
Enterprise and Regulatory Reform Act. (2013).
Equality and Human Rights Commission (EHRC). (2011). *Hidden in plain sight: Inquiry into disability-related harassment.* EHRC.
European Court of Human Rights. (1950).
Evans, J. (2003). *The independent living movement in the UK.* Farsta: Independent Living Institute. Retrieved May 4, 2019, from https://www.independentliving.org/docs6/evans2003.html#1.
House of Commons Justice Committee. (2011). *Inquiry report on "Government's proposed reform of legal aid": Third report of session 2010–11.* London: The Stationery Office.
HRA (Human Rights Act). (1998).
Ives, J. (2007, May 30). Campaigners hail treaty on disability rights. *The Guardian.* Retrieved May 4, 2019, from https://www.theguardian.com/society/2007/mar/30/disability.uknews.
JCHR (Joint Committee on Human Rights). (2011). *Implementation of the right to independent living for disabled people inquiry.* London: The Stationery Office.
JCHR (Joint Committee on Human Rights). (2012). *Implementation of the right of disabled people to independent living, twenty-third report.* London: The Stationery Office.
Kentish, B. (2017). Government cuts have caused "human catastrophe" for disabled, UN committee says. *The Independent.* Retrieved May 4, 2019, from

https://www.independent.co.uk/news/uk/politics/government-spending-cuts-human-catastrophe-un-committee-rights-persons-with-disabilities-disabled-a7911556.html.

Labour Party. (2019). *Election Manifesto*. Newcastle-upon-Tyne: Labour Central. Retrieved May 4, 2009, from https://labour.org.uk/manifesto/.

Law Commission. (2011). *Adult social care*. Law Com No 326, Law Commission, London.

Law Commission. (2017). *Mental capacity and deprivation of liberty*. London: The Stationery Office.

Low Commission. (2014). *Tackling the advice deficit*. London: Legal Action Group. Retrieved May 4, 2019, from https://www.lag.org.uk/about-us/policy/the-low-commission-200551.

Martin, W., Michalowski, S., Jutten, T., & Burch, M. (2017). *Achieving CRPD compliance*. Colchester: Essex Autonomy Project, University of Essex. Retrieved May 4, 2019, from https://autonomy.essex.ac.uk/wp-content/uploads/2017/01/EAP-Position-Paper-FINAL.pdf.

Massie, B. (2006, January 30). *Achieving equality and social justice—A future without disability?, Speech*. London: Westminster Central Hall

MCA (Mental Capacity Act). (2005).

MHA (Mental Health (Discrimination) Act). (2013).

MHA (Mental Health Act). (2007).

MHA (Mental Health Alliance). (2005). *Towards a better mental health act: The mental health alliance policy agenda*. London: Mental Health Alliance. Retrieved May 4, 2019, from http://www.mentalhealthalliance.org.uk/pre2007/documents/AGENDA2.pdf.

NatCen. (2017). *British social attitudes survey*. London: NatCen Social Research. Retrieved May 4, 2019, from http://www.bsa.natcen.ac.uk/latest-report/british-social-attitudes-34/key-findings/context.aspx.

Newton-Howes, G., Lacey, C. J., & Banks, D. (2014). Community treatment orders: The experiences of Non-Maori and Maori within mainstream and Maori mental health services. *Social Psychiatry and Psychiatric Epidemiology, 49*(2), 267–273.

NHS England, LGA, ADASS. (2015). Building the right support a national plan to develop community services and close inpatient facilities for people with a learning disability and/or autism who display behaviour that challenges, including those with a mental health condition NHS England.

NHS Digital (National Health Service Digital). (2016). *Inpatients formally detained in hospitals under the Mental Health Act 1983 and patients subject to supervised community treatment: 2015/16, Annual fig-*

ures. Leeds: NHS Digital. Retrieved May 24, 2019, from https://digital.nhs.uk/data-and-information/publications/statistical/inpatients-formally-detained-in-hospitals-under-the-mental-health-act-1983-and-patients-subject-to-supervised-community-treatment/inpatients-formally-detained-in-hospitals-under-the-mental-health-act-1983-and-patients-subject-to-supervised-community-treatment-2015-16-annual-figures.

NHS Mersey Care. (n.d.). *No force first*. Liverpool: Mersey Care NHS Foundation Trust. Retrieved May 24, 2019, from https://www.merseycare.nhs.uk/about-us/striving-for-perfect-care/no-force-first.

O'Hara, M. (2008, March 5). Route to equality. *The Guardian*. Retrieved May 4, 2019, from https://www.theguardian.com/society/2008/mar/05/disability.equality1.

ODI (Office for Disability Issues). (2006). *First annual report to the prime minister's office for disability issues*. London. Retrieved May 4, 2019, from https://careappointments.com/care-news/england/78529/office-for-disability-issues-first-annual-report-to-the-prime-minister/.

ODI (Office for Disability Issues). (2008). *Independent living: A cross-government strategy about independent living for disabled people*. London: Office for Disability Issues.

ODI (Office for Disability Issues). (2009). *Roadmap 2025: Achieving disability equality by 2025*. London: Office for Disability Issues. Retrieved May 4, 2019, from https://www.disability.co.uk/sites/default/files/resources/roadmap-full.pdf.

ODI (Office for Disability Issues). (2011). *UK government initial report on the UN convention on the rights of persons with disabilities*. London: Office for Disability Issues. Retrieved May 4, 2019, from https://www.gov.uk/government/publications/un-convention-on-the-rights-of-persons-with-disabilities-initial-report-on-how-the-uk-is-implementing-it.

ODI (Office for Disability Issues). (2013). *Fulfilling potential—Building a deeper understanding of disability in the UK today*. London: Office for Disability Issues. Retrieved May 4, 2019, from https://www.gov.uk/government/collections/fulfilling-potential-working-together-to-improve-the-lives-of-disabled-people.

ODI (Office for Disability Issues). (2017). *List of issues in relation to the initial report of the United Kingdom of great Britain and Northern Ireland: Government response*. London: Office for Disability Issues. Retrieved May 4, 2019, from https://www.gov.uk/government/publications/disabled-peoples-rights-information-for-the-uks-first-periodic-review/list-of-issues-in-relation-to-the-initial-report-of-the-united-kingdom-of-great-britain-and-northern-ireland-government-response.

ODI (Office for Disability Issues). (2018). *Policy paper: Progress on the UK's vision to build a society which is fully inclusive of disabled people: Letter from the minister for disabled people, health and work*. London: Office for Disability Issues. Retrieved May 4, 2019, from https://www.gov.uk/government/publications/disabled-peoples-rights-information-following-the-uks-first-periodic-review/progress-on-the-uks-vision-to-build-a-society-which-is-fully-inclusive-of-disabled-people-letter-from-the-minister-for-disabled-people-health-and-w.

Office for Disability Issues (DWP). (2013). Fulfilling potential—Building a deeper understanding of disability in the UK today. Retrieved from https://www.gov.uk/government/uploads/system/uploads/attachment_data/file/320515/building-understanding-main-slide-deck.pdf.

OHCHR (Office of the High Commissioner for Human Rights). (2016). *CRPD inquiry procedure*. Paris: OHCHR. Retrieved May 4, 2019, from http://www.ohchr.org/EN/HRBodies/CRPD/Pages/InquiryProcedure.aspx.

OP-CRPD (Optional Protocol to the Convention on the Rights of Persons with Disabilities). (2006). Retrieved May 4, 2019, from http://www.ohchr.org/EN/HRBodies/CRPD/Pages/OptionalProtocolRightsPersonsWithDisabilities.aspx.

Owen, G. (2016, November 6). Controversial UN task force slams britain's welfare cuts and says disabled people are "unfairly bearing the brunt" of austerity. *Daily Mail*. Retrieved May 4, 2019, from https://www.dailymail.co.uk/news/article-3909276/Controversial-task-force-slams-Britain-s-welfare-cuts-says-disabled-people-unfairly-bearing-brunt.html.

Paul Maynard Taskforce. (2016). *Paul maynard taskforce recommendations*. London: UK Government. Retrieved May 4, 2018, from https://www.gov.uk/government/publications/apprenticeships-improving-access-for-people-with-learning-disabilities/paul-maynard-taskforce-recommendations.

PMSU (Prime Minister's Strategy Unit). (2005). *Improving the life chances of disabled people*. London: Prime Minister's Strategy Unit. Retrieved May 4, 2019, from http://webarchive.nationalarchives.gov.uk/20130402160115/https://www.education.gov.uk/publications/eOrderingDownload/1968-2005PDF-EN-03.pdf.

Powell, A. (2018). *People with disabilities in employment*. House of commons library briefing paper No 7540. London: House of Commons. Retrieved May 5, 2019, from http://researchbriefings.files.parliament.uk/documents/CBP-7540/CBP-7540.pdf.

Pring, J. (2017, September 7). DPOs consider boycott of government engagement over "misrepresentation" at UN. *Disability News Service*. Retrieved May 4, 2019, from https://www.disabilitynewsservice.com/dpos-consider-boycott-of-government-engagement-over-misrepresentation-at-un/.

Pring, J. (2018, May 3). Mental health act review "is just tinkering around the edges" of reform. *Disability News Service*. Retrieved May 4, 2019, from https://www.disabilitynewsservice.com/mental-health-act-review-is-just-tinkering-around-the-edges-of-reform/.

ROFA (Reclaiming our Futures Alliance). (2017a). *List of issues in relation to the initial report of the United Kingdom of Great Britain and Northern Ireland*. An Alliance of Disabled People and Our Organisations in England. Retrieved May 5, 2019, from http://www.rofa.org.uk/list-of-issues-in-relation-to-the-initial-report-of-the-united-kingdom-of-great-britain-and-northern-ireland/.

ROFA (Reclaiming our Futures Alliance). (2017b). *Shadow report on the UK initial report on the UN convention on the rights of persons with disabilities, an alliance of disabled people and our organisations in England*. Retrieved May 5, 2019, from https://www.inclusionlondon.org.uk/wp-content/uploads/2017/03/ROFA-Shadow-report-UN-CRPD-Periodic-review-UK-March-2017.pdf.

Scope. (2017, August). *The disability employment gap is static*. Retrieved from https://www.scope.org.uk/press-releases/disability-employment-gap-static.

Scottish Government. (2015). *Summary statistics for schools in Scotland: No 6*. Edinburgh: Scottish Government. Retrieved May 4, 2019, from https://www.gov.scot/publications/summary-statistics-schools-scotland-6-2015-edition/.

Scottish Government. (2016). *A fairer Scotland for disabled people—Our delivery plan to 2021 for the United Nations convention on the rights of persons with disabilities*. Edinburgh: Scottish Government. Retrieved May 4, 2019, from http://www.gov.scot/Publications/2016/12/3778/3.

Special Educational Needs and Disability Act. (2001).

Spectrum. (2017). *Spectrum 2017 disability manifesto out now!*. Southampton: Spectrum. Retrieved May 4, 2019, from http://spectrumcil.co.uk/uncategorized/spectrum-2017-disability-manifesto-out-now/.

Spencer, S. (2005). Partner rediscovered? Human rights and equality in the UK. In C. Harvey (Ed.), *Human rights in the community: Rights as agents of change*. Oxford: Hart.

Stats Wales. (2017/18). *Pupils by local authority, region and type of school*. Retrieved May 4, 2019, from https://statswales.gov.wales/Catalogue/

Education-and-Skills/Schools-and-Teachers/Schools-Census/Pupil-Level-Annual-School-Census/Pupils/pupil-by-localauthorityregion-typeofschool.
The Legal Aid, Sentencing and Punishment of Offenders Act (LASPO). (2012).
UK Government. (2017). *Government to set out proposals to reform care and support.* London: Press Release, UK Government. Retrieved May 4, 2019, from https://www.gov.uk/government/news/government-to-set-out-proposals-to-reform-care-and-support.
UK Government. (2018a). *The independent review of the Mental Health Act.* London: UK Government. Retrieved May 4, 2019, from https://assets.publishing.service.gov.uk/government/uploads/system/uploads/attachment_data/file/703919/The_independent_Mental_Health_Act_review__interim_report_01_05_2018.pdf.
UK Government. (2018b). Modernising the Mental Health Act Increasing choice, reducing compulsion Final report of the Independent Review of the Mental Health Act 1983.
UK Government Office for Disability Issues (ODI). (2018, September). Concluding observations on the initial report of the United Kingdom of Great Britain and Northern Ireland—Initial government response. Retrieved from https://www.gov.uk/government/publications/disabled-peoples-rights-information-following-the-uks-first-periodicreview/concluding-observations-on-the-initial-report-of-the-united-kingdom-of-great-britain-and-northern-ireland-initial-government-response.
Welsh Government. (2014). *Framework for action on independent living.* Cardiff: Welsh Government.
WRA (Welfare Reform Act). (2007).

15

The Role of Disabled People's Organisations in Promoting the CRPD in Indonesia

Dina Afrianty

1 Introduction

When Indonesia ratified the United Nations (UN) Convention on the Rights of Persons with Disabilities (CRPD 2006) in 2011 through the introduction of Law No. 19/2011 on Pengesahan CRPD, there was high hope among persons with disabilities (Nursyamsi et al. 2015; Wardana and Dewi 2017). Many believed it would lead to a new beginning in the way the Indonesian Government and the community would respect and protect the dignity, interests and rights of persons with disabilities to independence, equality, freedom and participation in Indonesia's socio-economic and political development.

Five years after Indonesia ratified the CRPD, the Indonesian Government introduced a new law on disability, Law No. 8/2016 on Penyandang Disabilitas or 'People with Disabilities', which acknowledged the obligation the Government has to remove forms of discrimina-

D. Afrianty (✉)
La Trobe Law School, La Trobe University, Melbourne, Australia
e-mail: D.Afrianty@latrobe.edu.au

E. J. Kakoullis, K. Johnson (eds.), *Recognising Human Rights in Different Cultural Contexts*, https://doi.org/10.1007/978-981-15-0786-1_15

tion and barriers that hinder persons with disabilities from participating fully and effectively in society on an equal basis with others. Historically, Indonesians with disabilities have been subjected to discriminatory policies which emanate from local tradition, culture and the state political ideology. Under the authoritarian Government, human rights were heavily suppressed and persons with disabilities were one of the groups whose rights were extremely violated as they were treated as 'objects' of charity in many of the State's policies and regulations. The Law No. 11/2009 on Social Welfare, for example, regulates that persons with disabilities, including those with physical and mental disabilities who cannot live independently should be subject to the State's policy to put them in a special place that provides 'rehabilitation' services (Colbran 2010; Nursyamsi et al. 2015).

This chapter discusses the work of disabled peoples' organisations (DPOs) in monitoring the implementation of the CRPD in Indonesia. It discusses some of the DPOs' important achievements at the local and national levels and the progress that they have contributed to in the mobilisation of social inclusion in the community.

2 Discrimination Against Persons with Disabilities

Discrimination towards person with disabilities is clearly illustrated in a case involving Indonesia's fourth President, Abdurrahman Wahid (1999–2002), who is also popularly known as Gus Dur. The late President Abdurrahman Wahid, who was also at the time the chairman of Indonesia's biggest Muslim organisation, 'Nahdlatul Ulama',[1] was elected to power in 1991 as he received more votes from the male-dominated members of

[1] Nahdlatul Ulama or NU is the second Muslim-based organisation that established itself in 1926 following the establishment of the first, progressive and moderate Muslim-based organisation, Muhammadiyah in 1912. Muhammadiyah and NU since then are known to represent the moderate and tolerant faces of Indonesian Islam. Muhammadiyah owns thousands of schools and hundreds of universities and health services. NU is considered by many analysts of Indonesian Islam as more grassroots with strong followers in rural Indonesia with its strong traditional character of Indonesian Islam. NU owns thousands of traditional Islamic boarding schools known as Pesantren. See Hefner (2000) for more accounts on this.

the People's Consultative Assembly (or 'Majelis Permusyawaratan Rakyat (MPR)') than his female political rival, Megawati Sukarnoputri. President Abdurrahman Wahid had impaired vision and had suffered a stroke. It was interesting that despite his disabilities, President Abdurrahman Wahid received more votes from the members of MPR than Megawati Sukarnoputri, whose party had in fact won the 1999 general election.[2]

The election of President Wahid sent a positive signal to the disabled community as Indonesia then had a Head of State and national figure who had a (visible) disability. Human rights activists saw this as a good sign for Indonesia's democracy and human rights in that everyone was equal to run for public office (Irwanto and Thohari 2017). Many in the general public saw the election of President Wahid as a demonstration that despite the social stigma towards disability, it was not seen as an obstacle for an Indonesian wishing to be a political leader. Women's rights activists saw this differently, as women's leadership at that time was seen as against tradition and Islamic teaching, because the public rhetoric during the election was that women were considered unfit to hold high public office, let alone to become a president. However, Wahid's presidency was short lived as only three years later he was impeached by the same members of the Consultative Assembly for alleged corruption. Wahid was replaced by his Vice President, Megawati Sukarnoputri, making her Indonesia's first female President.

In 2002, Indonesia introduced a new electoral law to allow Indonesians to directly elect their political leader. Following this, Wahid announced that he would run in the 2004 presidential election. With support from his own party and the members of Indonesia's biggest Muslim organisation, Nahdlatul Ulama, he was confident about his chances. Nevertheless, his intention to become a President for the second time was immediately

[2] Indonesia's 32-year authoritarian President General Suharto was forced to step down in May 1998. It ended the centralised and militaristic government and led to Indonesia's political reform. During Suharto period, Indonesian President was elected by the members of the People's Consultative Assembly or MPR who represented three political parties. Following Suharto stepped down, new political parties were established. The first general election following Indonesia' political reform was conducted in 1999 and 44 political parties competed in the election. At the time, the President was still elected by the member of People's Consultative Assembly in 1999. It was only in 2004 that Indonesia introduced direct election to choose its national and local leaders. See, for example, Aspinall and Mietzner (2010).

challenged. The National Election Commission (or 'Komisi Pemilihan Umum (KPU)') introduced Regulation No. 26/2004 on Presidential Candidacy, stipulating that only physically and mentally healthy candidates can run as a presidential candidate.[3] This regulation immediately sparked public debate as many considered it discriminatory and argued that it contradicted Indonesia's commitment to human rights and democracy as enshrined in the Amended 1945 Constitution and Law No 39/1999 on Hak Asasi Manusia or Human Rights. The term 'physically and mentally healthy' (in Indonesian: '*sehat secara rohani dan jasmani*') is understood to exclude persons with disabilities (Hukum Online 2004a).

This Presidential Candidacy regulation was obviously introduced based on the political interests of Wahid's rivals in order to remove the possibility of him becoming Indonesia's President for a second time. It neglected the implications this had for the disabled community. The public was divided in their responses to the new regulation. The National Awakening Party (in Indonesian: '*Partai Kebangkitan Bangsa (PKB)*'), which was founded by Wahid, challenged the regulation in the Constitutional Court, arguing that the regulation went against Indonesia's commitment to international human rights. However, the Constitutional Court rejected the challenge resulting in Wahid's failure to become a Presidential candidate (Hukum Online, 24 April 2004b).

Democracy activists and political supporters of Wahid saw this regulation as in contradiction to the agenda of political reform and promotion of democratic values as it is highly discriminatory (Liputan 6, 23 May 2004). However, others supported the Constitutional Court's decision, arguing for the importance of having a 'physically healthy' (or a 'sehat') leader and further asserting that it did not contradict the Indonesian Constitution. It could be argued that the latter response was due to the well-entrenched and established stigmatisation against persons with disabilities as incapable, dependent and unproductive. This public view strengthens the idea that only 'healthy' Indonesians can run for public

[3] The regulation is set by the KPU and it defines disability to include mental, physical disabilities. See Viva News, 2009, 'Calon Presiden harus Sehat Jasmani dan Rohani', 19 February, accessed on 20 September 2017 from: http://www.viva.co.id/berita/politik/31804-calon-presiden-harus-sehat-jasmani-dan-mental.

office and that those with disabilities are not fit for office and hence incapable of holding public roles.

This example of discriminatory regulation is one of the many examples of discriminatory treatment against persons with disabilities in Indonesia, which prevents them from fully participating in public life. It demonstrates that the treatment of persons with disabilities is not only influenced by cultural traditions and belief systems embedded in society but it is also shaped by a lack of political will, commitment and awareness on behalf of political leaders. One thing that came out of this political event was that Indonesians began to have public discussions about the socio-economic, legal and political rights of persons with disabilities.

Following the ratification of the CRPD in 2011, people with disabilities and other civil society activists started advocacy awareness campaigns that targeted both the Indonesian Government and the wider community. This continuing campaign is to ensure that the Indonesian Government fulfils its obligations as enshrined in the CRPD. Among their initial campaigns was one which demanded that the Indonesian Government introduced a new legal framework, which would ensure that persons with disabilities live independently, participate equally in society and promote social inclusion by providing accessible infrastructure. It also promoted rights-based awareness of the needs of persons with disabilities.

Campaigns by disability rights activists have resulted, albeit slowly, in Indonesia making some significant progress in terms of promoting the rights of persons with disabilities. Some local governments introduced local regulation to support the national policy in promoting the rights of persons with disabilities (Irwanto and Thohari 2017). A result of this has been that local governments have started building accessible infrastructure, transportation and schools (Nursyamsi et al. 2015, pp. 29–30). Inclusive education has become a new theme in reforming Indonesia's education and academic curriculum, and Government budgets have allocated more funding to promote inclusive education (Saputra 2014). Further, in order to improve the civic participation of Indonesians with disabilities, the Government has reformed its electoral policy which now guarantees better opportunities for persons with disabilities to vote in elections (Mann 2014). In 2016 the Constitutional Court decided that citizens with mental, psychosocial or intellectual disabilities had the right to vote in the regional election (Election Access 2016). Prior to the 2019 general election, some in the general public were questioning the policy to allow people with mental disabilities to vote in the general election (Farisa 2018).

Despite the positive policies that the Indonesian Government has introduced, there is still a lot of work that needs to be done in order for the policies to be implemented, so that progress in fulfilling the rights of persons with disabilities can be achieved.

3 Changing Language: A Step Towards Social Change

As a State Party to the CRPD, the Indonesian Government is required to play a pivotal role in promoting, protecting and ensuring the full and equal enjoyment of the human rights and fundamental freedoms of persons with disabilities, by introducing and promoting legal, administrative and other measures to fully implement the provisions of the Convention (CRPD 2006, Art. 4). This also strengthens the Constitutional obligation of the Indonesian Government to guarantee the rights to equality for all its citizens.

The 1945 Indonesian Constitution guarantees that every individual has the right to achieve their fullest potential in all aspects of their life including in education, employment, health and equal participation in socio-economic, legal and political development. Up until 2016, the Indonesian Government had introduced 15 pieces of legislation, which regulated the rights of persons with disabilities in the areas of education, employment, health services and political rights (Liu and Brown 2015). They include, for example, Law No 39/1999 on Hak Asasi Manusia or Human Rights (L. 39/1999), Law No. 4/1998 on Penyandang Cacat or the Handicapped (L. 4/1998) and Law No 3/2003 on Pendidikan Nasional or National Education (L. 3/2003). However, there is also national legislation that is inconsistent with the principle of equality as enshrined in the Indonesian Constitution and which discriminates against persons with disabilities. Law No. 1/1974 on 'Perkawinan' (or Marriage Law) stipulates that when a wife becomes disabled the husband is allowed to take another wife (L.1/1974, Art. 4). However, this does not apply if it is the husband who becomes disabled. This is clearly a double discrimination.

The failure to protect and promote equality for persons with disabilities also stems from the fact that Indonesia's policy towards disability is largely based on a 'social-charity' approach, ignoring the potential of persons with disabilities to engage with, and participate in the community. The ratification of the CRPD (2006) has paved the way for the adoption of a 'rights-based' approach. The social-charity and medical approaches constitute persons with disabilities as 'objects' of charity, pity and rehabilitation which perpetrates the idea that persons with disabilities are incapable, dependent and not 'normal'. This perception is the result of cultural and traditional understandings towards persons with disabilities, which tend to discriminate and exclude them from pursuing similar life paths to their non-disabled peers.

Some traditional cultural practices view persons who are born with a disabilities as suffering a form of punishment from God, thus it is sinful and disgraceful for the family (Wardana and Dewi 2017). The common practice, especially in rural areas, is for families to hide their family member who has a disability from public view. For example, in 2016, international media reported how Indonesians treat their mentally disabled family members by secluding them in a confined room or having them shackled in chains (Jenkins 2016).

In urban areas, where people are more open-minded, children with disabilities receive more support from their families and have better access to education. The availability of special schools as regulated in the Law on National Education allows parents to send their children to get an education. However, special schools are located mostly in urban places, and the lack of accessible facilities, such as public transport, has become a serious challenge and a major barrier for children with disabilities from poor families in rural areas to experience their own mobility and get access to education (Irwanto and Thohari 2017, p. 95). They can only go to school if their parents or other family members take them. This situation leads to many children with disabilities staying at home and not getting the opportunity to enjoy public space as their non-disabled peers do. The result is that the lack of access to education from primary to higher education has resulted in persons with disabilities continuing to live in poverty and remaining dependent on their family (Wardana and Dewi 2017).

The major development following the ratification of the CRPD was the adoption of the concept of 'disability' by the Indonesian Government (Suharto et al. 2016). This term was also introduced by DPOs to the wider community as 'disabled' and 'disabilitas'. The introduction of the concept of 'disability' is expected to replace the old derogatory term such as 'the handicapped', 'the impaired' or the 'crippled' (in Indonesian: '*orang cacat*'), which carries with it the meanings of 'dependent, not normal and unequal'. Campaigns for the use of the term 'disabled' (in Indonesian: '*disabel*'), to be used in public, also aims to introduce a new understanding that disability is about 'access' and 'opportunity', and not about the physical appearance of an individual. Following the description in Article 1—Purpose of the CRPD (2006), the concept of 'disability' emphasises access and participation; therefore, the introduction of this term aims to address the negative stigmatisation towards persons with disabilities as being 'unproductive, unreliable and dependent', which was attached to the term 'crippled' (in Indonesian: '*orang cacat*').

A study by Suharto et al. (2016) discusses at length the evolution of the terminology used in Indonesia concerning persons with disabilities over a period of time. According to their study, while the community in general have continuously used the term 'handicapped' or 'crippled' (in Indonesian: '*cacat*'), the Indonesian Government has used different terms for persons with disabilities over a period of time. Influenced by the subtle and modest Javanese culture, which is very dominant in influencing Indonesia's socio-political culture, the Old Order (1945–1965) and the New Order (1966–1998), for example, introduced the phrase 'people who have physical or mental deficit' (in Indonesian: '*orang dengan kekurangan jasmani atau rokhani*') and the use of the term impairment (in Indonesian: '*tuna*') in various regulations and policies. These terms are considered as euphemisms for the term 'handicapped' (in Indonesian: '*cacat*'). Nevertheless, all those phrases and terms still carry with them a negative stigmatisation as a person with disabilities is still seen as 'disadvantaged, handicapped, dependent, useless, has no individual mobility, and has the inability to survive' (Suharto et al. 2016, p. 698).

Prior to the introduction of the term 'disabilities' (in Indonesian: '*disabilitas*'), Indonesian disability activists in the Province of Yogyakarta had introduced the term '*difabel*' or 'difable', which stems from the concept of 'differently abled person' (Suharto et al. 2016, pp. 700–701). Suharto et al. (2016) commented that there are some disabled community groups in Indonesia who prefer to use the term *difabel* instead of 'persons with disabilities' or 'orang dengan disabilitas' or 'penyandang disabilitas'. Two major DPOs based in Yogyakarta, for example, continue to use the term '*difabel*' in their names, such as the Centre for Integration and Advocacy for Difabel (in Indonesian: '*Sasana Integrasi and Advokasi Difabel (SIGAB)*') and the Center for Advocacy on Women's Difabel and Children (in Indonesian: '*Sentra Advokasi Perempuan Difabel dan Anak (SAPDA)*'). Despite the different terms that are used interchangeably by disability activists, it is clear that the key in raising community awareness of the rights of persons with disabilities is the promotion of the use of concepts of access and participation (Suharto et al. 2016).

Suharto et al.'s work (2016) reveals that problems with concepts and terminology play an important role in influencing Government policies in providing access to education, health services, employment, legal and political rights. These problems contribute to the difficulty of categorising the types of disabilities, resulting in difficulty in getting exact information or data regarding the number of Indonesians living with disabilities and the categories of disability. Up until 2016, many Government offices published different numbers of Indonesians living with disabilities. Thus, the adoption of the term and concept of 'disability' (in Indonesian: '*disabilitas*') is expected to overcome this problem and would lead to significant improvements in advancing access and participation of persons with disabilities.

4 Implementation and Monitoring of the CRPD

Disability activists from various DPOs together with human rights-based civil society organisations demanded a new legal framework and mechanism to implement the principles of the CRPD (Nursyamsi et al. 2015). The previous national Law on the Handicapped (L. 4/1997) was no longer seen as relevant as it was framed under the concept of 'social charity'. The new legal framework according to activists is needed to enable

Indonesia to introduce the rights-based approach. The drafting process of this new law began in 2012 and was introduced in 2016 as the Law on People with Disabilities (in Indonesian: '*Undang-Undang Penyandang Disabilitas*') (L. 8/2016).

This law is the latest, broadest and most comprehensive commitment of the Indonesian Government to fulfilling the rights of persons with disabilities. Consistent with the CRPD, it defines persons with disabilities as follows:

> every individual experiences limitation be it physical, intellectual, mental, and or sensory for a period of time which in his/her interaction with their environment present barriers and difficulties to participate fully and effectively with other citizens based on the equal rights. (L. 8/2016, Art.1; my translation)

The law also stipulates that disability can be the result of poor knowledge of health care during premarital age, pregnancy, delivery and child development, lack of occupational safety at employment, health hazards such as tuberculosis and leprosy, life styles which cause strokes, arthritis, diabetes mellitus and higher possibilities in Indonesia of environmental disasters such as earthquake, volcano and tsunami (Kusumastuti et al. 2014).

Given these definitions, the law guarantees equal opportunities and access for persons with disabilities to enable them to fully exercise their capacity in every aspect of development and engagement in the community. It calls for the need to abolish different forms of discrimination, which include discrimination, harassment, marginalisation and alienation on the basis of disability resulting in the limitation or abandonment of enjoyment in the lives of persons with disabilities. The law also guarantees the rights of all persons with disabilities to privacy, the rights to legal protection, education, employment, health, political participation, religious activities, sports, culture, accessibility, social welfare, public services, protection from natural disaster and rights to rehabilitation (L. 8/2016, Art. 5). It also stipulates the role of Government institutions, the community and DPOs in promoting the rights of persons with disabilities.

In addition to advocating for a robust and comprehensive legal framework to the national and local Government institution, DPOs also work with the community, including the religious groups, human rights and civil society organisations to monitor the implementation of the CRPD. In 2014, DPOs together with a legal aid organisation in Jakarta protested to the Ministry of Education which had allowed public universities under its authority to regulate that only those who are 'healthy' and not 'physically impaired' can enrol into tertiary education and undertake the entrance exam (Saputra 2014; Irwanto 2014). This regulation is discriminatory and contradicts not only the CRPD that Indonesia has ratified but also the law on National Education. Disability and human rights activists threatened to submit a lawsuit against the Ministry of Education for its discriminatory policy against students with disabilities.[4] It resulted in the Ministry changing its policies and requiring universities to allow the enrolment of students with disabilities in tertiary education (Khalisotussurur 2014).

This discrimination towards persons with disabilities to access higher education is an example of ongoing challenges faced by them despite Indonesia's ratification of the CRPD (Afrianty 2019). Many elements within Government institutions abandon their legal responsibility and obligation to promote equal access to persons with disabilities. Recruitment in many public offices is another serious challenge, as they continue to discriminate against applicants with disabilities. For example in 2014, some Government offices still made it public that they only accepted applicants without disabilities (Republika 2014). This structural barrier limits the opportunity for persons with disabilities to access employment). Obviously, the lack of access to tertiary education leads to limited employment opportunities but the latter also discourages persons with disabilities from pursuing higher education, as they think that it is pointless.

A report published by the Ministry of Health in 2014 reveals that based on the national survey conducted in 2012 and research conducted by the Ministry of Health in 2013, the level of participation of persons with disabilities in education becomes lower the further up the level of

[4] Ferri, Oscar, 2014, 'Tak dibolehkan ikut SNMPTN Penyandang Disabiltias Protes, *Liputan6*, 29 April, accessed 14 February 2017 <http://news.liputan6.com/read/2043613/tak-dibolehkan-ikut-snmptn-penyandang-disabilitas-protes> see also Detiknews 2014, '35 Organisasi Disabilitas Somasi Kemendikbud, Protes Syarat SNMPTN 2014, accessed on 14 February 2017, https://news.detik.com/berita/d-2521306/35-organisasi-disabilitas-somasi-kemendikbud-protes-syarat-snmptn-2014.

education. About 81.81 per cent of the total number of persons with disabilities have primary education and only 18 per cent have secondary education. The number becomes less when it comes to higher education. These two research studies, however, do not include the number of persons with disabilities in higher education but a report from the Ministry of Higher Education in 2017 reveals that out of the total six million Indonesians currently enrolled in higher education there were only 401 students with disabilities studying in tertiary education.[5]

In addition to the problems with access to education and employment, many Indonesians with disabilities have not been able to exercise their civic participation. Not only do they lack the access to participate in elections but they are also denied political rights to run for public office. A survey conducted by the Asia Foundation in the lead up to the 2014 general election found that of 2760 voters being surveyed about three quarters said they would not vote for a candidate with a disability. They argued that if there are 'healthy' candidates they should vote for the healthy ones because the 'unhealthy' would not be able to carry out their duties due to their physical limitations (Mann 2014).

DPOs also work with legal aid organisations in monitoring the implementation of the CRPD, focusing on the protection of legal rights. Article 12—Equal recognition before the law and Article 13—Access to Justice of the CRPD (2006), which guarantee the rights of persons with disabilities to legal protection and the obligation of the State to ensure that those rights are protected both when they become alleged victims or perpetrators of crime. A number of DPOs work with legal aid organisations, the Prosecutor Office, the Courts and the Police to raise awareness for a fair procedure and trials for persons with disabilities. Articles 28 and 29 of the Indonesian Law on People with Disabilities guarantee the rights of persons with disabilities to legal protection, legal aid, health protection and accommodation; they also stipulate that when they become involved in either criminal and civil legal matters they are entitled to legal protection (L.8/2016, Art. 28; 29).

[5] See information from http://kopertis3.or.id/v5/wp-content/uploads/Buku-Statistik-Pendidikan-Tinggi-2017.pdf and https://databoks.katadata.co.id/datapublish/2017/05/05/berapa-jumlah-perguruan-tinggi-di-indonesia.

Social stigma and the lack of awareness among the authorities have led to many persons with disabilities being prevented from exercising their legal rights (Colbran 2010; Komisi Yudisial 2018). Therefore, this has become one of the priority concerns of DPOs and rights-based civil society organisations in monitoring the CRPD's implementation.

Challenges to education, employment, political and legal rights are only some of the major challenges for persons with disabilities. An absence of access to education leads them to be alienated from many types of employment, and the barriers to holding public office have prevented them from being part of the socio-legal and public policymaking process. It seems that the only way for persons with disabilities to influence policymaking is through their activism within DPOs and through being part of the civil society movement.

5 DPOs Promoting and Monitoring the Implementation of the CRPD at the Local Level

This section discusses activities and campaigns by DPOs in the Indonesian Province of Yogyakarta. The Province is known for its strong commitment to accessibility, aiming to make its provincial capital the first 'Inclusive City' (in Indonesian: '*Kota Inklusi*'). This commitment is reflected in the enactment of a local Regulation on the Protection and Fulfilment of the Rights of People with Disabilities (L. 4/2012). The move by the Yogyakarta's administration is a reflection and result of strong local DPO activism, advocacy and awareness campaigns.

Local DPOs in Yogyakarta began their advocacy and campaigning almost two decades ago with a demand for local regulations to guarantee that persons with disabilities are granted equal access to education, employment, legal protection, health and public services.[6] As a result of this, Yogyakarta has become one of the most progressive cities in building accessible public facilities, such as schools, government offices and public

[6] See Solider: Beranda Inklusi and Informasi Difabel https://www.solider.id/ and SIGAB https://www.sigab.or.id/id/content/website-informasi-hukum-dan-difabilitas.

transportation. In terms of education, the local government has pushed educational institutions to provide access for persons with disabilities and to promote inclusive curricula in schools. One of the tertiary educational institutions, the Sunan Kalijaga State Islamic University has established a special unit to provide services for students with disabilities.

One of the prominent local DPOs in Yogyakarta is the Centre for Integration and Advocacy for Difabel (in Indonesian: '*Sasana Integrasi and Advokasi Difabel (SIGAB)*'). It was established in 2003, which was long before Indonesia signed the CRPD in 2007. The establishment of SIGAB is inspired by the experience of disabled community members whose lives have continuously been challenged by structural as well as cultural discrimination. They faced discrimination and marginalisation in their everyday lives as they were not treated as equals with other Indonesians because of their disabilities. Thus, the establishment of SIGAB was based on the realisation that as human beings and citizens, regardless of their physical and mental condition, they must be given the same opportunity and access to live equally as other persons.

Activists at SIGAB have diverse physical impairments and sensory impairments including visual impairment and deafness. They became part of, and work for SIGAB, as they feel the connection to others who are victims of marginalisation and discrimination. Most of the activists at SIGAB come from poor families who mostly spent their life living in villages across the province. Their experiences of living in villages and their interaction with the community has given them an understanding that one of the biggest challenges to social inclusion and participation comes from the cultural perception of the community towards disability, which strongly influences the way the community treats persons with disabilities. This has led SIGAB to prioritise its earlier work on advocating for awareness of the rights of persons with disabilities. Those who become activists at SIGAB are only part of the small number of persons with disabilities who manage to get into higher education. However, as most of them say, the only reason for them to be at SIGAB is because they were unable to get employment (Interview, Yogjakarta, 20 July 2013).

SIGAB is one of the DPOs that uses the term '*difabel*' instead of 'disabled' in its name as mentioned above. The use of '*difabel*' or 'differently able' in its name, according to SIGAB, is to emphasise the notion of the 'different ability' that an individual carries with them (SIGAB Website). The use of 'crippled' or 'handicapped' (in Bahasa Indonesia is 'penyandang cacat'), which is widely spread in the community, according to SIGAB leads to the dichotomy of 'capable' and 'incapable' persons. The problem, according to SIGAB, is that the community does not realise that the notion of 'capability' and 'incapability' is actually the result of the lack of access, or that it is the environment which does not provide the necessary support that persons with different abilities need (SIGAB Website).

In its awareness campaign on the need to change attitudes and perceptions towards persons with disabilities, SIGAB presents a story that someone with no hands can still produce a beautiful painting. Because every individual has different abilities, a person who has no hands would still be able to use their other body parts to paint. Hence, the problem is not with the absence of hands. It explains that an individual with no hands can still be productive and able to use their different abilities if they are given the access and opportunity to exercise and explore their skills and ability. SIGAB argues that access to materials and skills would give the opportunity for every individual to express and explore their different abilities. This story is used by DPOs like SIGAB to advocate the need for the community to change its perception towards persons with impairments. People in the community need to realise that every individual has her or his different abilities and it is the obligation and responsibility of the State and the community to give them access and opportunities to support them to participate and use their abilities.

Located in the capital of the province that is well known for its strong Javanese cultural tradition, SIGAB holds the view that the treatment towards persons with disabilities is primarily based on cultural practices and understandings that tend to see disability as a disgrace, which in turn had prompted parents and families to hide their family members with disabilities. Apart from advocating for awareness, SIGAB also works in providing counselling for persons with disabilities who experience discrimination. More recently it also began to work with local legal aid and other Government institutions advocating for legal protection for persons with disabilities. One of its major achievements is campaigning for protecting the legal rights for persons with disabilities who are not receiving equal treatment in the legal system, such as in the courts.

Since its establishment, SIGAB has worked with various international organisations that provide funding support for advocacy and activism. Some of the activities that SIGAB has carried out include organising weekly events involving village communities to promote awareness that persons with disabilities are as active as non-disabled persons. SIGAB organises meetings with village leaders on the rights of persons with disabilities and how the community and Government have the responsibility to stop discriminatory treatment towards their community members who have disabilities. Another important initiative that SIGAB has pioneered is the promotion of civic participation of persons with disabilities. Prior to the 2009 election, for example, it organised advocacy and campaigns through various dialogues and consultations with the political candidates, on the rights of persons with disabilities. This was undertaken because often during elections persons with disabilities are not given the access to cast their votes or to run as candidates.

Disability activism led by SIGAB has made Yogyakarta become the first province to have higher education institutions that provide services to students with disabilities. The Center for Disability Services (in Indonesian: '*Pusat Layanan Disabilitas*') at the Sunan Kalijaga State Islamic University was established in 2007. The Center was established by academics who shared concerns over the lack of access to students with disabilities studying at the university. The Center, although it runs on a limited budget provided by the University, manages to provide learning support and assistance for students with disabilities both in and outside classes. The Center recruits students to become volunteers to assist students with disabilities with tasks, such as note-taking and essay writing support. In an interview in 2015, the Head of the Center said that the challenges for students with disabilities in higher education remain difficult. For example, lecturers lack awareness of the rights of students with disabilities and are not inclusive in their teaching methods. Some have even told the Center that they were not willing to give reasonable accommodations to students with disabilities. In 2015, there were more than 50 students with disabilities enrolled at the University. Similarly to SIGAB, the Center also organises advocacy campaigns at the level of higher education institutions in relation to the need for inclusive curricula and for the university to provide more access to students with disabilities. Compared to other higher education institutions in many places in Indonesia, the Sunan Kalijaga State Islamic University is equipped with accessible infrastructure, which allows and facilitates access to students with disabilities.

6 Conclusion

DPOs have significantly improved the advancement of the human rights of persons with disabilities in Indonesia. They have become the main actors in advocating for progress and change in the way the Indonesian Government treats and approaches problems faced by persons with disabilities. The ratification of the CRPD in 2011 has allowed DPOs to campaign for the need for a movement from a social-charity approach to a rights-based approach. The rights-based approach requires the Government to promote inclusion, access and participation to enable persons with disabilities equal freedom and enjoyment to participate in public life. It has also allowed civil society organisations to take part in pressing the Government to promote the constitutional rights of persons with disabilities as they see the fulfilment of the these rights as part of the human rights struggle in Indonesia's democracy.

In the context of Indonesia's democratisation, DPOs have supported Indonesia's Government development agenda in terms of socialising and educating the community on the rights of persons with disabilities, as well as being the representative institutions of persons with disabilities who are still largely marginalised and alienated in social policymaking. The presence of DPOs is significantly important to represent the real concern, voices and interests of persons with disabilities since they do not have any representation in Indonesia's local and national parliament. As Ghosh (2016) argued "a political consciousness does not in itself constitute a social movement, as people may be aware of their own identity marker but not be able to posit a similarity in the conditions of oppression faced by them and other persons with disabilities" (Ghosh 2016, pp. 184–185).

References

Afrianty, D. (2019). Disability inclusion in Indonesia: The role of Islamic schools and universities in inclusive education reform. In G. Fealy & R. Ricci (Eds.), *Contentious belonging: The place of minorities in Indonesia*, (pp. 95–112). Singapore: ISEAS Yosuf Ishak Institute.

Aspinall, E., & Mietzner, M. (2010). Problems of democratisation in Indonesia: An overview. *Problems of Democratisation in Indonesia: Elections, Institutions and Society*. 1–20.

Colbran, N. (2010). *Akses terhadap keadilan penyandang disabilitias Indonesia*. DFAT Report. Retrieved from https://dfat.gov.au/about-us/publications/Documents/access-justice-2010-bahasa.pdf.

CRPD (United Nations Convention on the Rights of Persons with Disabilities). (2006). Adopted in 2006 by the United Nations general assembly.

Detiknews. (2014, March 10). *Organisasi disabilitas somasi kemendikbud, protes syarat SNMPTN 2014*. Retrieved August 10, 2019, from https://news.detik.com/berita/d-2521306/35-organisasi-disabilitas-somasi-kemendikbud-protes-syarat-snmptn-2014.

Election Access. (2016, November). *Constitutional court upholds right to vote of persons with pshycosocial or intellectual disabilities in Indonesia*. Retrieved January 24, 2019, from http://electionaccess.org/en/media/news/42/.

Farisa, F. C. (2018, November 20). *Perludem: Penyandang Disabilitas harus diberi hak pilih dalam pemilu*. Retrieved January 24, 2019, from https://nasional.kompas.com/read/2018/11/20/23173601/perludem-penyandang-disabilitas-mental-harus-diberi-hak-pilih-dalam-pemilu.

Ghosh, N. (2016). Disabled People's organizations in India: Assertions and angsts. In N. Ghosh (Ed.), *Interrogating disability in India*. New Delhi: Springer.

Global legal monitor. Retrieved from http://www.loc.gov/law/foreign-news/article/indonesia-disability-rights-group-seeks-new-law/.

Hefner, R. (2000). *Civil Islam: Muslims and democratization in Indonesia* (Alexander street anthropology). Princeton, NJ and Oxford: Princeton University Press.

Hukum Online. (2004a, April 24). *Terkait syarat kesehatan Calon Presiden Gus Dur Melawan Petisi*. Retrieved September 29, 2017, from http://www.hukumonline.com/berita/baca/hol10185/terkait-syarat-kesehatan-calon-presiden-gus-dur-melawan-dengan-petisi.

Hukum online. (2004b, 19 April). *Demi Gus Dur PKB Minta Fatwa MK Soal Sarat Menjadi Presiden*. Retrieved August 20, 2017, from http://www.hukumonline.com/berita/baca/hol10146/demi-gus-dur-pkb-minta-fatwa-mk-soal-syarat-menjadi-presiden.

Irwanto. (2014, March 18). *RI Shocking educational reality for people with disabilities*. The Jakarta Post. Retrieved June 15, 2018, from http://www.thejakartapost.com/news/2014/03/18/ri-s-shocking-educational-reality-people-with-disabilities.html.

Irwanto, & Thohari, S. (2017). Understanding CRPD Implementation in Indonesia. In L. C. Derrick & T. K. reuter (Eds.), *Making disability rights real in Southeast Asia: Implementing the UN convention on the rights of persons with disabilities in ASEAN* (pp. 95–118). London: Lexington Books.

Jenkins, N. (2016, March 21). Thousands of mentally ill Indonesians are imprisoned in shackles, report says. *Time*. Retrieved August 20, 2017, from http://time.com/4265623/indonesia-mental-illness-chains-pasung-hrw/.

Khalisotussurur, L. (2014, April 15). *Kemendikbud akhirnya perbolehkan penyandang difabel ikuti SNMPTN*. GresNews.com: Referensi Penting Hukum dan Politik. Retrieved June 30, 2018, from http://www.gresnews.com/berita/kampus/85386-kemendikbud-akhirnya-perbolehkan-penyandang-difabel-ikuti-snmptn-/.

Komisi Yudisial. (2018). *Akses hukum dan keadilan bagi difabel*. Jakarta: Komisi Yudisial Indonesia.

Kusumastuti, P., Pradanasari, R., & Ratnawati, A. (2014). The problems of people with disability in Indonesia and what is being learned from the World Report on Disability. *American Journal of Physical Medicine & Rehabilitation, 93*(1 Suppl 1), S63–67.

Liputan 6. (2004, May 23). *Gus Dur Tidak Lolos*. Retrieved September 20, 2017, from http://news.liputan6.com/read/78670/gus-dur-tidak-lolos.

Liu, E., & Brown, L. (2015, January–March). *Disability data and the development agenda in indonesia*. Inside Indonesia. Retrieved February 7, 2017, from http://www.insideindonesia.org/disability-data-and-the-development-agenda-in-indonesia-2.

Mann, T. (2014). 'Prejudice at the polling booth: Disabled Indonesians face barriers in Voting', In Asia: Weekly Insights and Analysis, The Asia Foundation. Retrieved from https://asiafoundation.org/2014/04/09/prejudice-at-the-polling-booth-disabled-indonesians-face-barriers-in-voting/.

Nursyamsi, F., Estu, D. A., Muhammad, F. A., Marutama, A., & Putri, B. (2015). *Kerangka Hukum Disabiiltas di Indonesia: Menuju Indonesia Ramah Disabilitias*. Pusat Studi Hukum dan Kebijakan. Retrieved June 30, 2018, from https://www.pshk.or.id/wp-content/uploads/2016/01/Kerangka-Hukum-Disabilitas-di-Indonesia.pdf.

Republika. (2014, October 17). *Seleksi CPNS dinilai diskriminasi penyandang disabilitas*. Retrieved June 20, 2018, from https://www.republika.co.id/berita/nasional/umum/14/10/17/ndl2aq-seleksi-cpns-dinilai-diskriminasi-penyandang-disabilitas.

Saputra, A. (2014, March 18). *Inclusive higher education: A dream for people with disabilities*. The Jakarta Post. Retrieved August 10, 2018, from http://www.thejakartapost.com/news/2014/03/18/inclusive-higher-education-a-dream-people-with-disabilities.html.

Suharto, S., Kuipers, P., & Dorsett, P. (2016). Disability terminology and the emergence of 'diffability' in Indonesia. *Disability & Society, 31*(5), 693–712.

Wardana, A. P., & Dewi, N. (2017). Moving away from paternalism: The new law on disability in Indonesia. *Asia Pacific Journal on Human Rights and the Law, 18*(2), 172–195.

16

The Process of State Party Reporting to the CRPD Committee: The Indian Experience

Amita Dhanda

1 Introduction

India ratified the United Nations (UN) Convention on the Rights of Persons with Disabilities (CRPD/Convention 2006) in October 2008 and as the time to submit the initial State Report in accordance with Article 35—Reports by States Parties (CRPD 2006) to the CRPD Committee started to draw near, the Ministry of Social Justice and Empowerment (Ministry)[1] invited bids from universities and other academic institutions to assist the Indian Government in the preparation of the State Report. The Centre for Disability Studies (CDS/Centre) that I

[1] In accordance with the Allocation of Business Rules of the Government of India, this Ministry was the Ministry in charge of disability affairs and hence was in charge of preparing the State Report that would be submitted on behalf of the Government of India to the Treaty Body. All references to the 'Ministry' or 'Minister' in this chapter refer to this Ministry alone. In order to avoid confusion other Ministries have been expressly named.

A. Dhanda (✉)
NALSAR, University of Law, Hyderabad, Telangana, India
e-mail: amitadhanda@nalsar.ac.in

E. J. Kakoullis, K. Johnson (eds.), *Recognising Human Rights in Different Cultural Contexts*, https://doi.org/10.1007/978-981-15-0786-1_16

head also sent in a proposal and we were selected to perform the job.[2] The involvement did not proceed as planned. However, the experience yielded some immense learnings, which need to be shared to enable a deeper reflection by those involved in implementing and monitoring the CRPD.

I am contributing this chapter to initiate reflection on State Party reporting, that is, the feasibility of the naming-shaming process, the reporting guidelines and the strategy of adjudging the authenticity of State Reports with the aid of data provided by the alternative or shadow reports (Alston et al. 2000; Poe et al. 2001; Goodman and Jinks 2003; Hafner-Burton 2005; Clapham 2006; Hungarian Disability Caucus 2010). This analysis is being undertaken on the strength of the India experience, and since India is not the world, it could well be claimed that the Indian experience does not speak to the entire universe of the UN. However, since India is home to the second largest number of people in the world, its experience has a quantitative ponderousness, which cannot be brushed aside. Having said that, I must admit that I am not writing this piece in order to make a State Party representation. Large parts of what I have to say may even seem like questioning the position taken by my country. Despite my disagreement, I am contributing this chapter to deliberate on why the political and permanent executive of my country approached the reporting obligations in the manner that I document here.

More importantly, this chapter documents the unsuccessful effort of an academic institution to assist its country in fulfilling its international obligations in a creative manner. Since I was in the driving seat, this exposition is informed by personal experience and the learnings obtained from it. This analysis is not claiming neutrality; it is informed by my standpoint on disability rights. I share the case study on the India State Report on the CRPD due to the credence accorded to experiential knowledge in Disability Studies (Kanter 2011).[3]

[2] The Centre was established as a disability research and advocacy centre at the National Academy of Legal Studies and Research in 2007. Though I had been working on disability rights over a lifetime, this was the first major research assignment of the Centre http: //www.disabilitystudiesnalsar.org/.

[3] Arlene S Kanter, 'The Law: What's Disability Studies Got to Do with It or an Introduction to Disability Legal Studies' (2010) 42 Columbia Human Rights Law Review 403.

I begin this exposition by first outlining why reporting seems to have been chosen as the preferred mechanism of obtaining compliance in International Human Rights Law. I next reflect on the accountability potential of the naming-shaming procedures and how realistic the expectations are as spelled out in the reporting guidelines. The reporting guidelines of Committee on the Rights of Persons with Disabilities (CRPD Committee) seek comprehensive information and ask States Parties to take stock of their performance on disability rights whilst blueprinting for the future (CRPD/C/2/3 2009). Such weighing up seems a reasonable expectation. Yet, my narrative of working on the State Report for the Government of India shows that it is not an expectation that is easy to fulfil. Hence, in this chapter I consider what makes the expectation difficult to fulfil and what can be done to make State Party reporting a deliberative, rather than an inquisitorial exercise.

2 Self Reporting by States Parties to Obtain Human Rights Compliance

Despite some recent challenges, State sovereignty remains the bulwark of International Law (Reisman 1990). Rules of international human rights law remain subject to this overarching principle. Consequently, the human rights regime binds States only to the extent that they consent to be subjected to it. The practice of reservations allows a State to opt for selective compliance. However, Article 46—Reservations does not permit a State to make a reservation that is in contravention of the object and purpose of the Convention (2006). Nevertheless, what constitutes 'object and purpose', and how 'contravention to such purpose' would be determined, remains a contentious issue (Tomuschat 2014).

Optional protocols allow individuals to approach the treaty body for the realisation of human rights, or permit the treaty body to conduct on the ground investigations and inquiries and thereby obtain enhanced international human rights monitoring. However, such monitoring cannot be undertaken if the State has not consented to the CRPD's Optional Protocol. State reluctance about enhanced international human rights scrutiny can also be assessed from the fact that whilst 177 countries have ratified the CRPD, only 92 countries have ratified its Optional Protocol.[4] A majority of the countries which have ratified the Convention are only agreeable to filing State Reports before the CRPD Committee. If accountability is what makes a legal mandate obligatory, then the periodic State Reports that have to be submitted by all States Parties that ratify a human rights convention assume critical importance. The arduousness of the task can be appreciated by the fact that even the CRPD Committee has delayed submissions,[5] many State Reports await review and several countries have not submitted their State Reports to other UN human rights treaty bodies even years after they were due.[6]

In order to make State Reports a powerful tool of accountability, the CRPD Committee, like other human rights treaty bodies, has detailed guidelines on the information required from the State Party. The reporting guidelines were first issued in 2009 (CRPD/C/2/3 2009), and in 2016 a revised version was issued (CRPD/C/3 2016). The later guidelines are more concerned with follow-up State Reports, whereas for initial State Reports the 2009 guidelines continue to apply.[7] An analysis of the reporting guidelines is not the purpose of this piece; however, I mention them to draw attention to their length. The 2009 version was 20 pages long and the more recent version extends to 24 pages (2016). And yet, keeping in view the time and resource constraints faced by the CRPD Committee, every State Party is required to submit its State Report in no more than 60 pages. Within those 60 pages, States are asked to not make only prose descriptions of their Constitutions and leading cases, but to

---

[4] https://www.un.org/development/desa/disabilities/convention-on-the-rights-of-persons-with-disabilities.htm (last visited 3rd September 2018).

[5] The lag between due date of report and its actual submission can be seen in the following list of the OHCHR https://tbinternet.ohchr.org/_layouts/treatybodyexternal/TBSearch.aspx?Lang=en&TreatyID=4&DocTypeID=29.

[6] An examination of the website of the Office of the Commissioner of Human Rights shows that only 33 countries have submitted all their reports and on time. For the rest it is a case of relative recalcitrance. https://tbinternet.ohchr.org/_layouts/TreatyBodyExternal/LateReporting.aspx (last visited 15th September 2018).

[7] In September 2013 in its Tenth Meeting the Committee adopted a simplified reporting procedure whereby countries whose reports were due from 2014 and beyond could opt to report on an identified list of issues. Since India is not reporting under this procedure, I am not addressing the reporting possibilities opened up by this simplified procedure. https://www.ohchr.org/EN/HRBodies/CRPD/Pages/Simplifiedreportingprocedure.aspx (last visited 27th January 2019).

also include quotations from their Constitutions and the landmark judgments pronounced under them (CRPD/C/2/3 2009). The reporting guidelines also require the State Party to list all the measures it has taken to realise the mandate of each CRPD article. Evidently, the CRPD Committee did not want any State Party to conceal its ineptitude beneath bulk, hence the restriction on the number of pages; but at the same time, it wanted to know everything. Article 33—National implementation and monitoring (CRPD 2006) provides for domestic monitoring, but other than asking the States Parties to report on the designated focal points and whether the authorities identified could be considered independent bodies, it asks no more. The 2016 reporting guidelines expressly refer to restricting the 'list of issues', depending on the situation on the ground in each country, whilst respecting the demands of transparency and equality. Even so there is no effort to forge a link between national and international monitoring. The CRPD Committee is not asking for the concerns expressed by the national monitor to be placed before it, so that it can limit its attention to only those issues which were inadequately addressed in national monitoring. Both in the reporting guidelines and in practice, the CRPD Committee continues to exclusively rely upon civil society organisations, disabled people's organisations (DPOs) and other entities, which do not identify with the Government.[8] Thus, even as States Parties are being exhorted to make full disclosure, there is an inner resignation that such disclosure will not happen. Therefore, the CRPD Committee is issuing reporting guidelines not just to the States Parties but to all those civil society players who will enable the CRPD Committee to perform its job effectively by submitting an alternative or shadow report to the CRPD Committee. I refer to this as the 'dynamic of

[8] Some of these reports have been uploaded on https://search.ohchr.org/results.aspx?k=shadow%20reports#k=shadow%20reports%20on%20the%20CRPD. An examination of these shadow reports shows following models: one that comment on the gaps in the State Report. See, for example, the NGO Report on Ukraine https://www.ohchr.org/_layouts/15/WopiFrame.aspx?sourcedoc=/Documents/HRBodies/CRPD/Future/GroupNGOs_Ukraine_CRPDFuture.doc&action=default&DefaultItemOpen=1. Two, those which claim to complement the State Report. See here the alternative report on Spain https://lib.ohchr.org/_layouts/15/WopiFrame.aspx?sourcedoc=/SPdocs/CRPD/5thsession/CERMI_Spain_5thSession_en.doc&action=default&DefaultItemOpen=1 And three which attempt to do an objective status of disability rights in the country report. See for example the Report from Hungary http://mdac.org/sites/mdac.info/files/english_crpd_alternative_report.pdf.

trust and mistrust' that subsists between the CRPD Committee and the States Parties, because it has a bearing on our effort at attempting to formulate the State Report on the CRPD for the Government of India. It is to that experience that I now turn.

3 Preparing the State Report for the Government of India

3.1 The Identity of the Ghost Writer

In the Introduction, I referred to the fact that CDS undertook the responsibility for writing the State Report in purely contractual terms: The Government of India invited bids, CDS put in an application along with other academic institutions and we were selected. This narrative effaced the conflict and dilemmas those of us working at the Centre were faced with in assuming the role. By implication the Centre would be the ghost writer of the Report. Hence, I and my team would be writing on behalf of the Government but we were not the Government. Rather, we were an advocacy cum research organisation which had contractually undertaken the responsibility for scripting the State Report. This position raised a number of questions for us: Would this freshly assumed responsibility cause our identity to be subsumed within the Government? Would we be expected to just perform a partisan job, with our critical faculties anesthetised? Or would we operate as the subject experts who would advise the Government of our country to fulfil its international obligations in an honest and transparent manner? The reporting guidelines of the CRPD Committee exhorted States Parties to use the report making process as an opportunity to take stock of where they stood in relation to the mandate of the CRPD and to plan for the future. We believed that these guidelines would allow us to perform our ghost-writing job in a credible manner without sacrificing our integrity. We decided that we would document the performance of the Government neither uncritically as may be the wont of Government officials, nor be stridently critical as often is the stance of civil society and non-governmental bodies. We therefore assumed the hybrid identity of a sagacious Government and a patient but balanced disability rights advocate.

3.2 The Dilemmas of Inclusion and Exclusion

Another major question before us was to decide on the players whose performance needed to be included in the report. If the report was to document the performance of the country, then the efforts of all governmental or non-governmental, central or state organisations needed to be included. It was also important to not just report on the schemes and programmes launched for persons with disabilities but also point to the extent to which disability was included in the general schemes and programmes of the government.

3.2.1 Inclusion of Non-governmental Efforts

We decided to start by focussing on the activities happening under each right specified in the CRPD (2006), without concerning ourselves on who was doing it. There were CRPD Articles such as support in situations of risk where the non-governmental initiatives were way ahead of any Government programme (CRPD 2006, Art. 11). Again, in relation to other rights, such as leisure and sports (CRPD 2006, Art. 30), the lead was taken by non-governmental players. The intention was not to shield the Government but to accord recognition to work undertaken in the country. Also, since the Government provided funds for several non-governmental initiatives, we did not consider it legitimate to categorise it as a purely non-governmental activity.

This approach of CDS did not go down well either with the Governmental or the non-governmental sector. The non-governmental sector felt that its work was being included in the report in order to let the Government off the hook, and to pass off the work of civil society as work being undertaken by the Government. Even though the Government pointed to its funding of several non-governmental efforts, it did not press for their inclusion in the Report, as the charge of 'passing off' civil society work as its own was seen to diminish Government efforts. After discussion we agreed to exclude all references to non-governmental work, as we realised that in the absence of a strong database and an authentic record of all non-governmental efforts, there was a real danger that a non-governmental effort could be included only because we knew about it, or excluded due to our ignorance. The arbitrariness of the methodology caused us to desist, especially as we only had a limited number of pages at our disposal. Our other suggestion of preparing a comprehensive national report on the status of persons with disabilities[9] did not have takers, so we abandoned this part of the enterprise.[10]

3.2.2 Inclusion of Efforts of Provincial Government

India being a federal country and disability being designated as a provincial subject,[11] every province of the country has its own set of scholarships and unemployment allowances for persons with disabilities. The Union came into the picture with the passage of the Persons with Disabilities Act in 1995 (PWDA 1995).[12] The statute was enacted in fulfilment of an international obligation and thus the Union Government came to play a role in the field of disability. This role has only magnified with India ratifying the CRPD and central enactments being remodelled in the light of the Convention. Considering this pivotal role of the Union, we needed to decide what space should be allocated to the initiatives of the provinces. We had decided on the principle of inclusion,

---

[9] Such an exercise had been undertaken for women in 1971. The Status Report on Women documented the social, economic and educational status of women in the country. That report can be accessed at http://feministlawarchives.pldindia.org/category/towards-equality/towards-equality-towards-equality/ (last accessed 2nd February 2019).

[10] The Hungarian Alternative Report supra note 7 can be categorised as such an effort by civil society.

[11] The Constitution of India has created lists in order to segregate the fields in which the Union and the Provinces have jurisdiction. Whilst the first List incorporates the items allocated to the Union, the second List spells out the areas of the jurisdiction of the Provinces. Item 9 of the second List accorded jurisdiction on 'relief to the disabled and the unemployable' to the provinces.

[12] The power to make laws in fulfilment of international obligations has been conferred on the Union by item 14 of the first List, and this power was employed by the Union to first enact the Persons with Disabilities (Protection of Rights, Equal Opportunity and Full Participation) Act of 1995 and then the Rights of Persons with Disabilities Act of 2016.

depending on the performance of a province, and gave the largest space to the province with the best track record. Whilst we also kept in consideration the political reality, whereby the party in power in a province may not be holding office in the Union.[13] It was also decided that we would adopt an 'equality line' and to tabularly include the schemes and programmes of all provinces. This method of reporting, tipped its hat at all provinces at least quantitatively. However, the opportunity of recording best practices and thus according international recognition to provincial initiatives was missed out.[14]

3.2.3 Disability Inclusion in Schemes and Programmes of Other Ministries

As already mentioned, we saw the occasion to submit the State Report not just as an opportunity to record what the country had done but also to draw attention to what India had failed to do. Herein significance was accorded to the inclusion or exclusion of disability entitlements. The exclusion could happen either by framing the scheme only for non-disabled persons or by failing to make the accommodation for persons with disabilities. Concomitantly this also allowed the reporting of occasions where a disability scheme was appropriately modified. For example, the Government of India floated a social security scheme for vulnerable persons which mentioned 'the aged, the socially and educationally backward' (National Family Benefit Scheme) but persons with disabilities were not expressly mentioned. Further, the governmental Sanitation scheme referred to the monetary support that shall be provided to families to build toilets, if their annual income was below the specified level.

[13] India is a federal polity with a parliamentary system. There are legislatures in the Union and the Provinces which are constituted by members who have polled the maximum number of votes in the constituency from where they stood for election. The political party who returns the largest number of candidates forms the Government in the Union or the Provinces. It is not necessary that the same political party forms the Government in both the Union and the Provinces. Since the Union Ministry was steering the report, it may depending upon political affiliations ignore the schemes and programmes of a particular province.

[14] Possibly, for this reason the final report did not include the disability initiatives of the provinces.

The amount for the toilet was calculated keeping in view the size of the toilet and the door. That a toilet used by a wheelchair user would need to be larger and fitted with accessibility and safety features found no mention. The fact that there was a prototype, which was oblivious to the presence of persons with disabilities in the family, needed to be highlighted in order to make other ministries cognizant of their obligations to persons with disabilities. However, the then Secretary of the Ministry of Social Justice and Empowerment was of the view that this was showing up his colleagues in other departments for not doing tasks which were not their primary responsibility. He remained unmoved on this position even though the PWDA (1995) had constituted a Central Coordination Committee, which had as members Secretaries of all Union ministries whose work overlapped with disability.[15] In contrast, to that Minister's approach, it is the overlap with the Central Coordination Committee, which explained why the Ministry of Labour had revised the work and wages norms of its Rural Employment Guarantee Scheme as it applied to persons with disabilities. Thus, whilst the quantum and type of work were made lighter in comparison to non-disabled persons, in recognition of the effort expended, the wages were kept the same. Whereas in direct opposition, the Ministry of Sports had reduced award money for medals won at the Paralympics in comparison to the sum awarded for the Olympics.

Upon reflection it is questionable whether the unwillingness of the Secretary of the Ministry of Social Justice and Empowerment stemmed from an in-principle objection to the critique, or because the critique would have found place in a report to be submitted to the UN. The policy of minimum disclosure seemed to inform the State's perspective in the matter, and we encountered it in greater or lesser degree at various stages of the report making process. The recurrent surfacing of this sentiment seems to point to something larger than the resistance of an individual official or a particular ministry. I will therefore return to this issue later in the chapter.

[15] These were departments of Welfare, Education, Woman and Child Development, Expenditure, Personnel, Training and Public Grievances, Health, Rural Development, Industrial Development, Urban Affairs and Employment, Science and Technology, Legal Affairs, Public Enterprises.

3.2.4 The Disability Division of the Ministry of Social Justice and Empowerment

By a process of elimination, we were now required to primarily report on the work undertaken by the Disability Division[16] of the Ministry of Social Justice and Empowerment (Ministry). This included both the work undertaken by the Ministry and the work it supported through its schemes and programmes. The most major of these were the Schemes Instituted under the Persons with Disabilities Act (PWDA 1995).[17] The Ministry had an impressive record of work undertaken under this scheme. Virtually every proposal, which had found place in the statute, had an accompanying scheme and programme. For example, section 66 of the PWDA (1995) required the appropriate government to promote research and development in institutions of higher education. This provision in the statute was used to launch a scheme whereby funding could be provided to educational institutions to undertake research. The Disability Division also had data on the money disbursed to various beneficiaries to undertake the tasks which were outlined in the PWDA (1995). The presence of the scheme or programme and the allocation of resources for it was only the first step of implementation. To report the matter to the CRPD Committee, it was necessary to have further data on how much of that money was disbursed; how much was spent; and how many beneficiaries received the intended benefit in how much time. Without access to such follow-up data, the schemes only indicated intention and did not show the realisation of intention. With access to the data, even if the Report was only limited to the Disability Division of the Ministry, the mandate of the CRPD Committee could be substantially realised at least in relation to the socio-economic rights included in the CRPD.

However, the Ministry, together with the provincial governments who received aid from the federal Government, could only provide information on the schemes and the monies disbursed under it. Regarding all the

[16] This division was upgraded in 2012 to a Disability Department with a full-fledged Secretary. Earlier disability was one of the divisions of the Ministry of social Justice and Empowerment.

[17] This was the overarching title accorded to a range of schemes instituted under any provision of the Act of 1995. The process was started with the enactment of the Act in 1995, and the bouquet of programmatic interventions kept expanding over the years.

other matters outlined above there was no systematic record keeping. An instruction that is routinely included in all project implementation manuals states that a project is not completed until all its successes and failures have been duly documented. This instruction was never followed. Subsequently, as the projects were completed, reports were filed to the funding Ministry. However, the data, which provided information on the impact of the particular scheme on the guaranteed right, was not culled out from the Ministry's reports and maintained accordingly. The status report was only evaluated on a standalone basis in financial terms, that is, whether the money disbursed to the particular agency was spent within the specified time, if there was any funding remaining and whether that had been returned or reallocated. The performance documented in the performance reports was not culled out and separately maintained in order to evaluate and report on the effectiveness of the particular scheme.

Confronted with this vacuum on vital data, we tried to gather data from diverse sources such as planning commission reports, annual reports of ministries, the census and the auditor general's reports. However, since these reports were also not written to evaluate the realisation of the rights guaranteed by the CRPD, we were not sure whether we could even make surmises, let alone draw conclusions on the basis of that data. We were of the view that the State should report its poor documentation to the CRPD Committee and resolve to rectify it by the next Report. Yet again, the designated Ministry was not comfortable in making forthright disclosures.

3.3 The Mandate on Civil Political Rights and the Right of Judicial Review

Prior to the CRPD, the civil and political rights of persons with disabilities had to be deduced in international human rights law from the International Covenant on Civil Political Rights (ICCPR 1966) and in national human rights law from the Constitution of India (Constitution 1950). The CRPD has inaugurated the process of recognising that persons with disabilities have civil and political rights on an equal basis with others. Since the PWDA (1995) did not include any provisions recognising the civil and political rights of persons with disabilities, it was necessary to look at how the provisions of the Constitution played out for persons with disabilities. The Constitution of India prohibits the State from making any law, which is in contravention of the fundamental rights guaranteed to the people and any law which is so made is to the extent of contravention, void (Constitution of India 1950: Art. 13). The Constitution also guarantees to the people the right to directly approach the Supreme Court or the High Court as the case may be, for appropriate relief if any of their fundamental rights are breached (Constitution 1950, Art. 32; 226).

In order to assess the meaning of these provisions for persons with disabilities, it was necessary to analyse, if and when these provisions were activated to assert the civil and political rights of persons with disabilities. Research revealed that the courts were primarily moved to challenge wrongful confinement or to seek an upgrading of psychiatric institutions. The petitions on wrongful confinement brought to the notice of the court how a person who was not mentally ill had been railroaded into a mental hospital or how persons acquitted on grounds of insanity had been in confinement for periods longer than those for which they could be punished. The Courts primarily relied upon the constitutional right to life and liberty in deciding whether to provide relief or not. The manner in which the Courts upheld this right was the primary evidence of the extent to which the right could be asserted by and for persons with disabilities. Since the right to liberty was primarily activated for persons who were incorrectly diagnosed as persons with mental disabilities, these cases were not included in our drafts. However, we did incorporate references to cases[18] where Courts were moved to upgrade living conditions. Our inclusion of the availability of the constitutional right was found to be in order; however, details of the relief being granted in individual cases was considered unnecessary.[19]

The Government of India had started the process of replacing the PWDA of 1995 and the Mental Health Act of 1987 with legislation

[18] *B. R. Kapoor* vs *Union of India* AIR 1990 SC 752; *Supreme Court Legal Aid Committee* vs *State of MP* AIR 1995 SC 204; *Aman Hingorani* vs *Union of India* AIR 1995 SC 215.

[19] Thus, whilst we made references to the judicial action in the field, the state report has only made generalised statements.

which was in accordance with the CRPD. However, the drafts of the two legislative Bills did not adopt a similar approach in interpreting the right to legal capacity and the matter of forced interventions. Whilst the new draft disability law was pressing for a complete embargo on forced intervention, along with universal legal capacity with support, the draft Mental Health law was pitching for compulsory care as a last resort, and substitute decision-making regimes only if required. We thought it was apposite to report this difference of approach in the Report as it would bring to the fore the difficulties countries were facing in the implementation of the CRPD.[20] However, the Ministry of Health insisted upon the discord not being included in the Report because in their view, the CRPD did not prohibit either forced or substitute decision-making (Freeman et al. 2015). This opinion has been voiced by several other States Parties; an express assertion would have helped deliberation but yet again diplomatic silence was preferred.[21]

The assertion of civil and political rights was contentious and their realisation, even with the intervention of the courts was far from easy. The reporting process required that such contentiousness and conflict should be reported. However, both the ministries for Social Justice and Empowerment, and for Health, were not agreeable to the documentation of the conflict; rather, they wanted the matter to be referred to in bland unproblematic terms.

As already mentioned, the PWDA (1995) was a legislative recognition of the social and economic rights guaranteed to persons with disabilities. These rights were to be realised through Government schemes and programmes. Whilst some statutory provisions made the floating of schemes to be mandatory by using the language of command, other provisions by using discretionary formulation left the matter to the choice of the

[20] At that point the two legislations were only being discussed and these differences surfaced as part of the deliberations. The enactment of these laws has been a much later process. Thus, the Rights of Persons with Disabilities Act was enacted in 2016 and the Mental Health Care Act in 2017. The problem of varied approach persists.

[21] During the negotiations on the CRPD in the Ad Hoc Committee, Don Mackay the Chair of the Committee in a private conversation did share how the dialogic mode in which the CRPD had been negotiated was the exception. As a rule, states choose to only make statements and there is general unwillingness to adopt positions. We experienced a similar unwillingness to take stands in the report making process.

government. Governments did not distinguish between mandatory and optional formulations and saw both kinds of provisions as aspirational—goals they would try to achieve. The aspirational tenor of the statute was turned around by the courts; they ordered the executive to float all the mandatory schemes and thereby rendered real the promise of the statutes.[22] We decided to include these judicial decisions, as the presence of remedies in our view demonstrated the robustness of the right. The reporting guidelines also required such judicial decisions to be included. The fact that the right was realised through the judiciary and not the executive was however seen as evidence of executive recalcitrance. We were thus asked by the Ministry of Social Justice and Empowerment to only report the realisation of the right and expunge the means through which the right was realised. It was at this point that we realised that we were not preparing a country report, which would allow us to report on all developments advancing the rights of persons with disabilities in the country whether undertaken by the State or Civil Society. Nor were we even preparing a State Report as that would allow us to include the initiatives of all organs of the State be it legislature, executive or judiciary. Rather, we were only preparing a Government report and thus could only write about the work on disability rights undertaken by the Central Government and most importantly by the Ministry of Social Justice and Empowerment who was the nodal ministry for disability rights.

3.4 Stocktake and Blueprint

As already mentioned, CDS took up the responsibility of ghost writing the State Report in line with the CRPD Committee's reporting guidelines, to take stock of the status of disability rights of the country and to provide a blueprint for the future. We thought that we could, with our understanding of disability and commitment to disability rights, be able

[22] Illustratively Section 43 of the Persons with Disabilities Act 1995 provided that "the appropriate governments and local authorities shall by notification frame schemes in favour of persons with disabilities for the preferential allotment of land at concessional rates..." By reason of this provision the High Court of Allahabad in *National Federation of the Blind* vs *State of UP and others* 2000 (2) Allahabad Weekly Cases 1234 required the State Government to frame a scheme and quashed the order whereby they refused to grant land on a concessional rate to a person with disability.

to both advise and persuade the Government to make a transparent weighing up of the status of disability rights in the country, in line with the stocktake and help in planning for the future, so that a vibrant disability rights regime could be set up. The narrative recorded above brings home that there was general unwillingness on the part of the Government to make statements that would concretely describe the situation. On several drafts of the State Report we received the following responses to our proposal to include a section that took stock of the status of disability rights in India and then outlined what should be done in the future.

In the spirit of the CRPD and in compliance with the reporting guidelines, the first draft of the State Report was shared at a civil society consultation.[23] If civil society had expressly appreciated this dimension of the Report, it may have caused the Government to make a commitment to its inclusion in the final Report. However, civil society largely ignored the stocktaking dimension of the Report and only concentrated on correcting the fine print. As already mentioned, there was public opposition to the mention of civil society initiatives in the State report,[24] because it could show the Government in a better light; significantly, the Report was not criticised for lionising the performance of the Government in the field.

The next draft version of the State Report was presented at the meeting of the Central Coordination Committee at which, unlike the civil society meeting, each ministry vied with the other to have every single one of its initiatives for persons with disabilities to be included in full detail in the Report. They felt any stocktake which was undertaken with incomplete data would not be an accurate assessment. De hors these individual assertions on particular chapters, we were advised that undertaking a stocktaking and blueprinting exercise for each of the rights was excessive and could be a stranglehold on the country for the future and hence should be avoided. It was suggested that a generic chapter which takes stock of the status of disability rights and blueprints for the future would fit the bill without unduly constraining the country. The Minister of Social Justice and Empowerment found merit in the suggestion and thus it was

[23] The various versions of the report can be accessed at http://www.disabilitystudiesnalsar.org/uncrpdreport.php.

[24] A number of civil society organisations privately expressed enthusiasm about their work being included in the Report.

decided to drop the evaluating section in each chapter and only a generic chapter on the status of disability rights was included.

After implementing the suggestions received from the Central Coordination Committee, we submitted the draft State Report and expected a quick final approval. Instead, we were put on a tailspin. The Government launched its own review process and we were taken off the radar. The final State Report we received from the Government had omitted the generic chapter on stocktaking and blueprinting; all narrations of judicial decisions had been deleted and any word or sentence which seemed remotely critical of the Government had been removed from the text. We protested at being side-lined and our expertise in the field ignored. We also alerted the Government to the real possibility of the silences in the State report being exposed in the shadow report. The officials of the Ministry were reconciled to a civil society exposure but were unrelenting in their opposition to self-disclosure. Our objection delayed the printing of the State Report and its submission to the CRPD Committee, but nothing else happened. In the end, we were forced to recognise that we were only agents, and as agents we had to act in accordance with the will and preference of the principal, that is, the Government of India. Thus, a contractual relationship which was started in enthusiastic idealism ended in disappointment, fatigue and sadness.

After the initial anger wore off, we at CDS were forced to look behind the resistance of the Government and its officials. Upon reflection we were able to see that our draft State Report had not encountered resistance all the way, in fact it had even received kudos from both the Central Coordination Committee and the Legal and Treaties Division of the Ministry of External Affairs. Hence, the resistance cannot be attributed to the entire Government, although it was practised by a sizable section. Since, the officials had no personal grudge against either CDS or me, it is important to reflect on the reason behind this defensive posturing, which renders the entire process of State reporting meaningless. It is to that analysis that I now turn.[25]

---

[25] Since, the work on the report was undertaken by my team and me, the article till this point has been written in first person plural. However, the analysis of the situation is mine and hence the following section has been written in first person singular.

4 A Relationship of Mutual Mistrust: The Reporting State and the Treaty Body

An examination of the reporting guidelines shows that the guidelines are addressed to both States Parties and civil society.[26] Through the State Reports the treaty body is accessing information from both the Government and non-government organisations. Since the primary reporting obligation lies with the State Party, the alternative report is being obtained in order to assess the silences in the State Report, and to obtain information on areas which a State has either neglected or attended to very scarcely. This model of State and alternative reports can be perceived as a way of ensuring that information be obtained from both the provider and the recipient of services so that the CRPD Committee obtains as complete a picture as is possible. Another way of viewing this practice is to see the alternative report as a mechanism for checking the veracity of the State Report. Such a procedure is being set up because it is believed that a State Party will not make full disclosure. Therefore, either to compel a State Party to make full disclosure or to not make the treaty body totally dependent on the information supplied by the State, a system of submitting alternative reports by civil society has been put in place. Irrespective of the explanation, the practice of State and alternative reports is premised on suspicion, if not mistrust. A State Party can counter this disbelief by proactively providing information to the CRPD Committee instead of waiting for it to find the same information through a process of discovery. The strategy of proactive disclosure, which we were advising the Government of India to adopt, requires that the recipient of the disclosure accords full respect for forthrightness, and lends support to the State Party to overcome the barriers it is recounting. If the State does not receive such a response, then the disclosure is treated like a confession, which can be used to pillory the State. By implication, States Parties are disinclined to make such disclosures.

Since, the cooperation of the States Parties is integral to the effective functioning of a treaty body, the constructive dialogue between the State

[26] In fact, the CRPD Committee whilst listing its business on the state report makes express reference to the reports from civil society it shall consider along with.

Party and CRPD Committee is a consummate performance of tact and civility. Treaty Bodies are generally though not always inclined to appreciate rather than denigrate a State making a disclosure. Since, the information in a State Report is in the public domain, States find themselves being shown up by other stakeholders, who believe that the expose would cause the State to fall in line and do its duty by the law.[27] It is this fear of a disclosure not being received in the spirit in which it is made that causes States Parties to remain in the denial mode. A State Party can disavow those facts that have been discovered by the treaty body; however, this option is not available for self-disclosed facts.

The aforesaid explanation enables me to understand the resistance of the Ministry and its officials to any self-disclosure strategy. I was repeatedly told that whilst they appreciated the sincerity of my suggestions, I did not understand the world of realpolitik, which operated on a different rationale than the space of academic study and analysis. It was this fear of disclosure being torn out of context, which caused State officials to operate on the minimum information mode. This reclusive approach is further exacerbated when Government officials believe that the world of human rights law enforcement does not treat all States similarly, that is, the omissions of some States Parties being treated more severely than those of others. My experience with the Government officials of my country caused me to conclude that the suspicions of treaty bodies caused States Parties to strike defensive postures and stonewalling strategies. However, once such strategies are adopted, it is often not realised by Government officials at which point they have crossed over from defensive positioning to passive aggressive posturing. The closing down of shutters by States Parties in no way advances the cause of human rights implementation and monitoring. In contrast, constructive dialogue requires respectful interaction, which cannot happen without trust. This raises the question, is it possible to redesign the International Human Rights Law monitoring process, so that it makes monitoring more

[27] This was the fear expressed by several Government officials during the process of deliberating on the report. This fear was also in evidence during the negotiations in the Ad Hoc Committee when several state parties did not want the informal negotiations to happen in the presence of civil society, disabled people and their organisations.

deliberative and less of a policing exercise? I address this concern in the next section.

5 Can the Background Conditions for the Constructive Dialogue Alter?

As already recounted, the alternative report, and the data it supplies, is an integral part of the International Human Rights Law monitoring process. In the reporting guidelines, the CRPD Committee has provided express guidance on its expectations to those who submit alternative reports. These encourage civil society to build alliances and to try as far as possible to submit only one report to the CRPD Committee. In order to enhance both the authenticity and the utility of the report, civil society organisations are trained on how to write an alternative report. Such capacity building programmes are high on the priority list of funding agencies. Thus whilst substantial investments are made in order to obtain a useful alternative report; other than providing reporting guidelines, little else is done by the CRPD Committee to obtain a useful State Report. All guidance on State Reports comes as part of the reporting process be it the settling of the 'list of issues' (LoIs) or the recording of the 'concluding observations' or seeking quick follow-up responses. All these procedures focus on what the State Party should do to fulfil its obligations under the CRPD and not on how it should report what it has done.

My muted criticism could be easily countered by pointing out how, despite some recent developments, State sovereignty remains the centre piece of international law. And, until that situation changes States Parties cannot be taught how to perform their reporting obligations. The truth of this response does not negate the validity of my objection. Although the reporting guidelines tell States Parties what the CRPD Committee requires, they provide no suggestions on how to do it. Just as a starter, a number of States Parties may need help on how to maintain and retain data on the information required by the CRPD Committee. In similar spirit it may be useful to share information on commonly encountered impediments and the successful strategies employed to overcome them.

In my view, the language of cooperation may result in more constructive engagement than an environment of confrontation. Many present and former members of the CRPD treaty body could say that the Committee has been positive in its approach and acknowledged every positive move made by a State Party.[28] This may well be true, but I am not referring to the formal process but to non-formal initiatives, which allow for learning to happen in a non-judgmental environment. Any initiative which is situated within the formal process of the UN gets coloured by it. As it stands, the relationship between the States Parties and the treaty body has combative undertones, which do not allow for trustful cooperation. It is imperative in my opinion that the International Human Rights Law monitoring process is not just about identifying wrongdoing and the wrongdoer but also about finding ways of correcting things. Matters can only be set right if what is wrong is understood and accepted. In my view the 'catch me if you can' fashion in which International Human Rights Law monitoring is undertaken needs to alter if such monitoring is to prompt the situation on the ground to be changed.

6 Conclusion

The purpose of filing State Reports to the CRPD Committee is to enable States Parties to fulfil their obligations under the CRPD (2006) in both letter and spirit. For this objective to be achieved, it is important that the State Party documents its achievements and failures with the maximum degree of honesty in its State Report. The work of CDS, Hyderabad, with the Government of India, shows that some governments may be unwilling to take the forthrightness route because they fear that their disclosures could be used to nail and not to assist them. It was also found that several wings of the Government in India do not have any understanding of relevant data and that there is a severe dearth of satisfactory documenting

[28] My own observation has been that the Committee has been kinder to recalcitrant States than to States who have been making a real effort to fulfil the mandate of the CRPD in both letter and spirit.

practices. It is necessary that each department of the Government is trained on the provisions of the CRPD and that the initiatives needed to realise the mandate of the CRPD and the manner in which Government efforts try to achieve these should be documented. Only with such training can the Government officials who are closest to the situation fulfil their obligations under the CRPD.

The conceptual burden of State sovereignty and the emotional baggage of nationalism prevent States Parties from participating in the Human Rights Law monitoring process in a positive manner. States Parties need to be persuaded to take the path of forthright self-disclosure through a series of non-formal sharing conclaves. The best practices and innovative remedies found by the CRPD Committee should be documented and widely shared. An exclusive reliance on 'naming and shaming' strategies causes governments to play 'catch me if you can', which robs the Human Rights Law monitoring process of its constructive potential. In order to restore the constructive spirit of the 'constructive dialogue', it is suggested that the treaty body interacts with the States Parties both formally and non-formally so to encourage compliance. Extensive investments have been made to build capacity to write robust alternative reports. Without denying the utility of that process, it is equally important to launch similar training initiatives which strengthen State Party's capabilities in preparing constructive State Reports. Since the primary responsibility of realising the mandate of the CRPD lies with the States Parties, with the State Reports being periodic records of that progress, it is important that the process of reporting should advance that progress. The aim of the submission of an authentic State Report should be to assist with compliance. This chapter has therefore narrated what in my view causes bland reports, which check boxes and provide no concrete details to be submitted and has suggested measures for overcoming the malaise.

References

Alston, John Norton Pomeroy Professor of Law Philip, Philip Alston, James Crawford, and Whewell Professor of International Law and Fellow James Crawford. (2000). *The Future of UN human rights treaty monitoring*. Cambridge University Press.

Clapham, A. (2006). *Human rights obligations of non-state actors*. Oxford: OUP Oxford.

Freeman, M. C., Kolappa, K., de Almeida, J. M. C., Kleinman, A., Makhashvili, N., Phakathi, S., Saraceno, B., & Thornicroft, G. (2015). Reversing hard won victories in the name of human rights: A critique of the general comment on article 12 of the UN convention on the rights of persons with disabilities. *The Lancet Psychiatry, 2*(9), 844–850. https://doi.org/10.1016/S2215-0366(15)00218-7.

Goodman, R., & Jinks, D. (2003). Measuring the effects of human rights treaties. *European Journal of International Law, 14*(1), 171–183. https://doi.org/10.1093/ejil/14.1.171.

Hafner-Burton, E. M., & Tsutsui, K. (2005). Human rights in a globalizing world: The paradox of empty promises. *American Journal of Sociology, 110*(5), 1373–1411. https://doi.org/10.1086/428442.

Hamelink, C. J. (2012). Human rights. *The Journal of International Communication, 18*(2), 245–265. https://doi.org/10.1080/13216597.2012.709929.

Hungarian Disability Caucus. (2010, August). *Disability rights or disabling rights CRPD alternative report*. SINOSZ, MDAC, FESZT.

Kanter, A. S. (2011). The law: what's disability studies got to do with it or an introduction to disability legal studies. *Columbia Human Rights Law Review, 42*, 403.

Poe, S. C., Carey, S. C., & Vazquez, T. C. (2001). How are these pictures different—A quantitative comparison of the US state department and amnesty international human rights reports, 1976–1995. *Human Rights Quarterly, 23*, 650.

Reisman, W. M. (1990). Sovereignty and human rights in contemporary international law. *American Journal of International Law, 84*(4), 866–876. https://doi.org/10.2307/2202838.

Tomuschat, C. (2014). *Human Rights: Between Idealism and Realism*. Oxford: OUP.

17

Conclusion

Kelley Johnson and Emily Julia Kakoullis

At a minimum, human rights documents like the CRPD can act as a kind of check list of relevant rights and obligations. The check list is a kind of practical pointer towards the organization of some version of an ideal world: it cannot guarantee a good life, but can guarantee a minimum framework in which fundamental needs are met and values adhered to so that a person with disability has as much chance as a nondisabled person of achieving a good life. But beyond functioning either as a check list or a description, the CRPD can act as a tool for the transformation of how cultures think about disabled people. Through the public discussion that, ideally, takes place as new policy documents circulate and key pieces of legislation are reported in

---

K. Johnson (✉)
Social Policy Research Centre, UNSW, Sydney, Australia
e-mail: kelley.johnson@unsw.edu.au

E. J. Kakoullis
School of Law and Politics, Cardiff University, Cardiff, UK

E. J. Kakoullis, K. Johnson (eds.), *Recognising Human Rights in Different Cultural Contexts*, https://doi.org/10.1007/978-981-15-0786-1_17

> *the media, new configurations of the social roles and practices associated with what is being regulated will emerge. And so legal and policy instruments, as well as reflecting current understanding of a topic, also have a potentially transformative effect.*
> *(Scully 2012, pp. 72–73)*

1 Introduction

In exploring the ways in which various cultures interact with the United Nations (UN) Convention on the Rights of Persons with Disabilities (CRPD/Convention 2006), this book provides a further endorsement for Scully's (2012) statement. It became clear as the book developed that the CRPD did provide a 'checklist of relevant rights and obligations' and a description of what might be possible in attaining 'a good life' for persons with disabilities. For some contributors it also became apparent that the CRPD could be transformative in a number of ways: through changes in law and policy, in the language used about persons with disabilities and in the possibilities for civil society, particularly for persons with disabilities and their organisations (DPOs), to take action for change. However, the book also reveals the complexities of the interaction between cultures (some internal to States) which either challenged or facilitated these changes and in some instances challenged the content of the CRPD itself.

When we developed the idea for this book, we were motivated by the understanding that there was not currently a strong literature which placed the concept of 'culture' (or cultures) centrally and explicitly in considering the journey of the CRPD from the international level to the domestic which would directly affect the lives of persons with disabilities. We began the book with a number of questions. These were not the basis for the chapters in the book, rather they served as a starting point for our own exploration and we came back to them for reflection as the book developed. The questions were the following: what is meant by the concept of 'culture' in relation to the human rights of persons with disabilities set out in the CRPD? How important are cultural contexts in shaping how the CRPD's provisions are interpreted and implemented by particular States Parties? What cultural factors facilitate or challenge the process of interpreting and translating the provisions of the CRPD into action for change during the processes of ratification, implementation and monitoring? At times the chapters challenged our original questions and led us to reframe them. Although we had initially seen the sections of the book as a series of 'snapshots' of the processes of ratification, implementation and monitoring, as we read the chapters as a whole we found there were a number of themes that addressed our questions indirectly and which emerged strongly across the different processes. We concluded that one of the key findings from the chapters read as a whole was that focusing on one aspect of the interpretation and translation processes for the CRPD (ratification, implementation and monitoring) did not allow for a consideration of the key themes that were strongly present across all of them. In this final chapter we consider these overarching themes and conclude by exploring their implications for the achievement of the CRPD in relation to providing a 'checklist of relevant rights and obligations' and a description of 'a good life' for persons with disabilities, and its transformative potential in various cultural contexts.

The overarching themes we discuss are: the complexity and diversity of cultures into which the CRPD is interpreted and translated, and the way these impact on and are affected by the CRPD; the diversity of ways in which the concept of 'disability' is defined and constituted within and between cultures and how this affects the development of the CRPD; the particular significance of individual provisions of the CRPD in different cultures, and the importance of the CRPD in supporting persons with disabilities to work for change in their particular culture.

2 The Impact of the Complexity and Diversity of 'Culture/s'

It is perhaps inevitable when considering the interpretation and translation of the CRPD into domestic culture, that the concept of 'culture' is sometimes seen in terms of nations or States. After all it is a State Party that ratifies the Convention and puts in place the laws and policies to support its implementation and monitoring, and these can be seen as reflecting particular values, beliefs and history. Many of the chapters reflect the ways in which the States Parties operate in relation to the development of law and policy. However, it became clear across sections of the book that decisions at a State level about the progress of the CRPD were not only or primarily motivated by a commitment to human rights. Other wider cultural issues and values could be stronger drivers in the way States made decisions. Some of these included: concern about potential risk to State sovereignty in relation to international treaties; the challenges to human rights promoted in the CRPD that were seen to run counter to religious or State-wide laws on particular issues, such as marriage and family; the impact of economic austerity and the economic consequences of implementing provisions in the CRPD, particularly in relation to the closure of institutions; and the pride and vested interests of States in relation to their history of services to persons with disabilities.

However, one of the key findings from this book is that viewing the concept of 'culture' in terms of nations or States reduces its complexity and ignores the often-conflicting cultural interests that operate within any State. In the light of this we came to the view that Bennoune's (2018) perspective that we should talk always of 'cultures', rather than 'culture', was a more accurate picture of the processes through which the CRPD progressed. Further, some of the contributors to the book conceptualised 'culture/s' in quite different terms to States: as a characteristic of a particular discipline, for example, Law or Anthropology; as a focus on the arts and their political impact; as a particular political and philosophical system, as in the welfare state or in relation to indigeneity. The chapters of this book suggest that a failure to recognise the complexity of cultures within one State Party may lead to simplistic views of how the CRPD is interpreted and translated into action. The challenges are not only in relation to the power and values espoused at State level; rather, the complexity of cultures within a State need to be given serious consideration.

3 The Impact of the Diversity of the Concept of 'Disability'

We found that throughout the book writers tended to discuss the concept of 'disability' in the way it is conceptualised in the CRPD. There were only some chapters that focussed on or included the particular needs of a specific group of persons with disabilities (persons with intellectual disabilities and war affected persons with disabilities). This lends some weight to the idea of disability culture/s where persons with disabilities use their shared experience and history of exclusion in a struggle for human rights across different contexts.

Considerable emphasis was given across sections of the book to the way in which persons with disabilities were constituted within different cultural contexts. Historical adherence in some States to a medical or charity model of disability was seen as posing a significant obstacle to the movement towards a human rights approach to disability. The ways in which these historical approaches were challenged recurred across the different sections of the book. Where there was a strong history of human rights, it seemed that the progress of the CRPD was facilitated. However, this was not always the case, as while the US has strong rights legislation in relation to disability, its perceived broader national interests prevented the ratification of the CRPD. The importance of a human rights lens in viewing the requirements of persons with disabilities for a good life was stressed across all sections and chapters of the book.

The importance of language in relation to persons with disabilities was given considerable emphasis by a number of contributors. The need for a shift in language, from descriptors which constituted persons as 'helpless', 'dependent' or 'lacking capacity', to persons 'having human rights', was seen as an important step in advancing the CRPD. This was not only at State level, differences in perception of persons with disabilities were also seen within different cultural groups, including the way in which specific disciplines identified persons with disabilities, the various views of particular cultures within a State, for example, Indigenous people, and the views of families and service providers which sometimes ran counter to the laws and policies of the State Party.

4 The Impact of Particular Articles in the CRPD

There was some emphasis (particularly in the implementation section of the book) on discussion of particular articles of the CRPD. When this occurred, two articles in particular were the subject of discussion: Article 12—Equal recognition before the law and Article 19—Living independently and being included in the community (CRPD 2006). The selection of these articles for particular consideration is perhaps unsurprising considering the 'synergy' between these two provisions "which centres on the notion that in order to live independently in the community everyone's legal capacity to make decisions and have those decisions is respected" (O'Donnell and O'Mahony 2017, p. 285), and that they are provisions central to achieving the CRPD's 'paradigm shift'. The selection of these articles by contributors reflected the priorities or concerns of their particular cultures, for example, Article 12 challenges historical views of persons with disabilities and the ways in which they have been subject to legal culture. The focus on Article 19 reflected the concerns of some States Parties in relation to community living, and the closure of large institutions. However, in one instance the focus was on the challenges to closing large institutions and in another the State's historical success in deinstitutionalisation was seen as an obstacle to future changes.

5 The Impact of Action by Persons with Disabilities

Both this book and other literature (Lord and Stein 2008; Soldatic and Johnson 2019) have documented what Scully (2012) refers to as the 'transformative effect' of the CRPD, particularly in relation to the involvement of persons with disabilities taking action towards the implementation of their human rights. The CRPD emphasises the importance of participation by persons with disabilities in all stages of its implementation, and across all sections of the book authors documented how persons with disabilities were either asserting their right to participate or were facing challenges in doing so. The forms of these activities were diverse, ranging from direct political action, to the use of theatre, to seeking change in specific institutions, such as education. There were discussions about how DPOs were taking initiative in a movement towards developing a human rights lens in relation to disability in their States Parties, and their achievements were acknowledged in terms of changes to domestic institutions, legislation and policies. However, this was not always accomplished without a struggle, and it was apparent that in some cultural contexts persons with disabilities were not included in some of the CRPD-related processes. We noted that particularly in later stages of the process of implementation of the CRPD, a number of chapters revealed an increasing initiative and involvement in the struggle for human rights by persons with disabilities, with a particular focus on moving States into a more human rights-based approach. At times it seemed as if the actions of DPOs aimed to move States into a more human rights-based approach. However, it was also apparent that in some instances the attempts by persons with disabilities to work collaboratively, that is, with other rights organisations, with families and with specific disciplinary representatives were challenging or problematic. There were also questions raised about the diversity of organisations which sought to represent persons with disabilities at State level. The need for work to bring together DPOs and to recognise the common and diverse disabilities cultures was an issue that underlay some of the chapters.

One of the important issues that was raised throughout the book was the fact that we are all situated not just in one culture but in many, and that at both an individual and group level we need to find ways of balancing the sometimes different priorities of our multiculturalism. A tendency to only view the concept of 'culture' as national or State ignores the complexity of this issue. The other important finding was the need for persons with disabilities to be able to self-identify with their particular culture/s and to have that acknowledged and respected.

6 Conclusion

This book has taken us as editors on a complex and sometimes challenging journey. It has led us to an appreciation as to why some previous literature about disability and culture does not always deconstruct what the concept of 'culture/s' means. This book suggests that a failure to consider the complexity of the cultures in which persons with disabilities live and their diversity means that many of the challenges which confront those working towards the successful implementation of human rights for persons with disabilities are not recognised. We are encouraged by the strength of purpose which the CRPD, once ratified, has given persons with disabilities and the changes that have occurred in some of the cultural contexts discussed by the contributors to this book. Nevertheless, the struggle for human rights of persons with disabilities continues, and we consider that there is a need to both recognise and give careful consideration to the variety of cultural challenges which will need to be resolved if the human rights of persons with disabilities are to be achieved. We hope that this book will initiate discussions on this issue and lead to positive action that will support the transformative potential of the CRPD. Understanding and having knowledge of the complexities of the diverse cultural contexts in which the CRPD is interpreted and translated is a step towards achieving this.

References

Bennoune, K. (2018). *Universality, cultural diversity and cultural rights. Report of the Special Rapporteur in the field of cultural rights*. Presented at the 73rd Session General Assembly UN.
CRPD (United Nations Convention on the Rights of Persons with Disabilities). (2006). Adopted in 2006 by the United Nations general assembly.
Lord, J. E., & Stein, M. A. (2008). The domestic incorporation of human rights law and the United Nations convention on the rights of persons with disabilities. *Washington Law Review, 83*, 449–479.
O'Donnell, S., & O'Mahony, C. (2017). The UN convention on the rights of persons with disabilities: exploring the synergy between article 12 and article

19. In C. O'Mahony & G. Quinn (Eds.), *Disability law and policy an analysis of the UN convention*. Dublin: Clarus Press.
Scully, J. L. (2012). The convention on the rights of persons with disabilities and cultural understandings of disability. In J. Anderson & J. Philips (Eds.), *Disability and universal human rights: legal, ethical, and conceptual implications of the convention on the rights of persons with disabilities*. Utrecht: Utrecht University Netherlands Institute of Human Rights.
Soldatic, K., & Johnson, K. (2019). *Global perspectives on disability advocacy and activism. Our way*. London: Routledge.

Index[1]

A

Activism, 71, 180, 187–190, 192, 193, 195, 261, 263, 265, 303, 304, 322–324, 345, 348
Anthropology, 45–60, 380
Austerity, 13, 298, 303, 308, 322, 322n19, 380
Australia, 4, 98, 122

B

Bangladesh, 12, 283n21, 289
Brunei, 58, 59

C

Charity-based approach to disability, 183
China, 11, 203–224
  Contract Law of the People's Republic of China (Contract Law, 1999), 211
  General Provisions of the Civil Law of the People's Republic of China (General Provisions of the Civil Law, 2017), 210–212
Civil rights, 103, 109, 110, 111n31, 113n34, 123n49, 251, 303–304, 322, 323

[1] Note: Page numbers followed by 'n' refer to notes.

E. J. Kakoullis, K. Johnson (eds.), *Recognising Human Rights in Different Cultural Contexts*, https://doi.org/10.1007/978-981-15-0786-1

Civil society, 10, 12, 13, 32, 135, 137–146, 151, 152, 158–162, 173, 180–182, 187–189, 193–196, 248, 251, 299, 305, 310, 318, 337, 341, 343, 345, 349, 357–360, 360n10, 368–370, 368n24, 370n26, 371n27, 372, 378
  activism, 187–190, 192, 195
Community, 8, 10, 11, 24, 40, 43, 49, 56, 57, 65, 67, 73, 74, 80–85, 87, 89, 91, 100, 110, 111n31, 122, 133, 143–145, 149, 151, 152, 180, 182, 186, 192, 194, 214, 227–232, 234–237, 240–242, 247–250, 252, 257, 258, 260, 265, 276, 279, 280, 286–289, 287n23, 288n25, 288n26, 302, 304, 307, 309, 317, 333–337, 339–343, 346–349, 382
  community-based services, 232, 253, 257–261
Committee on the Rights of Persons with Disabilities (CoRPD), 34, 36, 115, 134, 159, 232, 298, 355
  Concluding Observations, 115, 135, 142, 211, 236, 240, 318–322, 372
  constructive dialogue, 235, 316, 370, 372–374
  examination, 13, 298, 307, 313–321
  General Comments, 37, 38, 140, 142, 159, 207–209, 215, 232, 309
Consultation, 10, 137, 148, 149, 151, 159–161, 163, 164, 168, 169, 172–174, 180, 188, 189, 195, 299, 306, 318, 348, 368
Convention on the Elimination of all Forms of Discrimination Against Women (CEDAW, 1979), 25n4, 97n1, 98, 98n4, 98n5, 135, 191
Convention on the Prevention and Punishment of the Crime of Genocide (Genocide Convention, 1948), 98n4, 101, 104n18
Convention on the Rights of the Child (CRC, 1989), 97, 97n1, 97–98n2, 98, 98n4, 98n5, 104, 105n19, 107, 117, 136
Convention on the Rights of Persons with Disabilities (CRPD, 2006)
  adoption, 2, 5, 21, 80, 228, 339
  Article 1 (Purpose), 4, 340
  Article 4 (General obligations), 158, 168, 171, 173, 251, 251n22, 271n1, 300, 338
  Article 5 (Equality and non-discrimination), 309
  Article 6 (Women with disabilities), 90
  Article 7 (Children with disabilities), 90, 117
  Article 8 (Awareness-raising), 269, 271n1
  Article 9 (Accessibility), 271n1
  Article 11 (Situations of risk and humanitarian emergencies), 359
  Article 12 (Equal recognition before the law), 7, 10, 11, 20,

24, 25n4, 26, 33–38, 40, 43, 56, 203–224, 229, 237, 238, 282n19, 301, 309, 344, 382
Article 19 (Living independently and being included in the community), 10, 11, 49, 227–254, 257–265, 289, 307–309, 382
Article 23 (Respect for home and the family), 46, 49, 54, 120
Article 24 (Education), 49, 117, 117n41, 271n1, 282, 289
Article 25 (Health), 119n45, 120, 271n1, 289
Article 29 (Participation in political and public life), 49
Article 30 (Participation in cultural life, recreation, leisure and sport), 10, 73, 74, 269–290, 359
Article 33 (National implementation and monitoring), 12, 135, 158
Article 34 (Committee on the Rights of Persons with Disabilities), 115
Article 35 (Reports by States Parties), 12, 135, 235, 306, 353
Committee on the Rights of Persons with Disabilities (CoRPD), 34, 36, 115, 134, 159, 232, 298, 355
declarations, 149
drafting of, 139
implementation of, 5, 6, 10, 12, 14, 73, 116, 159, 191, 235, 243, 258, 261, 264–265, 297–324, 334, 343–349, 366, 383
monitoring of, 135, 148, 151, 299
Optional Protocol to the CRPD (OP-CRPD, 2006), 2, 134, 166, 305
Preamble, 4, 74, 90, 158, 288
ratification of, 3, 8–10, 99, 151, 152, 157–174
reservations, 149
Council of Europe (CoE), 32, 33
CRPD, *see* Convention on the Rights of Persons with Disabilities (CRPD)
Cultural relativism, 5, 29, 47, 53, 59, 60
Culture(s)
concept of, 2–3, 6–8, 47, 64–67, 70, 73, 378–380, 383, 384
deaf culture, 8, 70, 72, 74, 83
disability culture(s), 7, 8, 64, 67–75, 381
legal culture, 7, 20–43, 206, 207, 212, 382
welfare culture, 12, 258, 263–265, 380
Cyprus, 3, 4, 10, 157–174
The consultation process of state and other services on matters that concern persons with a disability law of 2006 (L. 143(I)/2006), 161, 163, 165, 173
The Convention for the Rights of Persons with Disabilities and Related Matters (Ratification) Law of 2011 (L. 8(III)/2011) (Cyprus), 172
The persons with disabilities law of 2000 (L. 127(I)/2000), 162, 162n1, 163, 168

D

Deaf culture, 8, 70, 72, 74, 83
Decision-making
assisted decision-making, 21n3, 36, 144
substitute decision-making, 33, 34, 36, 37, 141, 149–150, 209, 211, 217–221, 366
supported decision-making, 21, 35, 140, 142, 209, 217, 238, 301, 309
Deinstitutionalisation, 11, 227–254, 257–259, 261, 264, 382
institutionalisation, 42, 230, 232, 237, 249, 279, 317
institutions, 11, 20, 42, 65, 85–88, 104, 148, 185, 228, 230–237, 231n2, 233n5, 240–252, 254, 257–260, 263, 264, 278, 299, 342, 343, 346–349, 353, 354, 358, 363, 365, 380, 382, 383
Disability
concept of, 4, 47, 50, 51, 59, 174, 340, 341, 379, 381
charity-based approach to disability, 183
definition, 46–48, 68, 116n38, 207, 233n4, 336n3, 342, 379
intellectual disability, 12, 30, 35, 39, 40, 163, 222, 233, 243, 259, 260, 269–290, 337, 381
medical model of disability, 252
social model of disability, 4, 52, 168, 174, 230, 252
Disability movement, 10, 72, 150, 173, 187, 261, 304
Disability studies, 50–53, 281n18, 354
Disabled people's organisations (DPOs), 4, 10, 12, 13, 75, 88, 89, 107, 151, 159–163, 165, 166, 168, 169, 171–174, 171n3, 298, 301, 302, 304, 306, 307, 310, 312–321, 333–349, 357, 371n27, 378, 383
Domestic Decision-Making Legislation
Assisted Decision-Making (Capacity) Act (ADCA, 2015) (Ireland), 36, 142, 151
Contract Law of the People's Republic of China (Contract Law, 1999) (China), 211
General Provisions of the Civil Law of the People's Republic of China (General Provisions of the Civil Law, 2017) (China), 210–212
Mental Capacity Act (MCA, 2005) (England and Wales), 301, 321n18
Mental Health Act (MHA, 2001) (Ireland), 144
Mental Health Act (MHA, 2007) (UK), 302
Mental Health (Discrimination) Act (MHA, 2013) (UK), 312
Domestic Disability Legislation
Act Concerning Support and Service Provision for Persons with Certain Functional Impairments (LSS, 1993) (Sweden), 259
Act on services for disabled people with long-term support needs (38/2018) (Iceland), 259

Americans with Disabilities Act (ADA, 1990) (US), 107n24, 108, 114, 118, 123n49, 275, 275n7
Americans with Disabilities Amendment Act (ADAA, 2008) (US), 108, 113
Education for All Handicapped Children's Act (EAHCA, 1975) (US), 118, 118n42, 118n43
Individuals with Disabilities in Education Act (IDEA, 1990) (US), 118n42, 118n43
Individuals with Disabilities in Education Improvement Act (IDEIA, 2004) (US), 118
Persons with Disabilities Act (Protection of Rights, Equal Opportunity and Full Participation) (PWDA, 1995) (India), 360, 360n12, 362–366, 367n22
Persons with Disabilities Law (PDA, 2000 (Cyprus), 162
Protection of the Rights of Persons with Disabilities Act of 1996 (PRPDA, 1996) (Sri Lanka), 185
Rights of Persons with Disabilities Act (RPDA, 2016) (India), 360n12
Rights of Persons with Disabilities (RPD, 2018) (Indonesia), 149, 333
Domestic Ratification Legislation
The Convention for the Rights of Persons with Disabilities and Related Matters (Ratification) Law of 2011 (L. 8(III)/2011) (Cyprus), 172
DPOs, *see* Disabled people's organisations
Dualism, 134, 191

E

Equality, 24, 35, 37, 39, 45, 46, 48, 109, 111n31, 113, 147, 181, 184, 191, 260, 265, 274n6, 285, 300, 301, 303–306, 311, 312, 320, 333, 338, 339, 357
Equal recognition before the law, 7, 10, 11, 24, 37, 56, 203, 207–209, 213, 214, 229, 237, 309, 344, 382
European Commission, 239–242
European Convention on Human Rights (ECHR, 1950), 23, 24, 136, 309
European Structural and Investment Funds (ESIF), 11, 239, 240, 240n12

F

Family, 46, 49, 54–56, 81, 82, 84, 88, 119, 120, 141, 144, 184, 217–222, 228, 231, 232, 234, 242, 276, 339, 346, 347, 361, 362, 380, 381, 383

G

Global North, 47, 49, 51, 53–55, 58–60, 79, 80, 88–89
Global South, 48, 51, 80, 88

Guardianship, 11, 21, 21n3, 32–36, 42, 142, 204, 207, 209–212, 217–221, 237, 237–238n6, 238, 249
guardian, 21, 211, 215, 217–222, 238, 276 (*see also* Legal capacity)

H

Human rights, 2–14, 20, 24, 25, 25n4, 31, 32, 34, 35, 37, 45–49, 53–56, 60, 63, 65, 66, 69, 72–75, 80, 89, 91, 97–111, 97n2, 98n4, 98n5, 100n8, 102n9, 103n14, 104n15, 105n20, 105n21, 111n31, 112n32, 113n34, 115, 117n41, 121, 123, 134–136, 140, 144, 159, 169, 171, 174, 180–182, 184, 188–196, 204–206, 208n4, 212, 213, 223, 230, 235, 237, 240, 241, 258, 259, 261, 264–265, 269, 271–273, 275–277, 280n14, 285, 287, 289, 290, 298, 299, 302–304, 307, 308, 310, 312, 313, 317–323, 334–336, 338, 343, 349, 355–358, 364, 371–373, 378, 380–384
Hungary, 11, 227–254

I

Iceland, 11, 12, 257, 258, 260
Impairment, 4, 21, 50–52, 59, 70–72, 81–88, 91, 161, 212, 213, 215, 219, 220, 229, 242, 275, 304, 311, 319, 321, 340, 346, 347
Implementation of the CRPD, 5, 6, 10, 12, 14, 73, 116, 159, 191, 235, 243, 258, 261, 264–265, 297–324, 334, 343–349, 366, 383
Inclusion, 46, 82, 111, 111n31, 149, 159, 163, 182, 186–188, 190, 191, 228, 229, 236, 239, 240, 249, 277n12, 288, 289, 321, 323, 324, 334, 337, 346, 349, 359–365, 368
Inclusive education, 117n41, 272n2, 282, 289, 316, 318, 337
Independence, 49, 110n27, 110n29, 161, 259, 333
Independent living, 52–53, 111, 111n31, 229n1, 230, 232, 239n10, 246, 249, 258, 260, 261, 263, 265, 301, 304, 307, 309, 310, 316–319, 323
India, 13, 205, 353, 354, 356n7, 360, 361, 368
Indigenous, 8, 74, 79–91, 90n1, 381
indigeneity, 8, 79–91, 380
Indonesia, 13, 333–349
Institutionalisation, 42, 230, 232, 237, 249, 279, 317
Institutions, 11, 20, 42, 65, 85–88, 104, 148, 185, 228, 230–237, 231n2, 233n5, 240–252, 254, 257–260, 263, 264, 278, 299, 342, 343, 346–349, 353, 354, 358, 363, 365, 380, 382, 383
International Covenant on Civil and Political Rights (ICCPR, 1966), 31, 97n1, 98n4, 104, 116n38, 135, 364

International Covenant on Economic, Social and Cultural Rights (ICESCR, 1966), 31, 97n1, 98n4, 99n6, 104, 105n19, 135
International Law, 9, 28, 57, 66, 101–103, 102n10, 105, 115, 121, 122, 134–135, 163, 171n4, 228, 355, 372
Iran, 58, 98n3
Ireland, 9, 10, 21n3, 33, 34, 56, 133–152
  Assisted Decision-Making (Capacity) Act (ADCA, 2015), 36, 142, 151
  Mental Health Act (MHA, 2001), 144

L
Legal capacity, 7, 11, 20, 23, 33–42, 67, 139–142, 151, 167, 170, 203–224, 229, 237, 238, 249, 272n3, 366, 382
Legal culture, 7, 20–43, 206, 207, 212, 382

M
Malta, 57
Māori, 8, 80–85, 88, 89
Medical model of disability, 252
Mental capacity, 7, 37, 140, 141, 208, 211, 215, 216, 309, 313
Monaco, 55, 57
Monism, 171n4

N
New Zealand (NZ), 80–82, 84, 88, 90, 91
Nordic states, 11, 12, 257–265
Norway, 11, 12, 257, 258, 260

P
Personal assistance, 143, 229, 232, 234, 236, 253, 257–263
Personhood, 7, 21, 22, 24, 25, 29–32, 35, 38–41, 67
  shared personhood, 40
Persons with intellectual disabilities, 12, 30, 39, 163, 233, 259, 269–290, 381
Polynesia, 80, 84, 85

R
Ratification of the CRPD
  ratification process, 3, 8–10, 99, 151, 152, 157–174
Religion, 27, 52, 54, 58, 59, 65, 74, 81, 84, 85, 90

S
Social change, 3, 5, 271, 278, 338–341
Social model of disability, 4, 52, 168, 174, 230, 252, 304
Sri Lanka, 10, 179–196
State (Party) Report, 12, 235, 306, 353–374
  alternative report, 135, 192, 310, 313, 315, 354, 357, 369, 370, 372, 374
  shadow report, 135, 192, 310, 313, 315, 354, 357, 369, 370, 372, 374

States Parties, 2–6, 8, 11, 12, 21, 34, 35, 37, 46, 48, 54–59, 115, 117n41, 119n45, 158, 185, 190, 207n1, 207n2, 208, 208n3, 208n4, 209, 228, 232, 235, 251n22, 254, 269, 275n8, 287–289, 288n26, 306, 308, 338, 353–374, 379–381, 383
Sweden, 11, 12, 257, 258, 260, 263
Switzerland, 12, 289

T

Theatre, 12, 69, 270, 271, 274, 277–286, 289, 290, 383

U

United Kingdom (UK), 3, 13, 98, 123n49, 297–324
  Disability Discrimination Act (DDA, 1995; DDA 2005), 123n49, 300, 300n2
  Equality Act (EA, 2010), 300n2, 301, 320
  Mental Capacity Act (MCA, 2005) (England and Wales), 301, 321n18
  Mental Health Act (MHA, 2007), 302
  Mental Health (Discrimination) Act (MHA, 2013), 312
United Nations (UN), 9, 24, 25, 25n4, 31, 32, 45, 49, 57, 63, 80, 87, 91, 97–99, 97n1, 98n4, 101, 103, 106, 107, 121, 134–136, 143, 165, 171, 190, 235, 354, 356, 362, 373
  United Nations Declaration on the Rights of Indigenous Peoples (DRIP, 2007), 90, 90n1
  United Nations Office of the High Commissioner for Human Rights (OHCHR), 98n3, 137, 159, 160, 168, 169, 171–173, 181, 190, 308, 356n5
United States (US), 9, 12, 97–123, 205, 230, 253, 274n6, 289, 381
Universal Declaration of Human Rights (UDHR), 49, 50, 80
Universalism, 47, 48, 53, 59, 60

W

War, 182, 188, 381
Welfare state, 11, 12, 30–31, 257–265, 380
  Welfare culture, 257–265
World Health Organisation (WHO), 46, 50, 57, 66, 67

The manufacturer's authorised representative in the EU is Springer Nature Customer Service Centre GmbH, Europaplatz 3, 69115 Heidelberg, Germany. If you have any concerns regarding our products, please contact ProductSafety@springernature.com

Printed and bound by CPI Group (UK) Ltd, Croydon, CR0 4YY
25/09/2026
02222881-0005